# MAXIMUM VOLUME

# MAXIMUM VOLUME

## THE LIFE OF BEATLES PRODUCER GEORGE MARTIN

### THE EARLY YEARS, 1926–1966

KENNETH WOMACK

An A Cappella Book

First hardcover edition published 2017
First paperback edition published 2019
Published by Chicago Review Press Incorporated
814 North Franklin Street
Chicago, Illinois 60610
ISBN 978-1-64160-005-7

The Library of Congress has cataloged the hardcover edition as follows:
Names: Womack, Kenneth.
Title: Maximum volume : the life of Beatles producer George Martin, the early years: 1926–1966 / Kenneth Womack.
Description: First edition. | Chicago, Illinois : Chicago Review Press, [2017] | Includes bibliographical references and index.
Identifiers: LCCN 2017000470 (print) | LCCN 2017000894 (ebook) | ISBN 9781613731895 (cloth) | ISBN 9781613731918 (Pdf) | ISBN 9781613731925 (Epub) | ISBN 9781613731901 ( Kindle)
Subjects: LCSH: Martin, George, 1926–2016. | Sound recording executives and producers—England—Biography. | Beatles. | LCGFT: Biographies.
Classification: LCC ML429.M34 W66 2017 (print) | LCC ML429.M34 (ebook) | DDC 781.66/149092 [B] —dc23
LC record available at https://lccn.loc.gov/2017000470

Cover design: Marc Whitaker/MTWdesign.net
Cover photo: Associated Newspapers/REX/Shutterstock
Typesetting: Nord Compo

Printed in the United States of America
5 4 3 2 1

For Tortle:
P.S. I Love You!

Music should humbly seek to please; within these limits
great beauty may perhaps be found.

—Claude Debussy

# CONTENTS

# PROLOGUE

# "GOOD GOD, WHAT'VE WE GOT 'ERE?"

IT WAS WEDNESDAY, June 6, 1962, and George Martin was flummoxed.

For the most part, it had been a fairly quiet day in the life of the Parlophone A&R man, who, at age thirty-six, had become inured to working "artists and repertoire." On most days, he navigated a breakneck schedule of back-to-back meetings and recording sessions—one after another and often from dawn until well after dusk.

But today was relaxed by comparison, quiet even. George had taken a morning meeting with David Platz, a music publisher with whom he shared several ongoing business interests. They were natural collaborators, being two thirtysomethings having made their names on the London music scene as young execs on the rise. After lunch, George's afternoon had been devoted to his hilarious mates from *Beyond the Fringe*. Together, George and the comedy troupe had struck gold after the A&R man recorded their stage act on one of EMI's mobile units back in 1961. Under George's supervision, Parlophone enjoyed a hit record with the zany quartet of Alan Bennett, Peter Cook, Jonathan Miller, and Dudley Moore. And the future looked even more promising for George's clients, who were set to open *Beyond the Fringe* on Broadway in just a few short months.

For George, good old British comedy had proven to be his salvation, saving his beleaguered record label in the bargain. But what he really wanted, truth be told, was to handle a beat group. He was absolutely driven by the notion of landing a rock combo, ferreting out hit songs for them, and generating one chart-topper after another. In his heart of hearts, what he longed for most was something along the lines of Cliff Richard and the Shadows, the beat music wunderkinds who recorded for Norrie Paramor, George's opposite number with EMI's Columbia imprint. George was incredibly jealous of Norrie, especially since the Columbia A&R man had scored one chart sensation after another with Cliff Richard, who had emerged as Norrie's apparently unstoppable hit-making vehicle. That's what George wanted all right—to develop a beat music juggernaut to rival Paramor's and enjoy the good life for a change. Who wouldn't? It was well known around the EMI corridors that Norrie tooled around the city in his brand-new E-Type Jaguar—when he wasn't driving his sports car out to his seaside place on the Sussex coast, that is. Oh, George definitely wanted a Jag. Of that he was certain.

After a dinner break, George made his way to Abbey Road with Ron Richards, his assistant A&R man, strolling beside him. It was an early summer day in London as the two Parlophone colleagues contemplated the evening's recording session. How had they found themselves in such a position in the first place, having signed a contract with the very same Liverpool beat group that George had rebuffed back in February? George didn't hear anything earth-shattering in their sound, as he had told their manager, Brian Epstein, on that very first day when he played their acetate in his office. Walking toward the studio on that June evening, George and Ron still couldn't wrap their minds around the band's strange-sounding moniker. "Bloody silly name that is, Beatles," Richards said. "How corny can you get?" For the life of him, George couldn't figure out how they would even go about marketing them. "Was it going to be John Lennon and the Beatles, or Paul McCartney and the Beatles?" George wondered.[1]

When they arrived at Abbey Road, Richards made his way to the studio, while George occupied himself in the canteen. Let Ron, his more-than-capable assistant, handle the session—Ron fancied himself as Parlophone's resident rock 'n' roll man, after all. It's not like George was missing out on some groundbreaking moment in the presence of the next Elvis, as Brian Epstein had boasted back in February. Besides, EMI was incurring all of the session and production costs, which would never hit George's Parlophone budget. And what was the Beatles' contract worth anyway? It was a penny-per-record deal—no great investment on EMI's part. As Brian eagerly scanned the agreement in May, George knew something that the novice manager probably hadn't fully grasped: the Beatles' contract called for recording a mere six "sides"—nothing more, nothing less. How long, really, would it take to knock off a half dozen measly songs anyway—a few wasted hours at most?

And that's when tape operator Chris Neal found George in the canteen, telling him that he was wanted in the studio. Apparently the Beatles had already caused quite a stir around Abbey Road. "Good God, what've we got 'ere?" balance engineer Norman Smith had muttered to himself when the bandmates ambled into Studio 2. Their equipment was so ratty and tattered that Abbey Road's white-coated personnel had to rig up a series of work-arounds just to get the session started. As Richards and Smith stared in wonder verging on outright disgust, the Beatles had ripped off a cover version of "Bésame Mucho" before playing a composition of their own called, of all things, "Love Me Do." When did beat bands begin writing their own tunes—especially beat bands from Liverpool?[2]

Moments later, George made the scene, joining his EMI colleagues in the control room above the studio floor. There they were, standing before him for the very first time: twenty-one-year-old John Lennon on rhythm guitar, nineteen-year-old Paul McCartney on bass, nineteen-year-old George Harrison on lead guitar, and twenty-year-old Pete Best on drums. As George looked on, the band played two more original compositions called "P.S. I Love You" and "Ask Me Why." With four songs under their belts, the band members joined George and his team up in the control room. Without saying a word, the lanky ex-navy man commanded their full attention. Towering over them in his neat, well-pressed suit, George looked, for all intents and purposes, like pure, upper-crust London to these rural, North Country Scousers from Liverpool. And when he opened his mouth, George spoke with a posh accent to boot. He couldn't have been any more intimidating if he tried.

As the boys fired up their cigarettes, George took the floor. And for the next twenty minutes, he lectured his much younger charges, mercilessly critiquing nearly every aspect of their performance, from the slipshod nature of their vocal delivery to their sloppy musicianship. He even took issue with the way John Lennon played his harmonica during "Love Me Do." Eventually, the veteran A&R man brought his lengthy, scathingly candid diatribe to an end, and he actually began to feel sorry for the Beatles, having railed against them for so long.

"Look, I've laid into you for quite a time, and you haven't responded," said George, as the group members waited quietly before him in the control room. "Is there anything that *you* don't like?" For a moment, the four Beatles glanced back and forth at one another, nervously shuffling their feet. After giving Martin a hard, lingering stare, guitarist George Harrison retorted, in perfect deadpan: "Well, for a start, I don't like your tie."[3]

After an awkward moment, everyone in the room, which had lapsed into an unearthly silence, erupted with laughter. As the tension briskly evaporated, *everyone* was in on the hilarity, with George joining the Beatles in a moment of uproarious merriment. Later, after the band had left the studio for the evening, George remained in the control room with his Parlophone brain trust, trying to make sense of what they had just witnessed. Norman spoke up first, saying, "Phew! What do you think of that lot then?"[4]

In his mind, George had already decided that "they were rotten composers" and that "their own stuff wasn't any good." Yet sitting there with Richards and Smith, Martin admitted to his colleagues, "There is something special about them. I can't tell you what, but there *is* something there."[5]

And while he didn't quite know what that something was just yet, he knew that something very unusual had transpired on that early summer evening in Studio 2. During that one instant, Harrison had very possibly saved the Beatles from the EMI dustbin. Martin was quite sure that he didn't like the group's musicianship or their original material, but after years of toil at Parlophone Records, he knew comedy, and these guys, if nothing else, were funny. Even in the darkest of moments, when the chips were down, they knew how to laugh at themselves, as Harrison had so clearly revealed. And Martin could work with that.

They may be funny, these Liverpool Scousers, but were they worth the risk? That was the signal question that he pondered as he made his way back to his apartment that night. To his ears, they still weren't very good musicians. But that McCartney fellow had a sweet voice, and Lennon's was loaded with texture. He wasn't sure if he cared for Harrison's voice at all, and Best, the drummer, was awful, losing the beat several times during the session. Could there be anything worse, really, than having a drummer who couldn't keep steady time in a beat band?

And that's when he got back to the original, vexing question that he had posed to Ron during their walk to the studio: How do you structure this band? By contract, George was obliged to work with them—if only for the duration it would take to record six songs—so he might as well sort out how to frame them for the record-buying public, assuming, that is, that they'd ever sell any records. For a moment, George toyed with the idea of making McCartney the leader, but that meant redefining the band's chemistry. After that bout of hilarity back in the studio, chemistry was clearly the best thing that they had going for them. No, he thought to himself, he would approach this band differently. It couldn't hurt—and anyway, the risk was so negligible as to be almost nonexistent.

And besides, who really cared if they were "Paul McCartney and the Beatles" or "John Lennon and the Beatles"? To remake them into something else, George reckoned, would be to alter the essential nature of the group. "Why not keep them as they were?" he thought. As far as he knew, marketing a successful beat band without a front man as its leader hadn't been done before—at least not in the United Kingdom. To George's way of thinking, that aspect was truly appealing. In many ways, it was the very same argument that had led him to try his hand at recording Britain's funnymen. "I'd made a lot of records that hadn't been 'done before,'" George reasoned. "Why not experiment in pop as I had in comedy?"[6]

Perhaps the Beatles just might be worth the risk after all. And anyway, how big was the gamble, really, if you had nothing to lose?

# 1

# MADE IN GREAT BRITAIN

LONG BEFORE HE EMERGED as the most acclaimed producer of his generation, George Martin revealed himself to be a childhood prodigy. In contrast with the scruffy lads from Liverpool who strode into the stately halls of Abbey Road Studios on that fateful evening in June 1962, Martin had enjoyed many years of genuine musical promise, but like the Beatles, he, too, had seen his share of working-class toil and anguish. His earliest memory of music was at age "three or four," when he "gravitated" toward the family's upright piano and began playing "funny Chopsticks things." At the tender age of eight, he wrote his first composition, "The Spider's Dance," after half a dozen lessons on the old upright. A quick-spirited ragtime number, "The Spider's Dance" seemed to herald great things to come in young George's life.[1]

But in truth, no one in his family had an aptitude for music. "My parents weren't at all musical," he later recalled. "I guess I was a one-off." The piano had found its way into the Martins' life because of an uncle's job in a piano factory. Nothing more, nothing less. And while the person who greeted the London record business some twenty-four years later would sport a pleasingly posh accent, his upbringing was decidedly blue collar. He was working class all the way. The man history now knows as "Sir George" was born George Henry Martin, the youngest child of Henry and Bertha (née Simpson) Martin, on January 3, 1926, at the Royal Northern Hospital in Holloway Road, North London. At the time of his birth, the Martin family lived in a tiny converted garage in Highbury Mews, just off Holloway Road. For Henry and Bertha, infant George and his older sister, Irene, aged three and a half, were more than just the product of a growing family—they were two mouths to feed in truly burdensome times. As the Great Depression mounted across the 1930s, Henry, who went by Harry, found work as a craftsman carpenter to be in increasingly short supply. In the meantime, he moved his young family from the converted garage to nearby Drayton Park. Young George's earliest memories find their roots in his first real home, the second apartment on the top floor of a semidetached house. In later years, he recalled the nearby Sunlight Laundry and, just around the corner, a church hall run by Donald Soper—"a young man with patent leather hair," in Martin's recollection, who found fame as a BBC television personality and religious activist.[2]

The Martins' new home was a two-room apartment with an attic and a large sitting room with windows overlooking the road. In the rear was his parents' bedroom, while George and Irene shared a foldaway bed in the sitting room. But that is where any luxury that might be found in the Martins' new accommodations ended. As it happened, their apartment had no electricity. Instead, they were forced to rely on coal fires and gas lighting. The sitting room itself was lit by two wall-mounted gas brackets that bookended the fireplace. George remembered having to be very careful in handling the delicate gas mantels so as not to damage them. Any misstep might leave the family without light and warmth, not to mention an invoice that, as the depressed 1930s wore on, would be extremely difficult to pay.

Perhaps even worse, the Martins' apartment lacked both a kitchen and a lavatory. Indeed, there wasn't a bathroom in the entire building. A sink with cold running water was available on a half landing down a flight of stairs, while the lavatory itself awaited three floors down in the back of the house, where the Martin children took their baths in a tin tub. Without a proper kitchen to prepare the family's meals, Bertha had to make do with a communal gas stove on the landing. But for all of the apartment's shortcomings, it featured one redeeming aspect: the tiny attic rooms where Harry created a makeshift workshop to carry out his trade.

In George's memory, his father was "the most honest person I have ever known." As one considers the breadth of the extraordinary career that awaited young George—and the unflinching manner in which he would invariably conduct his life and business—it is not difficult to ferret out his father's indelible influence. In George's early years, Harry made his living as a highly skilled wood machinist and a gifted carpenter. In those days, he worked for a firm that fitted out public houses and bars, particularly the finely crafted mahogany trimmings associated with the most stately and glamorous pubs of that era. For Harry, the real attraction was the wood itself. As George recalled, his father not only adored his work but also had a "love affair" with wood. "He used to bring home a piece of wood and encourage us to feel it," George wrote. "He was absolutely besotted with the stuff, but because of that he was always very poor, finding it very difficult to get work."[3]

And by the time that the Depression was in full swing, finding work had become all but impossible for Harry. For two long years, he was out of a job, and the family had little money to call their own. Things came to a head during George's fifth year, when he contracted scarlet fever. Under British law, his parents were required to report the disease. Yet Bertha, nicknamed "Cissie" by her relatives, took the law into her own hands, preferring to care for her young son at home rather than subjecting him to the trauma of going to a hospital. As a nurse during the First World War, she had learned to hate hospitals and refused to subject her son to their misery. In one of young George's earliest memories, he recalled seeing a vendor passing by on the street below their apartment on a Wall's tricycle, complete with a wooden chest balanced on the front wheels and brimming with ice-cream treats. Still recovering from his bout with scarlet fever, George begged his mother for an ice cream. To his great confusion, Bertha broke into tears, saying, "Darling, I haven't got any money." As he bluntly recalled, the young family was "that broke." George would long remember his father's desperate efforts to comfort his son against the raging elements during one particularly frigid winter of his youth. "I have a vivid memory of a very cold winter," he said. "My feet were freezing, and he knew this, and we didn't have a hot water bottle. So he got an old can, which used to hold petrol or oil, cleaned it out, filled it with hot water, wrapped it in towels, and put it by my feet." As George's eldest son would remark years later, things became so desperate at this point in their lives that the young Martin family's most abiding ambition "was simply to be warm," given their impoverished environs at the time.[4]

The Martins' rescue finally came in the form of Harry's job hawking newspapers on Cheapside, just opposite St. Paul's Cathedral. As George remembered, "I think he may have got that job through my mother's side of the family, which we always regarded as somehow the grander side. The men, my uncles and my grandfather, used to run the *Evening Standard* vans 'round London, and they earned quite good money for those days. I always regarded them as my rich relations." Earning Harry all of thirty shillings per week, the job "saved our bacon," George later wrote: "I recall going with my mother to take him some sandwiches one icy winter's day, and seeing him standing on that freezing corner with the wind howling around him, trying to keep warm. I felt sorry for him." Finally, after the worst years of the Great

Depression had abated, Harry found work again in the wood machinery business in London's East End. Having suddenly returned to his element, Harry was happy again. In addition to his work as a wood machinist, he took private commissions to build custom furniture. As George remembered, Harry "was a marvelous craftsman," and "he made us tables, and sideboards, and cabinets, and beds, and toys for Irene and me. But never chairs. For some reason, he never made chairs." In yet another early memory, George recalled accompanying his father on a delivery in which Harry borrowed a fruit vendor's wheelbarrow to transport a custom-made wooden cabinet to a far-flung customer. For young George, the long walk made for "quite an adventure." Afterward, his father pushed the wheelbarrow back across London with little George as its only passenger, having fallen asleep atop some loose sacking.[5]

In addition to building the Martins' own furniture, Harry designed several pieces for sale, including one extraordinary item—"a standard lamp that looked rather like Nelson's Column, with a fluted column and a square base with claw feet." George recalled, "It was beautifully done, all bas-relief in mahogany, and my mother loved that lamp." As for Bertha, she was independent minded and, like her husband, determined to make it in spite of the social and economic despair of 1930s England. Along with Harry, she was resolute in providing the best of everything for her young family. She worked as a seamstress and a maid to make extra money. In spite of their lack of disposable income, Bertha and Harry worked tirelessly on behalf of George and Irene while always ensuring that they were properly clothed and fed. "Although we had no money," George later recalled, "I never thought we were poverty-stricken, and we never went without." Indeed, in spite of everything, "we lived comfortably enough. It was a pretty normal childhood."[6]

In 1931 circumstances forced the family to move yet again—this time less than a mile away to a three-room apartment above a working dairy on nearby Aubert Park, just to the east of the Arsenal football club's behemoth stadium. The accommodations were about the same as the family's previous apartment, only this time they had four gas mantels suspended in the middle of the sitting room, providing much more light than the two around the fireplace back on Drayton Park. Aubert Park also marked the first time that young George enjoyed the benefits of having electricity. Better still, life in the new family digs was also marked by the presence of that piano. According to his sister, Irene, the family originally purchased the instrument from a beloved uncle's piano company back when they lived at Highbury Mews. As George recalled, "A piano then was what the television set has become now, not simply a piece of furniture but a focus for family gatherings, and we managed to acquire one through the good offices of Uncle Cyril, who was in the piano trade. He was the one who always played the piano at parties." When the piano arrived, George was instantly smitten: "I fell in love with it straight away, and went and made noises on it." While Irene began taking lessons from a relative, George had to make do at first with being self-taught, as the family had only enough money to cover one set of lessons. But no matter, George later recalled, "I just made my own music. And I made it rather well! I found I was able to listen to tunes and then pick them out on the piano. Music felt completely natural, and I didn't think there was anything special about it."[7]

When George finally earned his opportunity to enjoy a few piano lessons of his own, he quickly penned "The Spider's Dance," along with a pair of high-minded classical pieces that he whimsically titled "Opus 1" and "Opus 2." Having become a composer at the ripe old age of eight, "I supposed I used to think that I was a genius," he remembered. "You always do when you are a child. Such fanciful ideas." As he later surmised, "I wasn't taught music to begin with. I just grew up feeling music and naturally making music. I can't remember a time where I wasn't making music on the piano." But the lessons, alas, didn't last. "I didn't learn anything from them at all," he later admitted, "and then my mother had a row with the piano teacher, and I never went back."[8]

When he turned five, young George was enrolled in Our Lady of Sion, the school on Holloway Road that Irene attended. George's early education clearly reflected his mother's staunch Roman Catholic beliefs. Three years later, he was enrolled in St. Joseph's, a Catholic boys' elementary school in Highgate Hill. But for young George, the world changed irrevocably when at age eleven he earned a scholarship to attend St. Ignatius College in Stamford Hill. A Jesuit college where the schoolmasters were Jesuit priests, St. Ignatius challenged George in a variety of ways, ranging from the intellectual and the artistic to the social and the physical. The Martin family had recently moved yet again—this time to Muswell Hill. They lived on Hillside Gardens atop a steep road only a few miles away from St. Ignatius, where George found himself in a "whole new world." "I enjoyed football, and played some cricket too," he recalled. "I loved art and maths, and was fascinated by aerodynamics and aircraft design. I quite enjoyed languages, learning French, Latin, and Ancient Greek." He remembered his St. Ignatius teachers with a special fondness, particularly Father Gillespie, a "fearsome" presence who instilled a love of language in his young charges. Not surprisingly, George was especially taken with choir—so much so, in fact, that he sang every day during Easter week, staying at the college rather than going home for the night.[9]

When the Second World War broke out in September 1939, George was thirteen and Irene, now seventeen, had taken a job with Sun Life of Canada's London insurance office. With England's and France's declarations of war against Nazi Germany, the "Phoney War" ensued. During the eight-month period that comprised the Phoney War, there was nothing in the way of military land operations until May 1940, when German forces attacked France and the Low Countries. In spite of the relative quietude in London before the Blitz, Bertha was certain that Alexandra Palace, which was less than half a mile from the Martins' home, would be bombed. After St. Ignatius was evacuated to Welwyn Garden City, about twenty miles north of London, George and his mother temporarily relocated to Cambridge, while Harry and Irene stayed behind in London. When Sun Life of Canada shifted their offices to Bromley, on the outskirts of the southern English countryside, Bertha decided to move the entire family to Kent, where George enrolled in the Bromley County School.[10]

In spite of the dislocation associated with his family's wartime evacuation, George continued to pursue his various passions without interruption. As he later observed, "I had carried on with the piano on my own; once you are interested in something like that, you can find out about it without even going to the library and looking things up. A piano is a great tool for finding out about music, about the relationships between one note and another. I remember getting very excited when I discovered a new chord, and especially so when one day I realized that there was a natural cycle of chords." Years later, George would discover that he possessed that rare gift of perfect pitch. Also known as absolute pitch, perfect pitch refers to a person's natural ability to identify or play a particular musical note without benefit of a reference tone. As George later wrote, "I was also able to work out, for example, that there were only three diminished chords in the whole range, and that they had different inversions." This ability to distinguish between various sounds and intuitively understand their musical interrelationships would emerge as an asset throughout his formative years and beyond.[11]

For their part, the Martin family could hardly begin to account for young George's innate musical talent. "I started playing things like 'Liebestraum,' and various Chopin pieces, by ear. Where that gift came from, I don't know. There were certainly no professional musicians anywhere in the family. They just assumed 'George is the musical one . . . let him get on with it.'" Life at the Bromley County School proved to be a great boon for George's development as a budding musician. The district of Bromley benefitted from a large local musical society, and his school occasionally played host to the likes of the BBC Symphony Orchestra. In fact, he experienced an epiphany in 1941, when the BBC Symphony Orchestra, under the direction of Sir Adrian Boult, performed Claude Debussy's *Prélude à l'après-midi d'un faune* at fifteen-year-old George's school. "I thought it was absolutely heavenly," he recalled. "I couldn't believe human beings made that sound." But even in the early moments, George found himself enrapt with the *making* of music as much as with its aesthetic beauty. It was his first brush with the "tingle factor"—that uncanny instant when the human spirit is awakened by the aesthetic power of music. "I could see these men in their monkey-jackets, scraping away at pieces of gut with horsehair and blowing into funny instruments with bits of cane on their ends. But the mechanical things I saw simply didn't relate to the dream-like sound I heard. It was sheer magic, and I was completely enthralled."[12]

In addition to such high-minded pursuits, the Bromley County School also offered regular dances, which featured acts like the Squadronaires, the Royal Air Force's popular jazz band. On one memorable occasion, George recalled, "[I] hung around the stage, and when one of them asked if I was a musician myself, I seized my chance and said airily, if brashly, 'Oh, yes, I play piano, the sort of thing you're doing.'" When the Squadronaires called him on his "adolescent bravado," young George joined the bandmates on stage. "That was the only invitation I needed," he recalled. "It was an unbelievable feeling to be sitting up there playing 'One O'Clock Jump' with them."[13]

During this same period, George joined an amateur dramatic society called the Quavers, a lay activity sponsored by a local church in Bromley. He enjoyed performing in the Quavers' productions, including plays by Noël Coward, among others. While George hardly distinguished himself for his acting skills, his experiences with the Quavers took an indelible turn when the dramatic society began hosting dances. He and his friends good-naturedly organized a band to provide musical accompaniment: "We called ourselves the Four Tune Tellers, and then we expanded and became George Martin and the Four Tune Tellers. Fame! My father made us a set of music stands with a double-T design." During their time together, the group's personnel shifted several times. As George recalled, "I was its nucleus and organizer, even though I was the youngest. In those days, there was no amplification, so no electric instruments. We always had the drums, and a bass player if we were lucky. The very first group had a violinist, who was a part-time policeman, but he didn't last very long. The violin isn't really a good instrument for a dance band, and we graduated to saxophones after that. My sister Irene was the vocalist." While the group's lineup shifted periodically, George remained steadfast as the band's pianist: "I wanted to be George Shearing, and I also modeled myself on Meade Lux Lewis"—a pair of influences that merged young George's interests in jazz, on the one hand, and boogie-woogie, on the other. George's time in the dramatic society left him with yet another revelation, one that he would realize at key junctures throughout his young life: as he engaged in regular conversation with other members of the troupe, "I decided that I spoke appallingly." To remedy this essential part of his nature, he began self-consciously attempting to speak like the well-heeled BBC commentators he heard on the radio.[14]

Before long, George's band developed a steady following and a regular musical repertoire. "We played the standards by Jerome Kern, Cole Porter, and so on, things like 'The Way You Look Tonight.' Quicksteps were always the most popular, and we always ended with 'The Goodnight Waltz.'" The band's set list was mostly gleaned from hit songs that George picked up from listening to the radio. In addition to pieces like Kern's classic "All the Things You Are," the group specialized in American imports such as Woody Herman. For the most part, their gigs consisted of "socials or dances at schools, where boys and girls of 15 or so would dance arm in arm, and in pubs and halls in the area: the Bell in Bromley, the Green Man in Catford, Ravensbourne Country Club, which was rather posh, and various places in Southend, an area north of Bromley." Soon sixteen-year-old George and the Four Tune Tellers found themselves in fairly high demand, playing one or two regular shows each week. While the bandmates enjoyed the act of performance immensely, traveling far and wide to get to their shows proved to be more than a minor strain. As George recalled, "It was all quite good fun, but we did have to cycle everywhere. The double bass player used to ride with his bass on his back, and the drummer had a real problem. As the pianist, I was the only one who had no instrument to be carried around, so I used to cycle alongside him, with the bass drum carried between us. Rather dangerous, I must say, but we were rarely stopped by the cops!"[15]

While George's experience with the Four Tune Tellers imbued him with a newfound confidence—not to mention the pure joy of live performance—he was hardly satisfied with being a scratch pianist who made do with playing by ear. Eventually, he earned enough money from the band's gigs to pay for piano lessons from a Scotsman named Mr. Urquhart. As George remembered, "Mr. Urquhart had a marvelous Bösendorfer piano, and it was then that I really woke up to music." As it happens, young George was still vacillating between his new life as a budding professional musician and a young man's fantasy about achieving untold fame and immortality: "I suddenly realized that I had talent—though, to be honest, the realization was a mite unconfined: I used to romance about how, if I'd had the proper training, I would have been another Rachmaninov. I got that sorted out rather later, when it dawned on me that Rachmaninov's reputation was under no threat from G. Martin, but at the time I really fancied myself as a classical writer." Under Mr. Urquhart's tutelage, George learned to play Chopin etudes and Beethoven sonatas. Perhaps even more significantly, Mr. Urquhart also taught him how to chart musical notation. For the first time, George was able to transcribe—if only very crudely—the musical phrases that danced, unabated, within the staves of his mind.[16]

As it happens, George's life—not to mention the tension between his reality as a working musician and the pleasant, diverting fantasia of musical stardom—was quickly arriving at a crossroads of sorts. When he graduated from Bromley in 1941, he had achieved distinctions in French and mathematics. By his sixteenth birthday in 1942, his schooldays had come to a close, and he was on a collision course with the "big wide world." For his part, George's gaze most often drifted toward the sky, his interest in aviation having continued to grow since his years at St. Ignatius. While Bertha hoped to spare her family from the perils of war-torn London, she had succeeded, rather ironically, in affording her son a front-row seat as the Royal Air Force and the Luftwaffe skirmished overhead. As George recalled, "I watched the Battle of Britain unfolding over my head, and our classes were continually interrupted by air-raid warnings, the whistle of bombs, and the chatter of machine guns." Always ready and willing to immerse himself in the objects of his interests, George quickly fancied himself as "an expert aircraft spotter" who "could tell a Hurricane or a Spitfire from a Messerschmitt or Heinkel miles away. The dogfights made beautiful trails in the sky, and I never thought of the horror of their combat but marveled at the grace of the aerial ballet that had me as a spectator." On one unforgettable occasion, George "heard a terrific noise of planes and rushed into the garden just in time to see two Focke Wulf 190 fighter bombers sweep over our house at naught feet, firing their cannon. It was a great thrill, even if they were only shooting up a barrage balloon." Bertha, understandably horrified by the proximity of war, was thunderstruck by her son's cavalier attitude: "My mother was absolutely frantic, calling me a stupid fool for being so careless of my own safety. I thought it was rather a hoot!" George soon realized that his family's mortality was threatened by the aviation spectacles that took place in the Bromley skies—the ones to which he had responded so lightly: "I remember one day [after a bombing] a house about five doors down wasn't there anymore. And the house next door to it, on the first floor, there was a bathroom exposed, and the bath was dangling, holding on from its pipes. And I thought, 'Well, gosh, that could have been us.' But you accepted it."[17]

Although he continued to dream about a career in aviation, his parents, always influential, loving, and supportive, held decidedly different views about the course of his future: "While I had been at school, my parents were always trying to impress on me the importance of a job with security. I had always been good at mathematics and drawing, so now my mother suggested: 'Why don't you go in for architecture?'" Meanwhile, his father, Harry, had different plans in mind: "Why don't you go in for the Civil Service? You'll never get chucked out of a job then." As George recalled, "To him that was, understandably, paramount, having suffered so much unemployment, but in both of them there was the feeling that they wanted me to do better than they had, an 'Our George is going places' mixture of parental pride and ambition."[18]

As it turns out, the elder Martins' dream of a better life for their son would have to wait—at least for the moment. Young George didn't become an architect, and he didn't join the civil service either. While he continued to nurse a near-fanatical interest in the study of aircraft and aerodynamics, an early attempt to sign on with the vaunted de Havilland Aircraft Company failed to materialize after George learned that the firm required a £250 cash payment for their apprenticeship program in aircraft design. Although he was accepted into a similar program offered by Short & Harland in Belfast, George was loathe to relocate to Northern Ireland. Besides, he reasoned, it was 1942 during the heart of the war in Europe, and aircraft companies had little interest in taking on new designers given their ever-increasing manufacturing backlog. George temporarily worked for Mr. Coffin, a quantity surveyor in Victorian Street. Not surprisingly, George immediately grew bored, and despite Mr. Coffin's counteroffer of increasing his measly £2 5s weekly salary, George gave notice after only six weeks on the job.

As with so many young men of his day, Martin's ambitions quickly shifted to the omnipresent military effort that galvanized the nation. After passing the entrance exam, he joined the War Office's nonuniformed ranks as a temporary clerk grade three. Never straying very far from the sound of music, George continued to tickle the ivories with his dance band by night. Indeed, by this point, George Martin and the Four Tune Tellers netted a tidy sum for their gigs—especially in contrast with his meager earnings as a clerk. But after eight months, during which he mainly provided tea service and worked in the mail room of the War Office's Easton Square headquarters in London, he strolled into the recruiting office at Hither Green and, without first telling his parents, volunteered to join the Royal Navy. His reasoning, like many would-be recruits, was fairly simple: "It was inevitable I was going to be conscripted before long. The Army didn't appeal to me because I wanted to fly, but I didn't particularly want to go into the Royal Air Force because everyone was doing that. I though it would be different to join the Fleet Air Arm." Like so many young men, he later admitted to being inspired to join the Fleet Air Arm after hearing the awe-inspiring story of its success at the Battle of Taranto, which enjoyed national headlines in November 1940 for its crippling air attack on the Italian fleet using aerial torpedoes. On yet another occasion, he put it even more bluntly, saying that he "didn't want to be a poor bloody infantryman." When he went to the recruiting office, he announced that he wanted to be a pilot with flying duties in the Fleet Air Arm. "So I signed on." It was the summer of 1943, and George was promptly accepted into the Royal Navy. He was barely seventeen years old. When he announced to his mother that he had been inducted into the Fleet Air Arm—"Mum, I've joined up"—Bertha went pale and burst into tears. "Oh, my God, you'll be killed," she exclaimed, pleading with him that his enlistment couldn't possibly be true. But there was no turning back, of course. Trying to calm her breaking heart, he pleaded with her, saying, "Mother, I won't get killed. I promise you that." In short order, George shipped out to the HMS *St. Vincent*, a training station at Gosport on the coast of Hampshire in southern England.[19]

For the next eighteen months, George called Gosport home. During this period, his training was delayed for several months when he was felled by a case of the German measles, which had reached epidemic proportions among the new recruits. As it turned out, Gosport marked George's most extended stay during his years as a navy man. With the Allies gearing up for D-day, he "had no real leave because we were getting ready to invade France and the whole of the south coast was sealed off. I couldn't go home, and my parents couldn't come to Gosport, but for some reason they and I were allowed to go to Winchester," a Romanesque city some fifteen miles northeast of Southampton. Every few months, George and his parents would meet in Winchester for tea and cakes. After completing a radio course in nearby Eastleigh, he was transferred to Glasgow, where he soon boarded the *Nieuw Amsterdam*, a Dutch ocean liner that had been refitted as a troopship. Designed to accommodate fifteen hundred passengers, the *Nieuw Amsterdam* was crammed to the gills with more than eight thousand souls, including some three thousand

German prisoners bound for Canada. During George's voyage to New York aboard the ship, the German prisoners served the troops in the crowded mess halls. At night, George and his shipmates slept on hammocks draped along the open decks of the liner. For the duration of its three-week voyage, the *Nieuw Amsterdam* zigzagged across the Atlantic in an effort to avoid U-boat entanglements. When life aboard the "dormitory-diner" mercifully came to an end, George spent two weeks in New York City "being amazed by the skyscrapers" and settling into the HMS *Saker*, the Royal Navy's facility in the Brooklyn Navy Yard. George later recalled having "a whale of a time. It was like heaven after blacked-out England. We were treated like little tin gods: wherever we went compères would call out, 'The British Navy is here—give 'em a big hand!'" For George, the highlight was a visit to Broadway's Diamond Horseshoe. He enjoyed free drinks at the club before venturing to the Paramount, where he basked in the sounds of Cab Calloway and Gene Krupa. "Everywhere was bright lights and tasty food and fresh milk," he later wrote, "things we couldn't get in wartime Britain." During a weekend getaway to Manhasset on Long Island Sound, George finally got to play the piano and enjoy more American cuisine.[20]

From the Brooklyn Navy Yard, George shipped out yet again—this time for the island of Trinidad off the coast of Venezuela, where the young navy men endured nine months of flight training. By this point, he had been promoted from naval airman second class to leading naval airman. His first flight occurred in a Vickers Supermarine Walrus, an amphibian biplane that shook like the dickens. After getting over his initial fears and becoming used to the plane's machinations, George began to enjoy flying, which he found to be exhilarating. He trained on a succession of aircraft, ranging from high-winged, single-engined monoplanes like the Stinson Reliant to amphibian aircraft like the Grumman Goose, the Fairey Albacore, and the torpedo-bearing Fairey Swordfish. In Trinidad, George was assigned to be an "observer," a role that required him to serve as captain of the aircraft. As an observer, he was responsible for being fluent in all of the duties associated with his three-men sorties, including radio, radiotelegraphy, navigation, and gunnery. After completing his training in Trinidad, George earned his wings along with a promotion to petty officer. All the while, he never strayed too far from the piano, seeking out every possible opportunity to play for his mates in the naval canteen.

With Petty Officer Martin's stay in Trinidad having come to a close in the spring of 1945, his unit was transported back to New York City by an American warship. George fondly recalled the early evening of May 5, 1945, as the warship passed Cape Hatteras off the coast of North Carolina. "I was on lookout duty, and there was an incredible sunset," he remembered. "Just one lump of cloud over the sun and nothing else in the sky. As the sun was descending below the horizon, there was a huge shaft of light coming out from either side of the cloud, describing an enormous bright V in the sky." By an "uncanny coincidence," he had just learned over the radio that the Germans had surrendered, and "V for victory had been declared in Europe." As the war with Japan was still raging in the Pacific Theater, George and his mates continued their training unabated, returning to England on an aircraft carrier from New York.[21]

A fortnight stay in Greenwich proved to have a lasting influence on George's future, with both positive and negative implications. On the one hand, young George relished the company of the older commissioned officers with whom he enjoyed formal dinners in the station's exquisite Painted Hall, nicknamed "the Sistine Chapel of the UK" for Sir James Thornhill's elaborate murals. In addition to being schooled in the finer aspects of tableside etiquette, George began to self-consciously refine his unsharpened North London accent with the posh tones of the gentlemen-officers whom he chose to emulate. Years later, George would confess to having long been concerned about the all-too-overt "cor blimey" aspects of his lower-class comportment. He would recall having first heard his recorded voice at age fifteen and recoiling at its unpolished sound. But those evenings among the officers in the Painted Hall would inspire him to pursue a decidedly different path. Tall, lean, and fair-haired, George began to take on the full appurtenances of a civilized and cultured Englishman. In the class-conscious United Kingdom, it is difficult to imagine a more important guise. But no sooner had he completed his stay in Greenwich than he suffered an immediate, unexpected setback. "All my mates, with whom I had gone through all that training, were made Sub Lieutenants. But I was still too young for that exalted rank, so was made a Midshipman." As if to add insult to injury, George was forced to return a portion of his salary to the Royal Navy when his pay was backdated to his days earning his wings in Trinidad as a petty officer, which held a higher pay rate than a midshipman. For George, it proved to be a debilitating and humbling experience. "It was typical of many points in my life," he later surmised. "I always seemed to lose out on deals like that. And even when, three months later, I got my stripe, it still rankled." But he had hardly been left empty-handed by his departing mates, whom he would later credit as having "taught [him] to be a gentleman." It would prove to be one of the most pragmatic and socially expedient gifts that he would ever receive.[22]

In England, George's training continued with a radar course in Burscough, a provincial North Country village outside of Liverpool. His unit learned the cutting-edge technology aboard a squadron of Barracudas. For the navy men, radar was a welcome relief. "In Trinidad, there was no radar," George recalled, "and when you took off from an aircraft carrier you were on your own. Two and a half hours later you had to find the ship again, relying on your own navigational sense, and on the winds. You found your own winds, worked out what they were doing to the aircraft, and then navigated by dead reckoning." But before he could settle into life in the North Country, George was called back to London. As it happens, his piano prowess had attracted the attention of an entertainments officer during a sojourn back in the West Indies. To George's great delight, he was given a spot on a BBC program called *Navy Mixture*, a variety show hosted by future character actor and comedian Jack Watson, along with the BBC's Dance Orchestra conducted by popular bandleader Stanley Black. By then, George had gained his missing stripe and life had righted itself with his promotion. For the occasion of the BBC program, George selected an original composition—a three-minute ditty titled "Prelude." On July 26, 1945, he arrived at the Criterion Theatre on Piccadilly Circus, where Watson jauntily welcomed the nineteen-year-old composer and pianist to the airwaves: "Stepping off the Liberty boat this week is a bloke who's making his first broadcast, and who, incidentally, has just received his commission—and so it's a double celebration. He's a pianist, and after a great deal of persuasion—during which he held up our producer at the point of a gun—he's going to play a composition of his own, which he calls 'Prelude.' His name is Sub Lieutenant George Martin." And with Watson's bravura introduction dissipating into the sound of applause, Martin launched into his tune with great abandon, playing before a live audience of 3.7 million—and still more, four days later, when the episode was rebroadcast by the BBC General Overseas Service.[23]

Lieutenant Jon Pertwee, who also performed on *Navy Mixture*, was so impressed by Sublieutenant Martin's abilities that after the show, he invited him to join the Department of Naval Entertainments. While flattered, George was taken aback. He was days away from completing his training and seeing his squadron into action—a journey that had begun way back in Gosport, been delayed by the German measles, and now seemed finally to be nearing its end. Pertwee proposed that Martin join him on the SS *Agamemnon*, an amenity ship that was setting sail from Vancouver to the Pacific, where it would entertain the troops with "concert parties" consisting of live music and all the beer that they could drink: the *Agamemnon* was fitted out with a brewery capable of producing three thousand gallons of beer a day. While it was appealing, George declined the offer, preferring to stay with his mates in the Fleet Air Arm and to see out the war together. "I often wonder what would have happened if I'd accepted," he wrote years later, "because in retrospect it obviously had much more to do with my future career than flying bits of metal and wire in the sky."[24]

In August 1945, with their three-month radar course complete, George's unit was finally formed into an operational squadron. On August 9, they were preparing to travel east at Ronaldsway on the Isle of Man when they learned the news that the Americans had dropped the second atomic bomb over Nagasaki, bringing about the Japanese surrender and effectively ending World War II. For George, an additional eighteen months of service awaited him. After a "drunken farewell party" with his unit, his squadron was disbanded, and he returned to Bromley on leave. His tour of duty continued with an extended posting as a resettlement officer at the Royal Naval Air Station Donibristle in Fife, just north of Edinburgh. The cornerstone of his duties involved seeing his fellow troops "demobbed" or demobilized out of the service and back into civilian life. Hence, as more and more navy men left the service, George's job became progressively easier.[25]

During this time, he occasionally indulged his love of flying as an observer for several peacetime missions while also becoming heavily involved with a local choral society at the naval station. In addition to singing in the chorus, George composed various pieces for the group to perform. By this time, his skills as a composer had grown substantially thanks to his lengthy correspondence throughout the war years with Sidney Harrison, who served on the Committee for the Promotion of New Music, a London-based nonprofit organization dedicated to assisting young composers with their craft. Over the years, Harrison had established himself as a well-known pianist and BBC commentator. George came into Sidney's orbit after meeting Eric Harrison (unrelated), who held a piano recital in Portsmouth that George had attended during his Gosport days. After hearing George playing the piano after the recital, Eric suggested that the navy man share his work with Sidney. With a new Debussy-like piece called "Fantasy" in hand, George sent his latest composition to Sidney, who provided painstaking feedback. To George's great delight, Sidney "sent me back a criticism which extended to three foolscap pages. How remarkable to take all the trouble! He told me everything that was wrong with it, but also how to improve it. Above all, he urged me to go on writing." In addition to his inspiration and encouragement, Sidney counseled the novice composer to learn how to work with and compose for a range of instruments beyond the piano, thereby improving his versatility.[26]

During this period, George also came into the orbit of Jean Chisholm, a member of the choir, as well as the Wrens, the Women's Royal Navy Service branch. Chisholm served as the leading soprano at King's College Chapel in Aberdeen. Martin soon learned that he had a great deal in common with the twenty-five-year-old Jean—especially in terms of their mutual interest in music—and he became smitten with her beauty, not to mention her "very fine, Isobel Bailey type of voice." Born in February 1921, she was nearly five years older than the Fleet Air Arm officer. A brunette with piercing blue eyes, she was known as "Sheena" (Gaelic for "Jean") to everyone but her father, who used to sing to her, "I dream of Jeanie with the light brown hair." At one point not long after they met, George gave her a Jack Russell terrier that the happy couple called Tumpy, a name that—even years later—never strayed very far from George's senses.[27]

With Sheena, George was invariably attracted to the central place that music held in her life. Over the years, music had been the one constant across George's existence. But with his new love, he also realized the limitations that making sound could impose on those who lack the temperament for public exhibition. A classically trained musician in her own right, Sheena could be painfully shy and was never truly comfortable as a performer. She had attended the University of Aberdeen as a choral and organ scholar, and when she met George, they naturally bonded over music. While she had her own limitations, she quickly learned the source of her new boyfriend's. Although he could play virtually anything by ear, she recognized early on that he was acutely insecure about not being able to read music with the fluency of conventionally trained musicians. People in their circle understandably thought he was a very accomplished pianist, and with this in mind, he was occasionally invited to sit in with other players, a situation that left him feeling bemused by his inability to keep pace with anyone who held a more pronounced musical education.[28]

As George demobbed more servicemen from his unit, he increasingly enjoyed greater free time, which allowed him to write for and perform with the choir at his leisure. Sheena was equally smitten with George, whom she recognized as a gifted pianist. Yet she later confessed to being surprised to discover, as they played together in the choir, that his ability to sight-read music was still progressing very slowly. He could play the piano beautifully by ear, but when it came to accompanying the choir, he was at a decided disadvantage given his lack of formal music education. For Sheena, it seemed rather odd that a man with such talent and the crystal-clear accent of fine breeding was bereft of the fundamental musical knowledge that he needed to progress at his instrument.[29]

After serving as a resettlement officer for many months and later as a transport officer, George was finally posted as a release officer, a harbinger of his own impending demobilization. And so it came to pass that in January 1947, the newly minted twenty-one-year-old was tasked with the happy duty of releasing himself from the Royal Navy, thus ending his service on behalf of His Majesty's Forces. For all intents and purposes, George had experienced a "good war," avoiding injury and seeing no action. But he was suddenly at a loss about how to contemplate his future: "But of what I was going to do with myself I had no idea. It was a case of 'physician heal thyself.' I had no education to speak of. I wasn't trained for anything. It was too late to become an aircraft designer. So there seemed only one possibility, and in what was really desperation I turned to music."[30]

On tenterhooks about his future, he penned a letter to Sidney Harrison, his fairy godfather. Over the years, Harrison had marveled at the young composer's budding talent, and his letters had become increasingly insistent that Martin try his hand at a professional career in music. In 1947 Harrison was a professor of piano at the Guildhall School of Music and Drama. Founded in 1880, Guildhall was an independent arts conservatory located in London at the Barbican Estate. Having finally met Harrison in the flesh, Martin was impressed with the older man's confidence about his prospects for a life in music, possibly even as a teacher. "You can go and study for three years at a music college. I'll tell you what you do," he exclaimed to Martin. "You come along to the Guildhall, and play your compositions to the principal, and if he likes them as much as I do, you're in."[31]

Despite being riddled with self-doubt, Martin accepted an interview, arranged by Harrison, with Edric Cundell, the principal at Guildhall, in February 1947, less than a month after his demobilization. In short order, George was accepted into the school's "Three Years' Course for Teachers." Armed with a £160 annual grant from the British government for his service during the war, George could hardly believe his good fortune. Only a few days earlier, he had been bewildered by the bleak possibilities of an uncertain future. But now, with the likes of Sidney Harrison and Edric Cundell in his corner—not to mention his fledgling romance with Sheena—things were indeed looking up for young George. Looking back, he realized that he had grown up rather quickly from the young man who left Bromley not so long ago. "When I came back from the service," he later wrote. "I thought I was a grown man. The

Navy had been a shock to the system, because I had never been away from home in my life before. You grow up very quickly in that environment." In September 1947, he was set to begin his studies in composition, conducting, and orchestration. As George returned to Bromley that February, having bested his interview with the principal, it must have seemed as if his whole life were spread out before him.[32]

# 2

# THE BIG SMOKE

AS IT HAPPENED, settling back into civilian life in Bromley was fraught with difficulty for George. For the first three months, he remained unemployed, proudly preferring to be out of work rather than go on the welfare dole like so many young men of his era. With the next academic year set to begin in September, George took a temporary clerical position with the Iron and Steel Federation in Park Lane, alongside Hyde Park. For George, this meant making a regular commute into the heart of London—known as "the Smoke" for its overwhelming smog in those pre–Clean Air Act days. In this new role, he collated delivery notes for shipments of steel rods and processed wage sheets. "It was an arithmetical job, very boring, and the only way I could pass the time was to see how efficiently I could do it," he recalled. On one particularly effective day, he managed to make his way through more than seventy sheets, only to earn the chagrin of his coworkers for his unflinching productivity.[1]

Not surprisingly, only a week into his new job, a gruff veteran colleague took George to task: "What's your game, mate? Are you trying to be funny? You're checking 72 sheets a day and the average here is 30. I've checked your work and you're doing them all right. Just ease up a bit because you're making us look like idiots." The befuddled navy veteran offered a hasty, genuine response—"I was just trying to keep my mind alive"—only to receive a not-so-veiled threat in response: "You'd better watch it, mate." For George, the incident proved to be a rude awakening to life in the postwar world—a place in which jobs were scarce and tensions ran high. "I thought if you worked in a job you had to do the best you could," he later recalled, "but I was causing trouble in the department."[2]

But even worse, living at home with his parents proved to be a fractious decision, especially in light of George's many years of family solace at the homestead. As it turned out, the navy veteran experienced his most difficult period of readjustment with his mother, with whom he had always been an adoring and respectful son. For Bertha's part, George later wrote, "My mother thought I was still her baby. I had been very much a mother's boy, and loved her very much. But she was enormously suspicious of Sheena, believing she was the wrong person for me." Things deteriorated even further when she "started opening my love letters, and I found that quite intolerable and walked out, moving in with some friends in Berkshire. It was silly of her, and silly of me to walk out."[3]

During this period, Sheena experienced the tension firsthand while visiting the Martin family home at Bromley in the company of her new boyfriend, who was trying to make amends with his mother. Back in Scotland, Sheena had been reared in a lower-middle-class setting, which hardly prepared her for the sight of her new beau's working-class origins. In later years, she would confess to being shocked by the comparative poverty of their lives. To make ends meet, Bertha had started taking in foster children in exchange for government stipends. On the day of Sheena's visit, several orphans were in residence, including one young boy who had wet the bed. When Sheena tried to come to the child's aid, Bertha chased her around the house with a carving knife, threatening her for having invaded her household. To George's horror, the seeds of animosity had been suddenly and quite awkwardly sown between his mother and the object of his affections. Feeling that he suddenly no longer had any hope of saving his relationship with his mother, he quickly fled Bromley for London with an anguished Sheena in tow.[4]

Bertha's deeply apprehensive attitude regarding Sheena, former Wren and now George's steady girlfriend, was no doubt compounded by the head injury that she had suffered in the previous year during her son's last months in Scotland. Years later, George admitted that "she wasn't really herself, the person to whom I had always been so close." Chalking up his inability to understand her plight at the time to "the impetuosity of youth," George allowed that Bertha "was obviously only doing what she thought best for me." But he also recognized that his "absence in the Navy had been a great strain on her." Yet it was more than that, of course. It had to be. In the four years since he had left home for life in the Royal Navy, George had changed considerably, shifting dramatically from provincial lad to man of the world. Even more remarkably, he had changed from a whimsical youth who served a wide range of interests—music, aircraft, and mathematics, to name but a few—to a young man of increasing ambition and a healthy uncertainty about his future. And then there was the matter of his concerted effort to perceptibly alter his accent, which he had self-consciously restyled from a crude Cockney into an upper-crust gentlemanly enunciation.[5]

As George undertook his studies at Guildhall, Sheena joined him in London on a permanent basis, having left her family back in Scotland. The couple took their wedding vows on January 3, 1948, George's twenty-second birthday. Having proposed to Sheena in an "act of defiance" after his "rupture" with his mother, George had purposefully not invited his parents to the ceremony, only to discover that Bertha had found out about the upcoming wedding and made the trip up to Scotland, where the young couple's nuptials were held at the University of Aberdeen. Trying to make the best of it, George arranged for Bertha, who had scarcely traveled outside of Greater London before, to stay at a local bed-and-breakfast. To his surprise, Bertha, always used to having to scrimp and save, had insisted on sleeping on top of the bedding so as not to disturb the sheets. If George and Bertha had managed to reconcile by this point, it was short lived. As it happened, after his wedding day with Sheena, George would never see his mother again. Three short weeks later, Bertha died at age fifty-three from a cerebral hemorrhage. "It was very sad," George later wrote, "and I was filled with grief and guilt." Not surprisingly, his new marriage was suddenly and ineffably afflicted with the pain and guilt associated with Bertha's unexpected passing. To make matters worse, Sheena was besieged by a spate of maladies, including nervous dyspepsia followed closely by what George would later allege to be agoraphobia. Allegedly stricken with the deep-seated psychological need to be indoors, Sheena was homebound. Given the Greater London housing shortage in the postwar years, George held little hope of acquiring a house for her—attached, semidetached, or otherwise. In desperation, he took out a classified ad in the London dailies. "Down to earth with a bump," he wrote. "Fleet Air Arm officer unable to find anywhere to live." A well-meaning Londoner with a son who had served in the Royal Navy answered the ad and provided an apartment in Acton. "It was cheap," George later reflected, "and it was terrible, and it was our first home."[6]

To compound things, George's first months at Guildhall were fraught with difficulty. His course load consisted of conducting and orchestration, musical theory, harmony, and counterpoint, among other subjects. He took the piano, naturally, as his primary instrument. Given the requirement that Guildhall students take up a second instrument, George was advised to learn a wind instrument. After a great deal of consideration, he settled on the oboe, reasoning that he wasn't very fond of brass. Moreover, there was the issue of job prospects. To George's mind, mastering the oboe would allow him to seek out professional employment—the oboe was cheaper than a bassoon and less cumbersome to tote around. Besides, he figured that while clarinet players were a dime a dozen, solid oboe players were much harder to come by. Sure, there was the small matter of the instrument's inherent difficulties. But George felt that he was up for the challenge of mastering the oboe—"the ill wind that nobody blows good." To give himself an edge, George took private lessons with Margaret Eliot at her lavish apartment on Great Portland Street. The wife of vaunted British physician Richard Asher and the mother of three precocious children—Peter, Jane, and Clare—Eliot led a life of great culture and privilege. Visiting their exquisite environs must have been an eye-opener for the young Guildhall man who concealed a Cockney accent behind the posh veneer that he had acquired in the service. The differences between his station and the Ashers' must have felt even more acute when he returned to Sheena and his Acton flat on a very different side of town.[7]

With his second instrument underway, George planned to supplement his £300 married student grant through composition and evening gigs playing the oboe. As with his marriage, his dreams of finding success through live performance quickly began to take an inauspicious turn. While he always suffered from nervous bouts associated with playing in front of live audiences, his dexterity with the piano allowed him to overcome many of his fears. As he soon discovered, the oboe turned out to be another story entirely. His oboe examination at the Guildhall was conducted in front of Terrence McDonagh and Peter Graeme, two of Great Britain's preeminent oboists. While George managed to pass the exam, the experience left him stricken: "Sheer terror made me sweat so much that it was running down my fingers, and they slipped on the keys. There was no controlling it. That oboe became a live eel in my hands."[8]

While George never gained a genuine sense of confidence in his ability to work the oboe, his coursework provided him with ways of thinking about music that would have lasting professional value for him. In his years at Guildhall, he was most at home with his composition courses. In fact, he had been thinking about the act of composition for more than a decade by this point, having been prodded to continue his studies in this regard by Sidney Harrison, his fairy godfather. But for George, his tutorials in orchestration proved to be most valuable and life-altering. As part of his training, he would set the poetry of such luminaries as W. B. Yeats and Rupert Brooke to music to test out his muscle as composer and arranger. To complete the cycle, he would then compile full staves of orchestration for each of his poem-songs, thus taking the exercise to its full course.[9]

Indeed, as his surviving manuscripts reveal, he tried his hand at setting a wide variety of poems to music, including such works as Yeats's "Down by the Salley Gardens" and Brooke's "All Suddenly the Wind Comes Soft," as well as Ralph Vaughan Williams's "Linden Lea" and John Masefield's "Beauty." In order to further hone his skills as a composer, he created arrangements for Claude Debussy's "The Girl with the Flaxen Hair," one of the tunes that had thrilled him during his youth, and Johann Sebastian Bach's *Easter Oratorio* and Gavotte in D Minor, among others. He also tried his hand at arranging Domenico Scarlatti's sonata "Tempo di Ballo" and Edward Lysaght's Irish folk song "Kitty of Coleraine." In a lighter mood, he playfully orchestrated classic nursery rhymes like "Pop Goes the Weasel" and various Christmas carols. As he progressed in his studies, George began attempting more sophisticated original compositions such as a "Quintet for Woodwind" and the more ambitious "Fantasy in C Minor." While he suffered mightily as he attempted to take up the oboe, he found himself more at home during his Guildhall days as a composer—especially now that he had the musical vocabulary and technical skills to bring his ideas to life. It was as if the sounds that had lived inside of his head for so long had finally found a means for properly entering the world. More significantly, it was a far cry from his early days bashing about the piano in Scotland as Sheena closely observed him, sensing his unease at reading musical notation.[10]

Years later, George reflected on the signal differences between composition and orchestration, writing that "composition is a cerebral exercise of musical line and harmony, and whether it's performed on a synthesizer or by a hundred-piece orchestra, it's still the same music. What orchestration does is to give it life. And however you choose to do that coloring changes totally the way in which the audience receives the basic line." Above all, he learned at Guildhall that "when it comes to orchestration, what you do is to fill in all the subtle colorings, making the picture into a three-dimensional form." It was an idea that he had long harbored in his synapses—and it would be the making of him when he finally put it to the test. If George had misgivings about his Guildhall years, they involved the simple fact that he was a war veteran who happened to be more grown-up than many of the other students. Sometimes he "felt a little bit out of place" at the conservatory, he later reflected, "because I was older." Yet at the same time, Guildhall expanded his horizons in unexpected ways. In addition to the school's musical focus, it also served as a training ground for actors, affording George the opportunity to work with students in music and acting alike. Being comfortable with individuals from both of these artistic spheres would prepare him for his future in ways that he could barely imagine at this early vantage point.[11]

In July 1950, George graduated from Guildhall, his three-year coursework having been completed and his degree unfurled. Would he make a go of it with the oboe—that live eel let loose in his hands? *Certainly not.* While he had taken a series of freelance gigs playing oboe in parkside bandstands, he never held any illusions about becoming a virtuoso. Admittedly, he was "pretty well lost." Within a month, he had taken a job at the BBC Music Library at Yalding House on Great Portland Street. On the one hand, his new position allowed him to eke out a living—and it required him to call on his musical abilities, which counted for something. But on the other hand, it was, ultimately, a clerk's job—nothing more, nothing less. In many ways, George was right back where he had started after his demobilization: a bottom-rung wage earner, just like his days in a clerical position back at the Iron and Steel Federation. It was a source of great humiliation, to be certain.[12]

But then a most amazing thing happened—almost as remarkable as the emergence of George's fairy godfather, Sidney Harrison, during the war years when he needed him most. It was September 1950, and twenty-four-year-old George received a letter from Oscar Preuss, the head of Parlophone Records, a subsidiary of the EMI Group (Electrical and Musical Industries), the multinational conglomerate. It was a bolt out of the blue—the opportunity, *finally*, to land his first real job. If George knew precious little about Parlophone at the time, he could hardly be blamed. "I had no idea what EMI stood for," he later admitted. "I didn't know what it was." At EMI House, Parlophone was then regarded as the "third label"—a lower rung specializing in light orchestral works, jazz, and dance-band recordings, as well as a stepchild of sorts to Columbia, EMI's commercial juggernaut, and HMV, the blue-chip "His Master's Voice" label. The EMI Group actually held a fourth label among its subsidiaries—Regal-Zonophone, which produced Salvation Army recordings. Parlophone had been founded in Germany by the Carl Lindström Company before the outbreak of the First World War. In honor of the Swedish-born Lindström, Parlophone's logo featured a distinctive capital L as its moniker, which is often mistaken for a British pound (£) sign. In 1924 the British division of Parlophone was created under the leadership of Preuss, who served as the branch's first A&R manager. During the label's early years, Preuss established Parlophone as one of the United Kingdom's most successful jazz labels. Parlophone's association with EMI found its roots in the Columbia

Graphophone Company, which had purchased a controlling interest in the Carl Lindström Company in 1927. Four years later, Columbia Graphophone merged with the Gramophone Company, one of the United Kingdom's oldest recording firms, and EMI was born. In this way, Parlophone—in spite of being one of the lower rungs on the corporate ladder—was integral to EMI's corporate history. But EMI's employees knew the pecking order among the company's labels. As George noted years later, HMV had Elvis Presley, and Columbia had Doris Day. But Parlophone lacked such household names among its artist stable, holding the contracts of such myriad acts as jazzman Humphrey Lyttelton, orchestra leader John Dankworth, and the Scottish Country Dance Association.[13]

On November 28, 1950, George wore his old navy greatcoat as he cycled across London from the Acton apartment that he shared with Sheena toward 3 Abbey Road, the august address of Preuss's offices at EMI Studios. As he made his way through the rainy London weather that morning, George was quite literally heading into unknown waters. Nestled among the stately Edwardian homes of London's St. John's Wood, the studios had originally been built in 1830 as a luxurious residence that included five reception rooms, nine bedrooms, a wine cellar, a substantial garden, and servants' quarters. Purchased by the Gramophone Company in 1929 and rechristened EMI Studios, the facility officially opened its doors in November 1931—scant months after Columbia Graphophone had merged with the Gramophone Company and formed the EMI Group. In the early 1930s, English composer Edward Elgar conducted the historic recording sessions at EMI Studios for *Pomp and Circumstance*, the series of five marches that would immortalize his name—the march titled "The Land of Hope and Glory" emerged as a British sporting anthem, while "The Light of Life" became the signature melody for American graduation ceremonies. The EMI complex is composed of four studios constructed behind the original estate, which serve as the administrative quarters. The largest facility, Studio 1, which can hold a full orchestra and chorus, accommodates much of the orchestral recording into the present day, with Studio 2 and Studio 3 providing progressively smaller creative spaces.[14]

When George arrived for his first day of work at Parlophone as Oscar Preuss's assistant, he parked his bicycle in the forecourt and made his way into the white-painted mansion at 3 Abbey Road. As he announced himself at Preuss's office, he came face-to-face with Judy Lockhart Smith, the old A&R man's striking assistant—"a young and attractive girl with a distinctly cool manner." He would always remember being put off by the frosty distance inherent in her upper-class mien. Years later, he would learn that his intuition had been mostly correct. On first glance, she thought that he seemed rather square, uncool even. And she was definitely from a higher social station—not to mention a veteran member of the EMI staff, having gone straight to work at Abbey Road from secretarial college. George would soon learn that in addition to serving as Parlophone's staunch gatekeeper, Judy was the well-heeled daughter of Kenneth Lockhart Smith, the influential chairman of the United Kingdom's Film Producer's Guild.[15]

To his relief, Martin spied Preuss sitting in a far corner of the large, homely office behind an old rolltop desk. In short order, Preuss revealed that he had learned about Martin from an EMI colleague, Victor Carne, who had promised to ask around when the Parlophone head began looking for an assistant. As luck would have it yet again, Carne had asked none other than Sidney Harrison, who gave the newly minted Guildhall graduate a hearty recommendation. Not long after they met, Carne shared some advice with Martin that the young Parlophone assistant would reflect upon throughout his life. "Always remember, George, that if you are needed by the company you can do pretty much as you like," the older man counseled him. "But if you need the company more than they need you, then you really have to toe the line!"[16]

On his very first day at Abbey Road, Martin observed an afternoon session with Tommy Reilly, an ace harmonica player. During the session, Martin watched as Preuss and the studio's white-coated engineers recorded Reilly performing the tracks that would comprise his Parlophone debut in early 1951, including a medley that featured "Bibbidi-Bobbidi-Boo" and "Autumn Leaves," as well as arrangements of "El Cumbanchero" and "Midnight in Mayfair." George's new salary would amount to scarcely more than two pounds per week more than that of his student days, but he needed a job. And with his thirst for new adventure—rarely quenched, as he was easily prone to boredom—the position with EMI was simply too good to pass up. To make things even more interesting, Parlophone was in serious need of a boost. By 1950, Preuss had decided to transform the weak label into its top-grade status of old. His dire need of an assistant was palpable: before Martin joined the label, Preuss handled all of the administrative duties while overseeing production that "encompassed the whole world of music."[17]

At Parlophone, George's initial responsibilities included managing the label's catalog of classical recordings. The navy veteran must have seemed like a natural fit, having a background and education in classical music. But the learning curve associated with his new life at Abbey Road was a steep one. Preuss wasted little time in tossing Martin into the "deep end" of the business.

George knew that he had a lot to learn, being regarded by his new boss as "very '12-inch'—a reference to the old 78 rpm shellac records of those days, which had popular music on 10-inch and classical on 12-inch discs." First up for the old A&R man's new assistant was the London Baroque Ensemble, conducted by Karl Haas, a Jewish refugee who had barely escaped the tyranny of Nazism. For Martin, it would amount to a kind of trial by fire: taking an existing Parlophone artist and recording new output. Haas "was a lovely old man, a doctor of music," Martin remembered. "He had suffered badly in the war, was never very well, and in addition was always broke. But if he had any money at all on him, he would be off out to buy me presents like boxes of liqueur chocolates, or take me out to lunch." An unfailingly generous sort, Haas was a musicologist by training as opposed to being a talented conductor. He possessed a wide knowledge of baroque music, which he entreated Preuss to produce in spite of the fact that baroque remained very unfashionable in the classical music marketplace.[18]

Things took an interesting turn, though, when Haas met Peter Ustinov, the budding English actor on his way to having a legendary career of his own. As it happened, Ustinov was an ardent fan of baroque music. With the germ of an idea in his mind, Haas proposed that they form a London Baroque Society, with Ustinov serving as its president, Haas acting as conductor, and young Martin as secretary. Over the years, they spent many convivial lunches at EMI Studios chatting about baroque selections that the London Baroque Ensemble would shortly undertake. In such moments, Martin proved himself to be an able colleague, as well as highly adept at networking among the various strata of the British capital's moveable feast of musicians and composers. His budding relationship with Ustinov—as with so many that he developed in the ensuing years—would have far-reaching consequences indeed.

In an early triumph on 78 rpm, George oversaw a complex session involving the Luton Girls Choir, conducted by Arthur E. Davies, and the Band of the Irish Guards, conducted by Lieutenant C. H. Jaeger, in a stirring performance of "Princess Elizabeth of England" in honor of Her Royal Highness. Released in 1951, the record presaged Elizabeth II's gala coronation in 1952 as Her Majesty, Queen of England. Not long after working with Haas and the London Baroque Ensemble, Martin was tasked by Preuss with an even more formidable Parlophone artist, Sidney Torch and His Orchestra. By this point, Preuss had taken to entrusting Martin with more independence around stately Abbey Road, but the prospect of working directly with Torch rightly concerned him. Torch "had a reputation for extracting the very best out of a score. But woe betide anyone who stood in the way. He could be quite a prima donna, though his musicians had a healthy respect for him." When he first encountered Torch in Studio 1, Martin was so terrified that "I wanted the earth to open up and swallow me." In spite of Torch's reputation, the two became friends and made many records together over the years, many of them novelty confections like *The Waltzing Cat*. Torch also brought Martin into the orbit of Wally Stott, who composed the music for BBC radio's *The Goon Show*. Perhaps most interestingly, Martin developed such a close working relationship with Torch that the young A&R man eventually proposed trying some experimental recordings. Martin reasoned that Torch and his orchestra's sound could be embellished by double-speed tape techniques in order to afford them a unique presentation. While Torch was reluctant at first, he eventually gave in to the younger man's enthusiasm. "We laid down an initial track," George later wrote, "then I played it back at half speed while Sidney conducted the instruments that were being overlaid." George was surprised at the difficulty involved in synchronizing the recordings and dealing with such a lugubrious pace in order to bring the concept off. By this point, Torch had had enough. "He cursed me for it and eventually flung his baton right across the studio, nearly impaling the first violin in the process, yelling 'Bloody nonsense!'" While Torch's outburst brought a sudden end to young Martin's experiment, the idea of attempting multispeed recording again was never far from his mind.[19]

As George continued to find his way in the recording industry, he began signing artists on his own accord. One of his first discoveries was composer and conductor Ron Goodwin, who had already led a varied career as an insurance clerk, a music publisher, and later as a copyist and arranger for the BBC. Eventually, Goodwin began scoring music for documentary films while also working as a ghostwriter for such well-known bandleaders as Stanley Black, Geraldo (Gerald Bright), and Peter Yorke, among a host of others. By 1951, his career was on the rise after conducting for the Polygon company, for whom he arranged the recording of Jimmy Young's 1951 UK chart-topper "Too Young." At the same time, he managed to find his way into George's orbit, and the two developed a fast friendship. Ready to make his mark, the young recording manager signed the bandleader to a contract that called for arrangements and orchestrations for a dozen vocal singles, along with six singles with Goodwin's own orchestra. After so many years of toil—and a host of different professions—Goodwin was thrilled to have a regular gig. The bandleader was especially taken with the idea of recording six records of his own: George "also included in the contract that I would make six singles with what we called Ron Goodwin and his Concert Orchestra—session players, musicians booked for vocal backing sessions; I had an orchestral manager at the time called Harry Benson, and he would book the musicians, some of whom I would particularly ask for." In 1953 Goodwin saw his first release with Parlophone, an instrumental version of the theme from Charlie Chaplin's controversial film *Limelight*. In Goodwin's hands, the song topped out at an impressive number three on the British hit parade. Quite suddenly, George was starting to generate dividends from his accidental career with EMI.[20]

It is an invariable truism that the music industry is always changing, and the mid-1950s were no different. When his career with Parlophone began, there was simply no such thing as a "record producer"; rather, George was an "A&R manager" responsible for leading his artists through the recording process. For George, working artists and repertoire was formal suit-and-tie work at Abbey Road, where the technical engineers, donning sparkling white lab coats, prepared the instrumentation for recording—positioning microphones, amplifiers, and so on—while balance engineers operated the knobs and levers on the mixing desk in the control booth. In this way, EMI Studios was besotted with formality. As George later recalled, "It was rather like working in the Civil Service. Everyone wore a suit and a tie; there was no slopping around in jeans as there is today. You couldn't even take your tie off in the studio, and the engineers wore white coats, which made them look like surgical assistants."[21]

But big changes were afoot, threatening to upend this routine and the whole of the music world. Shellac discs were being replaced by cheaper and more durable vinyl compounds in a variety of formats: seven-inch, 45 rpm "singles"; seven-inch, 33⅓ rpm "extended-play discs," often adorned with artistic picture sleeves; and twelve-inch, 33⅓ rpm LPs or "long-players" that could accommodate more than twenty minutes per side. Even more remarkably, the entire industry had been transformed by the advent of magnetic tape as the primary recording medium. In the not-so-distant past, music had been recorded directly to disc—indeed, the notion of "cutting a record" was a literal process. Magnetic tape very quickly exerted a paradigm shift upon the business of recorded music. Effectively, the act of capturing sound was no longer a static event in which the goal was to preserve the subject as viably as possible. Magnetic tape afforded studio personnel the capacity for shaping and reshaping the subject after the initial recording had occurred. Additional sounds could be added at later and later intervals. No one was saying it quite yet, but the idea of "recording artistry" was in the air, waiting to be loosed upon a waiting world.

While industry stalwarts did their level best to contend with the implications of such incredible shifts, George quickly learned that EMI traditionally stayed behind the curve, preferring to remain conservative in the face of sweeping changes to their business model. As he later wrote, "When I entered EMI in 1950, I was entering a world in which there was already a great deal of controversy. Long-playing records had been pioneered by CBS in America, and in June of that year Decca had issued their first." As it happened, the EMI Group was having none of it. "The bigwigs at EMI stupidly refused to acknowledge that this was going to be a viable form of recording," George lamented. "They said that no one would want the tedium of having a very long-playing record, that it would be too expensive, and that they would be content to stick with their 78 rpm singles." As George would be loath to discover, EMI's prevailing corporate attitude about reacting to these kinds of technological changes would be par for the course. It would prove to be a genuine source of frustration that would limit his ability, time and time again, to conduct his work and stretch the boundaries of his creative imagination.[22]

EMI's cleaving to the 78 rpm single format forced George to adapt to the constrictions of discrete record sides that could barely accommodate four and a half minutes of audio material. This was a particular challenge for any A&R manager given classical music's tendency to stretch into lengthy movements. "I had to plan the music that was to be played, going through the score and deciding where to make the breaks. They were quite arbitrary, sometimes even in the middle of a movement. When the music had no natural break, I'd have to have the last chord on the first side played again to start the second side, to stop it sounding peculiar. It was absurd." While irritated, on the one hand, by the necessity of editing the music in such a fashion, George couldn't help being fascinated, on the other, by the technical, even creative process of structuring the musical breaks. He began to listen to classical recordings by other A&R men with an ear toward learning how they handled such constraints. More problematic, though, was the effect that EMI's stubbornness was having on their business. As other labels adapted to the new formats, the EMI Group became increasingly obsolete in terms of their recording practices. In short order, the conglomerate began losing vital parts of its catalog. In 1957, for example, the vaunted RCA-Victor back catalog was lost to Decca after nearly six decades in the Columbia label's hands. The implications of the move seemed to spell disaster for EMI—and especially for Parlophone, which was already resting on quicksand. Gaining control over RCA's masters meant that Decca held the exclusive rights to Elvis Presley's catalog.[23]

To George's mind, this turn of events proved to be "catastrophic." All in all, the EMI Group managed to pace itself some two years behind the rest of the industry. In addition to the EMI Group's conservative approach to technological shifts, George also attributed the company's failure to begin producing twelve-inch, 33⅓ rpm LPs to being "terrified" about the larger capital expenditures inherent in manufacturing them—that, in a sense, the company was too "cheap" to assume the costs associated with producing long-players. The man behind the shortsighted decision to cling to the 78 rpm format was Sir Ernest Fisk, who "will go down in history as the chairman who delayed the entry of EMI into the long-playing record market. What history may not record," George later wrote, "is the day I nearly got the sack as a result of not knowing what he looked like since he worked at the head offices." Things came to a head when George was working a session in the cavernous Studio 1 at Abbey Road. He was juggling a full choir and a spate of engineers while awaiting the appearance of a tardy organist. Suddenly, a man with a domed head carrying a music case showed up in the doorway. "It's about bloody time," George shrieked at him. "Do you realize we've been waiting for you?" As George chided him for delaying the session, the man suddenly said, "Do you know who I am?" And that's when it happened, George later recalled, as "a terrible doubt started to tug at the Martin mind." The man with the domed head went on to say, "My name is Fisk, and I am the chairman of this company." George felt a "ghastly silence" come over him as he contemplated the "great future behind" him.[24]

George's verbal gaffe with Sir Ernest was hardly his only mistake during his early years with Parlophone. As the newest and generally the youngest man on the EMI totem pole, he was forced to contend with a variety of egos and attitudes out of sheer necessity. Worse yet, he had to learn—on the fly, no less—how to become both shrewd and politically savvy. One of his earliest calamities occurred when the company sent him to see Mario Lanza singing "Be My Love" on the silver screen. "Being still very classically minded," he later wrote, "I was wholly offended by this man's singing, just belching it out with brute force and bloody ignorance. I hated every minute of it." After writing a derisive report in which he recommended against EMI taking on Lanza's performance of "Be My Love" for release, he had to watch in horror as it became a hit song for one of their competitors.[25]

Yet George's biggest blunder happened during a recording session with jazz great Humphrey Lyttelton and his band. As the group rehearsed one of their latest numbers, George felt himself becoming increasingly irritated by the bass player's finger work, which, to George's ears, sounded like a "dull thud." Perhaps even worse, the young A&R manager had the nerve to speak up, telling the bassist that he sounded like he was "playing with boxing gloves on." Hearing this remark, "Humph exploded. Calling me names of which I had not previously heard, he stomped out of the studio." Not knowing what to do, Martin hurriedly located Preuss, who demanded that he find Lyttelton and apologize profusely. And that's when the normally supportive head of Parlophone fed the bitter truth to his protégé. "If you lose us Humph, you've lost yourself your job," Preuss told him. In no time flat, George caught up with the jazz man, huffing and puffing along Abbey Road. He managed to bring Lyttelton back into the fold, but the lesson had been once and truly learned. "Musically, I was right," George reflected. "Diplomatically, I was wrong." It was an enduring philosophy that would serve him well across his career. "Tact is the *sine qua non* of being a record producer," he wrote years later. "One has to tread a fine line between, on the one hand, submitting to an artist's every whim, and on the other, throwing one's own weight about." For George, this aspect of his approach would be the first step toward a greater understanding of the business he had found himself in—a career for which, in one sense, he had never really prepared; and yet in another, it was the career for which George, with his long-standing fascination with music and the mechanics of sound, was seemingly made. "I had to learn how to get my own way without letting the performer realize what was happening. One had to lead rather than drive."[26]

# 3

# A HOUSE IN ST. JOHN'S WOOD

LIFE AT PARLOPHONE in the early 1950s fell into a steady routine as George traipsed between sessions in Abbey Road's studio spaces, more often than not finding himself in Studio 2—"Number 2" as it was affectionately known around the premises. George enjoyed the relative coziness of the space in comparison to Studio 1, which felt like the interior of a warehouse, or Studio 3, which seemed confining for all but the smallest of sessions. By contrast, Number 2 was ideal for George's acts, which generally consisted of small bands and half orchestras. He moved easily between the studio floor, where technical engineers handled the equipment, and the windowed control room up a narrow flight of wooden stairs, where balance engineers worked the boards and tape operators—"button pushers," in Abbey Road speak—staffed the machines. The staircase housed a storage closet filled to the brim with percussion instruments and all manner of attendant noisemakers. In terms of its overall size, Number 2 was relatively spacious, occupying some twenty-two hundred square feet with twenty-eight-foot ceilings. The powerful British Musicians' Union regulated the time and duration of studio work, with a maximum of three sessions per day and no more than twenty minutes of recorded output allowed. As a "closed-shop" organization, membership was compulsory, and the Musicians' Union specified session times from 10 AM to 1 PM, 2 to 5 PM, and 7 to 10 PM. Moreover, sessions ran "strictly to time," meaning that lunch and tea breaks were compulsory and that the session lengths were fixed. The concept of the producer as a kind of artistic director and collaborator had still not come into vogue at this point—and A&R managers like George weren't afforded royalties for their efforts, no matter how successful their records might be. On the rarest of occasions, standout A&R men would receive year-end bonuses to reflect the EMI Group's appreciation for their toil.[1]

When George started at Parlophone in 1950, A&R managers were basically supervisors. "Once an artist was contracted," he later wrote, "we had to decide on the repertoire—what piece should be performed—and we would work out in advance what kind of accompaniment was needed, organize the musicians for the session, book the studio, and brief the recording engineer. In the studio, we would control the session and encourage the artist to give a good performance." But in spite of the narrow expectations of his job and other strictures associated with life at Abbey Road, George found the work to be anything but dull. He especially enjoyed the act of bringing his artists' musical visions to life. He was always ready, willing, and able to pull out all the stops in support of their unbridled creativity. If anything, he preferred his sessions to present all manner of intellectual challenges rather than being simple rote executions of his clients' latest wares. The concept of using the studio as a means for creative problem-solving was exciting for the young A&R man, as evinced by his early efforts with Sidney Torch and multispeed recording.[2]

A prime example of George's innate sense of studio artistry came to light in 1952, when George decided to try his hand with experimental recording techniques yet again. This time around, he impressed Peter Ustinov, his colleague from the London Baroque Ensemble, to record a double-sided comedy single. In the early 1950s, Peter enjoyed a reputation for being the *enfant terrible* of British actors. Anxious to capitalize on his friend's notoriety, George recorded Peter's tongue-in-cheek "Mock Mozart," a three-minute mini-opera in which the actor sang all of the soprano, alto, and tenor parts. "For those days," George later reflected, "that was pretty adventurous. We didn't have multitrack recording, of course, so in order to produce the four-part ensemble he had to sing with himself." To accomplish this end, George instructed his technical engineer to dub Peter's voice from one tape onto another, mixing each recording as the process moved forward. In those pre-multitrack days, George recognized that the recording was certain to suffer generational loss as the tape deteriorated from successive recordings. Indeed, with each new pass, the signal-to-noise ratio worsened ever more perceptibly. The resulting record was an unusual release by any standards. At a monthly EMI meeting, he was summarily accosted for his experimental foray with Peter. "What do you think you're up to, George?" a colleague brusquely inquired. "It doesn't make sense. No one's ever made a record like this before." As it happened, George had the last laugh when he learned that the Oxford Street record shop had sold all three hundred copies of "Mock Mozart." "I was flying by the seat of my pants," he later admitted regarding the making of Peter's record. "I mean, I was doing things I wanted to do, hoping that the public would like them." By the time that EMI managed to press additional copies, the demand for Peter's confection had dried up. But for George, the lesson was clear and lasting: there was a commercial appetite, no matter how modest at the moment, for his experimental adventures—and especially in terms of good old tried and true British comedy. It was also confirmation of George's growing belief about a coming shift in his profession. "When I came to working as a producer, up to that time people had been making records as faithfully as they could, reproducing the original sound. What they were doing was making photographs. I said, 'Let's paint, instead of having photographs.'" With "Mock Mozart," George's paintings were beginning to come into more vivid relief.[3]

During this same period, Oscar Preuss suggested that Martin try his hand at record promotion in addition to his regular A&R duties. The first artist that he "plugged" was Roberto Inglez—Parlophone's "Latin American" Scot whose real name was Bob Ingles. Inglez specialized in "one-finger piano," low-register pieces like "Romanza," sophisticated, bouncy tunes with lush orchestration. In one unforgettable moment, with Inglez's latest records under his arm, Martin sped across town on his motorcycle to the BBC, where he attempted to persuade Jack Jackson to play Inglez's work on the *Saturday Night Show* featuring Tiddles the Cat. Martin remembered being "crushed" by his inability to place Inglez with the BBC. "Look, son," Jackson told him, "I don't want to be unkind to you. If you can bring me a record that's suitable for my program, I'd love to play it. But Roberto Inglez!" George soon realized that he wasn't very adept at record plugging. "I was a sheep among wolves, and didn't even realize it," he wrote. "In those days, there was a great deal of scandal surrounding the plugging business, and all sorts of people were taking backhanders. But that was not Oscar's style." As it turns out, using payola to push record promotion wasn't George's style either. There was no doubt that he was ambitious and wanted to succeed in the record business—the surprise career that Preuss had placed in his lap—but he had learned that, like his mentor, he was upright. He wouldn't be cutting any ethical corners. No, record promotion most certainly wasn't for him.[4]

With record plugging behind him, George continued to seek out new talent. But as it happened, big changes were brewing both at EMI and on the home front. In December 1954, Preuss grabbed a microphone in Studio 1 and announced his retirement during the annual EMI Christmas party. At his retirement dinner the following April, Preuss received the company's oddly underwhelming token of appreciation for a lifetime's service to the EMI Group: a copy of the *Encyclopedia Britannica*. Given everything that was to transpire in later years, George would have been well served to take special notice of EMI's decided lack of largesse during such an auspicious moment. Nevertheless, that same evening George learned that he would be promoted to head of Parlophone Records. He was shocked to have been selected, later remarking, "I thought that someone would come in and be put above me, so I was shaken to the core when they said I could have the job." At twenty-nine years old, he became the youngest label executive in EMI's history. Preuss was fond of telling Martin that "recording is a young man's business," and with his protégé taking the Parlophone reins, Preuss's words seemed to be as true as ever. Preuss also left his protégé with one parting bit of advice: "One thing you've got to remember, George. With artists, if you ever get thanks, it's a bonus."[5]

While George was pleased with his new position, he was well aware that dark clouds scudded on the edges of Parlophone's horizon. "Blimey," he thought. "Suddenly, I was head of Parlophone, and I had to make it work. I wasn't paid much, but I was given a free run." George well knew that the "third label" had continued to struggle throughout the 1950s, floundering in its effort to achieve any sense of pervasive identity while standing by as big-name artists and budding superstars signed with EMI's blue-chip labels—or went elsewhere altogether. George had long been aware of the internal pressures at EMI. When Preuss hired Martin as his assistant back in 1950, the older man had warned him that Parlophone's future rested on shaky ground within the company. As he took the reins in April 1955, George did so with his eyes wide open. "I knew perfectly well that I had to raise the level of the label and sell more records if I was going to survive," he recalled. "We were given a rap over the knuckles if a record didn't sell well, and most of the records I made sold only 3,000 to 5,000 copies, break-even point. If we sold 20,000, we had a hit on our hands." Worse yet, EMI was struggling in general with a declining market share in response to increased competition from the likes of Decca, the EMI Group's chief rival, as well as from the Dutch start-up Philips Electrical and the Cambridge-based Pye.[6]

If not for the promotion, George very likely would have left Parlophone behind. He had been strongly considering an offer from Decca Records, which seemed appealing for a number of reasons. First, Decca had enjoyed multinational successes since the 1930s and—at least from the vantage point of the mid-1950s—they seemed poised to continue riding high into the 1960s and beyond, in contrast with EMI. Second, and perhaps most important, George's young family with Sheena now counted a daughter, Alexis, among its number. Lovingly called "Bundy" by her doting parents, she was born on September 21, 1953. As for their homestead, the Martins had finally left their confining Acton apartment and taken up residence in a semidetached house at 53 Roe Green Close in Hatfield—some twenty miles north of London. George had long hoped to own a home of his own, and the idea became even more concrete after his assistant, Judy, who had grown up in the tony old section of Hatfield, slipped him a pamphlet about the area's housing boom. Hatfield had been selected by the government to be a "New Town" to help remedy the nation's paralyzing postwar housing shortage. Hatfield's selection made perfect sense given the growing and thriving aerospace industry in the region, which had begun in 1930 with the de Havilland Aircraft Company's factory—the same firm that George had opted out of years earlier when he couldn't muster the £250 apprenticeship fee. By 1960, Hatfield would develop into a full-fledged manufacturing center when Hawker Siddeley settled in the area, bringing thousands of aerospace jobs in the bargain. While George was excited by the prospect of home ownership, Sheena was mortified by the prospect of leaving London. She would later confess to having been much happier back in their cold-water apartment in Acton, where she and George had come to enjoy a wide circle of friends, many dating back to their Fleet Air Arm and Guildhall days. Determined to make his dream of having his own homestead a reality, George mounted his recently acquired Ariel VB 600 motorcycle, with Sheena riding along in the sidecar, and made the trip some twenty-two miles to the north to Hatfield. Never one to stand in the way of her husband's dreams, Sheena relented, and George secured a mortgage for the £2,400 house after borrowing money for the down payment from his in-laws and happily selling his much-reviled oboe.[7]

Shortly after George, Sheena, Alexis, and ever-faithful Tumpy moved into the tiny semidetached home, Judy and her parents stopped by to welcome the young family to Hatfield. After they left, George couldn't help noticing how awkward the Lockhart Smiths seemed to feel in the Martins' middle-class environs. "They treated this place like something you put up on a Friday night and took down on Sunday morning," he told his wife. But in short order,

George began renovating the first house he would ever own. As with his master-carpenter father before him, George enthusiastically applied himself to fitting out the house, even building an elegant fireplace and several pieces of furniture. With Sheena as his able assistant, he discovered that he was a real handyman about the young family's cozy home. Also like his father, George was a man of great economy, always looking out for a bargain—as much as for a way to be part of the process of not only making something but also making something new with his own hands. Years later, he would think back fondly about these simpler times. "It's always much more fun when you're having to do things for yourself," he mused, "when things aren't so easy and you don't have everything given to you."[8]

For Sheena, living in Hatfield took considerable time to grow on her. She had been relatively happy back in Acton, where she and George had enjoyed a thriving social life. As a "New Town," suburban Hatfield was still in the process of becoming a community, lacking sufficient sidewalks and forcing the young mother to push her daughter's pram through the muddy streets. Suddenly living so far from London, Sheena later confessed to feeling untethered without a telephone or a television and only the radio to keep her company as she raised a small child while her husband kept long hours back in the city. During this period, there was also a clear departure between George's ambitions to make his name in the recording industry and Sheena's simpler goals for establishing their homestead in a very different locale. To her mind, she felt marooned out in suburban Hatfield, with a young child as her only companion, while her husband was living an increasingly exciting life as he desperately worked to revive Parlophone and shift its fortunes toward genuine profitability.[9]

The family's relocation to Hatfield required George to buy a car to accommodate his commute into the city—especially given his erratic work schedule, which often demanded that he work evening hours to accommodate frequent recording sessions with his stable of artists. Having passed his driver's test in July 1954, he purchased a 1935 Austin Ten Cambridge sedan for sixty pounds. Proud of buying his first car, George gave Oscar Preuss a lift in order to show off his new prize. As they sped along the Finchley Road toward a traffic light, George went to shift gears only to find, to his horror, that the entire knob from the floor-mounted gearshift had come away in his hand. Not missing a beat, Preuss's protégé handed him the knob, saying in perfect deadpan, "Would you mind holding that for a moment?" as he brought his wounded vehicle to a rest—in third gear, no less—with the help of the Finchley Road curb.[10]

Having taken up the reins of Parlophone after Preuss's retirement, Martin intended to push the label's generic boundaries well beyond classical music. But first he had to contend with Preuss's standing roster of artists. George's work with Eve Boswell and Jimmy Shand typified his experiences during this period. A Hungarian-born pop singer, Boswell hosted a BBC radio show. Originally signed by Preuss, Boswell began working with Martin by the mid-1950s, and together they recorded several hit songs, including "Sugar Bush" and "Pickin' a Chicken," which cracked the British top 10 singles chart in 1956. Yet another artist that Martin inherited from Preuss, Shand was a Scottish accordion player and polka aficionado. As the resident Scottish label in the EMI Group, Parlophone handled an array of popular Scots artists, including Shand, Ian Powrie, Mickie Ainsworth, and Jimmy Blue. Parlophone enjoyed predictably impressive sales returns on their Scottish roster by keeping production costs to a minimum. "Bringing all these artists down to Abbey Road would have been expensive, and EMI was never one for spending money," George recalled. "So once a year we would take to Scotland in the EMI mobile recording unit." The five-ton vehicle was outfitted with a lathe so that George and his team could record the musicians directly to disc. George worked beside the engineers in the van's cramped interior, which was outfitted with a pair of loudspeakers so that they could monitor the artists' performance in a nearby hall, where they set up microphones to capture the sound. Without the watchful eye of the Musicians' Union, George and his crew could produce a sizable amount of music in a relatively short period. In one two- to three-day period, for example, they stockpiled twenty-four new Jimmy Shand master recordings—enough to supply Parlophone with reliable sellers for an entire year. With George behind the van's mobile recording desk, Jimmy recorded "The Bluebell Polka," which proved to be his biggest seller, breaking into the top 20 in 1955. They also became fast friends, sharing an interest in motorbikes. George regaled Jimmy with stories of his old Ariel VB 600 motorcycle, while Jimmy had a beaten-up motorcycle of his own, which he nursed back to life and sped around the Fife countryside.[11]

Having cut his teeth both at Abbey Road and now with the mobile unit, Martin was good and ready to seek out new talent in addition to working with Preuss's hand-me-downs. Dick James was an early example of Martin's capacity for sizing up new artists. A well-known figure among Tin Pan Alley—the assortment of music shops around Denmark Street in London's West End—James sang with vocal groups such as Geraldo's and the Stargazers but longed to establish himself as a solo act. With Martin in tow as his A&R manager, James hit pay dirt when he penned the theme for *The Adventures of Robin Hood*, the ITV serial that starred a host of British character actors; the show also marked the television debut for eleven-year-old Peter Asher and his younger sister, ten-year-old Jane—the eldest children of Martin's oboe teacher during his Guildhall days. For Martin, *The Adventures of Robin Hood* was a godsend. After all, the signature theme for a show about a swashbuckling archer was the perfect vehicle for some more of the studio wizardry that he was aching to try out. "I really wanted the 'William Walton sound' of all those arrows going through the air," he later reflected. "I actually got an archer in and put microphones all the way down Number 2 studio and had him fire an arrow past them and into a target at the other end—and it sounded awful. In the end we got the right noise by jamming a wooden ruler on the end of a desk, and going 'doinngg' with an elastic band on a mike, and slowing it down." In addition to deploying such improvised sound effects, George rounded up a posse of children, consisting of Dick's eight-year-old son, Stephen, and his schoolmates, to gleefully shout the theme's opening salvo, "Hooray, here comes Robin Hood!" As they listened to the playback, George good-naturedly provided Stephen and his pals with a sugar-themed session "fee" of cookies, chocolate candy, and lemonade. As it happened, Martin and James's association would eclipse their working relationship at Parlophone, with the Tin Pan Alley veteran later exerting a far-reaching influence upon the course of Martin's career.[12]

James's theme for *The Adventures of Robin Hood* not only resulted in a minor hit for Martin but also was proof positive that he could use the studio's environs to create impactful sonic pictures in the minds of his listeners. To this end, he was fond of employing an art metaphor for explaining the possibilities of musical production. "Drawing is not what one sees, but what one must make others see," he later observed, paraphrasing the words of French impressionist Edgar Degas. "In a way, that's what we do in sound. The recording is not what one hears, but what one must make others hear." As the years wore on, George's impressionistic metaphor proved to be a powerful realization for him. "Gradually, I got hooked" by the studio's artistic possibilities, he later observed. "I didn't want to leave it. It enabled me to be creative. I could do things that I found very enjoyable." But the real challenge, as he learned on more than one occasion throughout his life with Parlophone in the 1950s, involved walking the tightrope between A&R manager and creative director. His clients needed to believe that the ideas he stimulated and brought to life were theirs alone, but at the same time, he had to be as forceful as possible to get the best out of his artists. And all of this had to be accomplished, of course, within the boundaries of three discrete and highly prescribed sessions designed to produce a maximum output of the aforementioned twenty minutes. It made for a daunting task that George had to achieve with great tact, flattery, and efficiency—an unusual combination of personality traits by any measure. But George soon learned that he had all three qualities in spades. He was able to sublimate his artists' larger egos inside the contrastingly less-threatening space of his humble presence. And it didn't hurt that he was good looking—tall, blond, and well spoken, with piercing blue eyes and a staid demeanor. He quickly found that he commanded a quiet sense of authority and confidence from his artists. At times, they wanted not only to please him but also to act as genuine collaborators in the recording enterprise. His artists soon found that the "squarish" seeming man with the soothing voice and the pressed shirt and tie was one of them.[13]

Another early Martin success came at the fingers of John Dankworth, the jazz composer, saxophonist, and clarinetist. George was particularly proud of "Experiments with Mice," in which John made a musical progress through the signature sounds of the great bandleaders of yore. George also worked with John's wife, celebrated jazz chanteuse Cleo Laine, on the old standard "I Got It Bad and That Ain't Good."[14]

With his promotion now well in hand, George concentrated his energies on improving Parlophone's standing within the EMI Group, which was undergoing seismic shifts of its own at the time. At this juncture, EMI was finally beginning to manufacture long-players. Even more promising, the ultraconservative firm was beginning to market limited-edition "Stereosonic" records for release. But there were even more pressing events in the offing. Like Preuss, Ernest Fisk also decided to retire from the company, which wasted little time in appointing ambitious industrialist Sir Joseph Lockwood as the new EMI chairman. In one of his earliest moves, Lockwood spearheaded EMI's $8 million buyout of Capitol Records, the American juggernaut, in January 1955. The British musical press saw the move as a harbinger for EMI's British recordings to enjoy a more expansive American marketplace. As *Melody Maker* reported, "A new field is open for a greater distribution than ever before of EMI 'popular' records in America." Yet as part of the deal with EMI, Capitol ensured that the Hollywood-based label preserved its standing right to refuse to release UK acts unless Capitol execs felt that they could succeed stateside. The clause, already infamous among EMI's A&R men, was known as the "first turn-down option." And more often than not, the folks back in Hollywood did just that, having dismissed the vast majority of British records as being altogether incongruous with its distinctly *American* sound. As it happened, the latter issue was the least of Sir Joseph's concerns.

At the time, his primary motive in acquiring Capitol was to ensure that EMI controlled the American company's means of production—its massive manufacturing centers in Scranton, Pennsylvania, and Hollywood, California.[15]

With George's shift in stature, life at Parlophone changed in a hurry for the young label manager. In addition to the pressure of great expectations for Parlophone's success in the face of years of fading revenues, George had to build his staff. To his surprise, Preuss's longtime assistant, Judy Lockhart Smith, immediately turned in her resignation. "Now that you're setting up your own organization and your own department," she announced, "you'll want to make a clean sweep of it." But George knew far better than to let the remaining person with the most institutional memory stroll right out the door of 3 Abbey Road. "It would have been disastrous to get rid of the one person who knew more about Parlophone's business than I did," he later reflected. During this same period, George took to commuting to London with Judy in tow, giving the new record exec and his assistant ample time to plot a more promising future for the struggling label. Like Preuss before him, Martin also had the privilege of hiring his own A&R assistant. For this vital task, which grew to include signing new talent and conducting sessions at Abbey Road, he settled on Ron Richards. Three years George's junior, Ron had a background in music publishing, which George shrewdly recognized as vital in growing Parlophone's portfolio and as a much-needed complement to his own expertise. During this same period, thirty-two-year-old Norman Smith began working for EMI after answering a newspaper advertisement for a recording assistant. A Royal Air Force glider pilot during World War II, Smith had cut his teeth as a jazz musician before trying his hand at Abbey Road. "I got the job and was basically just a 'gofer' for the engineers and producers," he later remarked. "EMI had put a ceiling of 28 on the job, and I lied about my age to get in." Eventually, Smith "owned up about it, but I had the job by then and nobody seemed particularly bothered." Not long after taking over the reins of Parlophone, George also had to contend with shifting the label's headquarters from the old estate house in St. John's Wood to the EMI offices on Great Castle Street, a few miles away in the garment district.[16]

George wasted little time in trying to expand Parlophone's record sales. His work was more than cut out for him, as several Parlophone stalwarts had recently been lured away by Decca. George could hardly have been surprised given that he had very nearly left EMI for the greener pastures of Decca House himself. After all, George reasoned, Decca was "a very good and powerful label" in comparison with Parlophone, "a tinpot little label" that was now being "run by a man who was little more than a music student." Yet for all of his self-doubts, George clearly understood the magnitude of the new opportunity that Oscar's retirement had afforded him. He readily admitted that it had been "quite adventurous" of Sir Joseph to appoint "a fairly brash young man without much experience in the record business" like himself as Parlophone head. "But for me, it was an unbelievable chance," he wrote. "I was boss of a whole record label. I was on my own."[17]

In his first act as label head, George took stock of Parlophone's position: "I had to maintain allegiance to the artists we already had—Jimmy Shand, who was our biggest seller, Eve Boswell, Ron Goodwin, Jack Parnell, Johnny Dankworth, Humphrey Lyttelton." But more importantly, he quickly recognized that to leave his mark on the business—to set Parlophone on an even more powerful, possibly even uniquely *different* course—he needed to "get between the cracks" of the other labels in EMI's stable. Not surprisingly, George instinctively shifted his attentions toward comedy. He was proud of his work on Peter Ustinov's "Mock Mozart," and while EMI had bungled the opportunity, in his mind, of netting additional sales, he sensed a significant consumer appetite for clever, well-made comedy records. In retrospect, George later observed, the time was right for British comedy: "I hit upon the idea of making the kind of records that other people weren't making. And nobody was making comedy records in Britain. Stan Freberg and Bob Newhart were making comedy records successfully in America, but nothing much was happening in England." But George also recognized that time was of the essence if Parlophone was going to survive the internal politics brewing at EMI House. By the fall of 1956, a movement was afoot to place Parlophone in mothballs, transfer its revenue-generating artists to Columbia or HMV, and release the third label's less vital clientele. While musicians like Humphrey Lyttelton more than carried their weight—in 1956 the trumpet legend scored the first top 20 British jazz hit with "Bad Penny Blues," produced by Parlophone's Joe Meek—the lion's share of the label's clientele was hardly setting the world on fire. C. H. Thomas, the general manager of EMI's record division, was the primary force behind such radical cost-saving measures, even going so far as to propose that George be transferred to HMV as Walter Ridley's junior A&R man. George had no choice but to act quickly or sit idly by and watch as his standing at EMI became greatly diminished. Sure, he had a knack for bringing comedy to life on record. But as he would admit years later, he came to produce England's funnymen out of sheer desperation to save Parlophone—and his livelihood.[18]

As it happened, Martin didn't have to wait very long to find his next project. In early 1957, he attended a two-man show called *At the Drop of a*

*Hat* at the tiny New Lindsey Theatre near Notting Hill Gate. The show featured actor and singer Michael Flanders and composer, pianist, and linguist Donald Swann. *At the Drop of a Hat* took place on an empty stage, save for Flanders, who suffered from polio, in a wheelchair, and Swann seated behind the piano. Their repertoire consisted of fiendishly witty introductory comments and one hilarious song after another. For his part, Martin was simply bowled over by their performance. After a little persuasion, he succeeded in talking them into selling him the rights to record the show. And he did so in just the nick of time. On January 24, 1957, Flanders and Swann shifted *At the Drop of a Hat* to the Fortune Theatre in London's West End, and the comedy duo struck gold. The show ran at the Fortune for a remarkable 808 performances before moving to New York City in 1959. Excited by the opportunity to attach Parlophone to Flanders and Swann's hit revue, Martin recorded the duo live at the Fortune for five consecutive nights, later editing the material together to create a seamless whole. Rushed into stores, *At the Drop of a Hat* gave the struggling label some sorely needed success on the British charts. Perhaps Martin would find a way to get between the cracks and score some surefire hits for Parlophone after all.[19]

Reflecting back on those heady days in 1957, George felt that "it was a good time for comedy," reasoning that Parlophone's sudden bout of success could be attributed to radio enjoying its second wind in the face of television's initial onslaught. "Comedy records succeeded because sound dominated in the days before television got its grip on people." At that point, television was still "black and white, with very few stations and a limited number of hours of transmission per day. Radio was still king and listeners had aural imaginations: people could picture in their own minds what was going on." George shrewdly recognized that he had a genuine knack for bringing mental images to life. And perhaps more than that, he had a powerful talent for bringing them to fruition in the studio. He was also willing to work long hours to see a project through. As he later observed, "It was enormously hectic, but I was very keen, and I did so desperately want Parlophone to be a big label. I worked all the hours, and it was worth it because I thought I was doing something really worthwhile."[20]

Flush with the excitement of Flanders and Swann's success, Martin wasted little time in turning his efforts back to an old friend from his early years at EMI. Back in 1953, he had recorded *Jakka and the Flying Saucers*, a space fantasy play for children. Written by lyricist Ken Hare and with Ron Goodwin as its composer, the play included a wide range of whimsical voices and songs in a fairly limited story about a space boy, Jakka, who trolls about the sky on a space scooter accompanied by his five-legged space dog. One of the play's characters was voiced by Peter Sellers, who had made his start in radio on Ted Ray's weekly radio show *Ray's a Laugh*, later emerging as a member of the BBC Home Service's burgeoning radio program *The Goon Show*. Martin looked back at *Jakka and the Flying Saucers* with a sense of embarrassment: "It was a complete disaster, and I blush to think of it." While the record "sold 10 copies," he couldn't shake the memory of one sound in particular. In Sellers's hilarious impression—the record's only genuine bright spot—"the voice of God came out remarkably like Winston Churchill." As always, Martin's ear was fine-tuned for comedy, and Sellers had it in spades.[21]

In June 1955, he seized the opportunity to work with Sellers yet again—this time, in the company of fellow Goon Spike Milligan. With George's full attention, they pitched the idea of recording a parody of "Unchained Melody," which had been a smash hit in the United Kingdom the previous year. In fact, four different cover versions of the song by Al Hibbler, Les Baxter, Jimmy Young, and Liberace had simultaneously settled into the British top 20. As far as Sellers and Milligan were concerned, it was ripe for the pickings. For Martin, it was his chance to finally produce a record under the Goons moniker. But his hopes were just as quickly dashed at EMI's monthly supplement meeting, when he excitedly played the finished record for "the assembled EMIcrats, one of whom said: 'Well, of course, if we're going to put out that particular version of "Unchained Melody," we'll have to get permission from the copyright owners, because you are distorting the song a bit.'" As it happened, George and the two Goons weren't merely distorting the song "a bit"—they were lampooning the thing to high heaven, complete with madcap voices and a ukulele. George was truly flummoxed at EMI's reticence, arguing that they were going to be paying a copyright anyway in order to record the song. As George later wrote, "My view was 'Issue first, and ask questions afterwards'"—a practice that would come back to haunt him time and time again. But on this occasion, EMI contacted the publisher, who rejected the song in short order, declaring that they would never grant permission for their "gorgeous opus" to be defiled in such a heinous fashion. For his part, George was decidedly bitter about the turn of events, as were the Goons, who left Parlophone for Decca. Not long thereafter, the Goons released "I'm Walking Backwards for Christmas," one of their biggest hits, as well as a standout moment in Milligan's career.[22]

But as it turned out, all was not lost. A few years later, Martin managed to cajole Sellers back into the studio, where they recorded a single, "Boiled Bananas and Carrots" backed with "Any Old Iron." Sung tongue in cheek in mock-Cockney tones, "Boiled Bananas and Carrots" found Sellers in high-flying style remaking the old Harry Champion music-hall tune. In contrast with the unfortunate *Jakka and the Flying Saucers*, Sellers's single enjoyed modest sales. On the strength of "Boiled Bananas and Carrots," Martin pitched the notion of making an album with Sellers to the EMI brass. In spite of having relative autonomy as head of Parlophone, Martin needed the approval of the managing director and EMI record division in order to undertake a long-player, which was still considered a major label decision at the time. Once again, George's enthusiasm was crushed during a monthly marketing meeting. It was like Ustinov all over again. "A single is one thing, but making an album?" the marketing team asked. "Who is going to listen to a whole half-hour of that stuff?" Never one to remain daunted, Martin hatched a compromise—a bit of necessary "argy-bargy"—with EMI's top brass: in exchange for a limited production budget, he and Sellers would cut a ten-inch LP as opposed to the standard twelve-inch LP. The result would be cheaper both for the consumer and in terms of the EMI Group's manufacturing costs. More importantly for Martin, he would be able to showcase Sellers's talents in (mostly) long-playing form.[23]

The eventual album, which George titled *The Best of Sellers* to needle his EMI colleagues for their preemptive doubts about the project, consisted of one sidesplitting comedic confection after another. At times, the album even required George to engage in physical comedy, as with "A Drop of the Hard Stuff," in which Peter and George simulated an extended fight scene. With no other means at their disposal to generate the necessary sound effects, George, Peter, and the engineers "piled a heap of chairs and tables and music stands in the middle of the studio. Then, as Peter was doing his Irish bit, a chair was kicked away, and a music-stand was sent hurtling across the floor. Bedlam ensued." Joining in the melee, George found himself on the unhappy receiving end of a flying chair, courtesy of Peter. Listeners can even hear his shriek of pain on the record. "I really hurt my shin," George later recalled, when "Peter got carried away" with the stage fighting. As with his deployment of sound effects, George soon discovered that he could accent Peter's hilarious timing through well-placed, carefully honed incidental music. In such instances in his early career, George opted to work under pseudonyms. After trying out the exotic-sounding "Lezlo Anales," he toyed with "John Chisholm," the name of his father-in-law, before settling on "Graham Fisher," a moniker that he drew directly from the name of a childhood chum from his Bromley dramatic society days with the Quavers.[24]

For Martin, the skillful deployment of incidental music of his own authorship and arrangement was an essential aspect of bringing Sellers's comedic palette to life, as well as one of many ways to populate the real estate inherent in the magnetic tape of the recording studio. It was a lesson that would resound throughout George's work for years to come—and especially in the coming decade, when the notion of being a full-fledged record "producer" would finally come into full flower. With spoken-word comedy recordings, George felt as if he were truly finding his niche, recognizing that "this was something that nobody else in the country was doing." As an art form in its own right, it required a special kind of A&R manager, such as George, who was adept both at contriving innovative sound effects and composing evocative incidental music. George's comedy forays also allowed him to engage in the kind of experimentation that he longed to pursue in the studio. In "Shadows on the Grass," for example, Sellers pretended to be a Frenchman who meets an older woman in the park. Played by English actress Irene Handl, the whimsical woman unleashes a lengthy monologue punctuated by Sellers's comic interjections. With George's incidental music and requisite sound effects as its accompaniment, "Shadows on the Grass" came to life in the studio as George and engineer Stuart Eltham pruned the nearly twelve-minute recording down to a more commercially viable six minutes for the purposes of the long-player.[25]

In the making of comedy records, Martin enjoyed a special affinity with players like Sellers and Handl who joined him at Abbey Road. To George's great delight, *The Best of Sellers* emerged as a smash hit for struggling Parlophone—so much so, in fact, that EMI later commissioned a full-length twelve-inch version of the album at which the managing director had originally balked. And George simply couldn't get enough of it. "For the first time, I was the prime mover in a team of fun givers," he recalled. "It was my job to think up the title, the cover design, the style and content of the album and the creation of sound pictures which highlighted Peter's genius." As *The Best of Sellers* continued to chalk up impressive sales receipts, George was elated for a variety of reasons. For one thing, he was beginning to get Parlophone back on solid financial footing. EMI commissioned a full spate of comedy records in the album's wake, including additional titles by Sellers. In 1957 Parlophone released Sellers's second album, *Songs for Swingin' Sellers*—a humorous takeoff on Frank Sinatra's *Songs for Swingin' Lovers*—and the album accrued strong sales, filling George with a well-earned sense of vindication. "After *The Best of Sellers* had proved such a success—to the private chagrin of the EMI people who had said it would be a waste of time—those same people now asked me to do another record," George wrote. "It was a kind of accolade, which recognized Parlophone as the label for humorous people."[26]

In addition to Sellers, one of Martin's favorite funnymen was the diminutive Charlie Drake, a British comedian who found fame as the star of the BBC's television program *Drake's Progress*. In 1958 Drake recorded a spoof of "Volare (Nel Blu Dipinto Di Blu)," which Martin enhanced with a varispeed recording technique in which he captured the song's backing vocals at half speed only to play them back at full speed, enhancing the harmonies with a comedic feel befitting Drake's novelty track. It would hardly be the last time that George tried his hand at concocting such rudimentary studio effects. During this same period, varispeed recording would enjoy renown of a different sort after the Chipmunk's novelty act scored a seasonal hit with "The Chipmunk Song (Christmas Don't Be Late)." To create the illusion of the three chipmunks—the fictive Alvin, Simon, and Theodore—singing their trademark high-pitched vocals, creator Ross Badgasarian Sr. deployed varispeed to create the trio's anthropomorphic vocal stylings. Not long afterward, Badgasarian was rewarded with three Grammys for his efforts.

As for George and Parlophone, the "humorous people" began to flock to EMI's "third label" in veritable droves. By this point, all talk of mothballing Parlophone had ceased, with Sir Joseph Lockwood, a great supporter of George's, lauding the important role that EMI—and especially Parlophone—played in championing British talent across the record industry. Quite suddenly, Parlophone had emerged as the home for the premier British comedians of the day. Not surprisingly, Peter Sellers was quickly followed by fellow Goons Spike Milligan and Harry Secombe, along with actor Bernard Cribbins. As with Sellers, Martin delighted in his sessions with Britain's funnymen—right on down to dreaming up the artwork for their album covers. For Milligan's 1961 album, *Milligan Preserved*, the comedian was pictured with his head on a plate being "preserved" in a glass bell jar. "To do that," George recalled, "we had to have a special table cut with a hole in it through which Spike stuck his head. We nearly suffocated him when the jar was placed over his head."[27]

As with Flanders and Swann, Martin never shied away from scouting out new talent. On August 22, 1960, the *Beyond the Fringe* comedy revue premiered at the Royal Lyceum Theatre in Edinburgh before moving south to the Cambridge Theatre. The sidesplitting cast included Alan Bennett, Peter Cook, Dudley Moore, and Jonathan Miller. Martin recorded them over five nights in Cambridge, later capturing an additional set of shows at London's Fortune Theatre in 1961. The resulting album was a smash hit for Parlophone, ushering in a new era of satirical comedy in Great Britain. Martin continued to work in the short run with Moore, a gifted jazz pianist. In 1961 George produced a single, "Strictly for the Birds" backed with "Duddly Dell," by the Dudley Moore Trio, which also included drummer Chris Karan and bassist Pete McGurk. In addition to recording Moore's piano along with the Dankworth Orchestra, Martin produced an EP by the *Beyond the Fringe* cast. The extended-player included George's incidental music on the track "Sitting on the Bench," which the A&R man sagely featured in order to curry favor with DJs who might otherwise blanch at the idea of playing spoken-word tracks. As he later recalled of his work with his *Beyond the Fringe* mates, "All of these records sold tolerably well without setting the world alight, and I enjoyed every one." That same year, he hit modest pay dirt with Humphrey Lyttelton when he recorded the old jazzman's "Saturday Jump," which fell into regular rotation as the theme song for *Saturday Club*, the popular BBC radio program. And in the late fall of 1961, George landed a major hit with Charlie Drake's novelty record "My Boomerang Won't Come Back." Always one for employing studio trickery to bring his "sound pictures" to life, George conjured up the recording's vivid Australian outback setting by skillfully manipulating Abbey Road's existing equipment to establish the illusion of indigenous Aborigine instrumentation.[28]

As it happened, George's groundbreaking work with *Beyond the Fringe* aligned him with the emergence of the United Kingdom's "satire boom" in the early 1960s. In spite of his remorse over being left behind years earlier regarding his Fleet Air Arm promotion, he had a long-standing knack for good timing in his career—witness the deus ex machina penchant of his fairy godfather, Sidney Harrison, for entering his life at the most opportune moments. The satire boom marked just such an occasion, as Martin's comedy records with Sellers, Milligan, Secombe, and Cribbins found the A&R man making propitious forays into a cultural zeitgeist that many critics date to the debut performance of *Beyond the Fringe* back in August 1960. George's timing simply couldn't have been better, as he began notching bestsellers with a host of Great Britain's most esteemed funnymen. At its height, the satire boom became most closely associated with the intelligentsia, generally hailing from Cambridge and Oxford—namely, Peter Cook, John Bird, John Fortune, David Frost, and Bernard Levin, among others. Most of the satire boom's expositors date the movement's ebbing to the December 1963 cancellation of the BBC satirical *That Was the Week That Was*, a program that would later figure in George's professional life at the very moment in which it was making an unexpected ascent. With his posh-sounding voice and his patrician good looks, George easily fit in with England's "it" crowd. Indeed, he fit in so well that the A&R man found himself rather cannily moving about the satire boom's circle. Martin got along particularly famously with Milligan, with whom he enjoyed a long-running association, producing several albums by him and even serving as best man at his 1962 wedding.[29]

For George, *Beyond the Fringe* was a milestone in more ways than one. Perhaps most significantly, the album marked six years since his promotion. In that period, he had shown incredible, innovative leadership and returned Parlophone to far more secure standing within the always-competitive EMI Group. For Ron Richards, the shift in Parlophone's fortunes during George's tenure at the helm had been stunning. "We had gone from being known as a sad little company," he later recalled, "to making a mint of money." As for George himself, he saw comedy as a vital proving ground for the potential that magnetic tape held for transforming the studio and expanding its possibilities. He was keenly aware that it hadn't been so long ago that EMI clung to the idea of cutting records even as the rest of the industry shifted toward the wonders of tape. To George's mind, Parlophone's stable of comedians had "played a big part at teaching others at Abbey Road how to use tape. It was still in its infancy, and a lot of people at the studio regarded tape with a good deal of suspicion but we gradually learnt all about it, and working with the likes of Sellers and Milligan was very useful because, as it wasn't music, you could experiment. Our engineer, Stuart Eltham, got very closely involved with the whole thing and became our sound effects person. We made things out of tape loops, slowed things down, and banged on piano lids." For George, the idea of an A&R man—a record manager—suddenly held the capacity for evolving into something else altogether. As he later remarked, "Directors don't have to make films look like stage-plays, and I felt that we as producers could make our recordings differently." In short, the studio had the potential to become, in George's words, "a real magical workshop."[30]

# 4

# "FRUSTRATION HAS MANY FATHERS"

IN 1959 THE EMI BRASS had renewed George's contract without hesitation, given the great strides that he had made since his promotion. While he was happy to receive a new three-year contract for £2,700 per annum, he would have gladly accepted slightly less for the opportunity to earn royalties from his artists' sales receipts, thus giving him a stake in the overall success of his growing and increasingly prosperous stable. EMI's refusal to even so much as consider the notion of the most rudimentary kind of profit sharing was taking its toll on the Parlophone head's psyche. "Frustration has many fathers, but few children, among them bitterness, anger and resentment," he later wrote. "Those had come to be the unhappy ingredients of my feelings towards EMI." Yet for George, "it was not simply a straightforward question of my wanting more cash. I wanted participation, profit-sharing. I reckoned that, if I was going to devote my life to building up something which wasn't mine, I deserved some form of commission." When he inked his latest contract, which included a seventy-five-pound annual raise, thoughts about Oscar Preuss must still have been heavy in George's mind—his mentor had died on Christmas Eve in 1958, only three years into his retirement. George eulogized Oscar in *New Musical Express* (*NME*), remarking with admiration that "he invariably adopted the most rebellious tactics." For George, adopting "rebellious tactics" had clearly served as a guiding principle and arguably one of the key aspects in his revitalization of Parlophone. In only a few short years, Martin had bested Preuss's efforts to improve the third label's standing among the EMI Group, and he was hungry to do even more. Although royalties for A&R men had become routine business practices in the United States by this time, the EMI Group was having none of it, much to George's abiding chagrin. He harbored strong suspicions by this time that his counterparts at EMI and in Great Britain in general were supplementing their base salaries by various unethical means, and he vaguely minded any of his competitors succeeding where he couldn't on an inherently uneven playing field.[1]

As George signed his 1959 contract, he was fully aware of how much more driven he had become since assuming the mantle of Parlophone's leadership. He was unapologetically ambitious, and he remained perpetually unsatisfied with his inability to land "the big one"—to score a truly world-breaking hit record. To his mind, such an achievement was only possible for Parlophone—and for him as a much-respected A&R man—with a surefire pop sensation. "The comedy records had been fine, and had begun to put Parlophone on the map," he admitted. "But I was looking, with something close to desperation, for an act from the pop world. I was frankly jealous of the seemingly easy success other people were having with such acts, in particular Norrie Paramor, my opposite number on Columbia, whose artist Cliff Richard was on an apparently automatic ride to stardom." George's envy was easy to understand. Born Harry Webb, Richard charted an incredible seventeen straight top 5 hits in the early 1960s. At the time, George used to joke that Norrie and Cliff were so successful that they could have taken "God Save the Queen" to the top of the charts. Indeed, it is impossible to overstate the sense of rivalry that George felt with Norrie, nearly twelve years George's senior and the über-bestselling A&R manager for EMI's Columbia imprint. But George was even more frustrated by his own inability to land an enduring act. To his mind, making pop records was decidedly less complex than producing comedy work. "It seemed to me that all that was needed, in producing [pop music], was a good song—whereas with comedy records, every one was a major production." George didn't merely crave a hitmaker; he wanted an easier genre to pursue than comedy records, which were "hard work. You had to get the right material, right script, right artists, and so on." Every new comedy album required "a completely new set of ideas each time," while pop artists simply sold whatever they managed to record. "What I wanted was a 'fireproof' act like that."[2]

In fact, for the past several years, he had been on an abiding search for the next "fireproof" wunderkind to turn the pop world upside down. And, in his own way, he had already come tantalizingly close on a few noteworthy occasions. As it happened, he had been pursuing an elusive hitmaker during the very same years in which he had been righting Parlophone's ship on the back of his successful comedy releases. Back in April 1955, shortly before his promotion to label head, George had signed the Southlanders, a London rhythm-and-blues act, to one of EMI's industry-standard penny-per-record-sold contracts—the kind of contract that held very little risk for the record company and, save for an unexpected bonanza, little in the way of promise for the next would-be Elvis Presley. A transplanted vocal group from Jamaica, the Southlanders seemed to fit the bill. Hoping to capture the "American" sound for a British marketplace that hungered for anything that sounded like it hailed from the United States, George invited the Southlanders to Abbey Road, where they hastily recorded a cover version of the Penguins' smash hit "Earth Angel." Although he managed to coax a serviceable, smooth-as-silk recording out of the Jamaican group, George's production of "Earth Angel" lacked that certain something, and it hit the charts with a resounding thud. His gimmicky effort to capitalize on the Penguins' American hit not only was a misfire but also left him wide open to making similar errors in professional judgment in the future. Yet at the same time, George was occasionally rewarded for such maneuvers. A case in point occurred in January 1956, when he saw his Parlophone recording of Edna Savage's "Arrivederci Darling" land at number nineteen scarcely a month after Anne Shelton had cracked the top 20 for HMV, Parlophone's rival EMI label, with her own rendition. In 1958 George managed to find success with such tactics yet again—this time, with TV funnyman Charlie Drake's cover version of "Splish Splash," which had been a mammoth hit for Bobby Darin. Cowritten by Darin and American DJ "Murray the K" Kaufman, "Splish Splash" charted at number seven in Martin and Drake's hands. But as history would show, George wouldn't always be so lucky when it came to straddling the ethical line between being an astute businessman and an opportunist.

At this juncture, George attempted to rebrand Parlophone through a series of different innovations, including his concept for "Do It Yourself" discs. A forerunner of karaoke, Do It Yourself discs consisted of orchestrations of popular hits without lead vocals. In George's estimation, consumers would buy the discs, complete with lyric sheets, and sing the songs themselves with their friends in the comfort of their own living rooms. The unflappable Ron Goodwin recorded George's orchestrations with the Parlophone Pops Orchestra. While *NME* lauded Parlophone's Do It Yourself discs as George's "brainchild," the novelty only produced a handful of unsuccessful records in instrumental recordings of Bill Haley's "Rock Around the Clock" and Doris

Day's "Que Sera Sera." With the Do It Yourself discs quickly fading into history, George turned to the children's marketplace, for which he launched records by one Nellie the Elephant, voiced by Mandy Miller, as well as a comedy record with Spike Milligan and Eric Sykes singing the novelty track "You Gotta Go Oww!" He tried his hand at yet another comedy number with Libby Morris's minor British hit "When Liberace Winked at Me." Continuing this wave of eclecticism, he supervised Bert Weedon's guitar-tinged theme for the ITV hit game show *The $64,000 Question*, while later positioning Parlophone for unrealized holiday sales with Benny Lee's "Rock 'n' Roll Santa Claus." At one juncture, he even brought Sidney Harrison, his fairy godfather, into the studio to record an EP titled *Sidney Harrison Shows You How*. A reference to Harrison's short-lived BBC program *How to Play the Piano*—which aired in 1950, around the same time that Harrison brought young Martin into Preuss's orbit—the disc featured a standout track in the august piano teacher's performance of Frédéric Chopin's Prelude in C Minor. But still, as ever, the real hits seemed to elude the young Parlophone head as he attempted to right his foundering label.[3]

Never one to be daunted, in September 1956 George followed up on a tip from *Daily Mirror* columnist Noel Whitcomb about a new pop combo called the Vipers Skiffle Group. With Whitcomb in tow, Martin caught up with the band at the 2i's Coffee Bar in Soho. The Vipers were at the vanguard of the skiffle craze that had been overtaking the British Isles throughout the summer of 1956. A ragtag musical genre with roots in jazz, blues, and folk, skiffle was commonly played on makeshift instruments such as old washboards and homemade stand-up basses, with the occasional acoustic guitar and drum kit thrown in, depending on their availability. To George's mind, "skiffle was a harbinger of what was to come, three guitars bashing away, although they were acoustic." As it happened, George was only marginally impressed with the Vipers' Cockney lead singer Tommy Hicks. "He had a bright, smiling face and all the right movements, but I didn't think he sang or played the guitar particularly well," he later wrote. While he didn't have much use for the singer, Martin was partial to Hicks's band. After inking the Vipers to one of EMI's penny-per-record deals, George enjoyed the dubious honor of being the first A&R man to sign a skiffle band in an era dominated by Lonnie Donegan's "Rock Island Line" and little else. On October 4, he invited the Vipers down to Number 2 at Abbey Road, where the band recorded their plucky brand of homespun coffee-bar fare. While the results of their partnership with the Parlophone head were less than inspiring, they loved working with him. As guitarist Wally Whyton recalled, "George Martin was amazing. We were a fairly eccentric bunch and thought we were Jack the Lads. Every night the 2i's was packed out and everybody wanted to see the Vipers, so we were full of our own importance, but George was an absolute gentleman, a toff. He never got fazed if we fell off stools, or were late, or didn't have the money to get home."[4]

As it happened, the Vipers came out of the gate with a bang, scoring a top 10 UK hit with "Don't You Rock Me, Daddy-O"—a variation of the old standard "Sail Away Ladies." Two more singles releases managed to crack the top 30, including "Cumberland Gap" and "Streamline Train." But things took a turn for the worse after their next single—"Maggie May," a traditional folk tune about a Liverpool prostitute—was banned by the BBC for its sexually suggestive content. In 1958 George recorded the Vipers' performance of "No Other Baby," popularized by Dickie Bishop and the Sidekicks the previous year. But by then, the Viper's momentum had faded, and in spite of a well-timed dose of BBC publicity, "No Other Baby" failed to chart and their work with George faded almost immediately into obscurity. For Martin, the unkindest blow of all occurred shortly thereafter when Hicks refashioned himself as Tommy Steele and was signed by Decca's A&R team, led by industry stalwart—for the time being, at least—Dick Rowe. In his own way, Steele emerged as Great Britain's first bona fide rock 'n' roll sensation. How could George have missed the surefire hit when it had been right there, singing and dancing under his very nose on that fateful night at the 2i's?[5]

In 1957 George thought that he'd finally discovered the rock 'n' roller he'd been looking for—"my own answer to Cliff Richard and Tommy Steele," he later quipped. And for the briefest of times, it looked as if he were right. Like the rest of the nation, George had seen Jim Dale on the BBC's *Six-Five Special*, a rock 'n' roll television revue. On the strength of his appearance, Martin signed Dale to a penny contract, and they promptly recorded "Piccadilly Line"—a takeoff on Lonnie Donegan's skiffle hit "Rock Island Line"—which failed to chart. To Martin's great delight, Dale's follow-up single, a cover version of "Be My Girl," debuted on the singles charts in October 1957, eventually reaching as high as the number-two spot. Martin was elated and ready to ride the crest of Dale's career. But their partnership would prove to be short lived. A movie version of the *Six-Five Special* was in the offing, and Dale's agent glimpsed a future for him as a comedic actor. For his part, George was crestfallen. Dale's manager "exerted a Svengali-like influence over him," Martin remembered. "He had him tied up in more knots than I could count."[6]

Flushed nevertheless with the excitement of having come painfully close to topping the charts, George returned to New York City for the first time since 1944, when, as a member of the Fleet Air Arm, he had seen Cab Calloway on Broadway. Here he was, some fourteen years hence, as Parlophone head and working for the vaunted EMI Group. He was anxious to visit American recording studios and learn more about their production efforts. He also planned to make his way to the West Coast to meet with representatives from Capitol Records. His only interaction with the EMI subsidiary by this juncture had been the rerelease of a Parlophone single titled "Skiffling Strings." Credited to Ron Goodwin and His Orchestra, "Skiffling Strings" was George's creation. While the Vipers had been unsuccessful as a Parlophone artist, George opted to make a skiffle record with the "zinging string sound" of an orchestral arrangement. To his delight, "Skiffling Strings" managed to generate solid airplay and sales on the home front. When the opportunity to release the track in the United States emerged, Capitol Records chose, rather surprisingly, to market the song to an American audience, albeit under a new title, "Swinging Sweethearts." By this time, Capitol had established a long-standing reputation for turning down releases from the parent company, typically arguing, as always, that British acts were unable to tap into the "American" sound. "Swinging Sweethearts" managed to buck the trend, becoming an American top 20 hit and bolstering George's confidence in the process.[7]

After touching down in the States and going on an impromptu drinking tour with Capitol rep Roland Freiborghaus, George barely recognized the New York City of his war years. To his eye, it had become "very tawdry." The romantic images in his mind's eye from his late teenage years had been replaced with an enduring image that he witnessed in a souvenir shop: "There was a plaster statue of Jesus Christ with outspread arms, and right next to him there was a condiment set in the shape of a naked woman with her legs bent, her removable breasts being pepper and salt, respectively." While he may have been bemused by the images' stark juxtaposition, his American visit proved to be revelatory in terms of his professional outlook. During his West Coast swing, George finally laid eyes on the famous Capitol Records Tower, the thirteen-story Hollywood building designed to simulate a stack of records. While he chuckled at the tower's outlandish display of American chutzpah, he was bowled over when he had the opportunity to sit in on a Frank Sinatra recording session at the famed Studio C in Capitol Tower. Produced by Val Valentino, the session included such luminaries as Voyle Gilmore, the senior producer at Capitol who had invited George to attend the evening's proceedings, and Billy May, the orchestral conductor. George watched in awe as Frank Sinatra, with girlfriend Lauren Bacall in tow, completed five master tracks across a four-hour session that evening for his *Come*

*Fly with Me* album. "Sinatra impressed me enormously," Martin later recalled. "When he arrived, he knew just what he was going to do." Martin simply couldn't get over Sinatra's professionalism and efficiency. "It was terrific," he wrote years later.[8]

While he was captivated by Sinatra's "ultra-professional" attitude, Martin was even more excited by the prospect of working with the caliber of equipment that he had seen at Studio C. For one thing, he noted that the condenser microphones being deployed in Studio C had limiters and compressors in order to ensure the purest, brightest possible sound. But even more impressively, Sinatra's album was being recorded for a stereo release. In 1958 in Great Britain, stereo recordings were reserved almost exclusively for classical artists, not pop artists. But in the United States, it was a different story altogether. "American recordings were made on Ampex three-track half-inch tape," George discovered. "Val spread the orchestra over the two outside tracks as a stereo pair, mixing there and then as they recorded. He put the voice on the center track, so that during playback the voice was good and loud and Frank liked what he heard. But the three-track system also afforded Val the opportunity of altering the relationship between the voice and the backing at a later stage—after Frank had left—which would have been impossible with our two-track stereo" back at Abbey Road. Needless to say, George "thought it was a wonderful technique." The setup at Capitol Studios confirmed his long-held suspicions that EMI was operating in the technological dark ages of the recording industry.

George was accompanied on his trip to California by EMI engineer Peter Bown, who was enthralled by the American deployment of the Fairchild limiter, the compressor that assists studio personnel in decreasing the dynamic range between the loudest and quietest aspects of an audio signal. It was Bown's "first experience with the Fairchild limiter, which we still use to this day," the engineer later recalled. "We didn't have them at Abbey Road, we had nothing like that, so we weren't able to make records that were so dynamic. I came back from America telling everybody in England, 'We've got to do something about this, we've got to re-equip the studio, because without it, we're not going to make any good records, ever.'" When he returned to London, George wasted little time in proffering a list of recommendations, which EMI readily accepted but, as history would demonstrate, took many years to implement.[9]

Years later, George would recall his summer 1958 visit to Capitol Studios for yet another reason. Although Old Blue Eyes had been the picture of professionalism throughout the session and very nice to Martin on the only occasion when they met, the evening ended in a "blazing row" between Sinatra and Gilmore. Martin had noticed the way Gilmore had cozied up to the crooner throughout the session, dropping sycophantic remarks like "Great singer! Great team!" At the end of the night, Gilmore nervously presented Sinatra with the artwork for *Come Fly with Me*, which featured a painting of the singer donning a fedora hat. "In the background, was an airplane, and very prominent on the plane, almost as big as Frank's name, was the logo 'TWA.' Frank took one look at it and called Gilmore every name under the sun. He knew that Capitol had done a deal with TWA, and he walked out in a terrible huff, dragging Lauren Bacall after him." As with the other members of the session crew, Martin could only stand by in stunned disbelief as Sinatra traipsed out of the studio. "The cover was unchanged upon release," Martin recalled. "Soon afterwards, he started his own label, Reprise, with Warner Brothers. That was the incident that triggered it—I was there." Martin would never forget witnessing Sinatra's disgust at Capitol for selling him out to accommodate their commercial interests with TWA—how Old Blue Eyes' unparalleled professionalism so quickly crumbled in the face of what he believed to be his own record label's betrayal of one of its most lucrative artists.[10]

As with Sinatra's unremitting string of successes, *Come Fly with Me* soared to the upper reaches of the American LP charts in 1958, but it would be a few more years before Martin managed to land his first legitimate number-one hit. He had toiled for years in an effort to land a pop smash to rival the success of the great Columbia artists who routinely topped the charts. It may have been this very same sense of fervor that landed him in hot water in the summer of 1960, when he ignored his own well-honed sense of decorum and yen for originality to become, if only briefly, a bottom-feeder in an industry that would do absolutely anything, that would jump on the first available bandwagon, to net sales units. Having seemingly forgotten about his experiences some years back with "Earth Angel," George couldn't fend off his sense of professional envy when he heard the ersatz strains of the American smash hit "Itsy Bitsy Teenie Weenie Yellow Polka Dot Bikini" by sixteen-year-old Brian Hyland. Released in June 1960 by the independent Kapp Records, the novelty song would turn over more than a million copies stateside within months of its release. As the British recording industry struggled to keep up with their behemoth American counterparts, A&R men back on the sceptered isle latched onto the latest American gimmicks with unchecked gusto. In July 1960, that A&R man was George Martin. According to the July 1 issue of *NME*, Martin first heard Hyland's record on a Friday, concocted his own arrangement the next day, and recorded a cover version with eighteen-year-old Paul Hanford on Sunday. Within five days, Parlophone's recording was in English stores, where it competed directly with Hyland's American original, which Decca had released in Great Britain on Kapp's behalf. Suddenly, EMI and Decca were at war in the record outlets, with Parlophone playing up the stakes with an advertisement lauding Hanford's cover as "THE version of the new teenage novelty number." A front-page *NME* ad featured a photo of the clean-cut heartthrob, who was later depicted in a publicity photo strolling along Regent Street with a model wearing a polka-dot bikini.[11]

While George was merely engaging in the same kind of copycat behavior that his A&R peers had sunk to time and time again over the years to keep pace with a rapidly evolving industry, his zeal for keeping up had resulted in a terrible lapse in judgment. Indeed, in this case he had simply sunk too far given that Hanford's version of "Itsy Bitsy Teenie Weenie Yellow Polka Dot Bikini" was nearly identical to Hyland's American bubblegum hit. Accusing George of "piracy," *Melody Maker* stoked the fires of plagiarism allegations in the industry trade pages and challenged the Parlophone head to a televised debate with DJ Pete Murray on BBC TV's fledgling pop music program *Juke Box Jury*. During the debate, Murray questioned Martin's ethics and described his work with Hanford as "a shameful waste of his widely acknowledged skill." George continued the rancor after the program, admitting his disgust with his copycat recording and the reasons that had driven him to do it in the first place. "No A&R man worth his salt likes copying," he wrote, but at the same time "he is paid to produce financially successful records. British artists must 'cover' or be forced out of business. We are competing against the Americans on unequal terms." To George's mind, British megaliths like EMI and Decca were shackled to a strangely eclectic marketplace—the very same sales base that had afforded him the opportunity to score hits with comedy troupes and other unusual artists—and a dearth of talent. While Hanford's version of "Itsy Bitsy Teenie Weenie Yellow Polka Dot Bikini" failed to chart, Hyland's original scored a top 10 British hit. Ironically, George's production of the song enjoyed top 10 showings, via EMI's international licensing agreements, in Sweden, Portugal, the Philippines, South Africa, and New Zealand. In Mexico, it even managed to top the charts, giving George—in perhaps the most dubious manner possible—his first number-one song.[12]

While he may have understandably preferred to ignore the place of "Itsy Bitsy Teenie Weenie Yellow Polka Dot Bikini" among his A&R output—it receives no mention in any of his three book-length autobiographical works—George had learned a lesson that would have far-reaching consequences across his career. Yet as far as he was concerned, the song that finally secured the top spot for him in the UK was "You're Driving Me Crazy" by the Temperance Seven. It was May 1961, and the thirty-five-year-old Parlophone head had much to be thankful for on the professional and personal fronts in spite of the Hanford fiasco. Through a spate of hit comedy records, George had engineered the label's long road to recovery—so much so, in fact, that rumors about putting Parlophone in mothballs had all but faded at EMI House. Perhaps even more significantly, the zany humor of such label stalwarts as Peter Sellers and Spike Milligan had lent Parlophone a sense of identity in the industry, an aspect that it sorely lacked before George's promotion.

Although he would later characterize his marriage as being perpetually under siege because of Sheena's purported agoraphobia and the long shadow of his mother's untimely death, by 1961 George was the proud and doting father of daughter Alexis and son Gregory, born on January 21, 1957, whom he and Sheena lovingly called Poggy. Diagnosed at six months old with epilepsy, three-year-old Gregory can be seen on home movies as he frolics with Tumpy in the backyard at Hatfield and later as he played in the surf with his sister by the seaside in Lee-on-Solent, just west of Portsmouth, the provincial home of longtime family friends Joan and Graham Fisher. Filled with silliness and laughter, these home movies find George seemingly enjoying his marriage of "defiance" with Sheena. Having initially recoiled at the idea of living in suburbia, Sheena had come to cherish her life in Hatfield, where she and her children had made friends in the budding neighborhood.[13]

By July 1961, George could bask in the confidence of having righted Parlophone's sinking ship under challenging internal conditions at EMI—and having done so with his zany cast of strays and oddball musicians and comedians. He must have been rightly pleased when he was asked to contribute a column to *Eminews*, the company's in-house journal, on the life of a recording manager. Titled "You Know, It's Really Quite a Funny Job," George's feature story attempted to account for the many hats that he wore as Parlophone head, including running a label, discovering and signing new talent, and making records. "Don't let me give you the impression that it is one long, glorious tour through show business. It embraces a great deal of tedious work and thought, and sometimes unpleasant actions. I remember a very famous bandleader walking out of our studios once because I had criticized the playing of his bass player." With a clear sense of self-satisfaction, George goes on to note, for the record, that only a few weeks later, the bandleader fired that same bass player. Indeed, if George had an Achilles' heel, the understandable need to see his artistic instincts confirmed—and in public, no less—was it. But by this juncture, he had also learned that there was no substitute for coming into the orbit of as many artists as possible—and with an open mind. "There is no set rule for the uncovering of talent," he wrote, "you just keep your ears to the ground (when you're not recording, of course!) and hear as many new people as you can."[14]

That same month, the Temperance Seven played the Cavern Club, a jazz dive in a dank basement in faraway Liverpool. Supported by the Saints Jazz Band, the Temperance Seven took the stage with their usual eccentricities in full flower. With the bandmates dressed like funeral directors, the lead singer sang through an echo-laden megaphone while the drummer kept time with an oversized bass drum with coconuts and a tiny cymbal affixed atop the frame. That night, they performed "You're Driving Me Crazy" in fine style, along with their second single, "Pasadena," also produced by George, which was cruising its way up the British charts at the time. It would top out in the number-four spot. Riding their unexpected wave of success, the band even played the vaunted London Palladium that incredible summer.[15]

But for all of the personal and professional gratification that seemed to be at George's fingertips, landing his first bona fide number-one hit had felt like a dubious accomplishment for him. He was thrilled, of course, with the prospect of finally having achieved a long-held goal. But he was also extremely conscious of the fact that the Temperance Seven weren't even a pop act, much less an honest-to-goodness rock 'n' roll group. No, they were a fairly traditional jazz band. Despite their penchant for wearing spats and Edwardian frock coats, they were top-rate musicians, one and all. "You're Driving Me Crazy" had been produced in George's usual workmanlike fashion. "They played in a very authentic style of the 1920s," he later wrote, "and their musical mainstay was Alan Cooper, known affectionately as 'Hooter.' He was a genuine eccentric, who played various kinds of woodwind and was a master of the idiom. The vocalist was Paul McDowell, who sang through a megaphone, and in order to help the realistic feel of the recording, I grouped them all 'round one mike." George had recorded "You're Driving Me Crazy" in Number 2 back in February. By the week of April Fools' Day, it had broken into the *NME* charts, although nobody really gave it a chance. Nobody except for George, that is.[16]

Despite a healthy spate of skepticism from the EMI brass, George had trusted his intuition and released the record by the band with the funny-sounding name in spite of the company's usual coterie of naysayers. As for the Temperance Seven, "They all drank like fishes," George fondly recalled, "and of course there were nine of them in the band; hence the name." But all good humor aside, he felt deflated that a traditional jazz act was behind his first chart-topper. "This group was all that could be expected of me," he lamented. When he received word that "You're Driving Me Crazy" had topped the singles charts, George was away in Cambridge with his mobile production unit. To celebrate the occasion, he went out to dinner with Ron Richards, his assistant A&R man; Shirley Spence, a Parlophone staffer; and Judy, the longtime assistant whom he had met on that very first morning back at Abbey Road in 1950.[17]

As his closest friends and colleagues toasted the chart-topping success of "You're Driving Me Crazy" that evening in Cambridge, George's thoughts might have understandably drifted back to the previous year, when his zeal to land a pop hit had gotten the best of him, as evinced by the "Itsy Bitsy Teenie Weenie Yellow Polka Dot Bikini" incident that had landed him an embarrassing appearance on television. All in all, the same man who regularly confessed to being "squarish" still didn't quite feel like he belonged, that he didn't quite fit in with the business in which he wanted to not only assimilate but also truly succeed. Make no mistake about it: George was ambitious in every sense of the word. He knew that he had the talent, the drive, and the energy to make it among the industry's top A&R men–cum–producers. George had finally had his taste of the top spot. Sure it was a traditional jazz tune and hardly the stuff of American rock 'n' roll, but it had topped the charts nonetheless. And there was simply no doubt about it: he was hungry for more. Yet by the early summer of 1961, as the whimsical strains of "You're Driving Me Crazy" played on the British airwaves, other forces that had been gathering around George's life for the past several years began to come to the fore. His world was about to change dramatically—and in more ways than one.

# 5

# AN INSTANT FRIENDSHIP

WHILE GEORGE MAY have been understandably frustrated by his inability to land a successful rock 'n' roll act by the early 1960s, there were two factors worthy of consideration as the new decade came of age. First, in many ways Great Britain simply wasn't ready to handle big-time rock. Pliers of the trade had to be content with a music circuit that consisted of longtime industry stalwarts like Decca and EMI and a radio superstructure controlled by the state-run BBC, with notable incursions by offshore transmitters like Radio Luxembourg—both of which served as the de facto tastemakers of the day. In England, pop music was quickly finding its way in the age of television with the advent of the BBC's *Juke Box Jury*, which premiered in June 1959, and ITV's *Thank Your Lucky Stars*, which took to the airwaves in 1961. By 1962, *Juke Box Jury* attracted audiences more than twelve million strong every Saturday night. Arena rock was a long way off in the United Kingdom, a country whose performance venues consisted of two-bit clubs and tattered, aging ballrooms all across the British landscape. Moreover, its recording industry was small potatoes in comparison with the American juggernaut, as George had seen firsthand in the late 1950s. The Temperance Seven's "You're Driving Me Crazy" had sold two hundred thousand units across its chart-topping run. Although this was an impressive mark by EMI standards—and a dream come true for the Parlophone head, who was beginning to succeed at turning his long-suffering label around—it was the express result of an industry still in its relative infancy. In those days, George later wrote, "there was no real rock and roll in Britain. It was a very gentle kind of hit parade. By the end of the

Fifties, Elvis Presley was beginning to make a dent in the English market, but he was still more an American phenomenon. Jim Dale's 'Be My Girl' was as near as we'd get to rock and roll. Cliff Richard was just beginning at the end of the Fifties. There was also Skiffle, a craze in the late Fifties influenced by rock and roll. But American rock and roll was way ahead of us."[1]

As one of the industry's rising leaders, George had a lot to be proud of by this juncture in his career. He had stepped into Oscar Preuss's shoes and taken Parlophone from a label in jeopardy to the makings of a well-oiled financial engine. Sure, rock 'n' roll still eluded him, but he possessed the wherewithal to take a jazz band like the Temperance Seven, hear something special in their sound in spite of the naysayers in his own company, and steer them to the top. Indeed, by this point Parlophone was on truly solid footing, and it reflected the eclectic tastes of its leader, a man with an insatiable thirst, by his own admission, for variety in all aspects of his life. "I'm a person who gets bored quite easily," George remarked in later years, and "I don't like doing the same things over and over again." If anything, Parlophone was the living embodiment of its label head. By 1961, as "You're Driving Me Crazy" soared across the top of the charts, George had worked with acts of all genres and stripes, from spoken-word comedy and jazz to country, skiffle, and orchestral recordings. He had succeeded, quite simply, by following his own interests wherever they happened to take him—and in spite of Parlophone's weak financial picture throughout much of the 1950s, he was anything but risk averse. He was more than willing to take a chance on an act when it captured his imagination. And besides, it was a matter of great joy for him to discover something new and bring it to life: "I made a lot of what I call 'sound pictures' with actors and comedians because it was fun to do."[2]

In 1961 George's interest in working across a wide range of genres and making sound pictures took on new shades of meaning when he began experimenting with electronic music. And for the first time in his eleven-year-old professional career in the record business, he opted to take a chance on himself. During this period, he had begun exploring his interests in pushing the boundaries of the recording studio by playing with different tape speeds, altering acoustics, reverse echo, and backward recording. He was self-consciously trying his hand at *musique concrète* (translated as "concrete music") by treating instruments with various kinds of studio engineering to create new forms of electronic sound. While *musique concrète* had enjoyed a long history by this point—with musicologists generally crediting Pierre Schaeffer with providing the foundations for composition through electronic means in the early 1940s—George found himself in a moment of technological shift in which it became ever more possible to bring even more complex and creative revolutions to fruition in the contemporary recording studio. George was particularly influenced by pianist Winifred Atwell, who scored a string of boogie-woogie and ragtime hits on the English charts in the 1950s for Decca. Atwell was known to manipulate the sound of her piano by slightly detuning one out of every three strings. George took to treating his own instrument at Abbey Road, where he "tried newspaper woven between the strings, and tuned milk bottles, anything to give a new sound." Not content with his own experiments and stymied by what he perceived to be the electronic limitations at Abbey Road, he sought out the electronics wizards and gearheads at the nearby BBC Radiophonics Workshop, which had come to enjoy national renown because of their association with the soundtrack for *Doctor Who*. "Mind you, it was a far cry—light years from the extremes of computerized jiggery-pokery that can be achieved in this day of samplers and libraries of different electronic sounds," George wrote. The enthusiasts at the BBC Radiophonics Workshop "flew by the seat of their pants. Everything had to be made laboriously by hand, but it was a labor of love."[3]

For his own labor of love, George began with the automatic beat of BBC TV's time signal, originally created in the Radiophonics Workshop laboratories. The Parlophone head supplemented the "melody" of the electronic time signal with a Latin rhythm provided by studio musicians. The result was a moderately successful single titled "Time Beat" and credited to Ray Cathode, George's pseudonym. Playing up on the novelty of producing electronic sounds, EMI staged publicity shots featuring George posing with a robot named—naturally—Ray Cathode for an *NME* exposé. In an interview with *Disc*, George, unable to resist a good pun, observed that "electronic or 'concrete' music is not new in itself, but it is on pop discs. It is concrete music reinforced by musicians—so we're calling it reinforced concrete music." When "Time Beat" received its debut on *Juke Box Jury*, the guest panelists voted it as a "miss," although it enjoyed a fair amount of radio exposure on the BBC's Light Programme.[4]

As was his usual modus operandi, George continued to work with a variety of different acts—in addition, of course, to his regular sessions with his growing cavalcade of comedy stars. In yet another misfire in his attempt to land the next big pop sensation, George endeavored to make a star out of twenty-four-year-old Leo Maguire, an up-and-coming heartthrob from the British soap opera *Compact*. Working in tandem with the show's contemporaneous narrative in which Maguire's character hits the big time as a pop star, Martin recorded a session with the actor in which he sang "Crying for the Moon," which Parlophone swiftly released to coincide with the *Compact* story line. In spite of such carefully synchronized marketing, "Crying for the Moon" met the charts with a resounding thud.

While his dreams for turning Maguire into a pop smash came up empty, Martin fared much better with Rolf Harris, an Australian singer-songwriter who had enjoyed a massive hit with "Tie Me Kangaroo Down Sport" in his home country back in 1960. Ready to try his hand with the UK market, Harris recorded "Sun Arise" with Martin in front of a live audience of his Australian mates. Cowritten with Harry Butler, an Australian naturalist and the personality behind the television program *In the Wild*, "Sun Arise" proved to be a challenge for George, who was forced to contend with a host of studio limitations, not to mention a rowdy group of antipodean bystanders. Initially, Martin felt that the track was "very boring" as originally conceived by Harris, who pointed out that the impetus for his idea lay with the culture of the Aborigines, who would "repeat a phrase over and over again and it would become mesmerizing." With the notion of producing a truly "mesmerizing" track now on the table, Martin rolled up his sleeves to bring the images cascading around Harris's mind to life in a monumental four-hour session at Abbey Road. "To make [Harris] feel at home," Martin later wrote, "I got a load of Australians along for the audience. To make *them* feel at home I had cases of Swan lager specially brought in. That did it. We couldn't get them out of the canteen, and those who did make their way to the studio were trying to put cans of the liquid in the echo-chamber or anywhere else they could find. In the end, I appealed, 'Come on, chaps, we've got to get on with the recording.'" And this is where Martin really proved his mettle. The rowdy Australians notwithstanding, Martin skillfully mimicked the sound of an authentic didgeridoo by recording two cellos, a double bass, a piano, and Harris's guttural sounds. Meanwhile, he gave the singer's voice a series of rich textures by double- and triple-tracking his vocals. To George's great delight, "Sun Arise" skyrocketed all the way to the number-three position on the British charts. It was an impressive turn by another one of George's quirky band of hitmakers.[5]

With unexpected breakthroughs from the likes of Harris, 1962 had unfolded with a promising start for Martin, a winning streak that was heralded by his work on Bernard Cribbins's "The Hole in the Ground," which he had slaved over for several weeks. With lyrics by Myles Rudge and music by Ted Dicks, the comic song rose all the way to the ninth spot on the British hit singles charts, where it lingered for an impressive thirteen weeks. A tongue-in-cheek music-hall satire about class disjunction, "The Hole in the Ground" showcased George's growing abilities as an A&R man–cum–producer to create visual images through words and music, with his elaborate, behind-the-scenes studio choreography remaining all but invisible in the final product. As Cribbins himself would later observe about Martin, "He was a very tall person. He had a great air of serenity and authority about him." It was this essential nature that made it easy for him to leverage Cribbins's unusual comedic talents—and it would be a skill that would serve him well as the decade wore on. George's herculean efforts on "The Hole in the Ground" attracted the praise of no less than Sir Joseph Lockwood, George's well-placed supporter, who wrote an effusive March 21 memo stating that "the record is magnificent and everywhere I go I hear people talking about it, particularly in the City."[6]

Never one to turn down the opportunity to seek out new artists, George took a meeting in February 1962 with Brian Epstein, a novice talent manager out of Liverpool. Brian was working mightily to secure a record deal for his band with the funny-sounding name: a four-piece rock combo calling themselves the Beatles, an offshoot of a late 1950s-era skiffle group known as the Quarry Men. To the good folks at EMI, Brian was well known for being one of the most successful record retailers in the North Country. A few years earlier, his father had given him the reins of the family's NEMS (North End Music Stores) record outlet on Great Charlotte Street, and the twenty-seven-year-old, who had languished from one sputtering career effort to another, proved to be a natural record hawk. NEMS enjoyed a long history in the United Kingdom—dating back to 1886, when it originally opened as a piano store. Things really took off when the Epstein family opened a second location on Liverpool's Whitechapel Street. Run entirely by Brian, who toiled day and night to will NEMS into becoming a regional sensation, the Whitechapel outlet quickly caught the attention of the London record distributors. Brian threw himself into his life at NEMS—just as he would later do on behalf of his most cherished clients. "Sales at NEMS were mounting," he later wrote, "and the staff increased slowly by twos and threes to an eventual thirty, all working very hard. I built up a best-seller list which I checked twice daily and from this I expanded the pop music department and pushed the classical discs upstairs. I put in ridiculously long hours, working from 8 AM until long into the night and on Sundays I used to come into the store to make out orders."[7]

By 1960, Brian had negotiated cooperative advertising agreements with all of the big labels—Decca and EMI, most prominently—and the youngest son of the Epstein clan had finally found his mettle at last. Marking the opening of the Whitechapel location in its pages, the Liverpool *Echo* parroted one of

Brian's favorite boasts: "The ambition of NEMS is to supply ANY record that is named—and to produce it almost immediately." Indeed, Brian's promise of instant gratification dared to provide what almost every downtrodden Liverpool Scouser desperately wanted: easy access in a world dominated by monolithic London in the faraway south. And to his credit, Brian made good on his boast more often than not. In fact, that very same boast had put him on a collision course with his clients after one Raymond Jones entered the NEMS Whitechapel location and requested a copy of "My Bonnie" by the Beatles. When Brian didn't have a copy of the record in his inventory—indeed, he hadn't so much as even heard of "My Bonnie"—he sought out the Beatles, who regularly played at the Cavern Club only a few hundred feet away from NEMS. And when he saw them onstage during a lunchtime concert, he knew that he wanted to manage them. As Brian later wrote, "I thought their sound was something that an awful lot of people would like. They were fresh and they were honest and they had what I thought was a sort of presence, and—this is a terrible, vague term—'star quality.' Whatever that is, they had it—or I sensed that they had it." So in the early months of 1962, when the young record scion truly believed he had discovered hidden rock 'n' roll gold on Liverpool's cast-iron shores, he made his way to London, chin held high, to stake his claim within the industry corridors that he had worked so hard to engage—and, in terms of North Country music interests at least, essentially conquered—after so many had previously failed to make a dent in the Big Smoke.[8]

But even still, the fact that Brian was able to find his way into George's office was a minor miracle in and of itself. It all began, strangely enough, with the Beatles' rejection by Decca. Armed with the tapes from the band's failed audition, a dejected Brian found his way to the office of Bob Boast, who managed the massive HMV record store on Oxford Street in Central London. As Bob later recalled, "He said he'd had a very wearing two days visiting record companies. It seems they just weren't prepared to listen. I was, though it was beyond my powers to help him. But at that time we had a small recording studio on the first floor, where budding artists could make 78 rpm demonstration discs. I took Brian there and introduced him to our disc cutter, Jim Foy." For Brian, it made perfect sense to have the tapes transferred into acetates for easy demonstration to record execs. As Brian and Jim listened to the tapes, the disc cutter voiced his admiration for the songs. As was his common pitch at the time, Brian pointed out that many of the tunes were original to the band. Jim helpfully suggested that Brian visit the office of Ardmore and Beechwood, one of EMI's music-publishing arms, which happened to be located just upstairs, above the HMV shop. Moments later, Ardmore and Beechwood's general manager, Sid Colman, came downstairs and listened to the tapes for himself. Liking what he heard, he retired with Brian to the Ardmore and Beechwood offices with the freshly cut discs now in hand. For Sid—a music publisher, after all—the objective was simple: secure the copyright for the original material on the discs. Although his own interest had been piqued, Brian said that the publishing rights would only be in the hands of Ardmore and Beechwood if Sid could finagle a recording contract for the band. When Brian left HMV that day, Sid promised to see what he could do.[9]

Years later, Martin would write that Colman had served as the intermediary who brought Epstein into his orbit. In George's memory, Sid said to Brian, "Why don't you go 'round and see George Martin at Parlophone? He deals in unusual things. He's had a big success with the most unlikely recording acts. I'll give him a ring and make an appointment, if you like." Indeed, it was well known around EMI during this period that George was open to artists of all stripes. As Bernard Cribbins later remarked, "George Martin was the chap they sent all the weirdies to." For George, Sid's kind offer of a referral provided the impetus for Brian's subsequent meeting with the Parlophone head. But at this point, the story becomes decidedly hazy. Many years after the fact, record plugger Kim Bennett would suggest that this turn of events was all but impossible given the gossip that Sid actively disliked George, whom he found to be a bit of an upstart. Whatever the reason—whether because of Sid's generous offer of a professional referral or Brian's indefatigable persistence on his clients' behalf—shortly after Jim Foy cut the discs, Brian made his way back toward the very EMI brass that had rejected him out of hand back in mid-December on the strength (or what they perceived to be the lack thereof) of the Beatles' recording of "My Bonnie" with English expatriate Tony Sheridan. Indeed, on December 18, 1961, Ron White, EMI's general manager, had written the Beatles' manager to let him know that the company would not be pursuing the group any further. Perhaps Brian now felt more confident with the Decca acetates in hand and ready for demonstration. The world will likely never know.[10]

In any event, Brian arrived at EMI House in a most fortuitous moment when George was the primary A&R head in residence—his archrival, Norrie Paramor, was on vacation, as was Norman Newell, the EMI A&R man and former Columbia head who floated among the three labels and signed acts for all three. According to Judy Lockhart Smith's desk calendar—which erroneously listed the visitor from Liverpool as "Bernard Epstein"—it was on Tuesday, February 13, 1962, when George agreed to meet Brian in the Parlophone head's new offices in EMI House at 20 Manchester Square, having moved over from Great Castle Street. That morning, Brian quite naturally came into Judy's orbit first, as he attempted to wind his way into George's office. She later recalled him as being very well mannered, gracious, and well kempt—a stark contrast with the outsized egos that she typically associated with the entertainment managers who stood over her desk. For his part, Brian immediately took a liking to the amiable Judy, with whom he felt the pangs of an "instant friendship." Overrun with other appointments away from EMI House, George was late for the meeting. When he arrived, he and Brian retired to the A&R man's fourth-floor office, where Brian lapsed into his well-honed pitch about his Liverpool beat band, the Beatles, whom he had discovered the previous November in the sweaty environs of the Cavern Club, a former jazz club on Matthew Street. As George later recalled, "To start with, he gave me a big 'hype' about this marvelous group who were doing such great things in Liverpool. He told me how everybody up there thought they were the bee's knees. He even expressed surprise that I hadn't heard of them—which, in the circumstances, was pretty bold. I almost asked him in reply where Liverpool was. The thought of anything coming out of the provinces was extraordinary at the time. Then he played me his disc, and I first heard the sound of the Beatles."[11]

During this brief first meeting, Brian played one of the ten-inch demonstration records, most likely the acetate featuring "Hello Little Girl" on one side and "Till There Was You" on the other. In his autobiography, Brian whimsically recalled the moment of truth as George and Judy listened to the Beatles for the first time: "I liked the way he listened to the discs, his long legs crossed, leaning on his elbow, he rocked gently to and fro and nodded and smiled encouragingly. Judy also smiled her delicious smile, and I sat with a face like stone as if my very life was at stake. In a way it was." Scrawling on the record labels in blue fountain pen, Brian noted that "Hullo [*sic*] Little Girl" was by "John Lennon & The Beatles" and that "Til [*sic*] There Was You" was by "Paul McCartney & The Beatles." Brian later remembered that "George liked 'Hello Little Girl,' 'Till There Was You.' Liked George [Harrison] on guitar. Thought Paul was the one for discs." As it happened, Brian's recollections hardly jibe with those of George, who remembered things very differently, recalling, "I wasn't knocked out at all." Perhaps George had let the band's manager down too gently. Or, more likely, perhaps Brian was engaging in a moment of rudimentary wishful thinking, feeling hopeful in the presence of the kind and gentlemanly slightly older man. In any event,

Brian's association with George would, in all probability, have ended right then and there had it not been for a circuitous, unforeseen succession of—at times, unrelated—circumstances that would change their lives in dramatic and far-reaching ways.[12]

As the meeting came to an end, George recalled telling Brian, "Look, if I have to judge them on the strength of these demos then the answer is no." But always hedging his bets, the Parlophone head instinctively cracked open the slightest of windows for Brian's consideration. Seeing that Brian "looked crestfallen," George added, "If you care to bring them to London I will have a listen to them in the studio and see if there is anything I like." In this instance, George was following his own dictum that being an astute recording manager means that you "keep your ears to the ground," as he had written in his *Eminews* column the previous July, "and hear as many new people as you can." But for Brian, this solution simply wasn't expedient enough. On January 1, the Beatles had auditioned at Decca Records for A&R man Mike Smith, only to be rejected later under the proviso that "guitar groups were on their way out," a verdict often attributed to Decca's A&R head Dick Rowe. In any event, Decca instead signed Brian Poole and the Tremeloes, an East London beat group, leaving the Beatles in limbo. On some level, Brian must have felt the snub of English snobbery and regionalism playing a hand in the band's increasingly bewildering fate. As his brother, Clive, later commented, during this period of wholesale rejection, Brian had to "put up with rudeness and indifference and doors being slammed in his face."[13]

Desperate to win a contract for the Beatles after being declined by Columbia, Pye, Philips, Ember, Oriole, and now Decca, Epstein had no intention of presenting the bandmates with empty promises. He was well aware of the score: having been declined by juggernauts like Decca and EMI meant that essentially 80 percent of the British record trade had rejected his clients. In spite of this daunting reality, he was still determined to return to Liverpool with a signed contract in his hands. After all, the Beatles wouldn't be "bigger than Elvis," as Epstein liked to boast, without a deal. No, when Epstein left that day, his dealings with Martin should have, for all intents and purposes, been concluded—and possibly forever. After all, Epstein was a North Country resident with a thriving record business in Liverpool and its environs. If and when his dalliance with the Beatles fizzled out, he would likely step fully back into his role at NEMS. But it didn't happen that way, of course.

What Brian didn't know—couldn't possibly have known—was that "George was desperate to get something off the ground in the pop department," in Ron Richards's words. George was simply tired of being humiliated by glory-hound Norrie Paramor while Parlophone lagged behind as the EMI Group's third label. While Brian's Liverpool beat band would wait in the wings—at least for the moment—George continued on his long quest to take a pop act to the top of the charts and sustain their career. But he wasn't merely nursing this ambition to improve Parlophone's standing in the industry. He was dead set on making his name in the record business as a genuine hitmaker, an entertainment impresario who shared in the profits from his ability to recognize talent and take it to the big time.[14]

By the time that he met Brian, George had already begun working with a new artist who generally seemed to fit the bill, baritone cabaret singer Matt Monro, who, for the time being at least, would emerge as one of Parlophone's most significant acts. Previously a member of the Decca and Philips stables, Monro came into Martin's orbit during the sessions for *Songs for Swingin' Sellers*, for which Monro had recorded a demo in order to assist Sellers in delivering his sidesplitting imitation of Old Blue Eyes. Sellers loved Monro's vocal stylings and decided to include the original song on his album, for which he credited Monro—humorously, of course, this being Sellers and all—with the pseudonym Fred Flange. As it turned out, Monro initially had been reluctant to work in this capacity, feeling that crass imitation was beneath him. But the crooner eventually came around after his wife, Mickie, persuaded him to take the gig. As Martin later recalled, Monro "came in and did the job like the professional he was and he was so good at the job and so easy to work with. I paid him a measly 25 pounds and he did the job very quickly and very efficiently as he always did. I had to give him a pseudonym and Fred Flange came to mind. 'Flange' was one of my favorite nonsense words." Drawn to Monro's talent, Martin lured the singer to Parlophone, and they recorded a series of international hits. In short order, the Monro-Martin collaboration scored two top 10 singles in "Portrait of My Love" and "My Kind of Girl," the latter of which was named as the winner of ITV's *A Song for Britain* in February 1961. Under Martin's tutelage, the "Man with the Golden Voice" went from journeyman nightclub singer to household name in a matter of months. Nobody was more surprised than Monro regarding his unexpected bout of success, especially with "Portrait of My Love": "I was convinced that it was the most uncommercial number I had ever heard, but within two weeks, it was in the charts and stayed there for months." For his part, Martin adored working with Monro, who was unerringly professional and "had no tricks and no temperament and only had to be asked to do something once. When he sang he just expanded and the notes would come out and go on forever."[15]

Monro also afforded an even more valuable opportunity for Martin, who had long yearned for a creative outlet, as well as for a means to supplement his fairly static EMI salary. Over the years, George had been sporadically composing songs under Graham Fisher, his nom de plume. In this guise, he had cowritten Monro's modest hit "Can This Be Love?" As George later remarked, "Another of my favorite performances from Matt is a song I wrote under the pseudonym of Graham Fisher along with Herbert Kretzmer, who later wrote all the lyrics for *Les Misérables*." A hit single in its own right, "Can This Be Love?" was later included on the Parlophone EP *Matt's Kind of Music*.[16]

In 1961 George had also penned tunes for Ron Goodwin and Spike Milligan, later writing "Double Scotch" and "The Niagara Theme," which he copyrighted under his given name with the newly minted Dick James Music, a publishing company founded by his old partner in crime during his EMI salad days. Staked with £5,000, James had opened up for business in Charing Cross in September 1961 with the express intention of focusing his energies on supporting British songwriters. As he wrote in the mission statement for Dick James Music, "It is the intention of the company to pursue a policy of securing and exploiting works by British writers. It is probable that the company may well publish works of foreign origin but the accent will be on British works wherever and whenever possible."[17]

By the time that Monro's "Portrait of My Love" peaked in the number-three spot in the *NME* January 1961 charts, Martin's artists were flying high, with another Martin production, "Goodness Gracious Me!" featuring Sellers, who sports an Indian accent, and Italian actress Sophia Loren, also bubbling in the top 10. George had cannily asked David Lee and Herbert Kretzmer to compose "Goodness Gracious Me!" in an express effort to see it included on the soundtrack for *The Millionairess*, which Sophia Loren was starring in at the time. Ultimately, director Anthony Asquith opted not to feature the song in *The Millionairess*, although it served to publicize his romantic comedy anyway, as it steamed up the charts in the days leading up to the film's premiere. Martin also hastily produced Loren's cover version of "Zoo Be Zoo Be Zoo"—an English-language recording of "Zou Bisou Bisou," composed by Bill Shepherd and Alan Tew—as yet another publicity effort for *The Millionairess*. Ron Richards good-naturedly turned in a wobble-box performance for "Goodness Gracious Me!" which George produced in the cavernous Number 1 studio. When they recorded the duet, George sported his usual flair in setting his artists at ease: "Sophia was incredibly charming, fun to be with and easy to work with. In no way did she play the big star." With one hit following the other, it was as if, after so many years toiling away at the "third label," he could suddenly do no wrong. For the first time in his career, it was as if George had the golden touch, being able to consolidate talent in the service of commercial acclaim. Indeed, there was only one A&R man who seemed to outdo him at this juncture: the Columbia label head who existed as his chief rival, fellow EMI mainstay Norrie Paramor. At every turn, Norrie seemed to best George. In one memorable week in March 1962, George managed to see an astonishing three of his Parlophone acts in the *NME* top 20 only to watch Norrie surpass him with *four* hits for Columbia. And of course, Norrie enjoyed remarkable celebrity of his own for nursing Cliff Richard to stardom on the British pop charts. Beginning with the 1958 success of Richard's breakout single "Move It"—often credited as the first British rock record—Paramor steered the teen idol on a creative path that produced an incredible string of twenty-three top 10 UK hits. In the four-year period between 1958 and 1962, the Richard-Paramor partnership had produced sales in excess of five and a half million records, a staggering sum by any measure. George was admittedly jealous of Norrie's fame and success—not merely because of his standing within the EMI Group but also for the flashy lifestyle that Norrie led and that George, in spite of his better angels, coveted. Although they held similar salaries with EMI, George was making ends meet out in suburban Hatfield, while Norrie had a London home on stately Bishop's Avenue and a seaside place in Sussex, not to mention a slick new motorboat and a delectable E-Type Jaguar. "I had always been very envious of Norrie Paramor," George freely admitted.[18]

For Martin, the difference in their incomes was obvious—and it had everything to do with Paramor's unremitting string of chart-topping artists, namely Richard, for whom the Columbia A&R man extracted sizable and continuous royalties. Upon further inspection, Martin managed to suss out no fewer than thirty-six different instances in which Paramor had penned B-sides—under pseudonyms, of course—on his clients' hit singles. Martin was beside himself with anger, not merely at Paramor but at EMI for refusing—officially, at least—to afford its A&R men opportunities to supplement their income with residual income from songwriting and, in short, to directly accrue royalties from their artists' successes. His long-simmering anger at his colleague's practices—as well as for the way in which Paramor unabashedly flaunted his lifestyle—must have finally taken its toll. In March 1962, only scant weeks before the scheduled renewal of his three-year contract with EMI—his current deal was set to expire in April—George had lunch with twenty-two-year-old David Frost, a recent Cambridge graduate and a fledgling reporter for *This Week*, London AR-TV's current affairs program.

Frost plied Martin with questions about the contemporary state of the record business, especially about the growing influence of long-players in the UK marketplace, and as Martin downed his lunch, his companion got much more than he bargained for, as the Parlophone head spoke frankly about Paramor's shady activities through the guise of some three dozen aliases. For George, it was a moment of uncommon candor—an unusually brazen moment of jealousy and rumor-mongering from a man many in the industry saw as a gentleman above reproach. While Frost would sit on his scoop about Paramor's shenanigans for the time being—it would be nearly eight more months before the lid on the Columbia head's double-dealings would be blown sky-high—Martin's rare instance of reckless abandon hinted at something darker in the A&R man's world.[19]

Indeed, as he walked away from his lunch with Frost that day, Martin held a secret known to only a scant few: he had been carrying on an extramarital affair with his assistant, Judy Lockhart Smith, for more than four years. It was a discreet, albeit very dangerous, association that would threaten his standing as a captain of the record industry—even in the early 1960s, upstanding people simply didn't behave in that fashion. When he first met her as Preuss's assistant back in 1950, Martin had felt rebuffed by her presence, by what he perceived to be her cool exterior and standoffishness. But as the years passed, she emerged as his most treasured ally and a tireless promoter of him as he vaulted toward success among the hallowed corridors of EMI. Perhaps most of all, he was smitten with her upper-class station, not unlike the gentlemen officers whom he aspired to emulate back in the Painted Hall during his war years. "Judy had this incredible upper-class accent and George was clearly that way inclined," a colleague later remarked. "She used to say a raised *what?* at the end of sentences. He was dazzled by her and by her upbringing, completely dazzled."[20]

By the advent of the early 1960s, George had begged Sheena for a divorce but to no avail. She simply couldn't give up on their family life with Alexis and Gregory in modest Hatfield. Years later, he would attribute his wife's malaise during this period to a trenchant form of agoraphobia. Although George obviously lacked the formal training to make such a diagnosis—and there is no evidence to suggest that his wife was ever under a physician's care for such a malady—it is worth noting that people commonly mistake the meaning behind agoraphobia as being associated with being afraid of being out of doors as opposed to its true meaning, which involves a fear of being in public spaces—of having to contend with unfamiliar environs and uncontrollable social situations. Given the nature of the disorder, agoraphobia usually manifests itself in the sufferer through the onset of panic attacks. And while she was remembered by family and friends to be a shy and nervous sort at times, Sheena was known to have little problem making her way around Hatfield or even traveling into the city.[21]

By the time that Martin sat down for lunch with Frost, he had taken the even riskier and momentous step of moving out of his home with Sheena and his family and taking up quarters in a tiny bachelor apartment in Central London not too far from EMI House. Years later, his daughter, Alexis, would vividly recall the day her father left his family in the suburbs: "I remember standing at the top of the stairs at our home in Hatfield and listening to my mother begging my dad in the hallway not to go. She was saying, 'You can't do this. Please, please, don't leave me!' I was eight years old and did not understand what was happening. All I knew was that she was feeling so much grief."[22]

While this was a difficult time for George, who was torn over leaving his family in the suburbs, his adoration for Judy, and a deep sense of remorse, it resulted in an unexpected reunion of sorts with his father, Harry, who was a widower and had lived alone for some fourteen years. As George later recalled, when he lived apart from Sheena for the first time, "I took a pokey little flat in Upper Berkeley Street, London, and he came to share it with me. We got to know each other pretty well, and we even made some furniture together. I still have the sideboard we made. I used to take him along to recording sessions, which he loved." Eventually, Harry met Judy. "He became very fond of her and they got on like a house of fire." For George, living with Judy was simply out of the question back in those days, so for the time being he was left to seek out stolen moments at work or occasionally sleep on a "chair-bed" in the well-appointed apartment that Judy now shared with two other women, having also relocated from Hatfield to the city. Judy's comparatively opulent place sported a grand piano, where George would while away the hours writing new compositions that he would place with Dick James Music.[23]

With Judy's steadfast encouragement, George actively sought out extramural composing opportunities. With his growing frustration with peers like Paramor earning the big bucks outside of EMI's narrow salary strictures, Martin was eager to make his mark—and just as importantly at this juncture in his life, prop up his meager income, which he sorely needed to pay for his estranged family in the suburbs and his new bachelor life in London. As George's steadfast supporter, Judy managed to steer work his way courtesy of her father, Kenneth Lockhart Smith, a veteran of the British film industry since the late 1920s and chairman of the Film Producer's Guild, housed at Merton

Park Studios. With the elder Lockhart Smith's connections, Martin brought two film scores to fruition during this period, including the low-budget art flick *Take Me Over*, which highlighted the music of the Temperance Seven. He also composed incidental music for *Crooks Anonymous*—a slapdash British comedy that was right up his street. For his efforts, George earned the fairly paltry sums of £100 and £200, but the experience afforded him an entrée into an arena that had long been central to his interest: crafting music so as to create vivid mental images. With film, the task proved to be even more appealing to him given the requirements of taking an existing palette of filmic words and images. George delighted in the process of using incidental music to establish drama and depth, to enhance the existing storytelling features in new and often unforeseen ways. For George, this cut to the quick of music's power to move its listeners and heighten aesthetic experience.[24]

For *Take Me Over*, directed by Robert Lynn, George ended up earning a life lesson in composing incidental music and merging it with film. He later wrote about *Take Me Over* being his "Big Chance" for proving himself as a composer. Indeed, while he had saved Parlophone from EMI's scrap heap and seen the Temperance Seven top the charts, he was understandably besieged by self-doubts about making it in popular music. And besides, there was always the specter of Norrie Paramor writ large in the music trades. As it happened, he was generally happy with his work on *Take Me Over*. "The songs I wrote for them, and the incidental music, in a typical 20s style, worked out fine and suited the mood of the film very well," he later reflected. "But when we came to fitting the music to the picture my troubles started. It was done at Shepperton, and provided my first experience of a film studio; I had no conception of how hard it would be. I was not helped by the fact that the Temperance Seven were seen to be playing in the picture, and that I therefore had to fit the music to what they were doing on film. That was a basic error on the part of the producers. They should have recorded the music first, and then the band should have mimed to it on film, which would have been far easier. As it was, I was landed with having to do the thing back to front, with no idea as to how. It was the most exhausting, nerve-racking experience of my life, and I got through it by sheer hit-and-miss, trial-and-error methods." To make matters worse, the Temperance Seven's lack of sophisticated music training exacerbated the situation, as they were unable to follow his musical direction when he took up the conductor's baton in an effort to synchronize the incidental music with the images being projected overhead in antiquated Shepperton Studios. To George's chagrin, every mistake by the Temperance Seven—and there were many during their postproduction sessions with the

Parlophone head—required studio personnel to rewind the film and start all over again, thus wreaking further havoc on George's "already well-frayed nerves."[25]

After completing work on the production, George recalled saying "I never want to do another film again. If that's film music, you can have it!" George may have been dismayed, but by that time he would have far bigger things on his mind. While his experience with *Take Me Over* left him swimming in a sea of professional doubts, his incidental work directly led to his acquaintance with Muir Matheson, the renowned Scottish composer, not to mention a veteran conductor whose work had graced many British pictures over the years. Having been tapped to provide music for *Crooks Anonymous*, a comedy directed by Ken Annakin and starring Wilfred Hyde White, Leslie Phillips, and James Robertson Justice, Matheson needed a musical vehicle for Phillips, who was playing petty criminal Captain Dandy Forsdyke, to sing in the film. He may have been perturbed after working on *Take Me Over*, but George always knew how to recognize opportunity when it fell into his lap. "Why don't you write a song for Leslie Phillips?" Matheson asked. "We'll get him singing it over the opening titles, and then you can work with me on the film score. You do all the commercial bits, and I'll do all the snippety bits of fitting." For Martin, the job proved to be tough going with Phillips, who, by his own admission, wasn't a talented vocalist. Although Martin enjoyed his "happy little partnership" with Matheson and "learned a great deal from him about the techniques of film writing," when he settled into his seat at the film's premiere at the Odeon Acton, he was in for quite a surprise. "I was utterly amazed," George later wrote. "The opening titles were accompanied by the score I had done for the brash opening music for the song. That was fine. But when the voice was due to appear—nothing. Not a word. All I could hear was the accompaniment to a missing voice. It must have been a very full accompaniment, because no one else seemed to notice." George's work on *Take Me Over* and *Crooks Anonymous* led to additional film work, including *Calculated Risk*, directed by Norman Harrison, another caper movie for which George composed and conducted the soundtrack.[26]

Music undoubtedly acted as a salve for George's anguish at leaving his young family alone in the suburbs. The excitement that he no doubt felt over his intense, long-running affair with Judy, as well as over his career—which was happening almost exclusively in the city—must have been tempered by a deep sense of guilt. Eager to start his new life with Judy—living, as she did, in a world of wealth and privilege—he had beseeched Sheena for a divorce. As a non-practicing Catholic, he felt the pangs of such a momentous step, and

Sheena understood this implicitly, refusing over a period of years to allow him to end their marriage and fully take up his new life in London. She had her own reasons, of course. In spite of everything, she still loved him—still adored the Fleet Air Arm man who had swept her off her feet back in Donibristle during his heady, music-filled days of demobilization in Scotland. But Sheena also knew how to read a calendar—in February 1961, she had turned forty, a desperate age in the early 1960s for any divorcée, especially a single mother trying to raise small children in the suburbs.[27]

For some time, Sheena had nursed a secret suspicion about her husband's possible extramarital activities. When Sheena started to suspect he was having an affair in earnest, she ran the idea by Ron Goodwin, who thought the very idea of George seeing another woman was "ridiculous." Sheena finally learned the awful truth in late 1960 or early 1961. When she could no longer take the agony of her lingering suspicions, she arranged for a babysitter under the pretense of wanting to do some shopping in the city. George reluctantly brought her along on his morning ride into London. Their first stop, of course, was Judy's home in old Hatfield. For Sheena, the truth abruptly crystalized for her when George got out of his Austin Ten Cambridge sedan to knock on the door and fetch his assistant for the daily commute. He suddenly began making excuses, leaning over the wheel well, as if something were wrong with the car, when, to Sheena's mind, he was clearly flustered by the notion of taking his wife to his paramour's home. Until that very moment, Sheena hadn't even realized that George had been driving Judy into work every day.

After George had taken up residence in his bachelor apartment in the city, Sheena relentlessly begged him to come back to their family life in Hatfield. For nearly five years, she would refuse to grant him a divorce, knowingly tugging at his latent sense of Catholic guilt. She simply couldn't bear to let him go. For his own part, George easily consented to a long-running charade in which he and Sheena pretended to be together in wedded bliss, with George living in London while his family resided in the greener environs of the suburbs. As facades go, it was very plausible given the high demands of George's professional life at EMI. Every few weeks, Sheena would bring the children into London, where they would have lunch with their father and take in the sights of the city—perhaps going to a film at one of the Leicester Square cinemas or visiting the London Zoo. For the entirety of the charade, young Gregory remained wholly in the dark, believing his parents to be happily married, but Alexis came to know better. As the Martins' daughter edged toward teenagehood, she intuited the fractures in her parents' marriage that her younger brother, lost in the haze of boyhood, could not.[28]

During this period, Sheena later recalled feeling lost in Hatfield in more ways than one. Not only was she separated from a husband to whom she desperately clung, but also for the most part she had left her life and family back in Scotland, which seemed like a world away after some fourteen years as George's wife. The situation was exacerbated by the few friends who still bothered to visit her in Hatfield, including Joan and Graham Fisher, who were outraged by the idea of George leaving his family. As he watched the charade of their faux family life unfold over a period of years, Graham fumed—within earshot of a confused Gregory—"Those children don't have a father anymore!" For her part, Sheena simply didn't understand the lure of the record industry and the ways in which her husband had long been evolving away from her.[29]

During the weekend of March 24, 1962, George and Judy took a comparatively brazen step in their relationship, which they had so carefully guarded from the world for several years. Taking advantage of an unusual opportunity in the life of the Parlophone head, they went on a business trip together. George had been invited to represent EMI at a "festival of live and recorded music" at the Norbreck Hydro, a resort hotel situated on the cliffs above Blackpool. With company business in the offing, George felt that the festival afforded him a plausible reason for inviting his assistant to join him for the trip to the North Country. As part of the event, George was asked to give a lecture about innovations in the record business. At the appointed time, he took the dais with a gramophone player as his only prop and presented a speech about "Humor on Record" in which he detailed his comedy exploits with the likes of Peter Ustinov and members of the Goons, as well as the circuitous route via which the Indian embassy had assisted him in rounding up a sitar player for *Songs for Swingin' Sellers*. George's Blackpool talk even netted him a front-page story in *Eminews*.[30]

It was under precisely these circumstances that George finally met with EMI's managing director, L. G. "Len" Wood, to discuss the terms associated with his contract renewal in the spring of 1962. By that time, various forces had come to align against George in his professional and personal lives, which were shortly set to collide in vastly unexpected ways. For his part, George proceeded with the negotiations, intent on winning his long sought-after residuals. "I *always* felt we should have a royalty," George later recalled. "I was prepared to take a lower salary if I could have a proportion of what we sold, like the salesmen did. I was very angry about it and nearly didn't sign the contract renewal." At one point, the Parlophone head even went so far as to boldly state his intentions. "I'll have to leave, then," Martin told the managing director. "If you feel like that, be our guest," Wood coolly replied.[31]

But George couldn't leave EMI so easily, of course. He needed the salary. And his vulnerabilities at this time were many—although still secret to all but a precious few. George had succeeded in making his case all right, but it was all bluster. He had no real intention of walking away from his EMI salary at this juncture. In fact, he couldn't hope to continue leading his double life without it. Perhaps even more important, the world that he had fashioned at Parlophone afforded him far more than a mere livelihood. He had progressed too far as an A&R man, an orchestrator, an arranger—as an *artist*, even—to so easily sacrifice his central creative outlet because Len Wood couldn't glimpse beyond corporate policy and comprehend the Parlophone head's need to have a fiduciary role in his clientele's success. At least those were the circumstances, if only for the time being, in the spring of 1962, when George inked a new three-year contract that would take him into 1965 with a salary of roughly £3,000 per annum. In this one meeting with Wood, Martin was setting a series of events into motion that would change his life forever while also shifting the course and fortunes of Parlophone specifically—and the EMI Group in general—in long-standing and resounding ways. Indeed, it is all but impossible to exaggerate the significance of this strange confluence of events in George's future.

# 6

# "I DON'T LIKE YOUR TIE"

MEANWHILE, BACK ON OXFORD STREET, Sid Colman had not so easily forgotten the reason that Brian Epstein had found his way into George's orbit in the first place. Back in February, after he assisted Brian in meeting Jim Foy and cutting the acetates from the Beatles' Decca audition, Sid played the recordings for Kim Bennett, a hardworking record promoter for Ardmore and Beechwood who had once tried to make it as a crooner for Decca, only to see his own contract not renewed by the record conglomerate in 1957. Kim, who had been out when Brian visited Sid's office on the top floor of HMV, was known for his stubborn determination on behalf of the songs and the artists that caught his fancy, and one Beatles track in particular, "Like Dreamers Do," the first number from the band's January 1962 audition, sounded like the real thing to his ears.[1]

For his part, Bennett didn't plan to give up on his quest to land the rights to "Like Dreamers Do" so easily. With the crisp attack of what would later become known as the Merseybeat sound, the song seemed fresh to Bennett, who may have been taken in by the singer's voice, as Paul McCartney crooned about the destiny of falling in love with the girl of his dreams. A kind of hybridized fusion of rock 'n' roll, skiffle, and rhythm and blues, Merseybeat soared with the sounds of midtempo beat music, propelled by guitar and bass and, of course, by a strong and persistent backbeat. As Kim later recalled, "I said, 'I like that. What do they call themselves?' and Sid said the Beatles. 'Oh bloody hell, what a name to use!' He told me the song was available if we could get them a record release and I replied, 'I like it very much, Sid. I like that sound. If we can get them a record, and then if we can get it played, I think it could go into the charts. It's different.'" As it turned out, moving the Beatles forward proved to be a tall order for Colman and Bennett—just as it had been for Epstein over the past few months. Bennett learned this firsthand when Colman tried to interest the A&R men at EMI House, which was conveniently located just across the street from the HMV, in "Like Dreamers Do." As he played the acetate for EMI's various A&R personnel, Colman was soundly rebuffed for his trouble. As Kim recalled, Sid's "actual words were 'Nobody over there wants to know' and, as he didn't qualify that remark, I took 'nobody' to mean that he'd seen everybody." Not one to be so easily spurned, Bennett suggested another line of attack to Colman: "Why don't you go across to Len Wood and say that if EMI give us a record, we will pay for its cost. Because it's a group it'll be a straightforward studio production, no orchestra; we'll have got two copyrights for the next 50 years plus maybe a royalty on the record." But Wood wasn't having any of it, telling Colman that he and Bennett "should stick to publishing and leave EMI to make the records."[2]

But what seemed like a resoundingly dead end for Colman and Bennett suddenly rematerialized, as if by magic, several weeks later—perhaps in late March or early April—when Colman happened to discuss the matter of the Beatles and acquiring "Like Dreamers Do" with EMI's managing director. "Time went by since I'd floated my Beatles idea. Weeks," Bennett recalled. "Then one day Sid came to my office door with a grin on his face, and rubbing his hands. He said, 'I've just been talking to Len Wood on the phone: we're going to get our record made after all.' After a short, stunned silence, I asked, 'Oh? Who's gonna do it then?'" To Bennett's great surprise, Colman announced that it would be none other than George Martin. "The Beatles record was going to be made as a gesture to Sid, to give Sid Colman a sop," said Kim. "Len was going to bow to our wishes at last." The grin on Sid's face seems to provide further evidence, with the benefit of sober historical backcast, that he may have indeed had it in for George. But why would Wood go to all the trouble of affording Colman with a "sop" when, on behalf of EMI, Ron White had already rejected the Beatles out of hand? Indeed, by this point, the EMI Group had rejected them three times—first, on the basis of the Tony Sheridan recordings; second, by Martin's own words during his meeting with Epstein; and finally, when Wood himself had spurned Colman and Bennett's notion of taking the Beatles into the studio to record "Like Dreamers Do" on their own accord. Years later, Norman Smith, the EMI balance engineer who spent many an hour working side by side with George at Abbey Road, reported that "L. G. Wood didn't approve of people having affairs, and he certainly didn't approve of George going off with his secretary. Not at all. I think it offended his moral standards. L. G. virtually ordered George to record the Beatles." Is it possible that Len had discovered the truth about George's dalliance with Judy after their clandestine trip to Blackpool? Did the Beatles find their way back into EMI's good graces via the circuitous route of a secret romance and back-office politics?[3]

However it played out, Brian was summoned out of the blue—and most likely via a telephone call from Judy herself—during the first week of May 1962 to return by invitation to the Parlophone offices. For the first time, Brian was actually being *asked* to visit, as opposed to cold-calling the offices of a record company on the Beatles' behalf. For his part, Brian was simultaneously elated, transfixed, and overbrimming with understandable trepidation. By this point, Brian was truly desperate—Parlophone was, essentially, the Beatles' last-chance saloon. The day before the meeting, which had been set for 11:30 AM on May 9 at Abbey Road, Brian asked Derek Taylor, a Liverpool journalist and his close friend and confidant, "What's the point? Should I even bother going?" He then turned to Alistair Taylor, his colleague at NEMS, who urged him to stay the course. But Brian was nearly inconsolable: "Maybe we should just sell records, Alistair? We don't seem to be very successful at making them." In short, in spite of the seeming promise that the impending meeting held, Brian was riven with self-doubts after so many months of rejection—when great expectations had just as quickly been dashed by denial and regret. He wondered, quite frankly, whether he could bear much more of it, of having to return to Liverpool with another load of bad news. As he would later write in his autobiography, *A Cellarful of Noise*, by the time that the Beatles made the trip to West Germany for their regular Hamburg residency, John Lennon and Paul McCartney, in particular, had grown increasingly despondent about their chances of making it in the business. It was, indeed, a far cry from their earlier, halcyon days, as John remembered them in his own words, when "I would yell out, 'Where are we going, fellows?' They would say, 'To the top, Johnny,' in pseudo-American voices. And I would say, 'Where is that, fellows?' And they would say, 'To the toppermost of the poppermost!'" But those days were gone. By this point, the bandmates had to be wondering about the "real" jobs that would, sooner or later, come calling. One recent night in Joe's Restaurant back in Liverpool, Brian had lamented to the bandmates that every label had effectively turned them down. "Right. Try Embassy," John joked, referring to Woolworth's low-budget label, which recorded cheap cover versions of contemporary hits and didn't even bother signing new talent. As Paul later recalled, "It was all a bit bloody hell, what are we gonna do?" While George Harrison held out a sense of hope in contrast with his older mates, Lennon and McCartney were on the verge, lamentable as it may seem, of giving up the ghost of ever making a living, much less achieving fame and fortune in the record business.[4]

The night before his fateful meeting with George, Brian spent the evening at his uncle Berrel's Hampstead home in northwest London. "What shall I do?" he implored his uncle. "I've got one more appointment, but I don't know what to do. Shall I give it all up and go home?" For his part, Uncle Berrel was mystified by Brian's indecision. After all, he was only scant hours from his meeting with the Parlophone head. "Oh, just keep that last appointment," he told his nephew. As it turned out, the manager's anxiety would be short lived. When Brian sat down in George's office the next morning, the Parlophone head cut directly to the chase, announcing that he was prepared to offer the Beatles one of EMI's industry-standard penny-per-record contracts. Brian was ecstatic, of course—and greatly relieved at having finally secured a recording contract for the group. Likely never truly knowing the strange set of circumstances that had landed him back in George's orbit, Brian listened patiently as the A&R head meticulously outlined the particulars of their agreement. In the contract, EMI promised to record no fewer than six "sides" during the first year, which would comprise three 78 rpm singles releases, with EMI retaining ownership of the original sound recordings. As it happened, EMI would discontinue its 78 rpm line in June 1962 in favor of 45 rpm singles; hence, the Beatles would never see the light of day on a gramophone record from days of yore. By the terms of the contract, EMI would handle all of the production costs, and the band and their manager would receive no advance on the contract. Any royalties would result from one penny per "double-sided record" for 85 percent of total sales to be paid quarterly. Although George offered the Beatles a four-year contract—with an expiration date of June 5, 1966—EMI was not required to renew after the first year. While Brian didn't bother to do the math, the odds of the Beatles making any real money off the deal were all but impossible. Indeed, for the bandmates to come away with £750 apiece, they would have to sell a million records. The odds of anyone doing that—much less four Scousers with nary a track record—were too preposterous to even bother calculating them in the first place. For his part, George was all too aware of the "pitiful" nature of the contract that he had proffered that day. "I didn't even have to issue the songs," he later wrote. "I only had to record them, and that was no problem because we had the studios there at Abbey Road anyway. EMI took no great economic risk." It was "pretty poor stuff," to George's mind, "but it was typical of EMI's policy at that time"—a "penny-pinching attitude" that the A&R man knew all too well from his own recent contract negotiations.[5]

As soon as he left George's offices, Brian made a beeline for the St. John's Wood Post Office, where he posted a series of celebratory telegrams. He wrote to the Beatles care of the Star Club in Hamburg, where the band was in the midst of a seven-week residency. "CONGRATULATIONS BOYS EMI REQUEST RECORDING SESSION PLEASE REHEARSE NEW MATERIAL," the telegram read. In short order, the bandmates responded, with Lennon writing back, "WHEN ARE WE GOING TO BE MILLIONAIRES," McCartney saying "PLEASE WIRE TEN THOUSAND POUND ADVANCE ROYALTIES," and the ever-pragmatic Harrison asking for Epstein to "PLEASE ORDER FOUR NEW GUITARS." In spite of his friends' volubility, drummer Pete Best was oddly silent about the incredible news out of London. For his part, George had done the unthinkable, unwittingly playing a role in engineering the circumstances that led to EMI signing an act known to scant few outside of England's North Country. While Brian was understandably frolicking on cloud nine after their meeting, George likely didn't give it a second thought. But the day's events marked a monumental sociocultural shift, nonetheless, as the Beatles, with their North Country roots, were fortunate to have a contract—*any* contract—at all. As no less than Elvis Costello remarked years later, "The fact that four young musicians from Liverpool were assigned to the EMI comedy imprint, Parlophone, and the staff producer responsible for the comedy output, gives us a glimpse of a number of casual regional assumptions and the hierarchies of early '60s England."[6]

As it happens, that very same staff A&R head and his Parlophone cohorts hardly knew the band themselves, effecting a typographical error in listing them as the "Beattles" on the four-page contract that was posted to Epstein a few weeks later. Signing the agreement in front of an enthusiastic witness, Liverpool DJ Bob Wooler, Brian dutifully crossed out the extra *t* that was affixed to the band's name throughout the contract, which was set to commence on June 6, 1962, the date that Brian and George had agreed on for the group's first session at Abbey Road. At this point in the Beatles' unlikely story, Brian's dogged persistence had as much to do with their meager success in landing a contract as their talent. Although he would likely never know the circuitous route that had landed the agreement in his lap, Brian's professional association with George had been vital in moving the whole strange business forward.[7]

Indeed, in spite of the circumstances, swirling and backhanded as they may have been, George truly admired and respected Brian Epstein despite the novice manager's penchant for overstatement and bravado. While George found him to be far-fetched in this sense, he instinctively admired Brian's ambition and passion on behalf of the group. And besides, George would later admit, on numerous occasions he, too, had been looking for the next Elvis—just like every other A&R man across the whole of the Western world. But at the same time, he had become increasingly aware in recent years, and in spite of the hits he managed to score with increasing regularity, that he knew very little about pop, much less rock. And perhaps that is why he felt a kinship with the younger man—both were trying their hands at making it in a world where relatively few found real success. George would later admit that he was immediately and deeply taken with the Beatles' manager after meeting him back in February. Moreover, George admired the younger man's elegance, sense of class, and mannered ways. In spite of his boasts, Brian exuded a sense of charm, a kind of natural aristocratic bearing—a quality that both men shared in their professional lives. For his part, Brian felt equally at home in George's presence, writing, "Martin I liked immensely. He is a painstaking man with a magnificent ear for music and a great sense of style." He added, "I do not think he could produce a bad disc," once again revealing his penchant for overstatement.[8]

During the ensuing weeks, as the Beatles presumably rehearsed new material at Brian's urging, George went about the business of running Parlophone. In addition to continuing to leverage the careers of the likes of Matt Monro, the Temperance Seven, and his beloved Goons, George was likely still stinging over Len Wood's rebuff back in April, when the A&R head had begrudgingly inked the contract without having access to the much-desired royalties associated with his acts' records. He felt decidedly irked about not being able to have a financial interest in his clients' success, which was beginning to occur at a more frequent and impressive pace than it had in years past, when Parlophone was a less stable entity among the EMI Group's subsidiaries.

During this period, Ron White, EMI's general manager who had declined to pursue the band back in December, felt the need to write to Epstein. In retrospect, White's letter made for a truly peculiar effort to explain the company's odd position of having rejected the band outright only to sign them to a recording contract just six months later. Even stranger still, White takes great pains to blame the A&R men while absolving himself in the bargain. "I hasten to say that I am very pleased that a contract is now being negotiated as I felt that they were very good," White wrote, "but our Artistes Managers who heard the record felt at that time that they had the greatest difficulty in judging their quality from the record." At this point, White attempts to account for EMI's seemingly contradictory position vis-à-vis the Beatles. "My only reason for writing is to endeavor to explain what must appear to you an anomaly in our organization," he adds. "I can assure you that our Artistes Manager did hear the record but I know you will appreciate that even Artistes Managers are human and can change their mind!" For his part, Epstein—who was delighted to have the Parlophone deal in hand, or, for that matter, *any* deal—graciously wrote back, saying, "It is a great pleasure for me to be associated with EMI in this manner."[9]

As if to make matters even more confusing—and to render White's letter to Epstein even more suspect—Brian Mulligan, a member of the EMI press office staff at the time, recalled the day that "White came into the A&R meeting and said we had just signed this band called the Beatles. He was not terribly impressed with them but said we had to sign them because their manager was our number one HMV dealer in Liverpool." This turn of events seemed to suggest that Len Wood authorized the signing of the Beatles, if only partially, because of Epstein's perceived influence in the North Country record trade. It is difficult to understand why this fact only became germane in June 1962 after being seemingly irrelevant to the Beatles' cause back in December 1961. Was the group's signing truly "a sop" for Sid Colman, in Kim Bennett's words—a kind of interoffice payback, engineered by Wood in response to Martin's adulterous ways? Or does the entire episode speak bluntly about the EMI Group's convoluted business practices during an era when every A&R man in the business was desperate to catch the scent of the next big thing?[10]

In any event, by the time that Wednesday, June 6, 1962, arrived, George set his mind back to the matter at hand: the Liverpool beat group that he had scuttled back in February only to acquiesce to providing them with a contract, sight unseen, a few months later. For George, June 6 had been a fairly light day, including a midmorning meeting with music publisher David Platz and an afternoon session with the folks from *Beyond the Fringe*. Now it was the Beatles' turn. If George had been miffed by the turn of events, at having to sign the North Country band without benefit of a proper audition, he didn't show it. In truth, it was nothing to be embarrassed about—even, in fact, if he had known that Len's imperative for signing the Beatles had to do with his affair with Judy. George knew that EMI, as opposed to Parlophone, with a comparatively miniscule budget, would be incurring the session and production costs, and besides, he was never above taking a look-see where new talent was concerned. No, his problem as the 7 PM session approached was the same as it had been when he first met Brian. How, George still wondered, was he going to find a way to package the beat group from Liverpool with the odd-sounding name? "I desperately wanted my own Cliff," George said. "I was so hidebound by Cliff Richard and the Shadows that I was looking for the one voice that would carry them." Assistant A&R man Ron Richards later recalled their conversation as they made their way to the studio that evening: "George and I were walking along, talking about what the group should be called. Was it going to be John Lennon and the Beatles or Paul McCartney and the Beatles? We still weren't sure. I remember saying to George, 'Bloody silly name that is, Beatles. How corny can you get?'" As Ron awaited the band's arrival in Number 2, George intentionally busied himself elsewhere, possibly even scouting for a snack in the studio canteen.[11]

EMI staffer John Skinner later recalled the band's arrival in front of Abbey Road. "They pulled into the car park in an old white van," he reported. "They all looked very thin and weedy, almost undernourished. Neil Aspinall, their road manager, said they were the Beatles, here for a session. I thought, 'What a strange name.'" As Aspinall set up the band's gear, EMI personnel did a series of double takes as they watched the Beatles amble into the studio in their matching suits and, even more conspicuously, with their long hair and halting Scouser accents. The bandmates included twenty-one-year-old John Lennon on rhythm guitar, nineteen-year-old Paul McCartney on bass, nineteen-year-old George Harrison on lead guitar, and twenty-year-old Pete Best on drums. "Good God, what've we got 'ere?" balance engineer Norman Smith muttered to himself up in the control room. For their part, the Beatles were transfixed by the prospect of arriving at the studio—*any* studio—as artists with an actual recording contract to their name. McCartney vividly recalled that Number 2 had "great big white studio sight-screens, like at a cricket match, towering over you, and up this endless stairway was the control room. It was like heaven, where the great gods lived, and we were down below. Oh God, the nerves." For his part, Richards oversaw the session. "I used to do more of our rock and roll," he later recalled, "so George asked me to have first look at them."[12]

As Richards assisted the band in readying themselves on the studio floor, Smith requested a recording level to get things rolling. And that's when the first signs of trouble ensued, as McCartney strummed his bass and his five-foot-tall "coffin" amp and speaker components coughed a sound that was hardly suitable for professional recording standards. "They had such duff equipment," Smith later observed. "Ugly unpainted wooden amplifiers, extremely noisy, with earth loops and goodness knows what. There was as much noise coming from the amps as there was from the instruments." Technical engineer Ken

Townsend, wearing his white laboratory coat in adherence with EMI studio policy, remedied the situation by hauling a "very large, very heavy" Tannoy speaker in from its place in the basement echo chamber. With McCartney's bass rig under control, the studio personnel turned their attention to Lennon's amp, which emitted a noisome clatter, as well as Best's dilapidated drum kit. "We actually had to tie string around John Lennon's guitar amplifier to stop the rattling," Smith later recalled. "There were also problems with Pete Best's drums—his cymbals, I believe. But we eventually got everything sorted out and finally we started to record."[13]

For their part, the Beatles were thunderstruck by Abbey Road's unmistakable austerity—the studio's aura of sterile professionalism and propriety. "EMI was such a sort of funny place in those days. We thought of it in the same terms as the BBC—some huge, monolithic corporation," McCartney later remarked. "I remember when we used to go to the toilets. On each sheet of toilet paper, it said 'property of EMI.'" But for the Beatles, such oddities were minor issues at best. John, Paul, George, and Pete were happy to be holding a contract with *anyone*. The bandmates hardly felt that they were scraping the bottom of the barrel with Parlophone—although McCartney later admitted, "We did wonder why we got the comedy guy and not the music guy."[14]

As the session began in earnest, it is worth noting that Brian had helpfully provided George with a list of suggested tunes for the A&R man's consideration in advance, including references to an "opening medley" featuring "Bésame Mucho," "Will You Love Me Tomorrow?," and "Open (Your Lovin' Arms)." He also listed another thirty songs in the McCartney, Lennon, and Harrison vocal repertoires, including seven original compositions. Yet at some point, any notion of following Brian's presession notes must have been scrapped altogether, as the band ended up recording the old bolero standard "Bésame Mucho" followed by three original Lennon-McCartney compositions, "Love Me Do," "P.S. I Love You," and "Ask Me Why." What remains vexing, even years later, was the decision—by Martin, by Richards and Smith, or by the Beatles themselves—not to even bother recording "Like Dreamers Do," which had been the reason, even if only covertly, for the band's signing in the first place. Indeed, how could Ardmore and Beechwood capture the copyright to that much sought-after tune back in February without having it committed to tape and thus under the strictures and control of their EMI contract? The omission of "Like Dreamers Do" begs a few essential questions: Had Colman and Bennett's objective been adequately communicated to Martin—and if so, had he bothered to inform Richards? Or did Martin have something else in mind for this new act—the one that, as Epstein was known to proudly proclaim, wrote their own songs?[15]

With McCartney's amplification problems solved for the moment, Richards and Smith made final preparations before the Beatles broke into a throbbing, if uneven, rendition of "Bésame Mucho." As the session leader, Richards made several suggestions that the bandmates accepted, including the omission of the standard "cha-cha-booms" that they traditionally sang to punctuate the Spanish song's dramatic chorus. Almost immediately, Richards took issue with drummer Pete Best's cadence—or rather, his glaring inability to maintain one throughout the duration of the song. "Pete Best wasn't very good," Richards later observed. "It was me who said to George Martin, 'He's useless, we've got to change this drummer.'" Given that A&R men were known to record their artists' tracks in order of preference, Richards had likely selected "Bésame Mucho" as the Beatles' first singles release. During the next track, the Lennon-McCartney original "Love Me Do," which the band had rehearsed especially for the EMI session, Smith had heard enough from the new Parlophone act and decided to call for reinforcements. As tape operator Chris Neal later recalled, "After they'd run through a couple of tunes Norman and I were not all that impressed with, all of a sudden there was this raunchy noise which struck a chord in our heads. It was 'Love Me Do.' Norman said to me, 'Oi, go down and pick up George from the canteen and see what he thinks of this.'"[16]

A few moments later, George joined the other EMI staffers in the control room above Number 2, laying his eyes on the Beatles for the first time. And that's when he heard the slightest kernel of something that attracted him to their sound. "I picked up on 'Love Me Do' mainly because of the harmonica sound," he later recalled. "I loved raw harmonica and used to issue the records of Sonny Terry and Brownie McGhee." But with his many years leading bands through their paces, he quickly noticed something else as well—an awkward moment when Lennon had to shift, quite suddenly, from vocalist to harmonica player. Walking downstairs into the studio, George joined the Beatles, exchanged pleasantries, and got right down to business, exhorting John and Paul to switch their vocals on "Love Me Do" in order to allow John to transfer to his harmonica with more dexterity. As Paul recalled:

> I'm singing harmony then it gets to the "pleeeaase." STOP. John goes, "Love me . . ." and then put his harmonica to his mouth: "Wah, wah, waahh." George Martin went, "Wait a minute, wait a minute, there's

> a crossover there. Someone else has got to sing 'Love Me Do' because you can't go 'Love me waahhh.' Now you're going to have a song called 'Love Me Waahhh'! So, Paul, will you sing 'Love Me Do'!" God, I got the screaming heebegeebies. I mean he suddenly changed this whole arrangement that we'd been doing forever. . . . We were doing it live, there was no real overdubbing, so I was suddenly given this massive moment, on our first record, no backing, where everything stopped, the spotlight was on me. . . . And I can still hear the shake in my voice when I listen to that record! I was terrified. . . . John did sing it better than me, he had a lower voice and was a little more bluesy at singing that line.

Having rejoined Smith and Richards up in the control room, Martin listened intently as the session resumed, with the band completing "Love Me Do" with the new vocal configuration before recording "P.S. I Love You" and "Ask Me Why."[17]

While the verdict was still out on the bandmates' songwriting and vocal abilities, the EMI staffers up in the control room were now truly convinced about Best's ineffectiveness as a timekeeper. For a beat band—or nearly any musical fusion, for that matter—maintaining the rhythm of the beat is an essential requirement. As the session wore on, Best was failing to impress when it mattered the most. The surviving recording of "Love Me Do" from that evening offers brutal testimony of his inability to keep time, as demonstrated by his lagging "skip beat" and ham-fisted playing style. For the most part, the EMI personnel were decidedly unimpressed by the Beatles, with Martin disdaining "Bésame Mucho," while Richards seemed to have favored "Love Me Do," the song that—fleetingly, at least—had caught Martin's attention. As for "P.S. I Love You" and "Ask Me Why," the latter tracks were all but dismissed, with Richards rejecting "P.S. I Love You" out of hand because it shared a title with another hit song in recent memory. For his part, Smith summed up the experience as "20 minutes of torture—they made a dreadful sound!—and then they came up to the control room."[18]

As the Beatles joined the production team upstairs, everyone dutifully lit up their cigarettes—this being 1962 and all—and George, all business once again, launched into an extended monologue about the rudimentary ways of the recording studio. "He was giving them a good talking to," Ken Townsend later recalled, "explaining about the studio microphones being figure-of-eight—in other words, you could stand on either side of them as opposed to stage mikes which were one-sided." It was "a good talking to" alright, with the Parlophone head clearly having become exasperated with the band's seeming lack of studio professionalism. According to Smith, the Beatles remained mute for the duration of Martin's remarks. "They didn't say a word back, not a word," Smith recalled. "They didn't even nod their heads in agreement. When he finished, George said, 'Look, I've laid into you for quite a time, you haven't responded. Is there anything *you* don't like?' They all looked at each other for a long while, shuffling their feet, then George Harrison took a long look at George and said, 'Yeah, I don't like your tie.'"[19]

After the formality of George's lengthy diatribe, the room lapsed into an awkward silence. This was Abbey Road, after all, the studio where technical personnel wore crisp white lab coats, while administrative types like George donned coats and ties. At first, George didn't register the joke. He would later remember being especially pleased with the tie that he had chosen that day—a black number featuring a red horse motif. George Harrison briefly felt as if he might have crossed a line with his deadpan attempt at humor, later recalling, "There was a moment of ohhhhh, but then we laughed and he did too. Being born in Liverpool you have to be a comedian." Once everyone had joined in the merriment, the floodgates of the Beatles' penchant for humor and self-deprecation opened wide up. As Smith remembered, Harrison's moment of levity "cracked the ice, and for the next 15 to 20 minutes the Beatles were pure entertainment. When they left, George and I just sat there saying, 'Phew! What do you think of that lot then?' I had tears running down my face."[20]

It is impossible to say—given everything that was to happen, not to mention the improbability and impact of the journey that they would share together—how significant Harrison's one-liner may truly have been in establishing a foothold, no matter how slight, for the band with the Parlophone head. "I did think they had enormous talent," George would later allow, "but it wasn't their music, it was their charisma, the fact that when I was with them they gave me a sense of well-being, of being happy. The music was almost incidental. I thought, 'If they have this effect on me, they are going to have that effect on their audiences.'" In short, he was absolutely charmed by them, by their personalities far more than their music at this stage. As George later remarked, "You actually felt diminished when they left." For the Beatles' part, the Scousers from Liverpool were understandably intimidated by the thirty-six-year-old George—the tall fellow with the posh accent, a real educated type. "We hadn't really met any of these London people before, these people who talked a bit different," McCartney later remarked. "George Martin was very well spoken, a little above our station, so it was a little intimidating, but he seemed like a nice bloke." Harrison agreed, later observing, "We thought he was very posh—he was friendly but schoolteacherly, we had to respect him, but at the same time he gave us the impression he wasn't stiff—that you could joke with him."[21]

While he had scarcely given the session a second thought before June 6 came to pass, George could hardly think about anything else after the band had left the studio that night. "It was love at first sight," he later wrote. "John, George and Paul—I thought they were super. They had great personalities, and they charmed themselves to me a great deal. George was probably the most vociferous of the lot. Pete Best was very much the background boy—he didn't say much at all, he just looked moody and sullen in the corner." George went so far as to describe him as being "surly" even as the other members of the band fell into hysterics at the end of the session. Up in the control room, Norman Smith also recalled that "Pete Best didn't say one word. I got a feeling something wasn't right between them—it wasn't only that George and Ron found fault with him as a drummer." Indeed, at one point as Pete lingered outside the control room, George had informed Brian, within earshot of John, Paul, and George, that he would be inviting a professional drummer for their next session. In that very moment—although it would take more than two months for the ax to finally fall—Pete's fate was effectively sealed.[22]

As he made his way back to his bachelor apartment that night, George couldn't rid his mind of the Beatles. He simply couldn't get over the electricity that he had felt in Number 2 that evening. Could this strange group from Liverpool actually amount to something? Perhaps Norrie Paramor didn't have the British monopoly on beat-band talent, after all. George's mind was swimming with questions about how to structure the group for the marketplace. He was still ruminating about whether they should be "Paul McCartney and the Beatles," "John Lennon and the Beatles," or some such ilk. "My original feeling was that Paul had a sweeter voice, John's had more character, and George was generally not so good," he later wrote. "I was thinking, on balance, that I should make Paul the leader. Then, after some thought, I realized that if I did so I would be changing the nature of the group. Why do that? Why not keep them as they were?"[23]

# 7

# "LIVERPOOL? YOU'RE JOKING!"

As Brian and the Beatles made the long drive back to Liverpool, they understandably thought that "Love Me Do" would likely be chosen by George and his team as their first single. Always in PR mode, Brian had told *Melody Maker* that he expected a July release for the Beatles and Parlophone. But as the days and weeks passed, nothing materialized. Unbeknownst to the Beatles' brain trust, George had seen the first session—in spite of all its good-spirited laughter and conviviality—as a false start of sorts. Sure, he had a very good feeling about them, and he was enamored with their charisma, but he was also on a long-running quest to land a hit song in the rock world. To his ears, the material that they recorded on that unforgettable first evening didn't make the grade: "I was looking for a hit song and didn't think we had it in 'Love Me Do.' I didn't think the Beatles had any song of any worth—they gave me no evidence that they could write hit material." On yet another occasion, he put his initial impressions even more bluntly, remarking that he "was quite certain that their songwriting ability had no saleable future." After his many years at the Parlophone helm, he felt that the best course of action was to see what the professional songwriters over in Tin Pan Alley had to offer. To his mind, "Love Me Do" could, at best, be relegated to the band's first B-side. Besides, George had time and an iron-clad contract in his favor. The penny-per-record agreement merely required him to record six sides within the first year. During the June 6 session, they had managed to produce four, which meant that he had twelve months in which to complete two more recordings with the band and fulfill the basic terms of the contract.[1]

In the interim, George continued to ply his trade with his motley crew of comedians and fringe musicians. Exercising his gift for bringing sound to life in the service of storytelling, he enjoyed the act of dreaming up sound effects in a repeat engagement with the latest cast from *The Goon Show*. Deciding to commit a humorous BBC radio script to vinyl as a long-playing comedy album, George's old mates Spike Milligan, Peter Sellers, Jonathan Miller, and Peter Cook joined him at Abbey Road to record their parody of the 1957 film *The Bridge on the River Kwai*. Also featuring voice work by Peter Rawley and Patricia Ridgway, the album included incidental music by Wally Stott. As with their previous productions, George and the Goons, with the able assistance of EMI engineer Stuart Eltham, had great fun conjuring the album into life. In one instance, George needed to duplicate the ghastly sound of a head being chopped off—at Sellers's insistence, no less. In a moment of macabre genius, George sent Stuart out to buy a large cabbage, which the engineer dutifully chopped in two on the record. For George, Stuart was one of his most trusted allies during this period. A talented engineer, Eltham developed a number of advancements at Abbey Road during the 1950s, particularly in terms of testing and calibrating the studio's echo chambers, which would be at the heart of so many innovations in the ensuing decade.[2]

Unfortunately for Parlophone, the LP's release had been under fire after the producers of *The Bridge on the River Kwai* became incensed about the comedic treatment of their classic film and threatened the comedy troupe with a lawsuit. At George's recommendation, the setting was shifted from Burma to Wales and cleverly retitled as *Bridge on the River Wye*. The only problem was that the album had already been recorded. Never one to back down from a challenge, George painstakingly worked with Stuart to splice the *k* sound out of every instance in which anyone uttered the word *Kwai* on the master tapes. George and the comedy troupe's sense of fun abounded throughout the project—even down to the liner notes, which helpfully instructed listeners, "For best results, play this record in a circular fashion." Although the album failed to enjoy strong sales in the manner of his earlier efforts with the stalwarts from *The Goon Show*, George found his footing yet again with Bernard Cribbins's follow-up to "The Hole in the Ground." Entitled "Right, Said Fred," Cribbins's latest work echoed the class-conscious satire of his earlier hit, even snaking its way into the top 10. Years later, Cribbins would describe "Right, Said Fred" as "almost a musical record—a sketch" even. While his efforts with the Goons and Cribbins found him all too easily resting on the laurels of his earlier work, the Parlophone head—as with nearly everyone trying to ply their hand as an A&R man—was always keen on finding fresh (or sometimes not-so-fresh) content to keep the EMI machine fueled and moving invariably forward with new product. For George, "Right, Said Fred" proved to be particularly diverting, allowing him to take chances in the recording studio: "I loved doing that kind of work because you lose yourself in it. You don't follow any rules except your own hunch that you think is right."[3]

While Brian and the Beatles had little choice but to stand by in Liverpool and await the band's first singles release with Parlophone, George hadn't completely forgotten about them. In fact, within a day after their return to the North Country back in early June, he had dispatched Richards to Tin Pan Alley to find a vehicle for the group's first A-side. Unsatisfied with "Love Me Do" as the Beatles' singles debut, George hoped that Ron could find a catchy tune with which the band could make their mark in the pop marketplace. In short order, Richards happened upon "How Do You Do It" by Mitch Murray, the stage name of twenty-two-year-old Lionel Stitcher, a ukulele player from North London. As it happened, Tin Pan Alley had come up bust for Richards, who saw "How Do You Do It" fall into his lap when Murray made the rounds, stopping by EMI House to audition his latest wares. The song had already been declined by Adam Faith and Brian Poole and the Tremeloes, the band that had outplayed the Beatles for a shot with Decca only scant months before. By June 19, Richards shared a demo recording of the song with Dick James, the Parlophone artist whom Martin had attempted to groom for the pop charts. Now a music publisher, James managed "How Do You Do It" for Murray, who refused to hand over the song's copyright to Martin and Richards unless he could be assured that his composition would see the light of day as a singles release. More than a month later—with his latest work with the Goons and Cribbins finally out of his hair—Martin declared his intentions to record "How Do You Do It" with his quirky band of Liverpudlians. "I thought it was a good song," he later recalled, "no great work of art but very commercial." For his part, James was nonplussed when he heard the news. "Liverpool? You're joking! So what's from Liverpool?" he reportedly asked.[4]

If Murray and James were dumbfounded, the Beatles were even more astonished when they received the demo for "How Do You Do It" at the tail end of July, when Epstein finally heard back from EMI. With his plans for his next move finally taking shape, George posted an acetate of the song to Liverpool, informing the Beatles' manager that he expected "How Do You Do It" to be the A-side of their debut single and, accordingly, that the band should learn the song in preparation for recording it during an upcoming

September 4 session. When Lennon and McCartney played the demo, they could hardly believe their ears as they took in the upbeat, saccharine sweetness of Murray's composition. "We hated it," McCartney later recalled, "and didn't want to do it. We felt we were getting a style, the Beatles' style, which we were known for in Hamburg and Liverpool, and we didn't want to blow it all by suddenly changing our style and becoming run of the mill." With another visit to Abbey Road in the offing, Brian gave the bandmates their marching orders. "It's a nice song," he pleaded with them. "Please give it a chance." But John, in particular, wasn't having it. "Bollocks," he replied, "tell him [George Martin] to stuff it up his arse." Not missing a beat, Brian replied, "We can discuss it with George Martin when we're in London. Don't make him think you're difficult. We can work it out when we're actually in the studio. Making waves now could be most undiplomatic." After John tromped out of the room, Paul assured the manager that they would make the best of it in spite of his partner's tantrum. When they dutifully got down to business, John and Paul tried their best at making the song their own. Not content to play the number in its original form, they shifted the key signature, and, with Harrison's help, added much-needed guitar ornamentation to the song's middle eight, the musical bridge often associated with pop songs. The three guitarists pointedly didn't so much as bother to involve Pete Best in the process of attempting to reinvigorate Mitch Murray's sugary-sweet confection. The writing, as far as their drummer was concerned, was already on the wall.[5]

While the Beatles struggled mightily, albeit reluctantly, in their effort to revamp "How Do You Do It," George turned his attention back to finding a way—if there even was one—to transform the band into the hitmakers for which he had been looking for so many years. At this point, he still believed that their charisma was the ace up their sleeve—perhaps the only card that they even held, really. But still the question remained: How could he capture the energy and excitement of the band that had bowled him over with their unusual blend of charm and chutzpah back in the control room and bring it to the studio? The answer slowly began to emerge on Tuesday, September 4, 1962, when the Beatles arrived for two sessions with George at Abbey Road. During the afternoon session, they were allotted time to rehearse material for the evening slot, when they would commit their efforts to tape. Even as they walked into the studio that afternoon, George could detect something different in their chemistry—and eventually he came face-to-face with the evidence of their dramatic change in the form of their newly recruited drummer, Ringo Starr.

Born as Richard Starkey, he had been a long-standing member of Rory Storm and the Hurricanes, the Liverpool mainstays who had been unseated in recent years by the likes of the Beatles. Brian had notified Judy that the band's new drummer would be in tow, so George hadn't bothered to hire a professional drummer, as he had promised to do back in June. For Ringo's part, the situation was more than a little intimidating. He was well aware of Pete's fate during the Beatles' first encounter with George, and he was determined to make a solid impression right out of the gate. As it happened, Ringo's musical skills would act as a mere prelude to the fireworks that occurred at Abbey Road later that evening—but they were fireworks nonetheless. At one point, Ringo caved in to the pressure of working in the professional environs under George's watchful eye. "I was playing the bass drum and the hi-hat," he later recalled, "and I had a tambourine in one hand and a maraca in another, and I was hitting the cymbals as well, [like] some weird spastic leper, trying to play all these instruments at once." The moment wasn't lost on George, who would later admit that after the drummer's unfortunate, nerve-induced display, "I didn't rate Ringo very highly."[6]

In addition to Ringo Starr's presence, Martin couldn't help but notice George Harrison's glaring black eye, the result of an incident several days earlier back at the Cavern. Beatles folklore attributed his bruising to the fallout from Pete's ouster from the band. Pete's fans had taunted the remaining Beatles, chanting "Pete forever, Ringo never." Harrison reportedly told the enraged fans—the "cave dwellers," in Cavern speak—to "bugger off," only to receive a "Liverpool kiss" in the form of a head-butt as he walked backstage. While others would attribute Harrison's black eye to the work of a jealous boyfriend bent on exacting revenge against his betrayer, the wound would survive for all time in numerous photographs from that day's recording sessions. But beyond the appearance of Starr and Harrison's conspicuous bruise, Martin was still contending with the issue of whether or not to showcase Lennon or McCartney as the band's front man. Although he had dispensed with his original notion about altering their name, he couldn't let go of his predilection—no doubt inspired by industry prejudices at the time—that one person should act as the band's leader. So who, then, would be the voice of the Beatles? "Paul's was sweeter," George later reflected, "but John gave the combination its interest and sharpness. He was the lemon juice against the virgin olive oil." As events that day would show, one of those voices was poised to venture out onto a very precarious limb with the A&R head.[7]

Under Ron Richards's supervision, the band ran through several songs that afternoon, including "How Do You Do It," along with five Lennon-McCartney originals, "Tip of My Tongue," "Ask Me Why," "P.S. I Love You," "Love Me Do," and a new number called "Please Please Me," a slow tune with an unmistakable Roy Orbison influence. Martin and his team were largely unimpressed with "Tip of My Tongue"—the A&R head was especially dissatisfied with the arrangement that the band had prepared—and the EMI staffers had already heard "Ask Me Why," "P.S. I Love You," and "Love Me Do," although Martin was still smitten with Lennon's harmonica work on the latter. The real trouble came with "Please Please Me," which "badly needed pepping up." To Martin's ears, it was "very slow and rather dreary. I told them if they doubled the speed it might be interesting." In a moment of creative inspiration, Martin suggested that they take special care with the song's introduction to give it more punch and immediacy. "I told them what beginning and what ending to put on it," he later recalled. At the same time, though, he chided them for not having exacted their own improvements in advance of the session. For their part, the Beatles felt as though they had been put in their place. Worse yet, Paul later recalled, "We were a bit embarrassed that he had found a better tempo than we had." While McCartney and his bandmates may have been deflated, Martin took things in stride, treating the Beatles and their roadie Neil Aspinall to dinner at Alpino, an Italian restaurant on Marylebone High Street. During the meal, Martin shared comical stories about his recording sessions with Peter Sellers and Spike Milligan, which the group—Lennon especially—lapped up with glee. Years later, Martin recalled the evening vividly, remarking that "we all had spaghetti and the cost per course was about 3s 9d (19p). It wasn't exactly over-the-top, but they thought it was wonderful, real high living!"[8]

But the drama really began to unfold during the evening session, when the Beatles rolled up their sleeves to record "How Do You Do It," the cover version that Martin expected to be the band's inaugural singles release during the first week of October. The studio personnel had shifted appreciably, as Ron Richards had gone home for the night, leaving Norman Smith in service as George's balance engineer, along with second engineer Richard Langham and his fifteen-year-old junior assistant, Geoff Emerick, who had only been working at Abbey Road for a single week; he had landed a job with EMI after his career counselor at North London's Crouch End Secondary Modern School arranged an interview for the young electronics whiz with the record giant. In short order, he was hired as a novice "button pusher," as the assistant engineers were known in those days.

Before the session began, Smith arranged the Beatles in what would become their standard studio formation for twin-track recording purposes, with microphones placed in front of each guitar's amplifier and a fourth devoted to recording the sounds emanating from the drum kit. "What I tried to do was to create a live sound that captured what they would do on stage," Smith later recalled, "because I felt that if I didn't do this, then I would lose the excitement. To me, it was important to create their live sound as it happened, and I did set them up in the studio exactly the way that they would perform on stage." As Martin addressed the Beatles over the talkback system, the band set down to work on the song that they had loathed upon first hearing it. Martin instructed them to record the rhythm track first, followed by the addition of vocals. He accomplished this via "bouncing down" from one tape deck to another—these were still the days of twin-track recording, after all. Hence, for the second taping, Martin essentially had Lennon sing his lead vocal, with McCartney providing harmony, along with the prerecorded rhythm track. With work on "How Do You Do It" completed in just two takes, the Beatles and the EMI staffers turned their attention back to "Love Me Do," discarding the June version with Pete and starting from scratch. To his own great relief, Ringo turned in solid performances on both "How Do You Do It" and "Love Me Do"—a welcome contrast from his nervous antics earlier that afternoon. Although Martin still felt that "Love Me Do" was "pretty poor" in spite of the harmonica and some fifteen takes, he wasn't worried at this point—it was being relegated, in his mind at least, to the B-side.[9]

But as the evening's session ticked away, with both "How Do You Do It" and "Love Me Do" seemingly in their finished states in preparation for an October release, the Beatles couldn't take it anymore. In such moments, Lennon later remarked, "I had to be leader. Whatever the scene was, when it came to the nitty-gritty, I had to do the speaking." As George remembered, "John came to me and pleaded with me. He said, 'Look, I think we can do better than this.'" The A&R man was understandably taken aback. This was 1962, when studio personnel knew their very narrow place in a well-defined food chain. A&R men supervised the sessions and made all of the production decisions, professional songwriters composed the material, the musicians played the songwriters' resulting wares. That was the way it was—short and sweet, with no two ways about it. But the band wasn't having it. Years later, John recalled that "they forced us to do a version of 'How Do You Do It.' We wouldn't let 'em put it out. We said, 'We'd sooner have no contract than put that crap out'—all the tantrums bit. We thought it was rubbish compared with 'love, love me do.' We thought ours had more meaning." Quite suddenly, the Beatles had created an impasse with Martin—and at the tail end of only their second session at Abbey Road. As McCartney remembered, "I suppose we were quite forceful really, for people in our position. We said we had to live or die with our own song, 'Love Me Do.' We knew it wasn't as catchy, but that was the way we had to go. We couldn't face the people back in Liverpool laughing at us. We were trying to keep the integrity—a blues group with harmonica on our records."[10]

By this point, Martin was well versed in the Beatles' stubborn belief in recording their own material in spite of what he felt, at least at the time, was his best counsel for finding success in the eclectic British marketplace. "They wanted to write, and it was a kind of ego trip for them too," he later recalled. "They wouldn't accept that other people could write better material for them than [they] could do themselves. To begin with I saw no evidence supporting their ambitions. John and Paul later said that before I even met them they had already written lots of songs they never recorded. There were some pieces that later emerged after they'd worked further on them, but really most of the early material I did see was pretty primitive."[11]

While he may have been confounded by the sudden turn of events, Martin was resolute about releasing "How Do You Do It." "If you write something as good as that song," he told them, "I'll let you record it, otherwise that's the song that's going out." Having said their piece, the Beatles left the studio for the night, forlorn in the face of Martin's show of administrative force. They were scheduled to return to Abbey Road the following week, which would give them several days to contemplate what had transpired that evening. For Martin, it came down to what he perceived to be a solid business decision. The bandmates had made their case, and he held no illusions about their feelings on the matter. As he remarked years later, "They never shirked on jobs. They didn't really want to do it, but in the end they did quite a good job." As A&R head, he knew that he held all of the cards, in spite of their wishes, and he intended to play them as he saw fit.[12]

But for Martin, it was an impasse that would be decidedly short lived. Within a matter of hours, his strange adventure of bringing the Beatles to the marketplace would take yet more unexpected turns. The very next morning, George dutifully played the Beatles' version of "How Do You Do It" for the folks at Ardmore and Beechwood. Sid Colman was beside himself at the thought of "Love Me Do," the Lennon-McCartney original, being relegated to the B-side. Wasn't the point of getting the band under contract so that they could control the copyrights? A B-side would automatically mean a substantial cut in revenue. With Colman's objections in mind, Martin met with Dick James shortly thereafter, played "Love Me Do" for him, and suggested that they deploy "How Do You Do It" as the B-side. James was incensed. Like

Martin and Richards before him, James felt that Mitch Murray's composition had hit written all over it. By Friday, the dispute over the Beatles' first single had exploded into an all-out mess after Murray heard the acetate of the band's recording of "How Do You Do It." Disgruntled, to say the least, Murray refused to agree to Martin's B-side request, repeating his earlier claim that the song had chart potential. And besides, he wasn't fond of the way in which the Beatles had reworked his song without so much as asking for his approval. Suddenly, George had nowhere to turn. Neither EMI's publisher nor the songwriter were willing to concede to B-side status, which effectively left him with "Love Me Do," a song that George didn't really like. After his show of administrative backbone on Tuesday evening back at Abbey Road, he suddenly found himself right where the band had left him: in need of an original Lennon-McCartney tune to balance out the release. In the back of his mind, he still held onto the idea of releasing the Beatles' version of "How Do You Do It," but that gambit could wait for now. Ready to wash his hands of the whole business, he knew that the band would return to the studio on September 11 for a brief afternoon session with Richards, when presumably they would record a B-side for "Love Me Do" in deference to Ardmore and Beechwood's imperatives, not to mention the Beatles' predilection for their own material. Perhaps Ron could figure things out.

And that's when the Beatles found their mettle and impressed Martin in ways that might have even saved their career—an instance that was on par with Harrison's cheeky comment about Martin's tie back in June. Before returning to London, they shrewdly used their time off between Cavern performances to rehearse "Please Please Me." They had heard their posh new mentor loud and clear. He had bluntly told them to rework the song on their own time, and they took him at his word. In short order, they quickened the song's pace and refashioned the intro and outro sections as he had suggested. Their efforts were well served by the arrival of new Gibson "Jumbo" J-160E electric-acoustic guitars, which propelled "Please Please Me" from its Roy Orbison languidness into a tune with real beat-band fire.

When the bandmates returned to London on September 11 for their third session at Abbey Road, their new head of steam quickly dissipated when they saw a drum kit already set up and waiting in Number 2. The kit belonged to thirty-two-year-old Andy White, a Scottish session drummer in high demand among the London recording circuit. At first, Martin had attempted to hire Kenny Clair, "probably the top session drummer at the time," Richards later recalled. Clair "was a brilliant player and could do anything," but he was unavailable for the session, so Martin booked White instead. For the record,

Martin and Richards hadn't completely given up on Ringo Starr, who "had more zest to his drumming than Pete," according to Richards. "I knew he'd be able to handle recording—in time. But we had a record to make and I needed someone who could deliver exactly what the song required on every take."[13]

For their part, the Beatles likely believed that the threat of a professional drummer had seemed an idle possibility after failing to materialize during the previous week, but Martin and Richards weren't taking any chances after Starr's momentary, nerve-fueled debacle behind his Premier kit. Nevertheless, Starr was crestfallen, later remarking, "I was highly upset—highly upset. It blew my brain away." When the session began at approximately 5 PM, Ringo could only sit and sulk as the other Beatles, having girded themselves for the task at hand in spite of their fallen mate, got down to business. Under Richards's supervision—Martin didn't even bother to attend the session—they recorded a new version of "P.S. I Love You" as the B-side for "Love Me Do," which Martin had now slated for their debut release given the machinations with Dick James Music and Ardmore and Beechwood during the past week. The Beatles likely believed that Martin had conceded to their show of force over "How Do You Do It" rather than understanding the full extent of the ways in which the cards had quickly and quietly shifted in their favor.[14]

As they recorded "P.S. I Love You" for posterity, Ron threw Ringo a bone, casually instructing the newest Beatle to shake the maracas during the recording. "Ringo was sitting next to me in the control box, not saying anything," Ron later recalled, "so I said 'Go and play the maracas' and off he went to do it. He stood next to Andy, and the drum microphone picked up his sound." As the Beatles played, Richards had to have been impressed with the band's newfound fervor. Their September 11 recording of "P.S. I Love You" was their best recording yet at Abbey Road, easily outclassing their efforts on "Love Me Do" and "How Do You Do It." With crisp harmonies from John and George, Paul took lead vocals on the track, which they recorded in ten takes. At this point, they returned to "Please Please Me," which they played with renewed abandon, although the song still required additional polish—especially in terms of Harrison's lead guitar work. "George was playing the opening phrase over and over and over throughout the song," Ron remembered. "I said, 'For Christ's sake, George, just play it in the gaps!'" The result was a robust, rollicking version of the very same song that Martin had dismissed the week before for being too dreary. While they briefly toyed with the notion of releasing "Please Please Me" as the B-side of "Love Me Do," Richards felt that the song was still too roughly hewn for general release. For his part, Lennon agreed: "We were getting very tired, though, and we just couldn't seem to get it right." Given the lateness of the hour, they opted to use the remaining studio time remaking "Love Me Do" with White on the drums. The result was only slightly more up-tempo than the Starr version recorded a week earlier, with White essentially mimicking Starr's previous work. When the session came to a swift close, the Beatles had completed their first single, "Love Me Do" backed with "P.S. I Love You," which was slated for release on Friday, October 5.[15]

Although Martin was decidedly unhappy with the chain of events that had led to the single consisting entirely of Lennon-McCartney originals, he knew that he had at least one more shot at working with them to find the right vehicle. As for Brian and the Beatles, they may have remained blissfully unaware at this juncture that EMI had now fulfilled its obligation to the Liverpool combo, having recorded six sides in the form of "Bésame Mucho," "Love Me Do," "P.S. I Love You," "Ask Me Why," "How Do You Do It," and "Please Please Me." While Martin didn't hold out any hope for "Love Me Do" becoming a hit single, Sid Colman at Ardmore and Beechwood was delighted to serve Lennon and McCartney with a contract for the global rights to "Love Me Do" and "P.S. I Love You." With their signature—and a subsequent agreement with Brian—the two Beatles set into motion an arrangement that would result in Lennon and McCartney becoming household names. But no one could have seen that coming—not even Martin, who was very much on the side of promoting their group sound in a marketplace overcrowded with crooners and other would-be rock stylists.

What George couldn't begin to imagine was the amount of publicity that Brian was prepared to unleash on behalf of the debut single by his relatively obscure North Country act. George still didn't believe that "Love Me Do" was even remotely the best they could offer—and he was right, of course. For his part, Richards couldn't stomach another minute of the song, later remarking, "Quite honestly, by the time it came out I was pretty sick of it. I didn't think it would do anything." Hence, Parlophone's leading A&R men were understandably surprised when "Love Me Do" began to make a run at the British singles charts in the autumn of 1962. Ringo must have been doubly surprised when he received his copy of Parlophone R4949 and heard himself playing drums on "Love Me Do" after so much fuss had been made over hiring a professional drummer. Even years later, no one at Parlophone could explain the reasons behind the mix-up that led to the September 4 recording being released as the A-side. As for the song itself, EMI's PR arm gave up after securing a handful of plays on Radio Luxembourg, which left advertising support almost exclusively in the hands of NEMS. But in the case of "Love Me Do," the Beatles' secret weapon turned out to be Kim Bennett, who was not content to merely exercise the copyright but was intent on turning it into a hit in spite of a marketplace that didn't seem to care. He was determined, moreover, to prove that his instincts about the band had been correct, while others, including Martin at first, had been erroneous in their initial appraisals. But even still, "It was a bastard to get 'Love Me Do' played," Bennett later recalled, "because no one wanted to know. I believed in it—to me, the sound was different and needed to be heard—but all I got was 'I'm not having that bloody noise in my program, thank you.' But I felt it necessary to persist because I needed to prove I'd been right." While Bennett pushed the band's record with his trademark dogged persistence, "Love Me Do" enjoyed a major assist from the Beatles' sizable North Country following, which easily foisted the song to the top of the Liverpool charts and ensured that it gurgled in the lower echelons of music charts nationwide. Aided by some twenty-three gigs throughout the month of October and well-placed PR interventions by Bennett and freelance Liverpool journalist Tony Barrow, "Love Me Do" achieved the unthinkable at the end of October when it broke into the *NME* charts at number twenty-seven. For the Beatles, cracking the *NME* was a game-changer, resulting in a spate of new PR opportunities and an *NME* article proclaiming what was hitherto inconceivable at this juncture in the world of pop music: LIVERPOOL'S BEATLES WROTE THEIR OWN HIT. In that moment in the history of the recording industry, it could hardly be certain which aspect of the *NME* headline was more astounding: that the band composed their own material or that they hailed from Liverpool.[16]

Perhaps just as significantly, the unexpected success of "Love Me Do" had fully captured George's attention back in London. He hastily arranged a follow-up evening session with the band for November 26 at Abbey Road. George would have met with them as early as November 2, but they were contractually obligated for another Hamburg residency. It was at this point that George studied the band's remarkable ascent in the British charts and decided to meet with them face-to-face and as soon as possible—which turned out to be November 16, when their schedule briefly opened up—for a strategy discussion at EMI House. When they joined him in his fourth-floor office that day, having only just returned from Hamburg that morning, George was ready to begin things anew with the same band that he had tried to scuttle, only to have them foisted upon him, and now watched as "Love Me Do," in its sixth week of release, continued to mosey up the national charts. For his part, George was still surprised by the public's fascination with "Love Me Do." "I didn't think it was all that brilliant," he later recalled, "but I was thrilled by the reaction to the Beatles and their sound." As the meeting began, he offered one more push for "How Do You Do It"—he still believed in its hit potential, and history would prove him right just five short months later through his production of the song by a very different Liverpool band. In his charming, amiable way, he quickly scrapped the idea after the Beatles curtly rebuffed any notion of reconsidering Mitch Murray's composition. Just as suddenly, Martin shifted gears, suggesting that they move forward with recording a new version of "Please Please Me" at their upcoming session. For the past few weeks, he had been listening intently to the September 11 version and suggested that Lennon reprise the harmonica sound of "Love Me Do" as a further ornamentation. But Martin hadn't merely been listening to the acetate as a tactician attempting to diagnose the track's weaknesses. By this time, he was genuinely smitten with the selfsame composition that he had once maligned for being so "dreary." "I was thrilled to bits with it," he later remarked. "I thought it was wonderful." At this point, Martin made it crystal clear that Starr would not be upstaged by the unforeseen appearance of any professional drummer, and with that gesture of solidarity, the band was fully in his camp. After recommending "Ask Me Why" as the B-side for "Please Please Me" and fixing the single's release date as January 11, the A&R man dropped a truly unexpected bombshell on Epstein and the group: he suggested that they do the unthinkable in British pop circles and record a long-player.[17]

This was no mild recommendation by any stretch. George's plan went against every A&R man's firmest instincts in the record trade at this juncture. LPs were for adult listeners and consumers of nostalgia acts, not the youth demographic. Once more, twelve-inch albums were the medium of bands that had already proven themselves with a parcel of hits, and the Beatles only had one—and just barely—at this point. For George, it was a significant risk, but it was also a masterstroke. So many of his impulses with the Beatles had been flat-out wrong up until this point. Why not work against the grain, double down on the Beatles, and go for broke? After all, George had never shied away from making the most unusual of choices—whether it be backing members of the Goons into comedy stardom, trying his hand at a primitive electronica record, or seeing the Temperance Seven, of all groups, all the way to the top of the charts. Even more, George, Brian, and the Beatles had an implicit understanding that the album would consist, for the most part, of Lennon-McCartney originals. After all, the Beatles were the band who "wrote their own hit," as the *NME* headline had trumpeted. Why not play out the string? And besides—as the A&R head well knew—it was also a matter of pounds and farthings. If there was money to be made, they'd best make it quickly. Everyone plying their trade in rock 'n' roll during those early days was more than a little fearful about hitching their star to the latest flash in the pan. With the exception of Elvis Presley and Cliff Richard, most acts were here today, gone tomorrow.

For his final suggestion to Brian and the band, George said that he was considering the notion of recording the LP live at the Cavern. Flush with confidence after observing the gradual ascent of "Love Me Do" on the British charts and with the promise of even greater things to come with "Please Please Me," George was anxious to observe the Beatles down in that legendary Liverpool basement—their home turf, for all intents and purposes—and the idea of capturing the electricity of a live performance on a long-player seemed like a sure bet. Besides, George already had plenty of experience recording concert albums with mobile units, as evinced by the smash-hit success of his work with *Beyond the Fringe* back in 1960. Within a few days, George went public, reporting his outlandish idea to the music press. As he remarked to *NME*, "I'm thinking of recording their first LP at the Cavern, but obviously I'm going to have to come to see the club before I make a decision. If we can't get the right sound we might do the recording somewhere else in Liverpool, or bring an invited audience into the studio in London. They've told me they work better in front of an audience."[18]

Not long afterward, Martin held a private meeting with Epstein for the express purpose of discussing the Beatles' publishing interests—and more specifically, the fate of Lennon and McCartney, the band's principal songwriters whose works Martin himself had attempted to shun in favor of "How Do You Do It." During their meeting, George cut to the chase, blaming Ardmore and Beechwood—EMI's own publishing arm—for having ignored "Love Me Do" and done "virtually nothing about getting the record played," which couldn't have been further from the truth, given Kim Bennett's ongoing efforts, even at that point, to promote the Beatles' debut. Epstein pointed out that he had already been thinking of steering Lennon and McCartney toward Hill and Range, the American firm that handled Elvis Presley's publishing interests. Martin countered by suggesting a trio of Tin Pan Alley alums, Dick James, David Platz, and Alan Holmes. But the A&R head quickly showed his hand, wasting precious little time by championing Dick James Music, a British company in contrast with Platz's and Holmes's firms, which were field offices for American holdings. Martin moved swiftly in support of his old friend and collaborator, the actor-cum-publisher with whom he brought the theme from *The Adventures of Robin Hood* to life at Abbey Road. By the end of the month, Martin succeeded in bringing Epstein and James together, an association that would reach far into the present day, after both of the principals had long since died, in many unforeseen, circuitous, and even infamous ways. As George later recalled, "In the end I recommended Dick because he was hungrier than the others and his was a British company." In spite of his stated reasoning for driving Epstein into James's orbit, the veteran EMI man had all too easily thrown over his own company's publishing interests in favor of a novice outsider who had only recently put up a shingle for Dick James Music. As EMI presser Brian Mulligan recalled, "The general perception of Dick was that he was a struggling pop singer who became an equally struggling music publisher—but quite a nice bloke." At the same time, Mulligan added, "I don't think there was any real surprise when Dick got the Beatles' music publishing; in view of his friendship with George it sort of made sense."[19]

Later, when Kim Bennett learned that George had routed Brian away from Ardmore and Beechwood after Kim had toiled so hard on behalf of "Love Me Do," the hardworking record plugger was less conciliatory, seeing George's behavior for what it was. "When a song's been established in the charts, there's no reason to change the publishing setup unless you want to be spiteful," he remarked years later. "George was very *naughty* in getting them away from us." It is difficult, indeed, to imagine a plausible reason for George to use his influence with Brian to purposefully spurn EMI's own publishing arm in such a manner. Was it the ostensible bad blood between George and Sid Colman that prompted the break—or was it something deeper, something George would rather not say out loud? Was he doing his utmost, in a truly illogical move by industry practices at the time, to distance himself from the world of Colman and Bennett, the first people in the industry to recognize the promise of Lennon and McCartney as composers in the first place? In short, was he trying to put the idiosyncrasies of the Beatles' circuitous origin story, and his own strange role in its creation, behind him?[20]

Whatever his true motives may have been for navigating Ardmore and Beechwood away from the vicinity of Brian and his clients, George was suddenly moving very quickly on the Beatles' behalf. After months of working in fits and starts on their recordings, he had clearly experienced an epiphany. He was determined that they would have his full and undivided attention—no more sloughing them off on Ron Richards. The time was nigh for the Beatles to experience a proper professional session at Abbey Road, without any sideshows involving a moveable feast of drummers or pockets of dissension about whether or not they would record Lennon-McCartney originals. No, those issues were solidly behind them—George would see to that.

As it happened, the Beatles' session on November 26 exceeded his expectations. As they planned in advance, the band arrived early, at six, for the evening session, which was set to commence at seven in the now-familiar environs of Number 2. For the first time in their brief career together, George, Brian, and the Beatles were singing out of the same hymnal, with the shared goal of producing a new single, "Please Please Me" backed with "Ask Me Why," that evening for a January 11 release date.

Norman Smith arranged the bandmates in their prototypical setup, which he based on his intuitive belief, having been a performer himself, that musicians often play better within close proximity of one another. To this end, Smith later recalled, "I used microphones not right up close to things. And I relied quite a bit, to get in the right sort of balance and the right proportion, on splash-back off the walls, so one had kind of a natural reverberation. And that's how, in my view at any rate, the Mersey sound was born: placing the microphones further away or equidistant, shall we say, from their instrument and the wall, or the splash-back. In other words, not that great separation on each microphone." After an hour's worth of rehearsal and equipment preparation—and with Martin observing intently as his balance engineer worked the desk upstairs in the control booth—the band tried out their new arrangement of "Please Please Me," complete with Ron Richards's recommendations for Harrison's slick guitar ornamentation and Martin's equally, if not even more, brilliant suggestion that Lennon double the lead guitarist's melody with a harmonica part, which they subsequently edited in. When the song was mostly complete, having been recorded using the studio's twin-track system, Martin was beside himself. If the record-buying public had heard the faintest glint of innovation in "Love Me Do," then "Please Please Me" would positively bowl them over. With his passions stirred, George offered a daring prediction. Still sitting up in the control room, he activated the studio PA and announced, with great sincerity and aplomb, "Gentlemen, you've just made your first number-one record." It was an incredible statement, and he meant it—years later, he would describe it as a moment of "bravado"—but the idea of a national chart-topper was so far-fetched that the Beatles promptly broke out into fits of laughter. George had once again experienced that most elusive aspect of the human experience—the tingle factor. George had finally felt it with the Beatles—a kind of intuition, innately emotional in nature, that informs us that we are in the presence of something profound and extraordinary. With "Please Please Me," he had felt the first shivers of recognition that this foursome from Liverpool was something truly special.

But how could he capitalize on this propitious moment, consolidate their artistic instincts, and lead them toward new vistas of creativity?[21]

After the band remade "Ask Me Why" in short order, generally adhering to their earlier arrangement, they adjourned for the night. For Ringo, it must have been especially redemptive after the debacle of his first session at Abbey Road. On this night, he had played masterfully, nailing his fills in the high-octane "Please Please Me" and keeping the steady Latin beat required by "Ask Me Why." And for George, the entire evening had been a revelation. The planning session that he had led ten days earlier had laid the groundwork for their new working relationship. "It went beautifully," he later wrote. "The whole session was a joy." During a break in recording, he had taken a moment to provide a few off-the-cuff quotations for Alan Smith, an *NME* reporter, saying, "The thing I like about the Beatles is their great sense of humor—and their talent, naturally. It's a real pleasure to work with them because they don't take themselves too seriously. They've got ability, but if they make mistakes they can joke about it. I think they'll go a long way in show business." Back in February, he had told Brian that he wasn't "knocked out at all" by their sound. Just nine months later—and with the notable addition of Ringo—George was a true convert. And once more, he genuinely liked the boys from Liverpool who had already taken to calling him Big George in order to easily distinguish him from the other George, the one who played lead guitar for the band. In many ways, he was becoming one of them now. They liked him, too, and more important, they trusted him. And they would discover soon enough that the man with the posh accent had far more in common with their humble origins than they could ever have believed.[22]

# 8

# 585 MINUTES

AS GEORGE AND THE BANDMATES anticipated the January release of "Please Please Me," they took great heart in a new, well-timed burst of PR energy behind "Love Me Do." In addition to the efforts of Kim Bennett—who didn't know about his upcoming fate with the Beatles' camp—Brian's publicity machine succeeded in placing the band on a number of national profile spots, including a key appearance on the popular children's television show *Tuesday Rendezvous*, for which the band mimed "Love Me Do." As a result, the single rebounded from a recent stall to number nineteen. It was an incredible moment, to be sure, as a band from Liverpool, of all places, had landed a top 20 hit. For decades, rampant speculation would persist that Brian had propelled "Love Me Do" into the top 20 by purchasing thousands of copies via NEMS in order to inflate the single's success. As he later wrote in his autobiography, "There was a rumor—which lingered until it became acceptable currency—that I had bought the disc in bulk to get it into the charts. Possible though this would have been—had I the money, which I hadn't—I did no such thing, nor ever have. The Beatles, then as now, progressed and succeeded on natural impetus, without benefit of stunt or back-door tricks and I would like to make this quite clear."[1]

Meanwhile, as preparations for the band's first LP continued, George traveled by train to Liverpool on Wednesday, December 12, 1962, with Judy in tow. He was in town for the purpose of testing the Cavern Club's acoustics when the space was empty. As he strolled about the club, clapping his hands together in order to test the echo, the issues with attempting to make a proper live recording revealed themselves almost instantly. The echo problems notwithstanding, George's overriding concern turned out to be the basement club's notorious condensation. "The Cavern would have been a dreadful place to do it," he later remarked. "It wasn't a very good acoustic environment—not a very comfortable environment at all really. Very grotty." After briefly considering his earlier idea about simulating a live setting at Abbey Road, George decided that a prototypical studio album would be their best recourse. In his experience, the optimal number of tracks was fourteen, and the Beatles had already recorded four that could be included on the long-player: "Love Me Do," "P.S. I Love You," "Please Please Me," and "Ask Me Why." As he and Brian studied the Beatles' checkered tablecloth of a touring calendar over the coming months, only one date seemed to fit the bill—Monday, February 11. To bring the album to fruition, they would be required to complete ten new tracks in a single day's worth of sessions.[2]

During the last week of the year, "Love Me Do" had rebounded after yet another mini-swoon, finally peaking at a respectable number seventeen. At the time, the Beatles were away in Hamburg, finishing out their sixth and final residency in the West German port city, the postwar proving ground where they had toiled, night after night, as Martin sought out the next Cliff Richard in fits of desperation, interspersed with moments of triumph as he pushed his stable of unusual acts beyond industry expectations. Although George had enjoyed plenty of professional highs during his twelve-year career with EMI, the optimism that he felt about the promise of the Beatles had set his ambitions ablaze. Despite all of the excitement playing out in his life as 1962 came to a close, George couldn't possibly have missed David Frost's caustic remarks delivered on a late November episode of the satirical BBC program *That Was the Week That Was*. Clearly drawing on his interview with Martin earlier in the year, Frost took Norrie Paramor to task in front of a national TV audience, flaying the Columbia A&R man for taking credit for the work of other songwriters and reaping scads of residuals in the process. Worse yet, Frost chided Paramor for purposefully reducing pop music to something bland and ordinary. "Norrie is an *ordinary* man writing *ordinary* tunes with *ordinary* words," Frost deadpanned. "During the last ten years, Norrie Paramor has used all his power and all his influence and made everything *ordinary*." The resulting headlines in *Melody Maker* screamed—in all caps, no less—PARAMOR PILLORIED! It was a brutal diatribe that left the corridors of EMI House in a veritable uproar. While Paramor may have never learned the source of his betrayal, he felt the awful sting of public effacement for months thereafter. As for himself, George could take heart in his incipient work with the Beatles, which—even at this comparatively early stage—was never bland and ordinary. Indeed, compared to the other purveyors of English pop during that era, the four North Country lads were downright revolutionary.[3]

During their December 1962 visit to Liverpool in order to troubleshoot the Cavern's usefulness as a soundstage, George and Judy rode about the city with Brian, who gave the A&R man a tour of the local music scene. First up were Liverpool fan favorites Gerry and the Pacemakers, who were playing the Majestic Ballroom in Birkenhead. In contrast to his hesitancy about the Beatles back in February, George boldly encouraged Brian to ferry this new band down to Abbey Road for a January 22, 1963, commercial test that could very well result in a recording contract. Back at the Cavern, George, Judy, and Brian enthusiastically took in the Fourmost, the Beatles' opening act. The Parlophone head could barely contain himself, telling Brian, "I would like to meet them sometime and see if we can't make a hit or two." In short order, George offered to audition the Fourmost, as he had done with Gerry and the Pacemakers that same evening. And that's when the Beatles took the stage, and George and Judy saw them ply their stage act in person for the very first time. George was mesmerized by what he witnessed there—oh, the place was still "grotty" all right, but quite suddenly he understood the Beatles' magnetism far more profoundly:

> The walls were streaming with condensation. It was amazing that the boys didn't get electrocuted, because there was water everywhere—a combination of general dampness and sweat, evaporated and re-condensed upon the walls. The atmosphere too was what is frequently, though often inaccurately, known as "electric." They sang all the rock and roll numbers that they'd copied from American records, and it was very raucous, and the kids loved every minute of it. Up till then there had been nothing to involve young people to quite the same extent. The rock and roll gyrations of Tommy Steele and Cliff Richard were clinical, anemic, even anesthetic, compared with the total commitment of the Beatles, which somehow got down to the very roots of what the kids wanted.

For George, seeing the bandmates' impact on their audience confirmed what he had experienced firsthand back in June in the Abbey Road control room. And now, sitting with Judy in the audience, he was no doubt experiencing something akin to what Brian had felt back in November 1961 when he saw the group atop this very same stage, when he began to glimpse the vaguest kernel of his future. Could this have been the moment when George saw the germ of his life's work—however vague and shapeless at this early juncture—unfolding right in front of him?[4]

For George, the Beatles quite suddenly existed outside of his narrow experience with them back in the confines of Abbey Road Number 2. He found himself transfixed by the band that he had rejected out of hand back in February and only reluctantly signed—literally under duress—in May. The very same group that had failed to leave him "knocked out" had bowled him over in the Cavern Club that night. While his visit to Liverpool had succeeded in ending his plans for making a live recording in the dank basement club, the trip had ultimately emerged as a great triumph for George in more ways than one. On the one hand, George seemed to be genuinely excited by all of the untapped potential lurking on the shores of the River Mersey; yet on the other, he seemed positively determined to overcome the reticence that had colored his thinking when the Beatles originally landed in his lap. No, he would act more precipitously from now on. The old navy man had learned his lesson but good. As for Brian, the Beatles' manager never harbored any ill will over George's early standoffishness, already seeing himself as a kind of North Country entrepreneur who could grow a stable of future stars under George's tutelage given the older man's much-longer knowledge of the recording industry and its practices. According to George, "Brian thought I was the bee's knees. He was always on the lookout for new acts, reasoning that if he passed them over to me, I would be able to make a hit record with them. Brian saw us as a dream team: he would manage the artists, I would record them, and Dick James would publish the songs."[5]

While George seriously contemplated the notion of developing new talent from the hitherto untapped well of Liverpool beat bands, he found himself raging against a longstanding intracorporation problem with Capitol, EMI's mammoth American subsidiary. In spite of an established agreement that Capitol had the right of first refusal on the latest wares from Columbia, HMV, and Parlophone, more often than not the stateside executives opted against injecting the EMI output into the American marketplace, a practice over which George had seethed for years. In recent months, he had become especially angered by what he considered to be Capitol's intentionally manipulative behavior when they deigned to release *Beyond the Fringe*, one of George's highly successful comedy juggernauts. As George saw things, *Beyond the Fringe* received particularly paltry treatment after Capitol reluctantly agreed to release it in the United States only to send the record into the marketplace without any promotional oomph. In a December 31, 1962, memo to Len Wood, George wrote that "this is a serious indictment of Capitol's ability to promote albums of British artists. I would not wish to recommend Capitol Records to any impresario who was thinking of launching a future British show in the States."[6]

Meanwhile, back in the United Kingdom, the "Please Please Me" single was initially dealt a terrible blow by Mother Nature when the nation—indeed, the world—experienced the coldest month of January throughout the twentieth century. Don Wedge of *Billboard* magazine went so far as the write that "the severe winter conditions which greeted Britain with the New Year had an adverse effect on the record industry. It was worst in Southern England, where all pressing plants are, and distribution became difficult, although it was to an extent counteracted by the reluctance of consumers to venture out shopping." In London, the Thames froze over, and transportation across the country came to a virtual standstill. As it turned out, the weather actually worked in the Beatles' favor when, during the second week of the record's release, many Britons found themselves snowed in. Thanks to the Herculean efforts of Dick James, their new publisher, the Beatles were featured on the January 19, 1963, episode of the nationally syndicated television program *Thank Your Lucky Stars*, where they performed "Please Please Me" for the massive audience cooped up at home. After achieving that "tremendous coup," in George's words, the Parlophone head began to see some much-needed traction from the EMI marketing wing, of which he had long been an acerbic critic. "EMI finally got off their backsides and realized that [I] wasn't quite so crazy and that this was something worth backing," he later wrote. "They actually played the record on their Radio Luxembourg program, which was jolly decent of them. It reached the number-one spot very quickly, and suddenly the whole thing snowballed and mushroomed and any other mixed metaphor you care to think of. From that moment, we simply never stood still." Indeed, in an instant the Beatles fully transformed from a largely regional act into the makings of a national phenomenon. On the strength of their appearance, tour promoter Arthur Howes quickly booked the band for a bevy of British appearances—including their work as a supporting act for Helen Shapiro in February, the same month in which they were scheduled to make their first album. Quite suddenly, the threads of their success were beginning to come together. For his part, George's prophetic words in November seemed to be ringing true. Could he have found his own Elvis, much less Cliff Richard, at last?[7]

On Monday, February 11, as "Please Please Me" continued its remarkable upward ascent, the Beatles took a brief respite from their breakneck performance schedule and made their way to Abbey Road Number 2, their new home away from home, where they joined George for one of popular music's most thrilling days on record. Across 585 minutes—and during three sessions ranging from 10 AM TO 1 PM, 2:30 to 6 PM, and 7:30 to 10:45 PM—the Beatles planned to record the requisite ten songs in order to round out the contents of their first long-player, even going so far as to try their hand at an eleventh for later use. If the unthinkable happened and the group couldn't finish the LP that day, George had a backup plan up his sleeve. As Norman Smith later remarked, "Naturally, we hoped they would be able to get through everything in one day . . . but if they hadn't done it, then we would have booked another session later." While the bandmates were all young men at the time, they were exhausted from their heavy touring schedule. To make matters worse, Lennon suffered from a lingering cold, which had been festering since the Helen Shapiro tour. And there was no question of their work on the album slipping into the following day, as the Beatles were booked for a youth-club dance at the Azena Ballroom on Tuesday night in Sheffield, Yorkshire. But beyond the scheduling pressures at work that day, George recognized an even greater issue involving the band's shelf life. He knew full well that the Beatles' remarkable run could end at virtually any time, that there was no guarantee they'd ever see another hit record again. "After the success of 'Please Please Me,'" George later remarked, "I realized that we had to act very fast to get a long-playing album on the market if we were to cash in on what we had already achieved."[8]

In spite of the daunting odds of making an album at such an outlandish pace, George had already developed a remarkable sense of faith in the band at this relatively early juncture. And he was particularly impressed with the increasing quality of their new material. George had originally "thought their songs were inferior to those of the professional writers, but they learnt very quickly. They were like plants in a hothouse: they sprung up rapidly once they got going, particularly after they had some success." As the session got underway, George understood his role in their professional lives in very specific terms. "At the beginning," he later wrote, "my input into the Beatles' records as their recording manager was largely a question of tidying up their own compositions and their cover versions, organizing their arrangements to make them commercial. I taught them the importance of the hook. You had to get people's attention in the first 10 seconds, and so I would generally get hold of their song and top and tail it—make a beginning and end—and also make sure it ran for about two and a half minutes so that it would fit DJs' programs. Generally you had two or three verses and the chorus, with maybe an instrumental bridge that I might also organize."[9]

As it happens, George's organizational skills were in high demand on that extraordinary day as the group prepared to capture a barrage of material, largely culled from their live act, on tape. Indeed, George continued to cling to his original concept for the album, later remarking that the LP "was a straightforward performance of their stage repertoire—a broadcast, more or less." But first, they had to survive the long working day ahead of them. As Norman Smith recalled, the bandmates relied on an odd combination of lozenges and cigarettes to propel them through the day: "They had a big glass jar of Zubes throat sweets on top of the piano, rather like the ones you see in a sweet shop. Paradoxically, by the side of that, was a big carton of Peter Stuyvesant cigarettes which they smoked incessantly." As the Beatles huddled in Number 2, George mapped out a rudimentary song list. At one point, McCartney made a play for recording Marlene Dietrich's "Falling in Love Again" or, failing that, trying their hand once more with "Bésame Mucho," but the Parlophone head refused to yield, preferring to focus the group's sights on a slew of Lennon-McCartney originals, along with several cover versions from their live repertoire. The surviving outtakes from the February 11 sessions find Martin constantly pressing the bandmates forward. On numerous occasions, he instructed them to try another take after a botched vocal or guitar chord—"And again, from the top"—or ushering them back in line about matters involving tempo and song structure.[10]

During the morning session, they recorded several takes of the wistful "There's a Place," with Lennon on lead vocals, as well as McCartney singing "Seventeen," the working title for "I Saw Her Standing There," the rave-up tune that Martin would select to lead off the album. After completing work on the first two original Lennon-McCartney numbers, Martin announced that their lunch break had arrived, and he retired, along with Smith and second engineer Richard Langham, "for a pie and a pint" at the nearby Heroes of Alma pub. For their part, the Beatles lingered behind, sustaining themselves on milk—along with the throat lozenges and cigarettes. Langham was shocked to discover that, upon the EMI staffers' return, the band had been "playing right through. We couldn't believe it. We had never seen a group work right through their lunch break before." As the recording session resumed, the band turned to a cover version of "A Taste of Honey," the well-known Tony Bennett vehicle. After recording the basic track in five takes with McCartney's lead vocal accompanied by the band, Martin suggested that the bassist double-track his vocal by singing along with the original. The resulting mix, to McCartney's great delight, afforded his vocal with a fuller, more layered sound. Harrison sang lead vocals on the next track, the Lennon-McCartney original "Do You Want to Know a Secret," for which Lennon had drawn his inspiration from Walt Disney's *Snow White and the Seven Dwarfs*. After several takes of "Do You Want to Know a Secret," Martin turned the band's attentions back to "There's a Place," for which he asked Lennon to overdub a harmonica part. Martin continued the forward momentum by asking the bandmates to add handclaps to "Seventeen" before the Beatles prepared to record the Lennon-McCartney original "Misery," which they had originally penned for Shapiro during their recent tour with the British vocalist. For "Misery," Martin instructed Smith and Langham to record the song at thirty inches per second instead of the typical fifteen so as to accommodate the addition of a piano track during postproduction. As the Beatles would later discover, Martin had a trick up his sleeve.[11]

When the group resumed work during the evening session, they tried their hand at recording "Hold Me Tight," the last Lennon-McCartney number that they would attempt that day. After recording thirteen takes with McCartney on lead vocals, Martin suggested that they set the song aside for future consideration before leading the Beatles through a spate of well-honed cover versions from their live act. After recording a version of Arthur Alexander's "Anna (Go to Him)" in three takes, they easily dispatched Wes Farrell and Luther Dixon's "Boys," which had been popularized by the Shirelles. Featuring Starr on lead vocals, "Boys" was recorded in a single economical take. The Beatles continued their fusillade of cover versions with Gerry Goffin and Carole King's "Chains," a Brill Building–era composition, with Harrison on lead vocals, which they accomplished in three takes. The band returned to the Shirelles with a cover version of "Baby It's You" featuring Lennon, with his voice becoming ever more tortured and forced by the minute.

By this point, the clock in Number 2 had ticked past 10 PM, closing time at Abbey Road, and Martin and the Beatles had one more song to record. The group and the EMI staffers took a well-earned break in the studio canteen, where they noshed on coffee and cookies and recommended various songs for consideration, even breaking into a few spirited debates. As Norman Smith later recalled, "Someone suggested that they do 'Twist and Shout,' the old Isley Brothers' number, with John taking the lead vocal. But by this time all their throats were tired and sore—it was 12 hours since we had started working. John's, in particular, was almost completely gone so we really had to get it right the first time, the Beatles on the studio floor and us in the control room. John sucked a couple more Zubes, had a bit of a gargle with milk and away we went." For Martin, "Twist and Shout" made perfect sense, being the "one number which always caused a furor in the Cavern." As the EMI team observed from upstairs in the control room, Lennon stripped off his shirt and approached the microphone. "John absolutely screamed it," George remembered. "God alone knows what he did to his larynx each time he performed it, because he made a sound rather like tearing flesh. That *had* to be right on the first take, because I knew perfectly well that if we had to do it a second time it would never be as good." As it happened, the first take was a thrilling, high-octane rock explosion, with John delivering a searing vocal performance for all time. Up in the booth, Langham was thunderstruck: "I was ready to jump up and down when I heard them singing that. It was an amazing demonstration."[12]

Never one to hedge his bets in the recording studio, George signaled the band to attempt a second take, but it was pointless. John's voice was simply gone. But it scarcely mattered, of course. Take one of "Twist and Shout" had resulted in a recording for the ages. For their part, the Beatles were ecstatic, feeling the full-on rush of a once-in-lifetime performance. As Lennon rested his aching voice, they begged Smith and Langham to stay behind that night with them in the studio to listen to a playback of "Twist and Shout"—the song that Martin would invariably describe as a "real larynx-tearer." As they finally closed down the studio that evening, the Beatles had completed the principal production work on their first long-player in just under ten hours' worth of studio time. Just as he had vowed, George had them in and out of Abbey Road in a single day. But the buzz from their landmark sessions continued into the following day. Tape operator Chris Neal, who visited the control room during the recording of "Twist and Shout," couldn't stop talking about John's "amazingly raucous vocal." As he later recalled, "The next morning Norman Smith and I took a tape around all the studio copying rooms saying to everybody 'What the hell do you think of this!' And George Martin was heard to say, 'I don't know how they do it. We've been recording all day but the longer we go on the better they get.'" It was a sentiment that Martin would repeat, time and time again, as he contemplated their remarkable North Country work ethic. He could only shake his head in recognition as they pushed themselves well beyond any reasonable limits in the service of their creative drive and ambition. Many years later, Langham reflected back on that special night as the Beatles, buoyed by an otherworldly energy, blew through the end of the evening time slot. "Sessions never normally over-ran past 10:00 PM," Langham recalled. "At 10:05, you'd meet half the musicians on the platform of St. John's Wood station, going home." But not the Beatles.[13]

On Wednesday, February 20, George carried out the postproduction work associated with the LP. With Geoff Emerick in tow and Stuart Eltham, George's longtime partner on Parlophone's highly successful comedy records, acting as balance engineer, George set to work on overdubbing additional instrumentation to the Beatles' "Misery" and "Baby It's You." These overdubbing sessions, also known as superimpositions or SIs, were fairly limited in the era of twin-track recording given that any additional recording forced A&R men to "bounce" additional mixes in order to create new recording space for enhancements. In so doing, as each additional "bounce" accrued, the potential for generational loss increased. Contending with the limitations of twin-track recording had proven to be a long-running source of irritation for George, who felt that the studio practice of restricting four-track technology to classical recordings was shortsighted. It was an issue that he would return to, over and over again, with the studio brass over on Hayes Street. But for the time being, he would have to make do. "I found with the Beatles," said George, "that if I recorded all the rhythm on one track and all the voices on the other, I needn't worry about losing the voices even if I recorded them at the same time. I could concentrate on getting a really loud rhythm sound, knowing that I could always bring it up or down afterwards to make sure the voices were coming through."[14]

For Emerick, watching Martin work turned out to be a revelation. The not-so-old A&R man had learned a trick or two over the years, and one of his favorite techniques involved varispeed recording. As Emerick later recalled, "That session was my first exposure to George Martin's signature 'wound-up' piano—piano recorded at half speed, in unison with guitar, but played an octave lower. The combination produced a kind of magical sound, and it was an insight into a new way of recording—the creation of new tones by combining instruments, and by playing them with the tape sped up or slowed down. George Martin had developed that sound years before I met him, and he used it on a lot of his records."[15]

As Emerick and Eltham observed from the control booth in Number 1, Martin worked to enhance Harrison's opening guitar chord on "Misery" by layering it with his own efforts at the studio's grand piano. Recording at half speed posed a particular challenge for him, though, as he was forced to synchronize his own playing with the original recording. As Emerick noted, "Overdubbing a half-speed piano is not the easiest thing to do, either, because when you're monitoring at half speed, it's hard to keep the rhythm steady.

There certainly were more than a few expletives coming from George as he struggled to get the timing down while overdubbing onto the song 'Misery,' on both the spread chord that opens the song, and on the little arpeggios and chord stabs that are played throughout." As the opening strains of "Misery" reveal, George's piano work adds an attention-grabbing layer of sound, with his notes bristling with the noise of the tiny hammers striking the piano strings as they are being recorded at half speed. To George's ears, the resulting effect sounded like the music emanating from the windup music boxes of yore. With work on "Misery" complete, George turned to "Baby It's You," for which he added a celesta part. As with "Misery," he hoped to create new blended sounds on "Baby It's You" by doubling Harrison's existing guitar part using the bell-like keyboard instrument. "Again, he was trying to get a new tone by blending the two instruments together—and, again, nobody had ever heard a sound like that before," Emerick recalled. "Later on, he also tried adding some normal-speed piano to the song, but decided it wasn't necessary, so only the celesta made it to the record." In this small way, George first introduced the notion of recording artistry onto a Beatles record.[16]

The bandmates would also be absent during the Abbey Road session on Monday, February 25—Harrison's twentieth birthday, when the Beatles were riding in a van on their way to the Casino Ballroom in Lord St. Leigh, where Epstein had booked them for a dance party. Back in Number 1, Martin prepared mono and stereo versions of the album, with Smith serving in his regular capacity as balance engineer and A. B. Lincoln working as second engineer. During a pair of lengthy sessions in the control room, Martin and his team selected the best takes of the album's contents, and then, after completing the editing and sequencing processes, mastered them for release. At one point, he and Smith opted to use a fade-out for "Do You Want to Know a Secret," which, in its original version, had a full close. In the best take from the February 11 omnibus session, Harrison concluded the number with an added sixth chord, which Martin may have found to be too jarring. Interestingly, it would be the album's title track that would account for much of the workload that day, as preparing an acceptable stereo mix of "Please Please Me" presented unexpected challenges. The twin-track master tape used to mix the single no longer existed, which required Martin to make a tape-to-tape copy of an earlier, albeit inferior, take of the song. With this version in hand, he skillfully edited in different segments of "Please Please Me" from other takes until he had pieced together a new version, which he subsequently mastered for stereo.

As with the LP, which was recorded for the most part back on February 11, the entire album was mixed in a single day. As Martin looked on, Smith carried out the process and prepared the Beatles' music for release. "Mind you," Emerick later recalled, "since it had been recorded in twin-track mono, there wasn't much for Norman to do except balance the vocal levels against the instruments and tuck in some echo, but he did a fantastic job and it still sounds fresh and exciting." Years later, Martin explained his decision to record both mono and stereo mixes, which was not a standard EMI practice at the time. "The reason I used the stereo machine in twin-track form was simply to make the mono better, to delay the vital decision of submerging the voices into the background," he recalled. "I certainly didn't separate them for people to hear them separate!"[17]

With the album's contents in their finished state, the Beatles' brain trust turned their attentions to marketing the long-player for public consumption on the progressively successful heels of the "Love Me Do" and "Please Please Me" singles. Both George and Brian were not keen on using "Please Please Me" as the album's title, which the bandmates had lobbied for since George promoted the idea of making an LP. During that era, industry practices dictated that A&R men suggest ideas for not only album titles but also the artwork for long-players, along with song order and sequencing. But in George's world, change was already afoot, so he passed the problem on to the Beatles themselves to concoct a title for their LP debut. Not long thereafter, McCartney helpfully suggested "Off the Beatle Track," also providing a rudimentary cover design that featured the four Beatles along with two insect antennae poking out from the titular B in Beatles. In an effort to bring McCartney's idea to fruition, Martin came up with a clever cover idea of his own. As a fellow of the Zoological Society of London, he had made regular trips to the Regent's Park zoo in the company of Sheena and their family. "Rather stupidly," George later recalled, "[I] thought that it would be great to have the Beatles photographed outside the insect house. But the zoo people were very stuffy indeed: 'We don't allow these kind of photographs on our premises, quite out of keeping with the good taste of the Zoological Society of London,' so the idea fell down. I bet they regret it now." With the incredible success of the "Please Please Me" single mounting by the day, the album's title suddenly seemed moot, as it made obvious sense to synchronize the current marketing of the single with the forthcoming long-player.[18]

Still in need of album artwork, George turned to Angus McBean, a longtime fixture on the London portrait scene. More important, George knew full well that Angus had shot the first four album-cover photographs for Cliff

Richard and the Shadows, Norrie Paramor's perennial hitmaking machine. As George later recalled, working with Angus was like everything else associated with making the long-player: "We rang up the legendary theatre photographer Angus McBean, and bingo, he came 'round and did it there and then. It was done in an almighty rush, like the music." On March 5, Angus joined George, Brian, and the bandmates at EMI House in London's Manchester Square. Several different poses were attempted by Angus, including a shot of the Beatles arrayed on a spiral staircase and, later, another with them goofing around on the steps leading up to Abbey Road Studios. The photograph that was eventually selected for the cover shot was taken by Angus when he first arrived at EMI House. "As I went into the door I was in the staircase well," he remembered years later. "Someone looked over the banister—I asked if the boys were in the building, and the answer was yes. 'Well,' I said, 'get them to look over, and I will take them from here.'" As George and Brian looked on, the Beatles posed at the top of the stairwell, gazing downward for all time. "I only had my ordinary portrait lens," said Angus, "so to get the picture, I had to lie flat on my back in the entrance. I took some shots and I said, 'That'll do.'"[19]

The *Please Please Me* album was released on March 22, 1963. It had taken £400 to produce. For their efforts, the Beatles had been paid the standard Musicians' Union rate of £7 10s for each of the three February 11 sessions. It would be one of the finest investments that EMI would ever make. As "Please Please Me" remained in heavy rotation atop the singles charts, the long-player enjoyed a slow burn, taking some six months to ring up sales of more than 250,000 copies. *Please Please Me* finally reached the number-one spot on May 11, marking nearly fifty-two weeks since George had first presented Brian with the Beatles' penny-per-record agreement. "Waiting to hear that LP played back was one of our most worrying experiences," John later remarked. "We're perfectionists; if it had come out any old way we'd have wanted to do it all over again. As it happens, we were very happy with the result." With a number-one single and album to the Beatles' name among their three releases with Martin at the helm, the group had clearly tapped into a new sound. Beat music was fully on the move in the British charts, and Martin had quite suddenly emerged as its chief progenitor. For the first time, he no longer had to gaze at Columbia with envy. EMI's third label had just scored a bona fide sensation, and Paramor could follow Martin's lead for a change.[20]

# 9

# YEAH, YEAH, YEAH!

NOT CONTENT TO REST ON HIS LAURELS, George had begun pressing "the boys," as he called them, taking after Brian, to keep producing new material. Having won Big George's hard-earned respect for their original compositions, John and Paul were only too happy to oblige. On Tuesday, March 5, 1963—nearly three weeks before their first long-player would hit the stores—Martin and the Beatles returned to Abbey Road to try their hand at three Lennon-McCartney compositions, "From Me to You," "Thank You Girl," and "The One After 909." With Smith as balance engineer and Langham as second engineer, Martin recorded seven takes of "From Me to You," which had been inspired by a regular column that McCartney had seen in *NME* titled From You to Us. Initially, the Beatles had intended to begin the song with a guitar solo, but after hearing their original arrangement, Martin had other things in mind. As Ron Richards later recalled, "The Beatles had marvelous ears when it came to writing and arranging their material. But George had real taste—and an innate sense of what worked." To George's ears, the song's opening chorus was the hook. He recommended that Lennon and McCartney sing the song's opening motto—"da-da-da da-da-dun-dun-da"—to which the A&R man overdubbed a harmonica part by Lennon. Disc cutter Malcolm Davies helpfully loaned him a harmonica, later recalling that "artists never came to the cuts in those days but John popped up to see me because he wanted to borrow my harmonica, thinking it might make a better sound. He brought it back a little later saying that it tasted like a sack of potatoes!"[1]

For George, continuing the Beatles' harmonica sound with "From Me to You" was more than a mere creative decision. To his mind, it was invaluable in building their audience from "Love Me Do" and "Please Please Me" through their most recent effort. "It was an identifiable sound of the Beatles on those first singles," he later wrote. They were self-consciously drawing on Lennon's expertise as a "blues harmonica player." As George recalled, John played a "diatonic harmonica, one with no black notes. He had a number of different harmonicas tuned to different keys"—when he wasn't borrowing a mouth harp off Abbey Road's disc cutter, that is. Having made short work of "From Me to You," George and the band shifted their sights toward another new tune called "Thank You Girl," which went under the working title "Thank You Little Girl." Interestingly, Ringo had struggled to bring the closing drum fill to fruition, losing the beat in the process. Rather than rerecord the entire song, George deployed an edit piece in which the Beatles tried their hand at capturing the offending section. The edit was then spliced seamlessly into the master tape to save time. After completing the song in thirteen takes, they adjourned until an evening session in which they tackled "The One After 909," one of Lennon and McCartney's oldest compositions. They had also intended to try their luck with "What Goes On," another early songwriting effort, although they had run out of time at this point. But the real highlight that day was "From Me to You," which George had helped to transform into a hit with a few tiny but vastly significant alterations. By now, George had adopted a very particular and economical approach to working with the band. "I would meet them in the studio to hear a new number," he later recalled. "I would perch myself on a high stool and John and Paul would stand around me with their acoustic guitars and play and sing it—usually without Ringo or George, unless George joined in the harmony. Then I would make suggestions to improve it, and we'd try it again. That's what is known in the business as a 'head arrangement.'"[2]

After so many years of toil, George had found his mettle at last. He understood his role in a very narrow sense, in comparison with his early days as an A&R man when he functioned as a sort of jack-of-all-trades with no real sense of direction. He still carried out a wide variety of duties, but now he saw himself in a larger, supervisory sense. And it wasn't always terribly creative, he later recalled, as "there wasn't much arranging to do. My function as a producer was not what it is today. After all, I was a mixture of many things. I was an executive running a record label. I was organizing the artists and the repertoire. And on top of that, I actually supervised the recording sessions, looking after what both the engineer and the artist were doing. Certainly I would manipulate the record to the way I wanted it, but there was no arrangement in the sense of orchestration. They were four musicians—three guitarists and a drummer—and my role was to make sure that they made a concise, commercial statement." With "From Me to You," the Beatles' "concise, commercial statement" saw them fairly easily score their second chart-topping single. In contrast with the previous number-one single and album, though, "From Me to You" was a blistering success. At this point, George and the band had clearly captured a new sound, a new urgency in British pop that even outpaced the press. An *NME* critic admitted that "From Me to You" had "plenty of sparkle" but ultimately concluded, "I don't rate the tune as being anything like as good as on the last two discs from the group." The Beatles' national audience clearly saw things differently, as the song exploded onto the charts, opening in the number-six position and selling an astonishing two hundred thousand copies during its first week of release. Things were shifting in George's world, and his professional success was mounting at an astonishing rate.[3]

The release of "From Me to You" also saw George's not-so-subtle maneuvering of Brian and the Beatles toward Dick James Music finally come to fruition. The "From Me to You" backed with "Thank You Girl" single marked the first appearance of Northern Songs, which had been incorporated on February 22, 1963. Originally intended to be called "Northern Music" in deference to the bandmates' North Country roots, Northern Songs was finally selected after the principals learned that "Northern Music" was already in use. Northern Songs was split fifty-fifty between Dick James Music and NEMS, which included Epstein's interests along with Lennon and McCartney as the band's primary composers. When he first set up the deal, James went so far as to invite Martin to participate as well. As George later recalled, "Dick also offered me a share in Northern Songs, but I couldn't accept, as an employee of EMI, which was engaging the Beatles and Northern Songs. I would have had conflicting interests." To his great credit, the band's producer had "no regrets" about turning James's offer down in spite of how incredibly lucrative Northern Songs would turn out to be. "It wouldn't have been right," George later wrote.[4]

As it happened, the Northern Songs agreement may not have been right in more ways than one. According to NEMS employee Peter Brown, Brian and the bandmates held little understanding of the significance and value of music publishing. As Brown later remarked, "It was very much let's get what we can get—any deal would be a good deal, just the fact that we actually had a deal." Moreover, "as I understand it," Brown recalled, "Brian sat them down and told them what the structure of the deal was and they said fine." As events would transpire, Lennon and McCartney's agreement with Dick James Music would emerge as one of the most vexing subplots in the story of the Beatles. In retrospect, Brown imputed James with enacting "a clever deal" that succeeded in seeing the Beatles' manager "sign over to Dick James 50 percent of Lennon and McCartney's publishing fees for nothing." Years later, McCartney would attribute his easy compliance to sheer ignorance. "John and I didn't know you could own songs," he remarked. "We thought they just existed in the air. We could not see how it was possible to own them. We could see owning a house, a guitar or a car, they were physical objects. But a song, not being a physical object, we couldn't see how it was possible to have a copyright in it. And therefore, with great glee, publishers saw us coming." While the likes of Epstein and McCartney may have been suckered by James's deal, it is hard to believe that Martin, an industry veteran who had signed hundreds of Parlophone acts with their own attendant publishing interests, didn't know better. But of course, he may have had his own blinders on during this period, for he was also one of James's clients.[5]

But by this comparatively early stage, the Beatles were hardly George's only beat band under contract. Through Brian's Liverpool connections, George and Parlophone had gone from being pop music's lonely outpost to becoming the go-to label for cutting-edge rock. Up first was Gerry and the Pacemakers, the band that Brian had managed since 1962 and the very same Liverpool act that George had seen back in December at the Majestic Ballroom in Birkenhead. In Brian's description, "Gerry Marsden was one of the biggest stars in Liverpool, with a smile as wide as he was short, a huge generous personality and a fascinating voice, full of melody and feeling." For George, Gerry and the Pacemakers seemed like the perfect vehicle for "How Do You Do It," the Mitch Murray–penned tune that the Beatles had rejected the previous September. On January 22, 1963, George produced Gerry and the Pacemakers covering "How Do You Do It" at Abbey Road. For George, Gerry and the Pacemakers' version was proof positive regarding his initial belief in the song during the previous summer. In short order, the tune made its way to the top of the British charts. "Gerry recorded it, and it went to number one," George later recalled. "But in that was a little personal vindication of my faith in the song." The idea of confirming his pop instincts was of personal and professional significance to George, and it was a sentiment that he would find himself returning to several times across his career. For a time, Gerry and the Pacemakers' "How Do You Do It" held its own atop the British hit parade until it was unseated by "From Me to You," thus rewarding George with three number-one hits in the new year—and it was barely springtime. Their next two singles releases would top the charts as well, affording Gerry and the Pacemakers the distinction of being the only British act to see their first three releases achieve number-one status. After their second single, "I Like It," topped the charts with George's production, the Parlophone head recorded their cover version of the classic "You'll Never Walk Alone." Recorded on July 2, 1963, at Abbey Road, the Rodgers and Hammerstein tune from *Carousel* marked one of George's favorite non-Beatles recordings during this period. He was always fond of Gerry's rendition of the American standard. "He always got a great reaction from audiences when he performed it," George later wrote, "and it was Brian's idea to record it. For the first time, I backed Gerry with a large string orchestra, which was a great departure for him. He had been a very jolly rock-and-roll star, doing little two-beat songs, and suddenly here was this big ballad with which his voice could hardly cope. All the same, I think it was largely that record which was responsible for the song becoming the universal football crowd song it is today."[6]

As with Gerry and the Pacemakers, George found chart-topping success with Billy J. Kramer and the Dakotas, yet another Liverpool act in Brian's stable. By this point, George had developed a strong working relationship with Brian, whom he also regarded as a close personal friend. "I was totally caught up in the excitement of it all, and Brian Epstein was working 'round the clock," George remembered. "Naturally, we had to spend a lot of time together, and we became firm friends. I remember his telling me, 'We're going to have a tremendous partnership, George. With you recording my acts, we're unbeatable.'" The Beatles' manager felt that he had a knack for recognizing talent, but he held no illusions that he understood the record industry in the same way that the Parlophone head did. As Brian observed, "I believe I know a hit when I hear one, but George Martin knows the record industry infinitely better than I ever could; and because George has been at it for some time, he has an innate sense of the public mood." Brian's words proved to be true as ever during George's association with Billy J. Kramer and the Dakotas, although the A&R man found Kramer's voice to be lacking. "Billy was certainly a very good-looking boy," George later reflected, "but when I listened to him I was forced to the conclusion that his was not the greatest voice in the world." Although George attempted to quell Brian's interest in Billy's act, the Beatles' manager persisted in his support for the Liverpool singer, and George reluctantly pressed forward. For his initial recordings with Billy J. Kramer and the Dakotas, George selected two Lennon-McCartney originals, including "Do You Want to Know a Secret" from the Beatles' *Please Please Me* album and "I'll Be on My Way," which the Beatles performed on a single occasion during an appearance at the BBC's Paris Theatre in London. To George's mind, "Do You Want to Know a Secret" had hit potential. "In those days we had a policy that anything the Beatles recorded as an album title was not issued by them as a single, and vice versa," George later recalled. "The song had been on the *Please Please Me* album (we'd obviously made an exception in the case of 'Please Please Me' itself, to cash in on their new popularity), and the Beatles didn't want to issue it as a single. In any case, they could already see the advantage of having their songs covered by other people, and since it suited Billy down to the ground, we decided to make it with him."[7]

But he still had to deal with the matter of Billy's lack of vocal prowess, forcing George to devise a means for alternately capturing and disguising his voice in the studio. "I decided the only way I could ever make a hit out of him was always to double-track his voice—in other words, to record the song once and then have him sing it a second time, following his own voice," George wrote. Yet in some moments, even George's deployment of double-tracking failed to improve Billy's vocal performance on his Parlophone recordings. With Billy's basic track in hand, George resorted to his trusty windup piano technique in order to camouflage Billy's vocals. Recording his piano part at half speed and then doubling the tempo afforded George's instrument with a kind of harpsichord effect. "Where there was any offending phrase from the Kramer tonsils," George later recalled, "I put in a bit of this piano and mixed it a bit louder. For the inquisitive, I may add that I didn't pay myself for these pieces of gratuitous musicianship, since I reckoned that if I did so, I would be getting money that a musician should be getting." But it was more than that, of course: George's ego still clearly stung from his treatment by Len Wood a year earlier when the Parlophone head requested an aboveboard financial stake in his artists' recordings. To do anything less would have put him in the same class as Norrie Paramor, whom he found to be ethically reprehensible. It was an issue that George would have to forestall—at least for the time being.[8]

Issued on April 26, 1963, Billy J. Kramer and the Dakotas' cover version of "Do You Want to Know a Secret" shot straight to number one, proving that George and the Beatles' magic was truly portable by this point. Indeed, even in other artists' hands, Lennon-McCartney compositions were commercially viable. And with George's superlative A&R instincts, even their lesser material could be hit worthy. As Billy later remarked, "Nobody was more amazed than me when it ["Do You Want to Know a Secret"] turned out to be a big hit." Four months later, George and Billy were back at Abbey Road recording "Bad to Me," another Lennon-McCartney original. With Paul McCartney observing from the control room, Billy J. Kramer and the Dakotas made short work of "Bad to Me." After "Do You Want to Know a Secret" and "Bad to Me" topped the British charts, George couldn't help thinking that "the process was starting to seem almost inevitable." By this point, Brian was convinced that George possessed a truly magic touch in the studio—that he could turn any act into a bona fide star. "Brian was a great ego booster," George later remarked. "He brought me these artists and expected me to make hits with them—and when I did, he wasn't at all surprised. I was. Though I couldn't perform what these musicians were doing, I had a formula in the studio, a way of getting the sounds. And though I was a virgin as far as rock and roll was concerned, I quickly immersed myself in it. The Beatles taught me a lot."[9]

While Brian had plenty of Liverpool acts waiting in the wings for George to audition, the Parlophone head happily turned his attention back to the Beatles. The boys had been crisscrossing the country, playing one show after another, until midsummer, when they finally rejoined George at Abbey Road for a truly watershed moment on Monday, July 1, 1963. By this time, the Beatles had begun booking their sessions under the pseudonym the Dakotas in reference to Billy J. Kramer's backing group. As their fame grew by leaps and bounds, they had little choice but to try to conceal their movements. As Geoff Emerick later recalled, by mid-1963 "there always seemed to be at least a hundred girls camped outside the studio in hopes of seeing one or more of the group dash to or from their cars. How they knew when the Beatles were due to come in was a complete mystery to us," he added, "but clearly the fans had some kind of network."[10]

As it happened, the band's growing number of British fans had no idea what their idols had in store for them next. There was very little, if any, notion about the Beatles in the United States either, where *NME*'s Chris Hutchins published an international dispatch titled "From Liverpool?—You're a Hit" in vaunted *Billboard* magazine on June 29, 1963. While Hutchins doesn't call out the Beatles by name, he makes certain to highlight the phenomenon that they were just beginning to unleash in their homeland. "The British popular disk market is currently undergoing a sensational period with groups from one city—Liverpool—taking it in turns to top the chart. Sales of their records are abnormally high at a time when the industry is undergoing a sleepy period," Hutchins wrote. He took special note of "Parlophone recording manager George Martin," who "scored an unprecedented achievement here when he lodged disks by the three biggest groups in the Nos. 1, 2, and 3 slots. Now he has set the entire month of July aside for marathon sessions with those groups to wax several singles and an album with each."[11]

Of course, Martin had been working with one unnamed group in particular who were on the verge of blowing their fame wide open across the British Isles. Lennon and McCartney had begun composing their latest song, "She Loves You," in a Newcastle-upon-Tyne hotel room on June 26, and within a matter of days it was in Martin's hands. As George later recalled, "I was sitting in my usual place on a high stool in Studio 2 when John and Paul first ran through the song on their acoustic guitars, George joining in on the choruses. I thought it was great but was intrigued by the final chord, an odd sort of major sixth, with George doing the sixth and John and Paul the third and fifths, like a Glenn Miller arrangement." For Martin, the concluding chord structure seemed jarring, not unlike the original version of "Do You Want to Know a Secret," and he suggested that they reconsider the arrangement. But the Beatles weren't having it this time. As McCartney later recalled, "Occasionally, we'd overrule George Martin, like on 'She Loves You,' we end on a sixth chord, a very jazzy sort of thing. And he said, 'Oh, you can't do that! A sixth chord? It's too jazzy.' We just said, 'No, it's a great hook, we've got to do it.'" For his part, Norman Smith had seen the lyrics in advance and was duly unimpressed. "I thought 'Oh my God, what a lyric! This is going to be one that I do not like.' But when they started to sing it—bang, wow, terrific, I was up at the mixer jogging around." By this point, Smith had come to adore his working life among the Liverpool Scousers who had given him pause only the previous summer. "We all got on so well," he later recalled. "They used to call me 'Normal' and, occasionally, '2dBs Smith' because on a few occasions I would ask one of them to turn his guitar amplifier down a couple of decibels."[12]

Sitting up in the control booth with Martin and Smith, young Geoff Emerick had a ringside seat as the Beatles recorded what would emerge as one of the most successful singles in British history. As Emerick observed the proceedings, Smith made dramatic changes in recording the Beatles' sound. As he and Martin worked on "She Loves You," Smith deployed a compressor, an electronic device that reduces the dynamic range between the loudest and softest signals. In so doing, Smith allowed Martin to capture the sound of the bass and drums independently of each other as opposed to being compressed together. Moreover, Smith positioned an overhead microphone over Ringo Starr's drums in order to create "a more prominent, driving rhythm sound," in Emerick's words. As a result, "both the bass and drums are brighter and more 'present' than in previous Beatles records."[13]

The nature of the Beatles' sound had been an ongoing issue with the bandmates, who hungered for a decidedly more "American" quality to their output—especially in terms of undergirding their work with a general ambience of loudness. As Martin later recalled, "I did succeed in getting some of that loudness onto the early Beatles records, but I wanted more, much more. And the boys were snapping at my heels. They could hear the difference in the US imports just as well as I could. 'Why can't we get it like that, George?' they would chorus. 'We want it like that!'" Smith's efforts to position the microphones in such a way as to enhance the group's sound were clearly making a difference by this juncture, but as far as Martin was concerned, it wasn't nearly enough. He was determined to imbue the Beatles' records with a bigger, bolder, more robust sound. "Getting maximum volume out of those grooves became my major preoccupation. I used to wake up in the middle of the night thinking about it. Volume! That great sound!" But of course, his motives involved more than mere aesthetics or simply attempting to please the bandmates' dreams for a more forceful sound that would bowl over their audiences like those American imports they cherished. No, it was much more than that. George wanted a Beatles sound that would drive fans right from their transistor radios into the record shops. "You, the listener, would hear it over the radio for the first time," he later wrote, "and it would knock your socks off. Out you would go to the record store and buy it. That's the business." It was the business, in short, of creating maximum volume.[14]

As it happened, the Beatles' new and "brighter" sound served as the perfect palette for "She Loves You," which, like "Please Please Me" and "From Me to You" before it, benefited from the song's arresting opening phrases. Clearly, Lennon and McCartney were evolving quickly under Martin's tutelage into songsmiths with an ear for infectious pop hooks. Slated for release on August 23, "She Loves You" exploded into being with a chorus, one of George's favorite musical conceits, introducing the listener to the Beatles' vocal catchphrase, "yeah, yeah, yeah," that would soon see millions of Britons singing along with sheer glee. Having recorded the band's latest single in a matter of hours on July 1, George was anxious to get to work on the Beatles' next long-player. "Brian Epstein and I worked out a plan," he later recalled, "in which we tried—not always successfully—to release a new Beatles single every three months and two albums a year. I was always saying to the Beatles, 'I want another hit, come on, give me another hit,' and they always responded." While "She Loves You" would be waiting in the wings for the time being, Brian had been busying himself making plans to consolidate the Beatles' fame outside of Great Britain. A few days later, on July 5, Brian had signed a landmark deal on the Beatles' behalf to undertake a 1964 Australian tour.[15]

Wasting little time, the Beatles set to work on July 18 and began recording material for their follow-up LP to *Please Please Me*, which was still holding its own atop the British LP charts. As they had done with their initial concept for their debut album, they approached their new long-player with the notion of capturing the material associated with their contemporary set list, which, as with the group's early days in Liverpool and Hamburg, consisted of a range of American rhythm-and-blues hits and pop standards. And that's exactly where George and the Beatles started during their first, lengthy Thursday night session in Number 2. As the initial song that they recorded for the new LP, the group's cover version of Smokey Robinson's "You Really Got a Hold on Me" featured John on, arguably, his most powerful lead vocal to date. With Martin's Steinway piano propelling the melody, the Beatles captured the song in only eleven takes—seven of them complete—before just as quickly turning their attention toward "Money (That's What I Want)," Berry Gordy and Janie Bradford's Motown composition, which the group landed in an economical seven takes, along with a piano edit piece by Martin. Next up was a cover version of "Devil in Her Heart"—refashioned after the Donays' 1961 hit "Devil in His Heart"—with Harrison taking lead vocals and Starr on maracas. After completing the song in three takes and a handful of overdubs, the band concluded the evening with several stabs at the Broadway standard "Till There Was You," a McCartney favorite from Meredith Wilson's hit 1957 show *The Music Man*. Performed in the style of Peggy Lee, the Beatles' version of "Till There Was You" would remain unfinished for the time being, as Martin and the bandmates were unsatisfied with any of the takes. For Martin, it was a whirlwind session, to be sure, but there was already a different spirit in the air, a confidence and maturity to the band's sound in comparison to their work back in February on *Please Please Me*. Later, listening to the playbacks of those initial recordings for the group's new LP, Emerick could hear it, too. "As I sat in the control room listening to the tracks," he later wrote, "I was amazed at how much the Beatles had improved since their debut album, in terms of both their musicianship and their singing."[16]

Twelve days later, George and the band continued their sporadic work on the new LP, with morning and evening sessions separated by the Beatles' appearance across town at the Playhouse Theatre for BBC radio's *Saturday Club* program. The proceedings began with yet another cover version—in this case, a cover of the Marvelettes' hit single "Please Mr. Postman" with John taking lead vocals and nailing the song in nine takes. And that's when the

Beatles unveiled "It Won't Be Long," the first of two remarkable new Lennon-McCartney contributions on the day. As Paul later recalled, the idea for the song emanated from John, although both of them enjoyed the idea of injecting their lyrics with "plays on words and onomatopoeia." With "It Won't Be Long," the songwriters created an intentional "double meaning" through the juxtaposition of "be long" and "belong"—phrases that highlight the differences between the passage of time and romantic commitment. When they brought the song into the studio that day, the group managed to crank out ten takes of "It Won't Be Long" before heading to the Playhouse Theatre. For Martin, the song had been a revelation, finding the Beatles matching, if not expanding on, the power that they had revealed earlier in the month with "She Loves You," which would not be unleashed upon an unsuspecting world for several more weeks. To Martin's ears, "It Won't Be Long" exploded into being like a kind of rock 'n' roll "pot-boiler," as Lennon exchanged a call-and-response chorus of "yeah, *yeah*, yeah, *yeah*, yeah, *yeah*" with McCartney and Harrison, echoing their catchphrase from "She Loves You." After returning from their stint on BBC radio—where they rehearsed and recorded six tunes—the Beatles abruptly shifted gears into a remake of "Money (That's What I Want)" in seven takes before returning to "Till There Was You." For the latter remake, Starr eschewed the drums for a subtler bongo part. Recorded in five takes and the only song on the eventual album without any overdubs, "Till There Was You" was distinguished by Harrison's adept Spanish-inflected solo on a nylon-stringed José Ramírez classical guitar.[17]

As the band's incredible day's work continued onward into the evening, Harrison handled lead vocals on a cover version of Chuck Berry's "Roll Over Beethoven," which the group had been treating since their Quarry Men days in the late 1950s. At this point, the Beatles returned to "It Won't Be Long," which they brought to fruition after twenty-three takes since the day had begun. And that's when their efforts on that incredible Tuesday reached ever higher still, as they unveiled the second Lennon-McCartney original, "All My Loving." Written by Paul during the band's tour with Roy Orbison the previous May, "All My Loving" marked a rare moment when the Beatle had "written the words first. I never wrote words first, it was always some kind of accompaniment. I've hardly ever done it since either." While the composition had begun as "a little country and western song," "All My Loving" had quickly morphed into a spirited rock number about the joys of romantic reunion. Recorded in its entirety in eleven takes with three overdubs, "All My Loving" was marked by Martin's deft recommendation that McCartney double-track his lead vocal, lending his voice deeper, more powerful tones and textures.

As the Beatles put away their instruments that night, Martin had completed one of the most astonishing spate of sessions in his career. His chief creative vehicle had eclipsed their earlier heights in a single day, completing several new songs—and two stunning originals—with great economy and finesse. For George and the boys, July 30, 1963, was yet another watershed moment in a career that was already swimming with them. Only one year earlier, the Beatles had struggled back in Liverpool to wrap their minds around "How Do You Do It." And they had done so in a callow effort to please the Parlophone head's now passé approach to a business model that they were well on their way to rewriting right in front of him.[18]

After that incredible day at Abbey Road, the Beatles would hit the circuit yet again, winding their way across England from one ballroom to another throughout August and into the early days of September. In the meantime, George continued to work with Brian's ever-growing stable of beat bands. Up first was the Fourmost, a Liverpool act that Brian had signed to a management contract in late June. Years later, the band would remember their artists' test with George for their credulity at the time. As Dave Lovelady recalled, "We wanted to impress George Martin and show him that we were a cut above the other Liverpool groups. We began our audition with 'Happy Talk' from *South Pacific*. George Martin looked at us in disbelief and said, 'You do realize that you're playing the wrong notes.'" Not long afterward, the Parlophone head had signed them as well, giving them ready access to a number of Lennon-McCartney originals. By this time, it was well known that they held the best numbers back for the Beatles, but John and Paul's songwriting brand was already well on its way to becoming a household name in England. Produced by George, the Fourmost's debut single was a cover version of Lennon and McCartney's "Hello Little Girl," one of the compositions on the Beatles' acetate that Brian had played for George at their first meeting in February 1962. The song came into the Fourmost's hands after lead singer Brian O'Hara "asked John Lennon if he'd got anything, and he did a tape for me. He says, 'I wrote this one while I was sitting on the toilet,' and then sings 'Hello Little Girl' with just his guitar for accompaniment."[19]

After the single's release on August 30, the Fourmost enjoyed an auspicious start with "Hello Little Girl," which reached the number-nine position on the British charts. The Fourmost's sophomore effort, a recording of Lennon and McCartney's "I'm in Love," made its way into the top 20. By this point, it was as if Brian and George could do no wrong. The Liverpool manager seemed to have an endless stream of Merseyside bands at his disposal, and George quickly ushered them into the studio, where he would produce their recordings in breakneck fashion and hurry them into the record stores, where they would be greeted by a music-buying public with a seemingly unquenchable thirst for beat music.

And that was when Brian foisted a young singer named Priscilla White on the A&R head. White was one of the Cavern's loyal "cave dwellers"—Beatles fans who had grown up right along with the band in the sweaty basement venue. White was also, Martin feared, a "setback" in terms of their apparently unstoppable progress as British rock 'n' roll impresarios. Working under the professional name of Cilla Black, she reminded George of Billy J. Kramer. Indeed, "For me, she was even more of a problem child than Billy had been," George later recalled. Years later, Black remembered her first meeting with the Parlophone head with a special fondness. It was on a Sunday evening, and "George's office was littered with record sleeves, brown box files and piles of sheet music, and nowhere near as grand as I'd expected," she later wrote. "I was very impressed with George, though. He was a tall, thin, elegant beanpole of a man, and Brian had told me in the taxi that he had a magnificent ear for music, a great sense of style, and a brilliant reputation as an arranger, composer and oboist. After just a few minutes breaking the ice, I could tell that George had a really sincere attitude towards Mersey sound music and, over a cup of coffee and some tasty ginger biscuits, I also discovered that he produced the Goons for the radio, as well as the great Peter Sellers." After completing the introductions with Brian and Cilla, George took the young singer into the studio, where she auditioned with "Get a Shot of Rhythm 'n' Blues." At first, Cilla had trouble reading the A&R man's demeanor. Had she succeeded or failed at earning her big break in London, that "wicked city" in the south in Cilla's words? "George didn't say much during that audition," she recalled, "but I couldn't help noticing that his attitude was becoming reassuringly different—much more smiley, relaxed, and open. He also walked Brian and me to the lift, and, young though I was, I realized this was significant. Managers at BICC [British Insulated Calendar Cables, where she worked] in Liverpool only did that for people they respected or considered important." While Cilla had passed the audition and earned a Parlophone recording contract, it turned out that the A&R head still wasn't quite sure about how to proceed with the newest member of Brian's stable.[20]

"Although she had a good, if thin, voice," George later recalled, "she was a rock-and-roll screecher in the true Cavern tradition, with a piercing nasal sound. That was all right in itself, but finding songs for her was clearly going to be very difficult." Needing fresh material to move her career forward and keep Brian's stable purring, George turned to John and Paul to provide Cilla with a repertoire. He recognized that "the Beatles by this time were bubbling over with enthusiasm for their own works—and rightly so. We had opened the vent, the oil had started gushing up, and the well, which I had originally thought might soon dry up, simply kept on producing more and more." By this time, Cilla had taken to singing one of their older tunes during her Cavern appearances, an original Lennon-McCartney number from the Beatles' failed Decca audition titled "Love of the Loved." For George, this seemed like as good as any place to start, so he brought Cilla down to Abbey Road to record "Love of the Loved," for which he had composed a special arrangement for trumpets. And for the first time in many months, George and Brian came up short. "It didn't sell well at all," George later recalled. "It was not a number one." Indeed, it landed at number thirty-five, which, after the succession of smash hits that George and Brian had steered toward the British charts, seemed like an abysmal failure. For Cilla, the session with George at Abbey Road had been no easy process, as the singer later recalled. "It was the first time I'd faced 'real' musicians, playing from real sheet music, and I was so disappointed!" she wrote. "What I wanted from the backing group was a really good club band sound—a Cavern sound—but it seemed I could whistle for it. George had his own ideas. Feeling very small and more jittery than I'd ever felt before, I didn't enjoy a single moment of that session. Every time I sang 'thurr' instead of 'there,' George kept pulling me up. 'That word sounds much too Liverpudlian,' he kept saying." All in all, it took fifteen takes for Cilla to properly eradicate the Scouse from her singing voice. With his own class-conscious baggage, George was keenly aware of the need for Cilla to sound as cosmopolitan as possible on her debut record. But in the end, all of his good-natured coaching hardly mattered, as Cilla had entered the British charts with a middling thud.[21]

Like George, Brian had been flummoxed by Cilla's fruitless debut. Tireless in his efforts to extol the talents of his stable, Brian traveled to the United States to attempt to generate American interest in his clientele. By this point, he and George were positively irate over the treatment of their chart-topping British artists—namely, the Beatles—at the hands of Capitol Records, EMI's vaunted American subsidiary. And for the first time, George was able to connect a name with the wholesale rejection of his Parlophone artists. That man was Capitol's international A&R representative Dave E. Dexter Jr. In June 1962, as the Beatles met Martin for the first time, Dexter was the subject of a memo from Capitol president Alan W. Livingston, who ordered his staff to submit all imported music for the A&R rep's consideration and approval. As it turned out, Dexter didn't appreciate rock 'n' roll, which he had once described as "juvenile and maddeningly repetitive" in an internal memo. As it happened, Dexter's musical tastes ran towards the likes of Peggy Lee, Nat "King" Cole, and Stan Kenton. American fans of beat music simply didn't have a chance.[22]

By the time that the Beatles began topping the charts in early 1963, Dexter passed on releasing "Please Please Me," quickly followed by "From Me to You," which he pronounced as being "stone-cold dead in the U.S. marketplace." By the time that Martin had begun working with Cilla Black, Dexter had passed on "She Loves You," too. But "Brian Epstein and I refused to leave the matter there," George later recalled. "We took the view that if Capitol didn't want them, we'd send them somewhere else." With the assistance of Transglobal Music, a New York licensing agency, EMI placed "She Loves You" with Vee-Jay Records, a tiny label based in Chicago. As George later remarked, the single ultimately "didn't sell well, but at least it did something, and at least we had a record on the American market. 'For God's sake, do something about this,' we said [to Capitol Records]. 'These boys are breaking it, and they're going to be fantastic throughout the world. So for heaven's sake, latch onto them.'" While Capitol continued to stonewall the Beatles, Transglobal had managed to license the contents of the *Please Please Me* album with Vee-Jay, who held the long-player in abeyance with no official release date in sight.[23]

While Brian failed to make any headway on behalf of his stable during his visit to the United States, he didn't come back empty handed, returning with a composition called "Anyone Who Had a Heart" from American songwriters Burt Bacharach and Hal David. "I absolutely flipped," George remembered. "I thought it was marvelous. 'Brian,' I said, 'what a lovely song. Thank you so much for bringing it over.'" George's first impulse was to record the song with Shirley Bassey, a veteran Welsh singer with EMI's Columbia imprint whom George was itching to see into the next phase of her career. But Brian had other things in mind, hoping that George would record the song with Cilla. As it happened, George didn't take kindly to the idea right away, as he harbored doubts about the song's appropriateness for the young singer. As Cilla later recalled, "Brian told me later that George had said, 'I very much doubt that Cilla's ready for an emotional piece like this.' But Eppy stood firm and it was me, not Shirley, who recorded the song."[24]

Strangely, after having achieved one hit after another with Brian's artists for the balance of 1963, George was gun-shy about recording a follow-up to "Love of the Loved" with Cilla. And it wasn't just her inexperience that concerned him. George was equally uncertain about his own ability to bring the composition to fruition. In particular, he felt that his trumpet arrangement may have been subpar. "I wasn't then known as an orchestrator," he reasoned, "and with others around who had big reputations it would have been cheeky of me to assert myself too much. So I brought in Johnny Pearson, who did a marvelous score for the song." With George up in the control room, Cilla finally succeeded in recording "Anyone Who Had a Heart," and it became a number-one hit in early 1964, making her a star on the British music scene. No one was more surprised than Cilla herself, who later wrote, "When I first heard the song I liked it a lot and wanted to record it, but I didn't rate it as a chart-topper. Recording it was a piece of cake. We had what must have been a 48-piece orchestra, the biggest I'd ever worked with, and during the recording, I did feel there was some 'magic' for me in the song." All of a sudden, George's work on "Love of the Loved" had been redeemed by the sweet joy of success. Years later, Cilla recalled the moment that Brian gave her the news. "I've just got the latest retail figures," he informed her. "'Anyone Who Had a Heart' is selling nearly a hundred thousand copies a day, and you're the first girl since Helen Shapiro to be number one in the British charts."[25]

But Cilla's record was not without controversy, with charges of plagiarism that hearkened back to George's dismal experiences with Paul Hanford's cover version of "Itsy Bitsy Teenie Weenie Yellow Polka Dot Bikini." Several months prior to the release of Cilla's version of "Anyone Who Had a Heart," Dionne Warwick's American recording had resulted in a top 10 hit. After Cilla's version topped the British charts, George learned that Warwick "was furious because we had pinched her version. Well, yes and no. Most songs have something inherent about the way they're done which is in itself an arrangement. What Johnny did was to retain that part, which was absolutely right for the song, and then orchestrate it." In sharp contrast with the charges of plagiarism that he had endured over "Itsy Bitsy Teenie Weenie Yellow Polka Dot Bikini," he refused to accept Warwick's arguments that Black's version was a nearly note-for-note theft—even down to a moment when the American singer fumbled one of the original lyrics, which Cilla dutifully replicated in George's recording. "The two records sounded similar," George later admitted, "but I am sure that ours was better than the American one. Certainly from an orchestral point of view we had a much better sound, and it deserved to be number one."[26]

While he had thrown up his hands back in 1960, declaring on *Juke Box Jury* that "we are competing against the Americans on unequal terms," he no longer seemed to care now that he was a producer with a golden touch. Now, only a few years later, the only thing that mattered was the work itself, and George was overbrimming with confidence that, more often than not, his was indeed the better work. Even during that incredible year, he still managed to find the time to record Parlophone stalwarts like Ron Goodwin, Matt Monro, and Jimmy Shand. Yearning for new talent, George even dispatched Ron Richards to head out for the North Country, where he discovered an obscure band called the Hollies in—somewhat naturally in those Mersey-sound days—the Cavern Club. In short order, the band recorded a pair of cover versions of Coasters tunes, including the Hollies' debut record "(Ain't That) Just Like Me," which landed at number twenty-five, followed by "Searchin'," which bubbled just under the top 10. In a matter of months, they would finally reach number eight with a cover version of Maurice Williams and the Zodiacs' "Stay."

With the Beatles as the label's undeniable mainstay and a host of other acts churning out regular hits, Parlophone had truly made it, no longer simply playing third fiddle to Columbia and HMV. For the first time, they were the EMI Group's indisputable pacesetters. But with the Friday, August 23, release of "She Loves You"—the song that had lain in wait since the first steamy days of July—the Beatles blew everything up all over again. In what seemed like no time at all, Britons were singing "yeah, yeah, yeah!" with unchecked abandon. During the previous month, as Len Wood studied the manufacturing orders for the "She Loves You" backed with "I'll Get You" single, EMI's managing director balked at the number of pressings. "The marketing manager set the advance order at 350,000, which was an extraordinary number in those days," Wood later recalled. "I told him I thought it was way too high, but he stood his ground and eventually I agreed to 250,000." As events would have it, Wood's estimation had rather dramatically missed the mark. Within just eleven days of its release, the single had sold an astonishing five hundred thousand copies and would occupy the top spot on the charts on two separate occasions as "She Loves You" ruled the airwaves across much of the fall. Not too long afterward, "She Loves You" notched sales in excess of a million copies on its way to becoming the United Kingdom's bestselling single of the decade. With this incredible backdrop, the Beatles finally resumed work on their second, as-of-yet-untitled album on Wednesday, September 11, 1963. With Martin up in the booth and with Smith and Langham by his side, the Beatles began working on "I Wanna Be Your Man," a new Lennon-McCartney song written expressly to showcase Starr. Only the day before, John and Paul had offered the composition to the Rolling Stones, who planned to record it as their second single. After one take, the Beatles turned their attention to two additional new songs, including "Little Child," which they attempted for two takes, followed by "All I've Got to Do," which they completed in fourteen takes. The group's banner day at Abbey Road resumed after a dinner break, when they tried out yet another new composition, "Not a Second Time." As with "Little Child" and "All I've Got to Do," it was written primarily by Lennon, who was clearly on a roll. After recording five takes, Martin double-tracked Lennon's voice before overdubbing his own piano part as well. The Beatles ended the evening by taking a stab at Harrison's writing debut with "Don't Bother Me," which, after seven takes, they abandoned for the night.[27]

Martin and the bandmates resumed work on their new LP the next day, marking the first time in months that they managed to find themselves at Abbey Road, and not out on the ballroom circuit, on two consecutive nights. When the Beatles settled down to business that afternoon, they recorded nine more takes of "Hold Me Tight," which Martin had put aside after their whirlwind February 11 session. After taking a short break, they resumed work on Harrison's "Don't Bother Me," although Martin found himself increasingly dissatisfied with the distortion that Lennon had been achieving on his rhythm guitar part. Studio outtakes find Martin asking Smith about deploying other means to attain the "dark" sound that Harrison aspired for with his song. "Can we have a compressor on this guitar, Norman? We might try to get a sort of organ sound." With the compressor effect in place, "Don't Bother Me" came together over nine additional takes and an overdub with Paul on claves, Ringo rapping an Arabian bongo, and John on tambourine.[28]

Afterward, they resumed work on "Little Child," with Paul overdubbing a piano part and John on harmonica. After six more attempts at "I Wanna Be Your Man," Martin and the band closed up Abbey Road for the night, having finished five songs in the space of two days. By the end of the month as the bandmates took a much-needed break from the road, Martin gathered his team back at the studio to work on the material that they had amassed in September. With Smith and Emerick sharing the control booth, Martin made two attempts at overdubbing piano parts on "Money (That's What I Want)" and Hammond organ on "I Wanna Be Your Man." For the rest of the workday, they held a mixing session to complete the Beatles' latest batch of tunes. Years later, Emerick would look back on these sessions, remembering how he would imagine himself in Smith's shoes as the band's balance engineer. "My contribution to those mixes may have been minimal—all I was doing was changing tape reels and starting and stopping the tape machines—but I was learning a lot from watching Norman," Emerick recalled. "I knew enough not to make comments during the session, but I do remember thinking things like 'I hope Norman lifts the guitar solo up'; 'I hope he rides the vocal here.'

I was already starting to imagine how I would engineer the sessions myself, given the chance."[29]

But before George and the other EMI staffers managed to see the bandmates again back at 3 Abbey Road, yet another seismic shift occurred in the Beatles' lives—the kind of all-out reshuffling of the deck that had taken them from being North Country unknowns to the toast of British pop music. Amazing as it now seems in retrospect, they were about to become even bigger still. On the evening of Sunday, October 13, they played a four-song set on Val Parnell's popular ITV variety show, *Sunday Night at the London Palladium*, in front of an ecstatic television audience of some fifteen million Britons. After the Beatles performed "From Me to You," "I'll Get You," "She Loves You," and "Twist and Shout" inside the theater, the mayhem shifted into the night, where two thousand ecstatic fans gathered on Oxford Street. "Screaming girls launched themselves against the police—sending helmets flying and constables reeling," according to the *Daily Herald*. But the *Daily Mirror* scooped the world the very next morning, boldly proclaiming the rise of BEATLEMANIA! across the United Kingdom.[30]

# 10

# EL DORADO

WHEN THEY FINALLY made their way back to St. John's Wood on Thursday, October 17, the Beatles were on the verge of yet another landmark moment in a career that was already chock-full of them. Indeed, for George and the bandmates, it would be a trailblazing session in more ways than one. After playfully assembling their first Christmas record, which was slated to be distributed as a Flexi-Disc giveaway by their Liverpool-based fan club during the upcoming holiday season, the Beatles got down to business. That afternoon, they reached a turning point that would have far-reaching consequences across their career when EMI belatedly allowed them—a pop act, no less—to make the shift from twin-track to four-track recording. As it happened, Abbey Road had been in possession of a four-track recorder since 1959, when the studio purchased a German-made Telefunken four-track tape machine. For the first several years, it was almost exclusively used by A&R men producing classical and opera records. For their purposes, four-track recording allowed them to achieve greater balance and separation among certain instruments, as opposed to being used for multitracking, which involves the merging of different sound sources in the service of a single, coherent whole. For many contemporary A&R men, recording pop acts simply didn't merit the need for multitracking. When George began working with the Beatles, twin-track recording met his production needs just fine. He rarely had to engage in bouncing-down practices in order to accomplish the band's musical vision at this juncture. But something had clearly changed in George and the group's creative calculus. Since their whirlwind session back in late July, the Parlophone head's confidence in the band had only continued to grow. Moreover, most rock 'n' roll groups during this era recorded their wares in much the same way that the Beatles recorded the *Please Please Me* LP—as quickly and as efficiently as possible in order to minimize studio fuss. But the Beatles had already demonstrated themselves to be perfectionists, willing to put in the necessary time and effort to get every song exactly right and as close to their vision as possible. With four-track recording, they could achieve enhanced separation of their instruments while also having greater freedom to optimize their individual performances in the service of their artistry.

As George later recalled, "With the success of the Beatles adding weight to my continual demands, the EMI bosses decided to join the world of modern recording, and we got four-track. It had taken a long time." While George pressed forward into the world of four-track recording with the Beatles, Geoff Emerick was even more cynical about the studio brass's belated change of heart: "Apparently, the bigwigs at EMI had decided that the band had now earned sufficient monies for the label—many millions of pounds, for sure—to be afforded the same honor as 'serious' musicians, none of whom, I am certain, brought in even a fraction of the income that the Beatles did." Whatever the reason—whether it was an old industry bias for classical over beat music or simply a matter of corporate reluctance—George viewed four-track recording as a key aspect of the Beatles' growth as songwriters and fledgling recording artists. As Ken Townsend later remarked, "With four-track one could do a basic rhythm track and then add on vocals and whatever else later. It made the studios into much more of a workshop."[1]

For the Beatles, life in Martin's four-track workshop began with a flourish, as Lennon and McCartney unveiled a veritable classic right before the Parlophone head's eyes. But first, John insisted on trying his hand at a four-track remake of "You Really Got a Hold on Me," which the bandmates had originally brought to a state of completion back on July 18. After a single take, George interrupted the proceedings, arguing that the July version was more than satisfactory. "All right, George, we give up," John replied. "But you'd better come on down here and have a listen to our next number-one record." Even at this stage of their career—with a chart-topping album and hit singles to their name—this was a bold statement, rivaled only by Martin's pronouncement about "Please Please Me" the previous November. Taking his usual place on his high stool, Martin waited for the Beatles to play, for the very first time at Abbey Road, "I Want to Hold Your Hand," which Lennon and McCartney had only just completed in the London basement of Dr. Richard Asher and his wife, Margaret Eliot, the oboe teacher who had schooled young

George Martin in the art of playing the oboe some fifteen years earlier. Paul had recently become the Ashers' lodger after dating their daughter Jane, an up-and-coming actress. As Lennon later recalled, they composed the tune in the Ashers' basement, "eyeball to eyeball": "Paul hits this chord and I turn to him and say, 'That's *it!*' I said, 'Do that again!' In those days, we really used to absolutely write like that—both playing into each other's noses." "I Want to Hold Your Hand" had been in Lennon and McCartney's ether for several weeks before coming to fruition in the Asher basement. At one point back in late August, Billy J. Kramer eavesdropped as John strummed an early version of the tune. "Can I have that song?" Kramer asked, hoping to lay his hands on the latest Lennon-McCartney nugget, as so many acts in Brian's stable were wont to do back in those days. "No, we're going to do that ourselves," John replied.[2]

For George, it was a revelation as he watched the Beatles play "I Want to Hold Your Hand" in Number 2, the room where, just fifteen months earlier, they had slogged through "Love Me Do" with Pete Best, their erstwhile drummer. For the Beatles, it must have seemed like a lifetime ago. For his part, Martin was absolutely thunderstruck. There it was—the tingle factor yet again. As they continued work on "I Want to Hold Your Hand," Martin and Smith took full advantage of their new four-track possibilities, allocating one track for bass and drums, reserving another track for vocals, and combining Lennon and Harrison's guitar work on yet another. As he would do in future sessions, Martin held the fourth track back for dispensing additional effects—keyboards, harmonica, handclaps, guitar solos, or other forms of instrumentation. As they had done with "Don't Bother Me," Martin and Smith redeployed the compressor effect on "I Want to Hold Your Hand" to afford Lennon's rhythm guitar part with the sonority of an organ. Martin also suggested that the Beatles punctuate the new song's verses with a series of double handclaps, which Smith recorded using the available fourth track. Emerick later recalled the sheer joy of watching the bandmates below in the studio proper as they good-naturedly clapped along with their latest number: "As I watched the four Beatles gathered around a single mic, clowning around as they added the part, it was apparent to me how much fun they were having, how much they loved doing what they were doing."[3]

After recording "I Want to Hold Your Hand" across seventeen takes, the Beatles turned to "This Boy," the composition that would serve as the single's B-side. Featuring an exquisite three-part harmony, "This Boy" required additional studio time to perfect the vocal parts. With its complex harmonies, "This Boy" was the perfect vehicle for George, hearkening back to his days with Sheena and the choral society in postwar Aberdeen. In later years, he wrote that the Beatles "always experimented with close harmony singing." With "This Boy," he added, adopting his typically self-deprecating posture, "all I did was change the odd note." He was very cognizant of the Beatles' natural singing abilities and the ways in which they had subsequently honed their voices through performance. "I didn't teach them to sing harmony, because they were already good at that," he later wrote. "They had cut their teeth in Liverpool and most importantly in Hamburg, when they had performed for hours on end each night in a very rough and demanding environment, organizing a repertoire for themselves by including American records in the act. They tried out the harmonies they heard on records and became quite good at it, to the point where they were able to sing naturally in three-part harmony once the song was established."[4]

In terms of Martin's input into the vocal structure of "This Boy," Emerick observed something slightly different that night, later remarking that "there was a lot of tweaking because it was a pretty complicated song, sung in intricate three-part harmony that George Martin—with considerable input from Paul—kept refining. George spent a lot of time at the piano with Lennon, McCartney, and Harrison, carefully checking each part they were singing and occasionally suggesting that a note be changed." While he may have only suggested the alteration of an occasional note, Martin's careful attention to ensuring that the trio fine-tuned their parts along with the piano underscores the attention to detail that he and the Beatles were increasingly bringing to their work together in the studio. If Martin and the bandmates were to be thought of as developing an ethic in their creative lives in the studio at this juncture, painstaking efforts like their work on "This Boy" would be the cornerstone of their budding artistry.[5]

That same night, the Beatles completed "This Boy" in fifteen takes. Martin also supervised two overdubs that evening, the first of which involved the replacement of a solo that Harrison had contrived for the middle eight. Feeling that the solo didn't fit the song's mood, Martin suggested that they repurpose the middle section with an inspired vocal from Lennon. During the second overdub, Lennon double-tracked his vocals, affording them with even more power and warmth. When they were done with the recording, Martin and the Beatles had finished yet another monumental work—and in the space of just six hours, no less. After holding an October 21 mixing session for the "I Want to Hold Your Hand" backed with "This Boy" single, which was slated for release on November 29, George reconvened the band on the morning of Wednesday, October 23, to resume work on "I Wanna Be

Your Man," "Little Child," and "Hold Me Tight," which they finally brought to fruition. After some additional tidying up in the control room on "Money (That's What I Want)" on October 30, George completed final preparations on the Beatles' new long-player, which was cut at Abbey Road on November 4 and scheduled for a November 22 release. By this point, Brian, George, and the band had decided on *With the Beatles* as the title of the long-player. For George and the group, the notion of an album merely reflected the idea of assembling a collection of songs, as opposed to working from a unifying theme. "We weren't thinking in terms of an album being an entity by itself," George later recalled. As for the LP's title, George pointedly remarked that "the first album was really a recital of their repertoire, *With the Beatles* was the first songbook so to speak." On November 9—nearly three weeks before the single's release—George arrived backstage before the Beatles' show in East Ham, where he excitedly informed them that "I Want to Hold Your Hand" had racked up advance sales of more than a million copies. It was overwhelming news, to say the least—a historic moment for the British record industry in and of itself. For the Beatles, it was an incredible harbinger of things to come. With their upcoming single already achieving such great heights, could their new long-player be far behind?[6]

The famous shadowy cover photo for *With the Beatles* had been shot by Robert Freeman in late August at the Palace Court Hotel in Bournemouth. Photographed in black and white, the unsmiling Beatles were clearly adopting the pose of serious musicians, a demeanor that visibly matched their growing expectations in the studio. The Beatles originally proposed that the album's front cover feature Freeman's photo without reference to the LP's title, but EMI balked, suggesting that the Beatles hadn't developed the right kind of profile to support an anonymous cover. Hence, with the simple words WITH THE BEATLES adorning the album sleeve, the Beatles' second long-player hit the stores, having already racked up advance sales of some three hundred thousand copies. In its second week of release, *With the Beatles* managed to knock *Please Please Me* out of the number-one slot on the album charts, where it had camped for twenty weeks. George and the Beatles were wowed by the reviews, including Alan Smith's November 15, 1963, preview in *NME*: "The highlight of *With the Beatles*: To my mind, 'All My Loving,' this John Lennon–Paul McCartney original has an instantly recognizable melody line, taken at mid-tempo. Paul handles most of the vocal, with vocal accompaniment by John and George. The opening number is a strident shouter, 'It Won't Be Long,' sung by John and written by the prolific Lennon-McCartney team." Caught up in his own elation, Smith concluded his review by writing, "If there are any Beatle-haters left in Britain, I doubt if they'll remain unmoved after hearing *With the Beatles*. It's a knock-out."[7]

Within a matter of days, the Beatles would rule the top 40 with their fourth straight chart-topping single as "I Want to Hold Your Hand" settled in for its own extended stay atop the British charts. George and Brian soon realized that they enjoyed the advantage of having an embarrassment of riches with the Beatles and the other members of Brian's stable. "With all this talent on the move, Brian and I had to establish a working formula," George later wrote. Having already devised a yearly plan for releasing new Beatles product, they needed to work up a strategy for delivering the other members of their growing stable into the marketplace. "Having Gerry, and Billy, and Cilla as well, we had to stagger the issue of their singles too, so that as far as possible there was an overlap but no clash. It seemed to work. Out of the 52 weeks of 1963, we topped the charts no less than 37 times." By any measure, it was an astonishing record for the Parlophone head who just eighteen months earlier had been searching in vain for a pop sensation to call his own. By this point, Norrie Paramor wasn't really George's rival anymore. So profound and overwhelming was the Beatles' success that the Columbia producer and Cliff Richard were now only visible in George's rearview mirror. The producers' careers were now firmly going in very different directions—with Martin sailing into uncharted waters that even Paramor, who had enjoyed astonishing successes with Richard, could never even remotely have imagined.[8]

As that incredible year came to a close, the thirty-seven-year-old Martin can be seen in one publicity photo after another as he poses with the bandmates in a cascade of shifting settings with Lennon, aged twenty-three; McCartney, now twenty-one; Harrison, the youngest at twenty; and Starr, also twenty-three. There is one photograph that stands out in particular—a picture of the Beatles at a celebratory luncheon in the EMI boardroom on November 18. There they are: John, Paul, George, and Ringo posing with George Martin and the EMI brass—Sir Joseph Lockwood, the august chairman, along with managing director Len Wood. Behind them, hanging on the boardroom wall, is Francis Barraud's famous painting of his brother's dog Nipper listening to a gramophone playing his master's voice. For the Parlophone head, it must have been utterly remarkable to experience how quickly things had changed. In the spring of 1962, he had reluctantly signed a contract that held him to a straight salary with no promise of residuals. Back then, Wood hadn't so much as even bothered to demur when Martin briefly threatened to leave EMI for greener pastures. And yet there Wood stands, smiling for the camera in that November 18 photograph from the Manchester Square boardroom, posing just behind Ringo Starr's left shoulder, as if all were right with the world. And why shouldn't it be? In 1963 Martin had steered Parlophone into tens of millions of pounds of unexpected revenue on the backs of Epstein's North Country acts. Yes, everything should have been right with the world, just as that convivial photo seemed to project. But was it?

As that magical year came to an end for George and the bandmates, the Beatles made an appearance on comedy duo Eric Morecambe and Ernie Wise's popular ATV sketch comedy show, *Two of a Kind*. In a December 1963 episode to be broadcast the following April, the surging Beatles played "This Boy," "All My Loving," and "I Want to Hold Your Hand" in front of a rollicking studio audience. But the real highlight was a performance by the group, along with Morecambe and Wise, of "Moonlight Bay," the Alice Faye number from *Tin Pan Alley*. Costumed in boater hats and white striped jackets, John, Paul, and George shared vocals with Ernie Wise, while Ringo played the drums. All the while, Eric Morecambe—donning a collarless jacket and Beatle wig—repeatedly broke up the Beatles' mock-serious mood with a series of comedic interjections that lampooned the band's incredible rise on the strength of such hits as "She Loves You" and "Twist and Shout":

*We were strolling along (twist and shout!)*
*On Moonlight Bay (whoo!)*
*We could hear the voices singing (I like it!)*
*You said you'd stay (Keep up, Bongo!)*
*You have broken my heart (oh, twist and shout!)*
*So go away ("Have the Beatles gone?" "No, they're here!")*
*With your short, fat hairy legs*
*On Moonlight Bay*
*On Moonlight Bay*

As the group hammed it up on the stage at ATV Studios in Borehamwood, Morecambe poked fun at the Beatles' drummer, whom he good-naturedly referred to as "Bongo." For the Beatles and their producer, the December 1963 "Moonlight Bay" skit highlighted the kind of humor that had brought them together on that very first night at Abbey Road: a shared sense of good-time, comedic fun—the ability to laugh at oneself in spite of everything. The Beatles' senses of humor and love of irony were on full display that night as the bandmates revealed an easy transition from hitmakers to vaudevillians, just as Martin had done himself. He had a lot to be proud of as 1963 came to a close. By this point, the Beatles had emerged as the toast of England.

No less than the London *Evening Standard* proclaimed that "1963 has been the Beatles' year. An examination of the heart of the nation at this moment would reveal the name Beatles engraved upon it."[9]

But for George, in spite of everything that he had accomplished for Parlophone and the Beatles, 1964 would begin with a professional slight. At the tail end of every calendar year, EMI employees eagerly anticipated their annual Christmas bonus, which was roughly equivalent to a week's earnings. George looked forward to his bonus, too—especially given his incredible year. "That year, the first full year of the Beatles," he later wrote, "the directors of EMI announced with supreme generosity that everyone would receive four days' pay as their Christmas bonus. Four days' pay at the end of a year in which I had had the number-one record in the charts for 37 weeks! But I didn't even get that." In fact, George got nothing. But he hadn't merely been forgotten. When his bonus "failed to arrive, I phoned the accountants down at Hayes. 'There must be some mistake,' I said. 'My secretary has had her four days' pay, but I haven't had any myself.'" But he soon learned that something else was at work. The accountant's reasoning was simple enough: "Well, it's one of the rules of the company that people earning more than £3,000 a year are on a different salary scale to the others, and they're not entitled to a Christmas bonus. You're earning just over £3,000 a year."[10]

It was a monumental blunder on the EMI Group's part, to say the least, and the Parlophone head knew it. And worse yet for EMI, George knew that he was now worth a lot more than the salary he had agreed to back in the spring of 1962. George could feel the sting of unfeeling corporate ineptitude, of EMI's seeming inability to compensate him appropriately for making the records that now had the company's manufacturing plants working in overdrive. No, denying him a simple holiday bonus was a monumental blunder all right, and George would not soon forget it. "I naturally had a chip on my shoulder," he later observed. The convivial nature of his working relationship with the Beatles and their manager was his only solace. Since Brian and the band had come into his life, George had been "working every evening and almost every weekend. It was very tough, but still great fun, because at least I had successful records coming out of my ears. That was my only reward." But with the increasing momentum generated by "She Loves You," "I Want to Hold Your Hand," and two number-one albums—the full onslaught of unremitting British Beatlemania—George was beginning to feel that something even more powerful was in the offing, that the Beatles' phenomenon might grow bigger still. "If I thought that I had worked hard before," he later recalled, "it was nothing compared with the furious, frantic activity that was about to begin."[11]

And it began—as things seemed to do back in those days—with a bang. A couple of bangs, to be precise. First, there was the matter of the Beatles' incredible performance in 1963. As Parlophone's A&R head, George felt duty-bound to apprise his EMI superiors that should they decide to pick up the band's option, as the original May 9, 1962, contract with Brian stipulated, the Beatles were guaranteed a 25 percent raise for each successive option year. As George reasoned, it was the least that the EMI Group could do given the group's unexpected and unprecedented sales during the 1963 calendar year. Anything else, to his mind, would be "patently unfair." Doing his due diligence as Parlophone exec, he suggested to Len Wood that EMI double the band's royalty immediately. EMI's managing director approved, albeit with a single proviso: that the Beatles, in turn, agree to a five-year option. "No, you don't understand," George countered. "I don't want to ask for anything" in return. George reasoned that EMI should show good faith in the Beatles' achievements on behalf of the company and reward them unconditionally for having so dramatically altered the EMI Group's balance sheet. Wood was speechless. EMI didn't negotiate outside of a contract. How could George even stoop so low as to believe that such an accommodation was possible—even in the Beatles' extraordinary case? "From that moment on," George later recalled, "I was considered a traitor within EMI." But to the Parlophone head's great surprise, Wood acquiesced anyway. On January 31, 1964—the day after tiny Vee-Jay Records had rereleased "Please Please Me" in the United States in anticipation of taking advantage of something that the British press had recently described as "Beatlemania"—EMI optioned the Beatles' contract and doubled their royalty rate, just as George had recommended. But another die had been cast in George's increasingly tension-riddled encounters with the EMI brass—as it always seemed to do where money was involved. For his part, Wood couldn't let the matter pass without chiding Martin in an inter-office memo, writing that "surely we have given the manager of the Beatles just the ammunition he requires to secure an additional term contract from the Beatles for himself and in turn to give us further options. I should be glad if you pursue the subject vigorously on these lines and let me know how things develop because if we do not get further options all we have done is to give away a fair chunk of Company money."[12]

And then there was the matter of Paris. The Beatles were in town for an extended residency at the Olympia Theatre, where they shared top billing with French singer Sylvie Vartan and America's Trini Lopez. With Beatlemania having made its way to France, the group's concerts were a veritable mob scene. At one critical juncture, the gendarmes created a protective ring around the theater so the Beatles could make their escape into the Parisian night. As events would have it, back on Friday, January 24, 1964, Norman Smith executed a tape-to-tape copy of the basic rhythm track of "I Want to Hold Your Hand"—take seventeen, recorded back on October 17, 1963, to be precise. Within days, he traveled to Paris with Martin to conduct the Beatles' first EMI recording session outside of the friendly confines of Abbey Road. On the morning of January 29, they waited together in vain for the bandmates to join them at Paris's Pathé Marconi studios. It was a day that would begin with a spate of anger and end with the makings of yet another pop gem.

But on the morning of January 29, the Beatles were safe and sound, relaxing in their luxurious suite at the George V Hotel instead of working with Martin and Smith at Pathé Marconi. Along with translator Camillo Felgen, Martin and Smith were in Paris to record German-language versions of "I Want to Hold Your Hand" and "She Loves You." The recordings were the brainchild of Otto Demmlar, a producer with EMI's West German division, Electrola Gesellschaft. Demmlar intended to distribute the tracks via Odeon, EMI's German subsidiary. The Odeon brass contended that German translations of the Beatles' hits were a necessity, and as Beatlemania gathered steam in the United Kingdom, they began pressuring their parent company for a Beatles release in their mother tongue. "Odeon was adamant," George recalled. "They couldn't sell large quantities of records unless they were sung in German. I thought that if they were right then we should do it. The Beatles didn't agree, but I persuaded them. Odeon sent over a translator from Cologne to coach the boys although they did know a little German from having played there." On that fateful morning at Pathé Marconi, everyone was ready to go: Martin, Smith, and the German translator. Everyone, that is, save for the Beatles, who simply weren't having it.[13]

After waiting for more than an hour, George telephoned the bandmates at the George V, only to connect with roadie Neil Aspinall, who replied, "They're in bed, they've decided not to go to the studio." The preternaturally staid George was suddenly beside himself with anger. "I went crazy," he later recalled. "It was the first time they had refused to do anything for me." With Felgen in tow, Martin seethed as their taxi sped across the city. And that's when things took an even stranger turn. "I barged into their suite, to be met by this incredible sight, right out of the Mad Hatter's tea party," George reported. "Jane Asher—Paul's girlfriend—with her long red hair, was pouring tea from a china pot, and the others were sitting around her like March

Hares. They took one look at me and *exploded*, like in a school room when the headmaster enters. Some dived into the sofa and hid behind cushions, others dashed behind curtains. 'You are bastards!' I screamed, to which they responded with impish little grins and roguish apologies." In a matter of minutes, George corralled the mutinous Beatles into a taxi, and they made their way to the studio, where, in short order, they were coached by Felgen on their German pronunciation and dutifully began dubbing German-language vocals onto "Komm, Gib Mir Deine Hand" ("I Want to Hold Your Hand"), which took eleven takes to perfect. "Sie Liebt Dich" ("She Loves You") proved to be considerably more challenging given that the original twin-track from the July 1 session no longer survived, requiring the band to record a new rhythm track at Pathé Marconi before dubbing in the vocals under Felgen's supervision in thirteen takes. "They were extremely pleased to get it over with," Smith later recalled. "We all were. I found the studio very odd to work in, the equipment was alien to anything we were used to."[14]

The unfamiliar environs notwithstanding, the session ended in a triumph for George and the Beatles, as their sessions so often did during their heady early days together. And that's when Paul unveiled his latest composition, "Can't Buy Me Love," which he had written at the upright piano that Brian had helpfully provided during the bandmates' protracted sojourn at the George V. Lennon and McCartney had their work cut out for them, as Epstein had inked their first film deal back in October with United Artists, who—not surprisingly, given George's association with the Beatles and his previous soundtrack credits—commissioned him to provide the incidental music. The film's producer, Walter Shenson, had no illusions about the motives of Brian and the Beatles for so quickly branching out into cinema. As Shenson later remarked, they wanted to make the movie "for the express purpose of having a soundtrack album." Pointedly, the Beatles had agreed to make the movie with a certain sense of understandable trepidation. They had become pop stars in what, for the record-buying public at least, must have seemed like the blink of an eye. But they harbored no fantasies about becoming bona fide actors, realizing that music was their bailiwick. Lennon had stridently informed the band's manager, "We don't fancy being Bill Haley and the Bellhops, Brian," in a clear reference to *Rock Around the Clock*, the 1956 rock musical that featured Bill Haley and His Comets, the Platters, and the Bellhops.[15]

They had new tunes to write for their silver-screen debut, and their first effort out of the gate had resulted in a playful, bluesy tune called "Can't Buy Me Love." After hearing the song for the first time in Paris, without benefit of his trusty stool across the channel at Abbey Road, the A&R head offered his usual succinct diagnosis. In its original construction, "Can't Buy Me Love" was fairly loose, with backing vocals that echoed McCartney's lead. In an instant, Martin knew what must be done. "We've got to have an introduction," he told the band, "something that catches the ear immediately, a hook. So let's start out with the chorus." In such moments, George's innate sense of hitmaking—of the elements that draw listeners into the structure of a song—came to the fore. In this way, "I designed the opening phrase," he later wrote. "That was the tag, and it grabbed people. Only then did the song go into the verse." And that was it. In a matter of moments, Martin had put the finishing touches on a Lennon-McCartney composition that he had only just heard for the first time. After George recorded four takes in the space of an hour, "Can't Buy Me Love" was ready for mass consumption. It even had a nifty guitar solo from Harrison, who had struggled to find the right sound for "This Boy" back in October. But not this time. His latest effort was a masterpiece of high-octane rock 'n' roll, rendered even more potent, eerily enough, by the leakage from previous takes that can be overheard in the recording's extreme background. In retrospect, it may seem like an odd artifact in a Beatles recording, given Martin's penchant for care and perfection when it came to the band's work. But Harrison's staccato stabs of sound somehow render "Can't Buy Me Love" even more intriguing, a kind of found object in the recording studio that Martin shrewdly allowed to survive in the mix. It wasn't the first time that he had opted to leave well enough alone where the Beatles' sound was concerned—and it would hardly be the last.[16]

As it turned out, work on "Can't Buy Me Love" hadn't been completed after all. During a mixing session on March 10—nearly a month and a half after the Beatles had returned from Pathé Marconi and, pointedly, after another one of Beatlemania's seismic shifts had transformed their lives yet again—George discovered a technical problem in the Paris recordings. After playing the tapes of "Can't Buy Me Love," the A-side of their next single, slated for release on March 20, George detected an audible flaw in Ringo's hi-hat part. As Emerick surmised, "Perhaps because it had been spooled incorrectly, the tape had a ripple in it, resulting in the intermittent loss of treble on Ringo's hi-hat cymbal." With Smith and Langham in the control room, Martin's excitement over the track quickly turned to anguish. The EMI staffers were under enormous pressure to mix "Can't Buy Me Love" and turn it over to the folks at Hayes, the technicians responsible for supervising EMI's record-manufacturing activities. They could rerecord Ringo playing his hi-hat, but the Beatles' drummer wasn't available, as he was over in Twickenham, acting in a key scene during the production of their first feature film. As

George Martin, aged sixteen, during an amateur production by the Quavers, a drama troupe sponsored by a local church in Bromley. *Courtesy of Gregory Paul Martin*

LEFT: Known by George as his "fairy godfather," Sidney Harrison (1903–1986) was an accomplished pianist and Guildhall School professor. George's association with Harrison led to his introduction to the Guildhall School and, later, to EMI's Oscar Preuss. *Publicity photo/BBC*

RIGHT: In 1946 George met Jean "Sheena" Chisholm (1921–2014), who served in the Wrens, the Women's Royal Navy Service branch. Five years older than George, Sheena was the leading soprano at King's College Chapel in Aberdeen. *Courtesy of Gregory Paul Martin*

During the months before his demobilization in Aberdeen, George sang in the choir with Sheena at King's College Chapel. George is in the back row (second from the left) with Sheena standing directly in front of him. *Courtesy of Gregory Paul Martin*

George and Sheena in Aberdeen (c. 1946), with Sheena's father, John Chisholm, a name George later adopted as a pseudonym during his comedy production and film-scoring years. *Courtesy of Gregory Paul Martin*

George and Sheena on their wedding day at the University of Aberdeen on January 3, 1948, George's twenty-second birthday. *Courtesy of Gregory Paul Martin*

George, sporting a goatee, during his Guildhall School years with Sheena. *Courtesy of Gregory Paul Martin*

George and Sheena with John Chisholm during the young A&R man's early years with EMI. *Courtesy of Gregory Paul Martin*

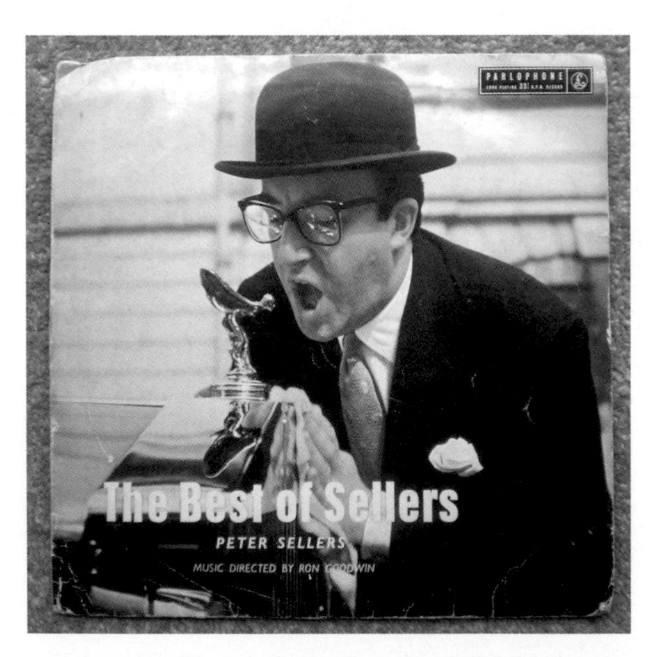


*The Best of Sellers* (1958), Martin's breakthrough comedy long-player with British comedian and actor Peter Sellers (1925–1980). A collection of sketches and comic songs, *Best of Sellers* was a top 5 hit on the UK charts. *Publicity photo/EMI*

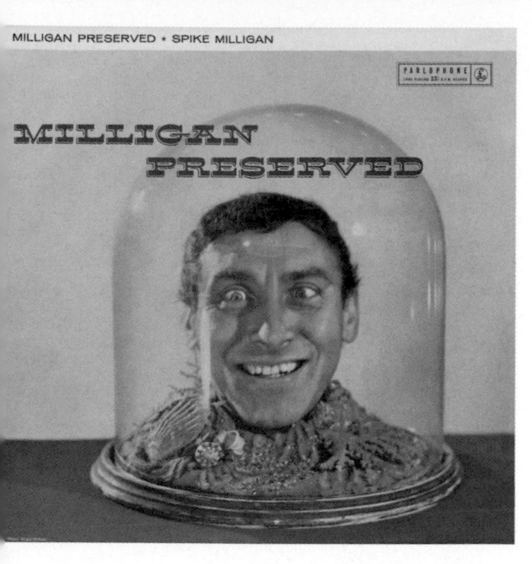


Produced by Martin, *Milligan Preserved* (1961) showcased the talents of Irish comedian and musician Spike Milligan (1918–2002), a member of the Goons along with Sellers, Harry Secombe, and Bernard Cribbins. *Publicity photo/EMI*

Martin's archrival at EMI, Norrie Paramor (1914–1979), was British producer and label head for Columbia Records. Paramor earned renown for his work with Cliff Richard nd the Shadows, with whom he enjoyed a string of hit singles on the UK charts in the late 1950s and early '60s. *Publicity photo/EMI*

A novice talent manager from Liverpool, Brian Epstein (1934–1967) first met Martin in February 1962 during his quest for a recording contract for a four-piece rock combo who called themselves the Beatles. At the time, Epstein was well known at EMI as one of the most successful record retailers in the North Country. *Publicity photo/NEMS*

During the Beatles' second session with Martin on September 4, 1962, the band was joined by drummer Ringo Starr. Under Martin's supervision, they recorded "How Do You Do It," along with five Lennon-McCartney originals: "Tip of My Tongue," "Ask Me Why," "P.S. I Love You," "Love Me Do," and a new number called "Please Please Me." *Getty Images*

Originally recorded by Martin and the Beatles in June 1962, the band's debut single was remade in September for an October 5, 1962, release on Parlophone. During the last week of the year, it peaked at number seventeen on the UK charts. *Courtesy of Adrian Brown*

The Beatles arrive at New York City's John F. Kennedy International Airport on February 7, 1964, in advance of their legend-making appearance on *The Ed Sullivan Show*, for which they enjoyed a television audience of seventy-three million viewers, not only the largest television audience in history at that point but also representing an astounding 40 percent of the US population. *Publicity photo/UPI*

Martin and the bandmates pose with gold discs marking their incredible record sales at the height of Beatlemania. In 1963 alone, Martin's acts held the number-one spot on the UK charts for thirty-seven weeks. *Getty Images*

George Harrison with Richard Lester (b. 1932), the American director behind *A Hard Day's Night*, the Beatles' feature film debut. Working with a $560,000 budget provided by United Artists, Lester shot the film in a cinema verité style using black-and-white film. *Publicity photo/United Artists*

Martin's second long-player, *George Martin Scores Instrumental Versions of the Hits* (1965), was recorded as part of his United Artists solo deal. *Publicity photo/United Artists*

Ringo was being filmed eating a stale sandwich and clumsily throwing darts in a Winchester Road pub, George and Norman were forced to improvise in a hurry. As Emerick recalled, they "took it upon themselves to make a little artistic adjustment. As I eagerly moved into the engineer's seat for the first time, Norman headed down into the studio to overdub a hastily set-up hi-hat onto a few bars of the song while I recorded him, simultaneously doing a two-track to two-track dub. Thanks to Norman's considerable skills as a drummer, the repair was made quickly and seamlessly, and I doubt if even the Beatles themselves ever realized that their performance had been surreptitiously augmented." As for EMI's meticulous records: the notation at Abbey Road's call sheets that morning merely referred to a performance by an unnamed "drummer" who received a standard musicians' union fee. As the release date for "Can't Buy Me Love" loomed only ten days later, the pressure under which Martin and Smith toiled was no small matter: by this point, there were more than a million advance orders for the Beatles' next single already waiting to be fulfilled. It was an incredible gauge of consumer demand by any measure, raising the stakes in a business that seemed to be changing—in terms of its size, scope, and even its institutional hierarchies—almost by the day.[17]

During this period, George—not to mention the whole of the industry in which he worked—still thought of and, in fact, referred to himself as a "recording manager" as opposed to a "record producer." The advent of multi-track recording in the service of popular music accelerated the concept of the producer as a creative director of sorts who worked on behalf of recording "artists" to bring their collaborative vision to life in the studio. As George and the Beatles fully entered the world of four-track recording, the Parlophone head saw his role transforming from supervising the band's work in the studio—the traditional bailiwick of the A&R man as chief organizer—into principally an artistic concern and less of a managerial one. George's experience in the United Kingdom was mirrored by the rise of the record producer in the United States, as evidenced by Phil Spector's growing reputation for creating an artificial "Wall of Sound" within the studio. In 1964 Spector had even gone so far as to self-consciously highlight the producer's role in the creation of the art object via advertisements for the Righteous Brothers' "You've Lost That Lovin' Feeling," which was pointedly attributed to "Phil Spector's Wall of Sound." Spector's cult of personality was so pervasive by this juncture that it nearly overwhelmed the Righteous Brothers' own part in performing the song, which was released on Spector's house label, Philles Records, and which the American producer had cowritten with Barry Mann and Cynthia Weil. For George, the idea of the record producer's imprint being as important as the artist's, if not more so, was absurd. Years later, he would write that "the producer's role has completely changed. He works with the engineer to create something which, in terms of normal acoustics, is not possible, something which is larger than life. He is there to superimpose his will on the artist, to steer the recording into the particular musical direction he wants."[18]

For George, the idea of a producer exerting any "will" over the artist was anathema—akin to Norrie Paramor deploying a series of aliases to procure unearned songwriting credits on his clients' B-sides. George saw the emergence of multitrack recording as an opportunity to make art come to life in the studio—a clear harking back to his Guildhall days when he began to see orchestration as a means for creating "subtle colorings" and to imagine music as a "three-dimensional form." He saw multitrack recording as a "great blessing" that gave him the "freedom to re-think. Like a painter in oils who doesn't like a couple of lines in his picture, he can go back over his work, erasing it and filling in with something new." Songs such as "I Want to Hold Your Hand" and "Can't Buy Me Love" were rudimentary examples of the studio's seemingly infinite capabilities as a creative space for genuine collaboration between artist and producer. The most effective kind of producer, George later wrote, "uses his own thoughts and those of the group, collating and assembling them and rejecting the ones that are no good. So another element in the make-up of a good producer becomes the ability to choose: to choose between what works and what does not work—and, what is most important, to choose quickly."[19]

For the Beatles' producer, this latter aspect had become truly paramount in the early weeks of 1964, as the band achieved unimagined heights of success and the demands on their time shifted from being merely onerous to becoming downright exhausting. As it happened, Martin and the Beatles didn't work together again until February 25, Harrison's twenty-first birthday. But by then, everything had changed—utterly. While they were still hunkered down for their extended stay in Paris, the Beatles got the news not only that they had achieved a much-longed-for American breakthrough but also that "I Want to Hold Your Hand" had blistered its way to the top of the US charts. As Martin later wrote, "America mattered. It mattered because, quite simply, it was the biggest record market in the world. In January 1964, when 'I Want to Hold Your Hand' reached number one in the American charts, it opened that market to us." Years later, he would wistfully recall the very moment when he learned the happy news. He was asleep in his bed at Paris's

George V Hotel when his slumber was interrupted by a telephone call from Brian, his voice besotted by drink. "We're number one in America on next week's charts. It's quite definite. I've been on the phone to New York." With the sounds of Brian's merriment ringing in his ears, George sank back into his bed and laughed with utter, unchecked abandon before hurrying out with Judy to join in the celebration.[20]

After toiling for fourteen years in the British record industry, George was keenly aware of the implications of having made the cross-cultural leap across the Atlantic. "If our excitement seems over-dramatic in retrospect," he cautioned, "it is important to remember that no British artist had got near breaking into that market in the same way. America had always been the El Dorado of the entertainment world. In the glory days of Hollywood we used to worship the British stars who went over there and managed to make it—Robert Donat, Madeleine Carroll, Ronald Colman, C. Aubrey Smith, Cary Grant, Ray Milland, and, of course, Charlie Chaplin. To make it big in the world, you had to make it big in America." Would George and the Beatles, with Brian as the band's canny rep, be able to make it in that twentieth-century El Dorado? Would they finally be able to catch a glimpse of that lost city of gold?[21]

# 11

# A REALLY BIG SHEW

WHILE THE STAGE was clearly set for the band's US debut, in truth it had been unfolding behind the scenes for months. Back on November 4, 1963—only a scant few days after Beatlemania had been born in the wake of their triumph at the Palladium—the group had performed their infamous Royal Variety Command Performance at the Prince of Wales Theatre. Before closing their set with "Twist and Shout," John impudently announced to the venue's regal audience, "For our last number, I'd like to ask your help. The people in the cheaper seats, clap your hands, and the rest of you, if you'd just rattle your jewelry." The fires of British Beatlemania had been mightily stoked within the space of a single week, and Brian took full advantage of the band's growing momentum. Having seen television turn up trumps for the Beatles in the form of the United Kingdom's *Thank Your Lucky Stars* and Val Parnell's *Sunday Night at the London Palladium*, Brian knew exactly where to go in order to try his luck with an American audience. Within days of the Royal Command Variety Performance, he was on a plane bound for New York City and a fateful meeting with American television personality Ed Sullivan. The music business had always been pocked with tales about lucky breaks, and the Beatles had one on the morning of October 31 at London's Heathrow Airport. As it happened, Sullivan had flown in from the United States to scout out talent for his popular CBS variety show when he and his wife, Sylvia, encountered the thousands of ecstatic fans who had gathered at the airport to welcome their idols home. He dutifully asked his son-in-law, producer Bob Precht, to do a little detective work and learn more about the

Beatles' UK phenomenon. By November 11, Epstein met with Sullivan in New York City, and the dueling impresarios hastily struck a deal: for $10,000, plus expenses, the Beatles would perform on three consecutive installments of Sullivan's program. In retrospect, the only sticking point during the negotiation involved the band's billing. Epstein insisted that the Beatles enjoy top billing for all three performances, although Sullivan's producer initially demurred, denouncing the idea as "ridiculous," Epstein later recalled, "because a group hadn't made it big in the States for a long long time and certainly not an English group." But Brian refused to give an inch, cleaving to his belief that "America would make us or break us as world stars." With the band slated to perform at the top of the bill on *The Ed Sullivan Show* in early February, Brian worked with pioneering promoter Sid Bernstein, who signed them for a pair of shows at Carnegie Hall that same week. For the moment, Brian's work was done, leaving things in George's hands as far as Beatles product went.[1]

With a major American television appearance in the offing for February 9, 1964, the ball was firmly in the EMI Group's court to ensure that the Beatles were ready for mass-market consumption in the United States. With a much-needed assist from the EMI brass, George aimed his sights at Capitol Records, the EMI subsidiary that had been rejecting the parent company's British releases since 1955. By this point, his disgust with his Capitol counterparts' practices was well known to Len Wood, who was finally ready to join the fight. According to George, in all fairness to Len "it had not been easy" to break through Capitol Records' red tape, an iron-clad barrier that Dave E. Dexter Jr. had been maintaining for years. "From the moment the Beatles broke in England in January 1963 we had tried terribly hard to sell them in America," George wrote, but "everything we attempted seemed to meet a resounding slap in the face. By then, of course, EMI had bought Capitol, so I was naturally enthusiastic about making use of our company in the States. Immediately following the success of 'Please Please Me' I had said: 'Right! Let's ship Beatle records over to the States and get them sold there.' I got a curt reply from Alan Livingston, the president of Capitol: 'We don't think the Beatles will do anything in this market.'" Things came to a head with EMI's American subsidiary in November, when Dexter continued his earlier stonewalling behavior—not to mention Livingston's bland dismissal of the Beatles—and rejected "I Want to Hold Your Hand" in his usual knee-jerk fashion in spite of the fact that the band's latest single already had advance orders for more than one million copies.[2]

By the time that Epstein returned to the United Kingdom—having succeeded in booking the Beatles on the most popular American variety show for three consecutive appearances in the new year—Wood had taken matters into his own hands and flown to New York City, where he summoned Livingston out from California for an urgent meeting. Having racked up nearly three hundred thousand advance orders for *With the Beatles* at that point, EMI simply could no longer wait for Capitol to come around. Given that EMI held 96 percent ownership of Capitol Records, the tenor of the meeting was decidedly in favor of Wood, who issued Sir Joseph Lockwood's mandate that EMI's American subsidiary release "I Want to Hold Your Hand" without delay. Having been informed that he would not be allowed to exit the meeting until he agreed to release the Beatles, Livingston had no choice but to adhere to Lockwood's dictate. After the meeting, Livingston originally planned to press a mere five thousand copies of "I Want to Hold Your Hand," but with *The Ed Sullivan Show* in the offing, Capitol saw the writing on the wall, hastily raised the number of pressings to two hundred thousand, and earmarked the unheard of sum of $40,000 to promote the single in the United States. By the time that the bandmates actually landed on US soil, Capitol had upped the number of pressings substantially, even going so far as to hire out their rivals' manufacturing plants to pick up the slack. By the end of January, still a week away from the band's arrival in New York City, American record stores had sold more than two million Beatles records. In retrospect, Livingston's decision to put money behind the Beatles' American debut would emerge as one of the shrewdest PR moves in entertainment history. But to Martin's mind, the irony in Livingston's belated moves—and under extreme pressure from Wood, no less—was difficult to accept, even with the incredible narrative that was shortly to unfold on the other side of the Atlantic.

Years later, George would vividly remember the Beatles' historic first visit to the United States in the early afternoon of Friday, February 7, 1964. Flying along with Brian, Judy, and the band, George had learned the astonishing news about the Beatles' ecstatic welcoming party moments before their Pan Am jet landed at New York City's John F. Kennedy International Airport. As McCartney later recalled, "The pilot had rung ahead and said, 'Tell the boys there's a big crowd waiting for them.'" And what a crowd it was: some four thousand fans, along with hundreds of police officers and journalists, waiting to get a glimpse of the group that had already taken America by storm—and yet hadn't so much as performed a single note on its shores.[3]

After making their way through the melee, the Beatles and their entourage paused in the Pan Am lounge, where the bandmates famously held their first press conference. As the Beatles hurled a spate of one-liners at the press about haircuts and Beethoven, George observed Capitol Records' support staff, who were there to handle the unprecedented event. "When the Beatles first arrived in America, and I with them, the Capitol people were embarrassed to a degree," he later recalled. "They had already been implying that the Beatles were their product, and my appearance naturally cast doubt on that point of view. Their reaction was to keep me out of the way." George made particular note of Alan Livingston, who "ran the whole show. He kept me away from the press, which I must admit seemed a mite peculiar. To top it all, he introduced the Beatles as Capitol recording artists, words which came ill from the lips of the man who had turned them down three times!" As for the Beatles, they soon fell into the orbit of "Murray the K" Kaufman, a DJ with WINS AM in New York City who just as quickly branded himself as "the Fifth Beatle," insinuating himself into their entourage for the duration of the band's American visit.[4]

But years later, George's most profound impression of those heady days in New York was the sheer mania exhibited by the Beatles' newfound American fans. "There was a complete, collective madness, which it is hard for anyone who was not there to understand," he would remember years later. "Middle-aged men were walking down Fifth Avenue wearing Beatle wigs to show how in tune they were. The boys were staying at the Plaza Hotel, at the top of Fifth Avenue on Central Park. There is a sort of pedestrian precinct outside the hotel, and, throughout the time the Beatles were there, this square was jammed solid with people, like Trafalgar Square on election night." Although George stayed at the Plaza Hotel along with the rest of the entourage, at the invitation of a friend, Judy stayed several blocks away at the Vassar Women's Club. Like George, she initially felt self-conscious about their reasons for being in the United States in the first place, as if being nearly two decades older than the Beatles' teenaged demographic was something about which to be embarrassed. Judy felt this most acutely at the Vassar Women's Club. "All the ladies staying there spent their time telling Judy the places of cultural interest she might visit while in New York," George later wrote. "She didn't like to reply that she was really there for the Beatles' concerts." For her part, though, Judy was no prude. As Cilla Black later recalled, "The Beatles loved her even though she was dead posh. She had an incredible sense of humor."[5]

As it happened, there was simply no escaping the Beatles that fabled weekend in New York City. Their music and image were everywhere George and Judy looked. While the couple had already experienced a healthy dose of Beatlemania in the United Kingdom the previous fall, it seemed almost incomprehensible that it was happening all over again—and on an even grander scale than they could ever possibly have dreamed. The Beatles were more profuse than ever, and George and Judy were teetering on a state of shock throughout that incredible weekend. "If you switched on the radio at any time of day or night, on any station, you would hear a Beatles song, and New York is certainly not short of radio stations," George wrote. "By then a year of recording had passed, and [in the United States] we had an album out, an EP, and five singles. I had recorded about 20 titles, and they played them all, all the time." But even more staggering was the climactic event on Sunday night when the Beatles performed "All My Loving," "Till There Was You," "She Loves You," "I Saw Her Standing There," and "I Want to Hold Your Hand" on *The Ed Sullivan Show*. Before the live broadcast, they had taped a brief set for the program's February 23 episode. Three straight weekends on Sullivan's popular variety show was a coup for any act. On a typical weekend, the program drew twenty-one million viewers. But on February 9, as the bandmates made their American debut, *The Ed Sullivan Show* enjoyed an audience of seventy-three million; not only was it the largest television audience in history at that point but also it represented an astounding 40 percent of the US population.[6]

For George, watching as the Beatles conquered American audiences on an unprecedented scale, it was a moment of stunning redemption—a validation of his first impression of the group back on that fateful day in June 1962, when he had been "diminished" simply because they had left the studio and disappeared into the night. "Of course, it wasn't the music alone which caused the hysteria, just as the music had not been the sole reason for my signing the Beatles in the first place," he later reflected. "That enjoyable charisma came through to the world at large, which was seeing something it had not seen before. It was an expression of youth, a slight kicking-over of the traces, which found a ready response in young people." For George and Judy, seeing that same hysteria writ large in New York City had, if only at first, a kind of distancing effect, as if they were suddenly realizing the initial pangs of the "generation gap" that would become a matter of ever more strident cultural conversation as the decade wore on.[7]

On Tuesday, February 11, George and Judy joined the Beatles on their train ride from New York City to Washington, DC, where the band played their first US concert at the Washington Coliseum. The group performed the event, which was being filmed by CBS for a March closed-circuit telecast in American cinemas, in the round. After every third or fourth song, the band's longtime roadie Mal Evans would shift Ringo's drum riser so that the Beatles could face a different quadrant of the audience. Everything worked fairly well until the drum riser became inexplicably stuck, briefly interrupting the festive proceedings. George later recalled that

> the audience, despite the various parental presences, was mostly teenage, and very hot. In the seat next to me, a little girl was bouncing up and down and saying, "Aren't they just great? Aren't they just fabulous?"
>
> "Yes, they are," I said, somewhat inadequately for her, I suppose.
>
> "Do you like them too, sir?" she asked.
>
> "Yes, I do rather," I said, all too aware that she couldn't understand what this old man was doing sitting next to her!

For George, it was a genuinely transfixing moment. The band that he, along with Brian, had slaved over to bring up from their comparatively primitive musical state when he first met them back at Abbey Road was bursting forth in full flower right in front of him—right in front of the world. And a few moments later, "when the boys played a song like 'I Want to Hold Your Hand,' and everybody in the audience started singing with them," George and Judy could no longer help themselves. They, too, had fallen under the Beatles' spell: "Judy and I just found ourselves standing up and screaming along with the rest." How could they possibly resist?[8]

Years later, George would find himself reflecting on the roots of Beatlemania. What, indeed, had caused a veritable mass of human beings to become so ecstatic about the Liverpool band? As he had previously observed, it couldn't merely be their music, as different and groundbreaking as it may have been. "That may sound daft," he later wrote, "but it was exactly the same screaming that adults do at football matches. And for us especially, in the midst of 60 thousand people who were all enjoying themselves to the full, identifying completely with the people who were performing, people we knew intimately, people with whom we had made all the records and every little bit of music—in that situation it was all too easy to scream, to be swept up in that tremendous current of buoyant happiness and exhilaration."[9]

But as events would demonstrate, there was a dark side to Beatlemania, too, and it became starkly apparent during the early morning of February 12, only scant hours after the band's exhilarating concert at the Washington Coliseum. Ringo's drum riser aside, the evening had been an incredible triumph. And an invitation to be feted by their countrymen at the British embassy promised something even more special: the opportunity to be accepted by the glitterati. The occasion was a gala benefit for the National Society for the Prevention of Cruelty to Children hosted by Lady Ormsby-Gore. Bleary eyed from the concert back at the coliseum, George and the Beatles trudged through the snow, finally making it to the embassy around one o'clock in the morning only to be greeted by a rip-roaring ballroom filled to the brim with three hundred well-heeled guests. Everyone there was posh—*very* posh indeed. "We want autographs!" they shouted, with one woman asking, not even bothering to conceal her deep tones of sarcasm, "Can they really write?" As Canadian journalist Bruce Phillips later reported, "There was more than a hint of the master-servant relationship in one [embassy official's] voice when he said: 'Come along, you there, you've got to come and do your stuff.'" For his part, George could not believe what he was seeing. As he later recalled, the room held a "full quota of chinless wonders who behaved abominably. They would approach the boys with an off-hand 'Oh, which one are you?'"[10]

And that's when things took a decided turn for the worse as the masked ball transformed into bedlam for the Beatles. As George, Brian, and Judy looked on in horror, one of the diplomats' wives sneaked up behind Ringo and, with her nail scissors at the ready, snipped a sizable lock of his hair as an impromptu souvenir. "What the hell do you think you're doing?" the usually amiable drummer shrieked. "It almost created a diplomatic incident," George wrote. Not surprisingly, the bandmates and their entourage beat a hasty retreat, with John later saying, "Some bloody animal cut Ringo's hair. I walked out, swearing at all of them, I just left in the middle of it." But of course, it was worse than that. In an instant, George and the Beatles had been reminded, in a deeply personal way, about the role of class in British social politics. Already keenly aware of their social station, the bandmates couldn't help but feel that the event had put them in their place. For his part, George couldn't help but feel the same pangs of effrontery. It was not so long ago that he, too, hailed from the wrong side of the tracks in North London, where a person was judged by the quality of their accent, not to mention the heft of their wallet. As Ringo stood there in the ballroom, the violation cut far deeper than his scalp. The incident made for yet another reminder, as the drummer would later put it, that to the kinds of folks who frequent high-society embassy soirees, the Beatles would always be "shitkickers from Liverpool." Perhaps even worse yet, it was how, in their darkest moments, the Beatles (and possibly even George, their elder statesman) still saw themselves. Photographer Harry Benson was especially struck by the group's reaction as they left the embassy that night. "They were very sad," he later remarked. "They looked as if they wanted to cry, John, in particular. They weren't pugnacious. They were humiliated." For Brian, the incident was nothing short of disaster. "Morale is vital," he later wrote. "I do everything I can to sustain it at the highest level, and though I can often ill-afford time away from the desk and the telephone, I travel thousands—tens of thousands of miles—to be with my artistes at important times and at times not so important." That moment in the embassy was clearly one of those important times. He was there, as always, to protect them, but there was nothing he could have reasonably done to prevent a sneak attack by a socialite with a pair of scissors. His only recourse would be to never place his most cherished clients in harm's way again.[11]

George would later describe the Beatles' fortnight stateside as "some giant three-ring circus from which there was no let-up." Even during these early moments, as Brian, George, and the Beatles watched in awe as their dreams of success came true, the Parlophone head could see something else emerging as well, something well beyond their ken. In short order, the Beatles found themselves under an extraordinary media microscope the like of which most people—save for Elvis Presley—could scarcely understand. "Every little snippet of information about what they ate, what they drank, how they slept, almost whether they breathed, was grist to the media mill," George wrote. "Interviews quickly became tedious, because they would be asked the same old questions again and again. On those rare occasions when a question was out of the ordinary, they would rise to it and try to score off it. For example, they might have been going through a stock run of questions like 'How do you write your music? Do you write the words as well as the music?' Then out of the blue some bright spark might suddenly ask, 'Well, now, do you think cornflakes are affecting the intelligence of the average American male?' Off the top of his head, John Lennon might come straight back with something like 'No, but I think cocaine might have done.' The next day the headlines would read 'John Lennon Advocates Cocaine.' Every little thing they said became translated into Beatle instructions as to how we should behave."[12]

George recognized that the bandmates simply lacked the kinds of life experiences to prepare them for the media onslaught, that the incident back at the British embassy was only just the beginning of their highly public tightrope walk. "After all, they simply didn't have the experience of a Jim Callaghan or Harold Wilson at parrying questions and spotting lurking dangers in their replies," he added. "So they were constantly being proclaimed as advocating things about which they knew little. Then, once attacked, they would be forced into a corner, and find themselves having to justify what they had said. For inexperienced people, it was a very tough ride." But the A&R head was also well aware of the fact that the Beatles had dared the world to open up its arms to their music, that they had made it to "the toppermost of the poppermost!" and beyond, and that everything they undertook was in the service of moving product. "Of course, people may rightly say that the hysteria and the adulation in themselves helped to sell records, and that selling records was what we were trying to do," George allowed. "But somewhere a balance should have been struck—and it never was."[13]

After returning via train from Washington, DC, to New York City, George and the Beatles prepared for the Carnegie Hall performances that Brian had booked with Sid Bernstein the previous November. With the group playing afternoon and evening shows on February 12, Capitol Records saw an opening for recording a live album at the fabled venue. After all, it was a special occasion given that the Beatles would be the first rock act to play Carnegie Hall. To George's mind, it was the perfect opportunity to finally capture the Beatles' stage show on record. Given the extraordinary electricity inherent in the band's live act, he and Brian had regretted their inability to produce a live album during the band's Cavern Club days. For them, Carnegie Hall was a plum chance for righting that wrong. On February 3, while George and the Beatles were still in England, Capitol fashioned a deal in which the Beatles' producer would oversee the recordings with Voyle Gilmore, Capitol's East Coast A&R head. After securing permission from Carnegie to record on the premises with a pro forma $600 fee, Capitol began making preparations to have a mobile unit on hand. But it was all for naught. Before George could so much as adjust a microphone, the American Federation of Musicians registered its objection to George's participation given that he would be acting as nonunion personnel in a recording session. While Capitol dutifully offered to cover the Englishman's union dues, the union simply wasn't willing to establish a precedent. As far as Brian and the bandmates were concerned, no George meant no Beatles. And with that, the live album was kaput.

The Beatles had long exercised a simple form of democracy à la the Three Musketeers: it was always all for one and one for all. And that didn't just go for Lennon, McCartney, Harrison, and Starr—but for Epstein and Martin, too. It would be the mantra that would see them through some of the diciest situations that would come their way, but it would also at times be to their detriment. As far as the February 12 Carnegie Hall shows went, it turned out that their inability to record a live album was a godsend. As Lennon later recalled, "Carnegie Hall was terrible! The acoustics were terrible and they had all these people sitting on the stage with us and it was just like Rockefeller's children backstage and it all got out of hand. It wasn't a rock show; it was just a sort of circus where we were in cages. We were being pawed and talked at and met and touched, backstage and onstage. We were just like animals."[14]

George and the Beatles finally enjoyed a respite when they traveled south for the comparatively balmy environs of Miami Beach. The following Sunday, the bandmates appeared on *The Ed Sullivan Show* yet again—on this occasion, playing before a live studio audience in the Deauville Hotel. Along with Judy, George watched the Beatles, casually clad in their bathing trunks, as they rehearsed in the hotel's Mau Mau Club. Incredibly, the band attracted some seventy million viewers during their performance that evening, nearly equaling their record-setting pace the week before. For the Britons, one of the clear highlights involved a lazy day at a Capitol Record executive's beachside estate. They managed to sneak away to the seaside manse courtesy of a Miami cop, Sergeant Buddy Bresner, who arranged for the Beatles to escape the throng waiting outside the Deauville Hotel by stowing the group in the back of a butcher truck. George would never forget that day at the beach with Brian, Judy, and the Beatles. While the Capitol exec was absent, he left an armed security guard in his place to ensure the safety of his special guests. As George and Judy watched in a kind of mild horror, their bodyguard—with a cigarette dangling from his mouth and his shoulder holster plainly visible—grilled steaks on the barbecue. As George later recalled, "Brian was complaining about all the bootleg records that were coming out. Suddenly, this tough-looking guy who was barbecuing our steaks leaned forward and said, 'You want we should take care of them for you, Mr. Epstein?' It was a very sinister moment."[15]

While Brian and the Beatles stayed at the Capitol exec's estate, George and Judy found accommodations at a "crummy little motel" in Miami. As with their visit to New York City, George was being overtly careful about paying for his and Judy's travel expenses without asking for or accepting support from EMI, which had famously pinched every possible penny throughout his experience with the multinational conglomerate. By this juncture, his relationship with Parlophone's parent company was beginning to reach a fever pitch in spite of the unprecedented success that he had garnered for EMI via the Beatles. In point of fact, the matter of his 1963 holiday bonus still stuck in his craw. This was the state of circumstances that led to his stay at the bargain-basement motel in the midst of the Beatles' first conquering of America. As it happened, the couple's first night at the motel was interrupted by a knock at the door by the hotel's front desk clerk. George later recalled that it was about 10:30 PM and he was in his dressing gown when the clerk announced, rather sternly, "You haven't paid your deposit. I want 25 dollars." In George's memory, the clerk "obviously thought we might abscond in the morning before paying our bill. Feeling very irritated, I had to rummage around to give him the money." But Judy wasn't finished with the matter. The next morning, she sought out the manager to give him a piece of her mind. With a "stern glare," she remarked, "I have been in many hotels and many private homes in America, and I've always received the utmost of courtesy. I've always thought the Americans were a fine nation of people, very polite and helpful. Never have I encountered such a rude person, nor have I been treated so shabbily in any hotel." Instead of acquiescing to her understandable annoyance, the clerk said, "Don't stop lady," before summoning a colleague: "Hey, Al, come and get a load of this!" It was a strange conclusion, indeed, to that (mostly) magical first foray for George and the band on American soil. And after trying their hand at waterskiing and sparring for the cameras with boxer Cassius Clay (later immortalized as Muhammad Ali), the Beatles, with George and Judy safely in tow, flew back to the United Kingdom.[16]

As they made their ascent over the Atlantic, the group held the top two spots on the American LP charts with *Meet the Beatles!*—Capitol's repackaging of *With the Beatles*, along with "I Saw Her Standing There" and the "I Want to Hold Your Hand" backed with "This Boy" single—having settled into *Billboard* magazine's upper echelons for a lengthy residence. And then there was *Introducing . . . the Beatles*. Held in abeyance by Vee-Jay Records since the previous spring, the latter album had powered the tiny Chicago label all the way to number two on *Billboard*'s album charts. As far as George was concerned, the label deserved all the credit in the world for having the gumption to purchase the licensing rights to the contents of *Please Please Me*, courtesy of Transglobal, when Capitol wouldn't bother to get off the dime. As *Introducing . . . the Beatles* gurgled just below *Meet the Beatles!* on the US charts, all that the Parlophone head could see was a bitter reminder of Capitol's inability to recognize pop gold in spite of all of his impassioned pleas on the Beatles' behalf. And besides, he knew that he had been right all along. For George, the proof was *always* in the pudding.

By the time the band's third, prerecorded performance on *The Ed Sullivan Show* was broadcast, the Beatles were already back in London, where they were preparing for their first recording session in nearly a month. Having returned to the friendly confines of Abbey Road on February 25, George and the group tried their hand at a new song, "You Can't Do That," another number slated for possible inclusion on the soundtrack for their feature film, which was set to begin shooting on March 2. John had composed the tune during their sojourn in Miami Beach. In addition to producing the Beatles' songs for the unnamed rock musical, George was tasked with composing the orchestral interludes for the United Artists film, which was to be directed by

Richard Lester, an American transplant who had cut his teeth bringing independent programs to British television, most notably *The Goon Show*. By the time that they set to work on "You Can't Do That," it had been slated as the B-side for "Can't Buy Me Love." A twelve-bar blues tune in the vein of Wilson Pickett, "You Can't Do That" was a pulsating rocker that Harrison punctuated with his new twelve-string Rickenbacker, which he had been given during the band's bravura visit to the United States. Recorded over nine takes—of which only four were complete—the song featured Lennon playing a fiery guitar solo on his Rickenbacker Capri. Even more impressively, John turned in a rip-roaring, full-throated vocal for the ages. Years later, after journalist Ray Coleman complimented his vocal prowess, the Beatle was taken aback. "You really mean it?" he asked. "I can't say I ever liked hearing myself." For his part, Martin was invariably perplexed about Lennon's "inborn dislike of his own voice, which I could never understand."[17]

The February 25 session was also notable for the appearance of Dick James, their music publisher. He made his presence known during the recording of a new McCartney ballad, "And I Love Her," another track under consideration for the untitled movie's soundtrack. But James, it turned out, was more than a mere studio visitor. During a tape change in Number 2's control room, he told George that he felt the song was "just too repetitive." In apparent agreement, George met with the band downstairs in the studio, where he recommended that they add a middle eight to break up the monotony of the verses. As Dick later recalled, "I think it was John who shouted, 'OK, let's have a tea break,' and John and Paul went to the piano and, while Mal Evans was getting tea and some sandwiches, the boys worked at the piano. Within half an hour they wrote, there before our very eyes, a very constructive middle to a very commercial song. Although we know it isn't long, it's only a four bar middle, nevertheless it was just the right ingredient to break up the over repetitive effect of the original melody."[18]

It was unusual for the Beatles to accept many visitors during their hours in the studio with George. Even Brian, who was integral to the Beatles' enterprise, kept his distance during this period, when the group was forced to make the most of their increasingly few and far between opportunities to create new work at Abbey Road. James's inroad into Martin and the band's artistic process, which by all accounts seems to have been welcomed at this juncture, underscores the notion of the sort of "corporate authorship" that characterized the band's early years with Martin at the helm. While more often than not the songs they recorded were released under the Lennon-McCartney moniker, the band's sound benefited from elements of Harrison, Starr, and

Martin's creativity and craftsmanship throughout this period. Flush with the magnitude of their success, the Beatles seemed open to external influences—most significantly, George's—in the service of their music. When the group resumed work on "And I Love Her," they rehearsed the new bridge while recording two initial takes. Later that afternoon, they concluded the day's work with yet another new number—John's up-tempo "I Should Have Known Better," which they attempted across three takes. Lennon could barely make it through take two, which devolved into hysterics over his harmonica playing, and not long afterward they closed up shop for the night.

The next day, Martin arrived at Abbey Road early to supervise remixing sessions for "You Can't Do That" and "Can't Buy Me Love" with Smith and Langham. With Capitol now avidly seeking new Beatles product along with EMI, George had begun creating different mixes for different territories—that is the United Kingdom and Europe, on one hand, and the United States, on the other. In the case of "You Can't Do That," George prepared mono and stereo mixes, which were dispatched to the United States for distribution on March 16. George was especially concerned after getting word that Capitol's Canadian subsidiary was considering "Roll Over Beethoven" as a North American follow-up to "I Want to Hold Your Hand." After loudly registering his dissent with this decision, he managed to hold off any new Beatles product until after the release of the "Can't Buy Me Love" backed with "You Can't Do That" single, which, as George predicted, proved to be a global smash hit. In the United States alone, some 1.7 million advance orders preceded the single's release. "Can't Buy Me Love" debuted at number twenty-seven during its first week of release and topped the US charts during its second. It was an incredible leap that remains unmatched to this day. But as usual, the Beatles were only just getting started. While their trifecta of *Ed Sullivan Show* appearances had been a juggernaut all their own, the tidal wave of newly minted American Beatlemania would be registered during the week of April 5, 1964, when *Billboard*'s Hot 100 included a stunning twelve different Beatles singles. Even more impressively, the top five was rounded out by "Can't Buy Me Love" anchoring the toppermost of the poppermost, followed by "Twist and Shout," "She Loves You," "I Want to Hold Your Hand," and "Please Please Me." Surely, this was no flash in the pan.

Interestingly, George would revisit "You Can't Do That" some three months later, on May 22, when he would conduct his own piano overdub for the song, only to scrap the mix before it ever saw the light of day. While it may have seemed innocuous—especially since the single had already topped the charts and begun its slow decline by late May—the fact that George felt that he had the license to pursue his own creative instincts outside the band's earshot underscores the incredible freedom that he enjoyed during this era with the production of Beatles records.

Having put the finishing touches on "You Can't Do That," the bandmates joined George in the studio on the afternoon of February 26, and they resumed work on "I Should Have Known Better," which they perfected—but, for the most part, did not complete—across eighteen takes, most of which did not advance beyond the middle eight. They eventually selected take nine as the final version of the song. "And I Love Her" proved to be considerably more of a challenge as the session wore into the evening. As they worked to remake "And I Love Her," Starr shifted from behind his drum kit to play the bongos, with Harrison chipping in on the claves. Recording fourteen new takes of the song, in addition to the two original attempts the previous evening, George and the Beatles' work on "And I Love Her" finds them slowly but surely shifting away from the breakneck speed with which they made their earliest records into more deliberate, painstaking studio practices, which clearly coincide with their new era of four-track recording. At one point on the night of February 26, Smith announced the recording of take fourteen of "And I Love Her" over Number 2's talkback, to which McCartney jokingly answered, "Ha, take 50!" But the group's generally methodical pace from thenceforward was no joking matter. As George later remarked, "We don't stop until we're confident there is no possibility of further improvement."[19]

On Thursday, February 27, George and the Beatles got started fairly early in the morning at Abbey Road, where they resumed work yet again on "And I Love Her," completing work on the song during the second take of the day. Harrison contributed a melodic solo using his José Ramírez classical guitar, which he had previously deployed on the *With the Beatles* song "Till There Was You." At this point, with principal photography for their first feature film set to commence on Monday, they needed to record additional material for the soundtrack in a hurry. Up first was Lennon's "Tell Me Why," which Martin and the group completed in eight takes. "They needed another upbeat song and I just knocked it off," John later recalled. "It was like a black, New York girl-group song." In addition to marking the completion of "And I Love Her," the February 27 session found Martin and the Beatles beginning work on Lennon's latest ballad, the exquisite "If I Fell." The song's intricate chord structure necessitated several takes for the band to establish the song's timing. Moreover, Lennon and McCartney's complex harmonies necessitated their request to record their vocals with a single microphone, an idea that Martin sanctioned. By this point, he clearly supported their instincts, which he had initially rebuffed in such notable early moments as "Love Me Do" and "How Do You Do It."[20]

At this juncture, George fully recognized the ways in which the band and the producer possessed complementary skills. Indeed, he was so taken with each new gem they presented that he had become content to help shape their sound and structure their compositions during the recording process itself. To this end, George can be heard making intermediate suggestions on February 27 as the tender ballad evolved across fifteen takes that morning. By take three, he had suggested a more pronounced drum sound from Starr. He introduced Lennon's strident acoustic guitar intro by take eleven, when he also recommended Harrison's lead guitar outro. "Something like that, you mean?" Harrison asked as the take concluded. But as professionally as the bandmates worked across those fifteen takes, if there was any doubt about their relative youth in comparison to Martin's more advanced years, it came at the end of take nine, when Lennon, barely twenty-three years old, complained, "I've got an itchy bum."[21]

By take fifteen, Martin had structured the group across four tracks, with Lennon's acoustic guitar, McCartney's bass, and Starr's drums on one track, Lennon and McCartney's vocals on a second, Harrison's twelve-string Rickenbacker on a third, and a fourth track available for Lennon and McCartney to double-track their vocals, as well as for Harrison to add guitar ornamentation during the song's intro and outro sections. All in all, it had been an incredible day for George and the group, who had completed two new Beatles classics—"And I Love Her" and "If I Fell"—in the space of a single day. On its face, it is a remarkable achievement. But in a story that could only be as rich and profuse as the Beatles' at this early stage of their recording career, it was just the beginning. And besides, it would be only the first of many days in which they would complete multiple tracks that by themselves would be the envy of any other artist.

12

# THE FOUR MOP-TOPS

WHEN MARTIN AND THE BANDMATES reconvened three days later on the morning of March 1, 1964—the Beatles' first Sunday session during their nearly twenty-one-month association with Martin—they had no such luck. They were all too aware that they only had seven songs prepared for the soundtrack for their still-untitled feature film, which they were scheduled to begin shooting the very next day. By this point, the film had gone by a variety of potential names, including *The Beatles* and *Beatlemania*, although neither seemed to stick as far as Richard Lester and Walter Shenson were concerned. Compiling a forty-minute long-player necessitated some thirteen or fourteen tracks, which meant that George had his work cut out for him in terms of bringing the album to fruition in order to synchronize its release with the feature film, which was now slated for a July premiere. Moreover, he had to complete work on orchestrating the movie's incidental music for Lester, who was anxious to bring the elements of his eventual film together. Martin and the Beatles, especially Lennon, were great fans of Lester's work, dating back to *The Running Jumping & Standing Still Film*, a 1959 short flick starring Parlophone stalwarts Spike Milligan and Peter Sellers. Lester shot the movie over two Sundays on a shoestring budget of seventy pounds, which was worth its weight in gold, as the film was nominated for an Academy Award—and perhaps even better yet, it nabbed the attention of the Beatles, who counted it among their favorites and sought the auteur out after Epstein landed the deal with United Artists. As events would show, the thirty-two-year-old director was highly cognizant of the media attention that his movie was already receiving given the incredible popularity and visibility of his stars, and principal photography would only serve to shine an even brighter light on his work. Besides, the film wasn't merely the Beatles' feature debut; it was also Lester's first foray into long-form cinema.

For Martin and the Beatles, things got started on the morning of March 1 with "I'm Happy Just to Dance with You," an up-tempo Lennon-McCartney original that neither of the songwriters had any interest in singing. Years later, McCartney would deride it as a "formula" song intentionally written to spotlight Harrison's vocals in the movie. The band made swift work of "I'm Happy Just to Dance with You," which they dispatched in four takes. Martin made full use of the studio's four-track machine, reserving one track for Lennon and Harrison's rhythm and lead guitars, respectively, and a second for McCartney's bass and Starr's drum kit, which left two tracks for Harrison to overdub his vocals, giving his voice a fuller, more powerful texture. Their workmanlike approach to "I'm Happy Just to Dance with You" underscores its place as mere "filler" for the eventual soundtrack album, in contrast with, say, "And I Love Her" or "If I Fell," which they had slaved over. Having run out of fresh material, Martin and the Beatles turned their attentions toward a cover version of Little Richard's "Long Tall Sally," which had long been a staple of their road show, and "I Call Your Name," a Lennon-McCartney original that had previously been relegated to Billy J. Kramer and the Dakotas, second-stringers among Epstein's ever-growing stable of artists.

Knowing the group's protracted history with "Long Tall Sally," Martin self-consciously opted to give the recording a "live" feel, with Lennon and Harrison trading guitar solos while McCartney handled the searing lead vocal that he had been honing since their Quarry Men days. For "I Call Your Name," everyone got into the act, with Martin playing a mean piano part as the group captured the red-hot song in a single take. One of Lennon's earliest compositions, "I Call Your Name" had been recorded by Billy J. Kramer back on June 27, 1963, with Martin in the control room at Abbey Road, as the B-side for "Bad to Me." During a talkback conversation with Martin, Lennon can be heard to be hesitating over whether to use Billy J. Kramer's arrangement, "'cause it's our song anyroad, innit?" The group completed the recording, including a new ska-like solo from Lennon, thus differentiating their version from Kramer's, in a speedy seven takes. As the clock ran out on the day's session, George and the Beatles had added an eighth song to their tally for the feature film's soundtrack while also completing two other songs that they could feed to Capitol's execs, who were now hungry for more Beatles product whenever they could get it. After keeping the Beatles at arm's length for nearly a year, they simply couldn't inject enough of the band's work into an insatiable American marketplace. By this point, Capitol had been eagerly repackaging the Beatles' albums in order to maximize the amount of product that they could ship to US record stores.[1]

In short order, both "Long Tall Sally" and "I Call Your Name" would find a home on *The Beatles' Second Album*, Capitol's long-playing follow-up to *Meet the Beatles!*, which continued to hold down the number-one spot stateside as the bandmates joined Lester at London's Paddington Station on the morning of Monday, March 2, to begin work on their film debut. With a relatively low budget of some $560,000 provided by United Artists, Lester planned to shoot his movie in a cinema verité style using black-and-white film. Lester's set was a slow-moving British Rail car that would ferry the cast and crew around the rural West County for the next six days. As the Beatles met other members of the cast and crew, they hastily joined Actors' Equity—a union official filled out four membership cards while they waited on the platform at Paddington Station. For Lester, the movie was fraught with an element of risk. "The director knew we couldn't act, and we knew," Lennon later remarked. "So he had to try almost to catch us off guard." But as producer Walter Shenson pointed out, Lester and Lennon's concerns were all for naught, as "the Beatles fell right into it, they were naturals. And the script was so good, it sounded like they were making it up as they went along." While the band members turned in admirable performances, the real measure of the film's success belonged to screenwriter Alun Owen, who ingeniously fashioned the Beatles' essential nature—along with a healthy dose of their media-constructed personalities—into his narrative. In many ways, Owen's screenplay managed to capture the rudiments of the charisma that had fascinated Martin on his very first day in the band's presence. As McCartney later recalled, Owen's story line sagely appropriated the "little jokes, the sarcasm, the humor, John's wit, Ringo's laconic manner; each of our different ways. The film manages to capture our characters quite well." Owen's screenplay succeeds by telling the Beatles' story—but telling it slant. "We were like that," Lennon later allowed, but only to a point. Otherwise, the eventual film was "a comic-strip version of what was going on" in the rare air of their unique brand of celebrity.[2]

In its final form, Lester's movie was generally a caricature of the bandmates' experience, save for the movie's last, chilling scene. Years later, critic Peter Tonguette would write that in Lester's film "the group, expectedly, triumphs over the assorted numbskulls, dolts, and squares they encounter—but is there a sadder conclusion to a more life-affirming film than the Beatles' helicopter lifting up in the final shot?" For the world, it was the first glimpse of the group having become virtually imprisoned by their own fame. By the time they alighted in New York City on February 7, 1964, they had been irrevocably reduced to their image as the "mop-tops"—those four lads from Liverpool with the unusual hairstyle. It was the suffocating world of pop culture having gone viral in the mid-1960s United States. George had seen it for himself while walking along Fifth Avenue that very same weekend when he observed middle-aged men donning Beatle wigs in broad daylight.[3]

But the mop-top story hadn't made its way into the public consciousness by accident. Capitol had deployed its $40,000 promotional budget to great effect, with a few well-timed assists from NBC. On a November 18, 1963, episode of the *Huntley-Brinkley Report*, correspondent Edwin Newman presented the first stateside images of British Beatlemania in full bloom, with the Beatles shaking their mop-tops with great abandon. Things heated up considerably by January 3, 1964, with "I Want to Hold Your Hand" generating its own share of stateside buzz, along with the much-ballyhooed upcoming appearance on *The Ed Sullivan Show*. That evening, Jack Paar formally introduced the band to his talk show's sizable American audience with a four-minute report, including images of the shaggy-haired Beatles performing "She Loves You" for ecstatic British teens. Paar described the group and their "crazy hairdos" as a "sociological phenomenon," sarcastically concluding that "it's nice to know that England has finally risen to our cultural level." Capitol's promotion dollars would be translated, if only tangentially, in the print media, including widespread references to the "Beatle haircut." A late January 1964 article in the *Washington Post* made explicit note of the bandmates' "floor-mop" haircuts, while the *New York Times* foretold of the coming arrival of the "mop-haired Beat singers" in early February. Later that month, with the Beatles' images firmly implanted in American synapses, the *Christian Science Monitor* memorialized the band as "Britain's mop-head troupe," cementing their media-honed personae for the broadsheet's substantial daily readership. As events would show, this kind of narrowing of cultural focus would be both the making and unmaking of the band.[4]

But that would happen much later, of course.

As the bandmates shuttled about the countryside on Lester's rail-car set—with their mop-tops on full display—Martin held a series of mixing sessions back in the control room of Abbey Road's Number 2 studio. Like the Beatles, he was under the gun to ensure that the soundtrack came to fruition contemporaneously with the feature film. For George, this meant not only supervising production activities associated with new Beatles recordings but also composing and orchestrating the incidental music. For the past several months, he had been working closely with Lester, Shenson, and Owen to coordinate the project. "I made special recordings with the Beatles of songs which were going into the film," George later recalled, "producing them specifically with the film in mind. Then I had to knit it all together, and write the incidental music. That worked pretty well. What is more, whereas I had been disappointed that the film was to be in black and white, feeling that the first Beatles film ought to be in glamorous color, in the event that worked very well too. Dick Lester's zany editing, and especially his experience in commercials, which enabled him to snap everything into tight, hard-packed little sequences, was excellent."[5]

While Martin admired Lester's technical skills, working so closely with the director had proved to be tough going, particularly given the American's amateur musical background. As Martin later wrote, "The only trouble was that he [Lester] was something of a musician himself. He is the sort of person who, at a nightclub or a party, will go to the piano in the corner and play his idea of jazz to amuse people. He plays jazz piano tolerably well, and he gave me the impression that he considered me inferior to him musically. The adage that a little learning is a dangerous thing was borne out." Given his extraordinarily busy life as head of Parlophone and as the Beatles' producer, Martin sagely decided to disregard Lester's overbearing attitude, preferring to plug away at the latest array of recordings and prepare for the next onslaught as the film's premiere inched ever closer during those heady early months of 1964.[6]

On March 3, George settled into Number 2's control room to mix the latest batch of songs for United Artists' eventual release of the American soundtrack for the feature film. By this point, George's work as producer had become doubly complicated as he had to balance the Beatles' studio output with the divergent demands of the British and American marketplaces, with Parlophone's product line reflecting the group's artistic intentions and Capitol's releases designed to sate the incredible US appetite for the Beatles. The UK and US markets also differed considerably in terms of economic issues. In the United Kingdom, the contents of singles and LP releases generally did not overlap; hence, British fans weren't forced to purchase songs more than once. In the United States, singles acted as previews of sorts for upcoming album releases—as means for generating buzz on the radio to create blockbuster LP sales. And besides, at this juncture avid American fans seemed indifferent to the prospect of buying songs in multiple formats. The only thing they knew for certain was that they wanted new Beatles product as soon as possible. Industry standards regarding the length of long-players also differed in the UK and US marketplaces, with British albums typically including fourteen tracks while their American counterparts featured about a dozen. For Capitol, this slight discrepancy in the number of tracks per LP allowed EMI's American subsidiary to redistribute the band's catalog across more albums during the Beatles' early years, which in turn gave them ample opportunity to ring up much greater stateside sales. In the United States, a penchant for high-fidelity sound—or "hi-fi"—may have also been responsible for the fewer number of tracks on American LPs given the industry's fear of "groove-cramming," in which a record consists of so many songs that sound quality becomes sacrificed. Since the 1950s, American audio manufacturers had marketed the idea of high fidelity as a means of ensuring superior sound reproduction—not to mention as a platform for hawking sophisticated and eminently more expensive playback equipment to audiophiles. By the early 1960s, the latest wave of audio equipment was enhanced by the ability to reproduce stereophonic sound, and the notion of stereo began to slowly displace the cultural capital of hi-fi.

For his part, George was keenly aware of the variant industry practices in the UK and the US marketplaces, and in spite of his long-standing irritation with their preliminary treatment of the Beatles, he eagerly sat down to work with Capitol and United Artists, in the case of the forthcoming soundtrack, to afford them with product of the highest order. Indeed, one of the early hallmarks of his efforts on behalf of the group's recordings was the painstaking care that he unfailingly took in preparing them for release. During their early years together, he carried out these editing and mixing sessions alone or with Smith, as the group members expressed scant interest in the technical side of Martin's business. "The Beatles didn't get totally immersed in record production until later on," he recalled. Even during their twin-track days together, George edited superior moments of performance onto the best takes of particular tracks in order to produce a greater and, to the best of his ability and given the technology of the day, a seamless musical whole. The stakes grew ever higher as the band stacked up one chart-topping single and long-player after another, and George continued to rise to the occasion. With Smith by his side in the control room, he devoted the entirety of the March 3 session to mixing the six new tracks, which would join "Can't Buy Me Love" for consideration on the eventual soundtrack. To this end, George prepared mono mixes from the best takes of "I Should Have Known Better," "If I Fell," "Tell Me Why," "And I Love Her," "I'm Happy Just to Dance with You," and "I Call Your Name." He spent considerable time with "If I Fell," having discovered a flaw in McCartney's vocal in the instance when he reaches up high to sing the word *vain* at the end of the bridge. After several attempts, George remedied the situation by mixing out Paul's offending vocal, which squeaked as he grasped for the high note, during the second iteration of the phrase "new love was in vain." As a consequence, this new mix left John singing alone during the introductory phrases. It was a small price to pay for sanitizing Paul's vocal while also affording the song with greater drama as it slowly builds from John's solo voice into one of John and Paul's finest duets on record.[7]

During control room sessions on March 4 and March 10, with the bandmates still roving the countryside on Lester's slow-moving rail car, Martin returned to Abbey Road in order to experiment further still with the latest batch of Beatles recordings. On March 4, he had mixed a new mono version of "I Call Your Name," which remained unused. March 10 saw Martin and Smith create stereo mixes of "Can't Buy Me Love," "Long Tall Sally," "I Call Your Name," and "You Can't Do That," along with mono mixes of "Komm, Gib Mir Deine Hand" and "Sie Liebt Dich." Despite their efforts that day, not to mention their emergency work on behalf of "Can't Buy Me Love" and Starr's garbled hi-hat, Martin and Smith left most of the material in the EMI vault, save for "Komm, Gib Mir Deine Hand" and "Sie Liebt Dich," for which they created stereo mixes on March 12. In short order, the tapes for the German-language translations were dispatched to West Germany and the United States for release. The experiment that they had begun just a few months earlier in Paris no longer really mattered. By now, the Beatles were a truly global phenomenon, and German fans—like fans the world over—gobbled up the latest Beatles output with zero regard for the language of origin. Meanwhile, back in the United States, Capitol moved so swiftly during this period that cover artwork and copy were completed before they even received George's packages of new Beatles product. As soon as they arrived in Hollywood, the recordings were pressed into masters, which were dutifully shipped to the company's manufacturing plants.

George took a much-needed break from his work with the Beatles for the remainder of March. As Parlophone head, he had plenty of label business to address during his brief hiatus from the Fab Four, and besides, the world's thirst for new Beatles wares was shortly to be quenched on March 20, which marked the release of the hotly anticipated "Can't Buy Me Love" single. Not to overstate the heightened nature of their affairs at the time, but as April and the promise of new Beatles sessions loomed, George existed as the creative mastermind at ground zero of the most popular and groundbreaking musical fusion on earth. The pressure was understandably enormous, and George, after years of toil and hard-wrought experience at EMI, was the right person for the job. Years later, McCartney would attribute his success in molding the band during the early days to Martin's tenure in the Fleet Air Arm, where he learned—often under duress—how to bring people together in the service of a common purpose, as well as how to effect compromises and cooperation. "I think it is an incredible stroke of fate that he had that experience," Paul later recalled. "That's what a producer does. He doesn't write the songs or play them—he doesn't fly the plane—but he is in charge. And that, tied in with his music, made him the perfect producer for the Beatles."[8]

By the time that April 1964 rolled around, George's skills as arbitrator, supervisor, and interpersonal negotiator would prove to be in very high demand. By this point, George and the Beatles were laboring under pressures of a very different sort as principal photography had been completed for the band's untitled feature-film debut. On April 13, things became even more intense as director Richard Lester announced the film's title to the press. Quite suddenly, Lennon and McCartney were confronted with the greatest of songwriting challenges: having to compose a song to order—and more daunting still, a song to be titled "A Hard Day's Night"—given Lester's press conference on April 13. Three days later, on Thursday, April 16, George and the bandmates reconvened for the first time since that Sunday session at the beginning of March. It was a tension-riddled experience in many ways, yet at the same time, the day's events ultimately catapulted George and the Beatles even further along their already-impressive artistic trajectory. But they weren't alone in the studio that evening. Along with Smith and Emerick in the control room, Martin was joined by Lester, who was eager to see his movie's title track unfold in the recording studio. Journalist Maureen Cleave, a writer with the London *Evening Standard* and a close friend of the band's, was also present, having ridden to Abbey Road in the taxi with John.

As it happened, Lennon and McCartney had completed "A Hard Day's Night" only the day before. Finding its origins in a "Ringoism," as John liked to call the drummer's malapropisms, *A Hard Day's Night* emerged as the film's title during a lunch break in which the Beatles joked about Ringo's penchant for prolixity. As the Beatles' drummer recalled in a 1964 radio interview with DJ Dave Hull, he had originally uttered the phrase after playing with the band well into the wee hours: "We went to do a job, and we'd worked all day and we happened to work all night. I came up still thinking it was day I suppose, and I said, 'It's been a hard day,' and I looked around and saw it was dark so I said, 'night!'" After overhearing the story during the lunch break, one of the producers immediately latched onto the phrase. Not long afterward, Shenson approached Lennon, saying, "I'm afraid we're going to need a song called 'A Hard Day's Night,' something up-tempo that can be played over the main titles." The next morning, Lennon called Shenson into his dressing room. "He and Paul were standing there, with their guitars slung over their shoulders," the producer later recalled. "John fiddled with a matchbook cover on which were scrawled the lyrics to a song—'A Hard Day's Night'—which they played and sang to perfection. This was 10 hours after I'd asked for a song." When they'd finished playing the tune, Lennon glared at Shenson and said, "Okay, that's it, right?" After the producer weakly answered in the affirmative, John said, "Good. Now don't bother us about songs anymore."[9]

On the evening of April 16, Lennon arrived in Number 2 with the lyrics of "A Hard Day's Night" now scrawled on the back of a greeting card for his son, Julian, who had celebrated his first birthday back on April 8. Apparently, the lyrics weren't entirely complete, as Cleave later recalled. Scanning over the birthday card, Cleave couldn't get past the lines, "But when I get home to you / I find my tiredness is through, and I feel alright." To Cleave's ears, "my tiredness is through" seemed "feeble." Quickly grabbing a pen, John deleted the phrase and replaced it with "I find the things that you do will make me feel alright." With the title track for their film debut in the offing—and the lyrics hot off the press—the Beatles quickly set down to work. As Emerick later wrote, "From the band's perspective, the session was going smoothly, but there was a storm raging behind the scenes that they were blissfully unaware of." Up in the control room, as the group made their way through nine takes of "A Hard Day's Night," Lester made his presence known, turning to Martin with one suggestion after another. "Even with my limited experience," Emerick later recollected, "it appeared to me that Lester was acting inappropriately; he was constantly locking horns with George Martin and butting in where he didn't belong. For some reason, he seemed to think that because the song was being recorded for his film, that gave him the right to provide musical input and direction, and that was simply not the way things were done. George was being his usual polite self, but I could see that he was getting increasingly irritated. In particular, Dick kept insisting that something 'blockbuster' was needed for the opening of the film— hence John and George's crashing guitar chord that heralds the first notes of the song."

While he may have been perturbed with Lester's behavior, Martin came through with a blockbuster idea that brought "A Hard Day's Night" to life in an arresting and unforgettable style. "We knew it would open both the film and the soundtrack LP," George remarked, "so we wanted a particularly strong and effective beginning." For the Beatles, that incredible beginning came in the form of a G7 chord with an added ninth and a suspended fourth.[10]

As George later recalled, "In those days, the beginnings and endings of songs were things I tended to organize. We needed something striking, to be a sudden jerk into the song. It was by chance that [John] struck the right one. We knew it when we heard it." To execute and enhance the sound, Lennon and Harrison played F major chords with an added G on their Rickenbacker Capri and 360 twelve-string electric guitars, respectively, while Paul plucked a D on his Höfner bass. The powerful sound was doubled with acoustic guitar and piano overdubs after the principal rhythm track had been completed. As George later wrote, "The strident guitar chord was the perfect launch." But Lester wasn't to be deterred, and he continued to offer impromptu insights throughout the session. At one point, he instructed George to "tell them I need it to be more cinematic," and in the words of Emerick, the director "kept making one odd suggestion after another." To Martin's great credit, he managed to keep the peace in Number 2 that evening by placating Lester up in the control room while allowing the Beatles the requisite freedom and space to work their creative magic in the studio down below.[11]

For the session, George arranged the drum, bass, and guitar parts on one track while affording space on another for John and Paul's vocals. This left two tracks open for additional overdubbing, which, as events would prove, would be to George and the Beatles' great benefit. As George recalled, "With the great advantage of four-track we were able to overdub and put on secondary voices and guitar solos afterwards. By the time we did 'A Hard Day's Night' we would certainly put the basic track down and do the vocals afterwards. Invariably, I was putting all the rhythm instruments onto either one or two tracks, generally one track, so you would have bass lumped with guitar." As things progressed, the first take was largely successful, save for Paul's bass foibles during the second—"My middle-eight was crap," he complained afterward. While the next few takes were false starts that barely got beyond the opening chord, the fourth take offered a full run-through of "A Hard Day's Night," marking a vast improvement over the first three attempts. The only blemish—which would prove to be a telling one, as it led to a masterful opportunity a bit later in the evening—was Harrison's lackluster attempt at a guitar solo. At this point, Martin suggested that they overdub the solo later rather than attempt to capture the whole shebang in a single take. At the end of the next run-through, which was sloppy in comparison to take four, Harrison pointed out they hadn't resolved the matter of the song's ending just yet. For the moment, at least, they would bring the song to fruition via a full close. Take six collapsed after McCartney botched a series of bass notes, although he doesn't cop to his slipups, which Lennon and Martin can't help mentioning during break:

> Lennon: "I heard a funny chord."
> Martin: "So did I!"
> Lennon: "Not 'alf, you didn't!"

As his colleagues good-naturedly chuckled at his expense, Paul rehearsed the middle eight in preparation for the next attempt. During take seven, the Beatles experienced yet another breakdown as Lennon broke a guitar string and McCartney fumbled his bass line in the middle eight once again. Take eight turned out to be a false start, as McCartney suddenly halted the proceedings in order to rehearse the offending bass notes one more time. His last-minute rehearsal paid quick dividends as the Beatles made take nine one for the ages. With the sounds of take nine still echoing down below, Emerick observed, "Lennon announced that he was satisfied, and George Martin concurred. Dick Lester, not surprisingly, called for yet another run-through, but George Martin was smart enough to keep him well away from the talkback microphone and pretended not to hear his dissent." At this point, George invited the bandmates up to the control room, where they listened to the playback with well-earned delight.[12]

After taking a short break, George conducted an overdubbing session on track three, to which John and Paul double-tracked their lead vocals, John added an acoustic guitar part, and Ringo played the cowbell. He originally planned to play the bongos, but kept faltering in his effort to keep the beat. To help out, Norman Smith made a rare appearance on a Beatles record as he came down from the control booth to lend a hand with the song's percussion. As Smith later recalled, "I played the bongos. Ringo couldn't do it. I went down to the studio and showed him what to do, but he just couldn't get that continual rhythm. So I said, 'Okay, forget it, I'll do it.' We overdubbed it, and I left my Tape Op behind upstairs to operate the equipment." At this point, "A Hard Day's Night" was effectively complete save for the unrealized guitar solo and, as Harrison had earlier observed, the song's ending. Emerick later recalled, "we were ready to attack Harrison's solo. George must have been having a bad day—or maybe Lester's increasingly annoying presence was getting to him—because he was having real difficulty nailing it." At first, the bandmates discussed the notion of McCartney playing the solo, given his facility playing lead guitar—"McCartney was a fine guitarist himself, and seemed always ready to jump in and show up his younger bandmate," Emerick wrote—but then Martin happened upon an idea that would elevate the already potent title track to yet another level.[13]

Using the available fourth track for "A Hard Day's Night," Martin joined the Beatles downstairs in the studio with the intention of deploying his windup piano technique—the same production trickery he had used on the intro for "Misery" the previous year. It made for both a redemptive moment for Harrison—allowing him to bring his earlier stabs at a proper guitar solo to life in the relative comfort of half-speed recording—as well as the palette for one of the most remarkable moments of studio wizardry in Martin and the Beatles' career together. As Emerick later reported, "I was told to roll the tape at half speed while George went down into the studio and doubled the guitar solo on an out-of-tune upright piano. Both parts had to be played simultaneously because there was only one free track, and it was fascinating watching the two Georges—Harrison and Martin—working side by side in the studio, foreheads furrowed in concentration as they played the rhythmically complex solo in tight unison on their respective instruments." The result was magical, as Harrison's guitar and Martin's piano merged together at full speed, taking flight as a kind of hybridized electronic instrument. But the half-speed guitar/piano interlude existed as a signal moment in the Beatles' corpus in yet another way: together, Martin and the band had fashioned an instance of studio magic that would be next to impossible for Harrison to reproduce onstage. In and of itself, the complexity of the guitar solo on "A Hard Day's Night" would have far-reaching implications as the Beatles moved forward during the touring years. In essence, their capacity for making music in concert, given the technical challenges of the mid-1960s, would quickly be outpaced by their studio-enhanced abilities. This aspect of their groundbreaking efforts would be shortly revealed during their upcoming concert appearances, when Harrison would improvise less intricate attempts at the solo, or later during a July 14 BBC studio performance in which network technicians resorted to studio artifice and simply spliced in the half-speed solo from Martin's April 16 recording. But it was telling nonetheless. With "A Hard Day's Night," the Beatles' musical paradigm shift was happening in real time—and right in front of their very eyes, no less.[14]

At this point on that thrilling April evening, "A Hard Day's Night" seemed to be once and truly complete, but as Emerick later wrote, "Lester kept insisting that he needed a 'dreamy' fadeout in order to segue into the movie's first scene." In spite of his best efforts, George wasn't able to muzzle the director completely. But it made for a satisfactory turn of events as his suggestion resulted in yet another unforgettable moment on that remarkable night. This time, it was Harrison, the other George, who saved the day by concocting a brilliant arpeggiated guitar figure on his Rickenbacker twelve-string, which Martin sweetened by slowing down the recording ever so slightly across the fade-out. All told, the elements that came together that evening to bring a complex and infectious song like "A Hard Day's Night" to life were revelatory for Martin and the Beatles. As they closed in on their two-year anniversary together, the producer and his charges had clearly enjoyed an early and highly significant turning point in terms of their recording artistry. The recording session associated with the making of "A Hard Day's Night" also marked yet another occasion in which the group took a composition from start to finish during the space of a single studio date. By nearly anyone else's standards, it would seem all but impossible to fashion a classic in such a brief window, yet Martin and the Beatles seemed to accomplish such deeds with great regularity—and with a kind of unfathomable, almost inexplicable ease.[15]

During control room sessions on April 20 and 23 outside the bandmates' earshot, Martin and Smith created mono and stereo mixes of "A Hard Day's Night," which were quickly shipped out to United Artists, which was anxious to begin compiling the soundtrack for its gala American release in late June. And with that, Martin and the Beatles would take a month-long break from each other before reconvening to complete work on the UK *A Hard Day's Night* long-player, which, unlike its American counterpart, had already been envisioned as the band's next studio album.

But on the evening of April 16, they were truly flying high. The aura in the studio certainly wasn't lost on Emerick, who later recalled, "I hadn't been on a session with the Beatles for some six months, and I was impressed by how much more professional they had gotten in that relatively short span. Not only was their playing tighter, but also they were acting very much like seasoned veterans in the studio, knowing exactly what they were trying to accomplish and getting it done with a minimum of fuss, very much like a well-oiled machine." For her part, Cleave was equally mesmerized at the speed in which the song had come to life: "Three hours later, I was none the wiser about how they'd done it, but the record was made." Just like that, they had completed another classic, ready and waiting for public consumption and well-deserved adulation.[16]

Under George's guidance, what the Beatles were accomplishing in the studio by this juncture was nothing short of extraordinary. And it certainly couldn't have been lost on them that there was a growing discrepancy between their creative lives in old Number 2 and the increasingly confining world of their unique brand of celebrity as the Four Mop-Tops. By this point, the bandmates "were out of breath," in Cleave's words, as they shuttled from concert appearances and radio spots to film sets and finally to Abbey Road, where they managed to find increasingly narrow spaces in which to record the rock 'n' roll chestnuts that seemed to come so easily to them. "They had to run everywhere to escape screaming mobs of which they were understandably frightened," Cleave later remarked. "I used to wonder what would happen if one of them fell over. Would he be torn to pieces?"[17]

# 13

# MARTIN'S REVENGE

**FOR GEORGE, JUNE 1964** would have long-standing implications, forcing him to confront—*finally*—the professional demons that had plagued him for nearly a decade. But first, there was the small matter of completing the soundtrack for *A Hard Day's Night*. The American long-player was already slated for a June 26 release, featuring a spate of original material—the title track, "Tell Me Why," "I'll Cry Instead," "I'm Happy Just to Dance with You," "I Should Have Known Better," "If I Fell," "And I Love Her," and "Can't Buy Me Love"—along with four instrumental cover versions conducted by George and a studio orchestra. Fortunately for George and the band, they had an extra month's cushion before the LP's British release, which was scheduled for July 26 distribution in the United Kingdom, only a few weeks after the film premiere. But by the time the bandmates reconvened with their producer at Abbey Road on the afternoon of Monday, June 1, their backs were truly against the wall. While the US album was already being pressed at Capitol's manufacturing plants, George and the boys were still several songs shy of completing their third studio album. As if to compound their already tight schedule, they planned to finish work on a new four-song EP to be titled *Long Tall Sally* and distributed on June 19 as an intermediate release before *A Hard Day's Night* found its way into British record stores during the last week of July. And it all had to be completed—the album and the EP—within the span of two days, as the Beatles were scheduled to embark on their first world tour on June 4. George had found it to be increasingly difficult to cobble together time with the Beatles in the studio given the band's demanding touring schedule. "Brian would dole out time to me like he was giving scraps to a mouse," George later remarked. But those were the rough-and-tumble days of Beatlemania in its prime. The pressure to release new Beatles product at regular intervals was also the express result of Brian and George's plan, hatched what seemed like a lifetime ago back in early 1963, to do everything possible to avoid a time lag in seeing new music into the arms of a ravenous record-buying public that, for the moment at least, appeared to have no bounds.[1]

While George and the Beatles' time frame was indeed tight, it hardly rose to the same kind of extreme pressure under which they had recorded the *Please Please Me* long-player. To round out the British version of *A Hard Day's Night*, the band needed to complete five additional tracks before leaving for Copenhagen on June 4. The *Long Tall Sally* EP merely required two new songs, to be paired with the title track and "I Call Your Name," in order to be readied by Martin and Smith for release in three weeks' time. Sure, they didn't have many extra hours to spare, but by George and the Beatles' standards during this period, it was more than manageable. They also had the added benefit that the bandmates had returned from an extended holiday in which Lennon and McCartney had composed several new tunes. But they had begun the afternoon of June 1, quite ironically, by working on a cover version—and one that they had perfected in their stage act over the years. The first song that they attempted was "Matchbox," the old Carl Perkins tune produced by Sam Phillips at the legendary Sun Studios in Memphis. Slated for the EP, the song featured Ringo on lead vocals. The cover version was recorded in breakneck fashion given the band's familiarity with the tune. Ultimately, the song required only five takes, with Ringo singing and playing the drums simultaneously. As it happened, Perkins was making his way across Great Britain on a promotional tour at the time, and he had met the group only the night before at a party after their show at the Prince of Wales Theatre in London's West End. Having been invited to attend their session the next day, Perkins enjoyed the opportunity to briefly jam with the Beatles before observing them in the studio, with Martin pounding the keys, as they recorded the very composition that the American rockabilly star had originally released back in 1957.

With "Matchbox" in the can, George and the band quickly turned their sights toward "I'll Cry Instead," a new Lennon composition that Lester was considering for the "break-out" chase scene shot in Thornbury Playing Fields in *A Hard Day's Night*, which was still in postproduction. As Beatles recordings go, "I'll Cry Instead" was recorded in a most peculiar fashion, with George producing the song in two sections. "I'll Cry Instead" may have been recorded as two distinct parts in order to facilitate Lester's ability to overlay the number on the chase sequence, which lasted approximately two minutes. Working expeditiously, the band required six takes to complete "section A" and two takes to complete "section B." Each part featured the same instrumentation and similar track arrangement, leaving George to edit them together afterward in deference to the structural requirements of Lester's film, which existed in a rough cut by this point. As it happened, Lester ultimately opted to tap "Can't Buy Me Love" for the chase scene, thus relegating "I'll Cry Instead" as one of *A Hard Day's Night*'s parcel of nonsoundtrack numbers. Before taking a break that afternoon, George and the group recorded a cover version of "Slow Down," Larry Williams's 1958 rock tune, which they intended to round out the contents of the *Long Tall Sally* EP. Recorded over six takes, "Slow Down" featured Lennon providing a boisterous lead vocal against a surging rhythm track. On June 4, Martin overdubbed a piano track onto "Slow Down," but by then the Beatles were twelve hundred kilometers away in Copenhagen, where their professional lives had quite suddenly been thrown into a very unexpected state of flux.

After taking their afternoon break on June 1, Martin and the Beatles turned to another new composition during the evening session, a wistful Lennon-McCartney ballad titled "I'll Be Back," which Lennon had based on Del Shannon's 1961 American chart-topper "Runaway." That evening, the band recorded the song across sixteen takes. For the first several attempts, George and the group toyed with different arrangements and time signatures. Take two, for example, finds the Beatles trying their hand at recording "I'll Be Back" as a waltz in 6/8 time, with Ringo awkwardly attempting to maintain the beat throughout the effort, which forced John to fumble with the lyrics during the bridge. For take three, the bandmates abandoned triple meter and attempted "I'll Be Back" in straight 4/4 time. Without having devised an ending for the ballad yet, Lennon announced at one point that the others will know that the song is over "when I start going 'oh oh' about eight times." At this juncture, Lennon and Harrison had been playing electric guitars, but by the twelfth take, they have forsaken their guitar leads for the acoustic sound that would elevate "I'll Be Back" to a melancholy fusion of remarkable emotional power. While several of the latter takes would prove to be false starts, take sixteen would be sublime. In this final arrangement, one track featured Lennon's acoustic guitar, McCartney's bass, and Starr's drums, while yet another was reserved for Lennon and McCartney's shared lead vocals. The third track was reserved for Harrison's acoustic, in which he played the lead riff throughout the song, while a fourth track was allotted to additional acoustic guitar layering and Lennon's vocals for the middle eight. By the time that Martin and the Beatles retired for the evening, they had turned a subtle and very intriguing corner. Once again, they had demonstrated Martin's axiom that their working relationship often presupposed that their songs were never finished until they had put them through their paces. With "I'll Be Back," they had worked through several iterations until Lennon's exquisite tune had finally come into its own. In so doing, they had discovered new and powerful notes of beauty and sadness that had been previously unexplored in their work with the Parlophone head.[2]

When they reconvened the following afternoon at Abbey Road, the first tune that George and the Beatles attempted was John's "Any Time at All," an ecstatic rock song with a driving beat and space for a piano interlude courtesy of Paul, who suggested an innovative means for completing the number's middle eight. For "Any Time at All," Martin double-tracked Lennon's vocal while recording a rhythm track consisting of McCartney's bass, Lennon's acoustic guitar, Harrison's twelve-string Rickenbacker, and Starr's drums. They recorded seven takes of "Any Time at All" before abandoning it temporarily and turning to McCartney's new composition, an acerbic, mournful tune titled "Things We Said Today"—a bit of "future nostalgia," in its composer's words. Recorded over three takes, "Things We Said Today" was a masterpiece of economy, with the first take ending as a false start followed by a full realization of the song in only the second attempt. For the third take, George recorded Paul double-tracking his vocal with Ringo playing a tambourine and John on piano. Using the power of four-track recording, Martin opted to omit Lennon's piano part, although it still existed as a remnant through leakage onto McCartney's and Starr's microphones.[3]

After a dinner break, Lennon unveiled yet another new composition, "When I Get Home," an up-tempo rock number that the Beatles recorded in eleven takes, with the final attempt being marked as the best. "When I Get Home" would be especially remembered by seventeen-year-old Ken Scott, who was working his very first session that evening as a second engineer. Years later, he recalled being "completely and utterly terrified" at the prospect of working with George and the Beatles. As it happened, he also very nearly raised the ire of the Parlophone head, almost ending his tenure at Abbey Road in the same instant in which it began. As Scott later recalled:

> At that time, four-track tape machines were so large that there was no room for them in the control room. They were sited along the corridor

and the only contact you had with the session was via a talkback system. On this particular evening the Beatles were playing back their latest recordings to a few friends who had come in. George Martin was giving me the directions over the talkback and at one point I heard him say "home." So I put the tapes away, switched off the power, put my coat on and left the room. As I was walking along the corridor I saw George standing in the doorway.

"Well," he said, "is the tape lined up yet?"

"I'm sorry?"

"Is the tape of 'When I Get Home' ready yet?"

"Ah, hang on George, I'll just check and see."

I ran up that corridor, flicked all the switches and put the tape back on as fast as lightning, acting nonchalantly as if nothing was wrong!

With "When I Get Home" having reached a state of completion, George and the Beatles continued yet another incredibly prolific night at Abbey Road by returning to "Any Time at All." After recording four more takes, they finished yet another original composition, rounding out the contents for the *Hard Day's Night* long-player in the nick of time, although there was still some talk about recording a fourteenth track for the album the next day. In one of the song's most interesting features, McCartney's piano part comprised the available fourth track in which the Beatles' bassist doubled Harrison's Rickenbacker notes in the same fashion that Martin had devised using his windup piano technique back on "A Hard Day's Night." It was yet another turning point in which the apprentices were clearly and quickly learning at the hands of their master.[4]

But things suddenly took a turn for the worse on the morning of June 3. There would be no fourteenth song for *A Hard Day's Night* after all. As it turned out, the number of tracks would be the least of their worries. As Brian and the Beatles made final preparations for the upcoming world tour, the bandmates held a photo session with the *Saturday Evening Post*. For several days, Ringo had complained of exhaustion and a sore throat since his return from his lengthy sojourn with Paul in the Virgin Islands. In spite of experiencing bouts of dizziness, he had struggled through the past few days at Abbey Road. After Ringo suddenly fell to his knees during the photo session, Neil Aspinall spirited the Beatles' drummer to University College Hospital, where he was diagnosed with laryngitis and pharyngitis, throwing the upcoming world tour into a state of unexpected disarray. As Starr underwent treatment for his ailments, Epstein, Martin, and the remaining bandmates grappled with what seemed to be an untenable situation. It was an odd moment, to say the least. The well-oiled machine that Brian and George had been nurturing since the late fall of 1962 was suddenly descending into an unexpected sense of chaos. For Harrison especially, it seemed futile to even consider soldiering on without Starr. "Imagine, the Beatles without Ringo!" the guitarist remarked. According to Paul, "Brian argued with us for more than an hour to change our minds about abandoning the tour, pleading that thousands of Dutch and Australian fans had already bought tickets, and that it would be cruel to disappoint them." According to Harrison, the Beatles' producer was just as adamant that the group do everything possible to avoid scrubbing the tour. As Harrison contended, the band was "bullied by Brian Epstein and George Martin into accepting the situation that [they] had to go." At one point, Harrison upped the ante, remarking, "If Ringo's not going, then neither am I. You can find two replacements."[5]

For his part, the Beatles' producer was beside himself with anxiety. He was suddenly faced with a twelve-hour window, at most, to decide about how to proceed. The triumphs of *The Ed Sullivan Show* and the film shoot of *A Hard Day's Night* had been masterstrokes of coordination. All of Brian's careful preparation for their first world jaunt was suddenly awash in disarray. The idea of canceling the tour seemed unthinkable from his vantage point. And Martin intuited the attendant and myriad problems with canceling the tour in an instant, sharing the manager's angst about the hundreds of hours and reams of correspondence that had gone into planning and executing the multinational trek from Copenhagen to Brisbane. For the past several months, Brian had been working with promoters a world away in terms of arranging for venues, hotels, motorcades, security, and merchandising. There were no out-clauses in effect, and cancellation, to Brian's mind, meant the possibility of lawsuits—and worse yet, awakening the manager's lingering fears about a PR disaster that might upset the band's fame, which he was working tirelessly to consolidate worldwide.

For Brian and George, the issue of the Beatles' capacity for sustaining their reach was at risk. At this point, they had achieved a seemingly impossible feat, having taken a regional success and transformed it into an international phenomenon. As they stood vigil with Lennon, McCartney, and Harrison at Abbey Road, they had managed to accrue an incredible record—two straight number-one albums, five chart-topping singles, and a new LP and a feature film in the offing. But there were simply no guarantees that it would all last. By mid-1964, the Beatles were one of the very few pop sensations to experience any kind of shelf life. Most acts dried up and lost their sway within a year or two—or at most, after landing a few hits along the way. Brian and George had no real reason to be confident that the Beatles would enjoy a different fate, all of their incredible success notwithstanding. But to their minds, that is exactly what it was: incredible. Both of their careers—as manager and as A&R head, respectively—had been tough going. They weren't about to take any chances now. It simply wasn't in their makeup. And for George, it was yet another moment that "rankled" when he felt everything suddenly slipping away, like his Fleet Air Arm days when he was demoted to midshipman or more recently, when EMI denied him the face-saving compliment of a simple bonus after he'd turned in one of the most illustrious years that the multinational company would ever see. No, like Brian, he wasn't taking any chances. For him, the old show-business adage was never more true and seldom more prescient: the show must go on.

Not knowing how long Ringo would be in the hospital, the Beatles' brain trust immediately set about the quick work of finding a stand-in. Years later, Martin recalled the showdown at Abbey Road and Harrison's subsequent vitriol. "George is a very loyal person," Martin remembered. "And he said, 'If Ringo's not part of the group, it's not the Beatles. And I don't see why we should do it. I'm not going to go.'" McCartney's memories were surprisingly vague about the need to carry on with the tour. "For some reason, we couldn't really cancel it," he recalled. "So, the idea came up, we'll get a stand-in drummer." For the briefest of instances, the idea of recruiting Pete Best may have even been considered. Pete had only recently managed to right himself, forming the Pete Best Four and recording the band's first single, "I'm Gonna Knock on Your Door," produced by none other than Decca's Mike Smith. For his part, John quickly demurred, noting that the ousted drummer now had "his own group, and it might have looked as if we were taking him back, which is not good for him." At this point, Martin began flipping through his extensive Rolodex of London-area studio musicians—the same directory that had no doubt produced the name Andy White back in September 1962. After coming up empty on his first few tries, George phoned up an East End drummer named Jimmie Nicol, who played in the Shubdubs, a band whose only claim to fame was a minor hit single called "Humpity-Dumpity." Years later, Nicol vividly recalled "having a bit of a lie down after lunch when the phone rang." George knew Jimmie as a competent timekeeper, and just as important, he looked the part, with a Scouser-like appearance that would easily blend in with the Liverpool bandmates. Not leaving things to fate, George called the East Ender into Abbey Road Studios for a hasty audition.[6]

When Nicol arrived at Abbey Road that afternoon, Lennon, McCartney, and Harrison quickly turned back to business, clearly having acquiesced to Epstein and Martin's admonitions to press on with the tour. For his part, Jimmie was understandably thrilled to be in their presence, perceiving the opportunity as a very big break, although clearly a "mysterious" one. "I'm fairly well-known as a session drummer in England. I do quite a bit of sessions for big artists," Jimmie later recalled. "It was very mysterious—nobody wanted to commit themselves. So I had to go along to EMI and meet them all and just rehearsed about five numbers. And that was it." As it happened, John, Paul, George, and Jimmie rehearsed six staples from the Beatles' standard set, including "I Want to Hold Your Hand," "She Loves You," "I Saw Her Standing There," "This Boy," "Can't Buy Me Love," and "Long Tall Sally." While the session had been billed as an audition, Alistair Taylor knew the score, later remarking, "Jimmie passed the audition, although I don't know how he could have failed as we really had no alternative." Listening in from his well-worn place in the control booth, George was plenty satisfied with what he heard that afternoon: "Jimmie Nicol was a very good little drummer who came along and learned Ringo's parts very well. Obviously, he had to rehearse with the others. And they (Paul, John and George) worked through all the songs here [at Abbey Road]." After Nicol left the studio for a celebratory drink and to pack his bags for Copenhagen, Martin and the remaining bandmates—ever the workaholics, in keeping with their working-class upbringing—ran through a series of demos, including Harrison's "You Know What to Do," McCartney's "It's for You," and Lennon's "No Reply," which devolved into a cacophony of nervous laughter. They then carried out a few final overdubs on "Any Time at All" and "Things We Said Today," putting the LP's contents to bed—at least as far as the band members were concerned. There would be no fourteenth track, after all.[7]

As it happened, the Beatles' inaugural world tour proved to be a peculiar affair from the beginning, leaving many of the group's inner circle in varying states of consternation. Harrison continued to bristle at the notion of using a stand-in, while Starr himself, only barely into his recovery back at the hospital, was crestfallen. "It was very strange, them going off without me. They'd taken Jimmie Nicol, and I thought they didn't love me any more—all that stuff went through my head." In spite of his sudden spate of good fortune, Jimmie endured his own understandable level of anxiety at trying to fill Ringo's shoes—and, quite literally, his clothes. "The boys were very kind but I felt like an intruder," Jimmie later recalled. "They accepted me, but you can't just go into a group like that—they have their own atmosphere, their own sense of humor. It's a little clique and outsiders just can't break in." All told, Jimmie performed in eight concerts with the Beatles. He even donned Ringo's suit on stage to blend in with his temporary mates. In order to complete the masquerade, the group's roadies deployed strategically placed clothespins to ensure that his jacket fit. For Jimmie, life with the Beatles made a palpable, even surreal difference in his worldview. "The day before I was a Beatle, not one girl would even look me over," Jimmie later remarked. "The day after, when I was suited up and riding in the back of a limo with John Lennon and Paul McCartney, they were dying just to get a touch of me."[8]

If the Beatles had any doubts about Brian and George's steadfast decision against postponing the tour, their qualms were quickly extinguished by the adulation that they enjoyed in each successive country. With Jimmie in tow, the bandmates' motorcade was greeted by a tumult of Dutch fans upon their arrival in Amsterdam. The next morning, the Beatles made a ten-mile trek through the Amstel Canal on a specially designed glass-topped boat. "We passed at least 100,000 cheering people who lined the streets on each side of the water to wave, and sometimes almost touch, the Beatles as they passed," *NME* reporter Andy Gray wrote. "Six police boats accompanied us on the water and they were kept busy, picking up dozens of boys who swam to the boat, some climbing on to shake the Beatles' hands." Incredibly, things became even more raucous when the group arrived in New Zealand. On June 12, as Jimmie's time with the Beatles was nearing its end, the group rode in a convertible for a nine-mile parade along Australia's Anzac Highway, which was lined by 250,000 people—nearly half of Adelaide's population at the time. When they reached Adelaide Town Hall, the lord mayor welcomed John, Paul, George, and Jimmie to the city as some thirty thousand people jam-packed the square. Later, in Melbourne, they were greeted by 250,000 people, who braved the bitter cold to catch a glimpse of their idols. Local journalists reported that some 150 young women had fainted, with another 50 fans being treated for various and sundry injuries. When the band landed in Sydney a few days later, some five thousand fans withstood a severe downpour to see the band, who hopped aboard an open-air flatbed truck to make their way into the city to yet another unprecedented Aussie welcome. By then, Starr had recovered and returned to the fold, relieving Nicol of his short-lived duties and consigning him to the waiting, amnesiac arms of history. For Ringo, it was a homecoming that seemed to quickly assuage his fears about being marooned so far away from his mates: "It was fabulous in Australia, and of course, it was great to be back in the band—that was a really nice moment. And they'd bought me presents in Hong Kong." As for

Ringo's glaring absence from the fold across those eleven days in June 1964, the fans didn't seem to mind in the slightest, at times barely even noticing the stiff-jacketed fellow in Ringo's usual place atop the drum riser. Like on other stops on the world tour, the fans down under were there to participate in the Beatles' phenomenon, an experience that didn't appear to be lessened by the temporary shift in the group's calculus.[9]

When they returned to the United Kingdom in the beginning of July after playing a final sold-out show in Brisbane's Festival Hall, the Beatles had become a truly global sensation. Brian and George's gambit with Jimmie Nicol had proven to be a shrewd move that had paid off handsomely in terms of the massive crowds and public exposure that the band had enjoyed—particularly in Australia and New Zealand, where their fans had come out in droves merely for the opportunity to catch a fleeting glimpse of them. For George and the group, all eyes turned toward the upcoming dates of July 6 and July 10, respectively, when *A Hard Day's Night* was slated for release as both the film and the long-playing album of the same name. As the Beatles plowed through the dates on their world tour, Martin and Smith put the finishing touches on the forthcoming EP and LP releases back at Abbey Road. On June 4, as the Beatles and Jimmie Nicol prepared to open the tour in Copenhagen, George supervised mono mixes of "Any Time at All" and "When I Get Home" before trying his hand at superimposing a piano part on "Slow Down." On June 9, as the Beatles and Nicol were winging their way to Hong Kong, Martin, Smith, and Ken Scott prepared mono versions for United Artists' American soundtrack release, which was composed of new Beatles tunes "A Hard Day's Night," "Tell Me Why," "I'll Cry Instead," "I'm Happy Just to Dance with You," "I Should Have Known Better," "If I Fell," "And I Love Her," and "Can't Buy Me Love."

Meanwhile, the United Artists long-playing version of *A Hard Day's Night* would be rounded out by George's instrumental arrangements for "I Should Have Known Better," "And I Love Her," "Ringo's Theme (This Boy)," and "A Hard Day's Night." The instrumental versions were credited to "George Martin and His Orchestra," and they served as incidental music throughout the eventual film. As George recalled, "Later, when I was busy orchestrating the background score it was decided to use Beatles music in the background whenever possible. Hence, 'This Boy' became 'Ringo's Theme' in the towpath sequence, and 'A Hard Day's Night' was turned into a jazz waltz for Grandpa's chase scene from the police station. 'If I Fell' was not used orchestrally in the film, but I liked the tune so much I did a score anyway." As with the Beatles' original studio efforts, George's knowledge about musical notation had become essential to their enterprise together, although more often than not at this juncture in their career, they were baffled by it—particularly John. As Paul later remembered, "George was writing out 'Hard Day's Night,' 'cause he was going to do an orchestral version or somebody wanted it in sheet music, which we of course never required. The Beatles just read each other . . . we just learned a song and if we couldn't remember it, it wasn't any good, we junked it. So when George was scoring 'Hard Day's Night,' he said, 'What is that note, John? It's been a hard day's night and I've been work-*innnn?* Is it the seventh work-*innnggggg?*' John said, 'Oh, no, it's not that.' 'Well is it work-*innnggg?*' He sings the sixth. John said, 'No.' George said, 'Well, it must be somewhere in between then!' John said, 'Yeah, man write *that* down.'"[10]

The opportunity to score the soundtrack for *A Hard Day's Night* had seemed to fulfill a long-standing ambition of George's to carry out orchestral work for the silver screen. But in reality, he found Lester to be insufferable as a collaborator. The same persistently negative presence that had caused so much anxiety during the April Abbey Road session devoted to the title track had reared its unwelcome head during recording sessions for the incidental music. As Martin later recalled, Lester's behavior ultimately "led to a nasty split between us. There was one of my scores which he particularly disliked. That I wouldn't have minded, but he waited until the actual recording to tell me so." For Martin, it was "A Hard Day's Night" all over again as Lester made his presence known in a very public, irritating, and humiliating fashion. "I was on the rostrum in front of the 30-piece orchestra when he came roaring up and tore me off a gigantic strip. 'This is absolute rubbish you've written,' he ranted. 'What the hell do you think you're doing? You're a bloody fool. What do you call this—this—crap?'" For Martin, who had been working diligently to keep the band's musical direction together across a tumultuous year, Lester's outburst was just about the last straw: "I was very embarrassed, and very angry. '*This* is what you asked me to write in the first place,' I told him. But it did no good, and there ensued one of those stupid arguments which can benefit no one. So I did some quick revision there and then, and recorded something along his new line of thinking. After that, we were hardly on speaking terms." It was yet another one of those instances, as George would experience time and time again, in which he would alter his way of thinking in order to keep the general peace—in which he would, more often than not, be the one to acquiesce in the service of the greater good. As events would demonstrate, he was quickly burning to the end of what had once been a very long fuse.[11]

On June 10, as the Beatles and Jimmie Nicol played the Hong Kong Princess Theatre on the other side of the globe, Martin and Smith, with assistance from Langham, prepared a mono mix of "I'll Be Back" that was never used. At this point, the Beatles' producer was up to his ears working on the postproduction effort for *A Hard Day's Night*, especially in terms of bringing the incidental music to fruition for the US soundtrack release. By June 22, as the Beatles played New Zealand's Wellington Town Hall with Starr back behind the drums, Martin supervised a lengthy control room session at Abbey Road in which he and Smith, with Emerick assisting, mixed the entire UK long-player for Parlophone, along with the US LP for United Artists to be synchronized with the film's debut. In addition to the mono and stereo mixes, the trio prepared the *Long Tall Sally* EP for release. It was an incredible session, to be sure, but as time would tell, it wouldn't even come close to being the longest control room session for a Beatles album.

For the Beatles' inner circle, Monday, July 6, made for a British replay of the Australian megacrowds that the band had experienced down under during the previous month. That evening, Brian, George, and the primly tuxedoed bandmates arrived at the London Pavilion for the premiere of *A Hard Day's Night*, having jostled their way through a crowd of twelve thousand fans packing the streets around Piccadilly Circus. For their part, the Beatles adored Lester's final cut, at least initially, and although he still maintained that James Bond was better, Lennon couldn't help boasting that their film was better than the other rock 'n' roll musicals that had preceded it. While Martin still felt a chill over his treatment at Lester's hands, he had to feel buoyed, as had Epstein, that *A Hard Day's Night* had been not only a commercial success at the box office but also a critical success in the London newspapers. The *Daily Express* lauded the film as "delightfully loony" and noted that "there hasn't been anything like it since the Marx Brothers in the '30s." Meanwhile, the *Times* highlighted the movie's "off-beat" quality and praised it as an "exercise in anarchy." The Americans quickly fell in line, with the *New York Times*' Bosley Crowther celebrating Lester's film as "a whale of a comedy" with "such a dazzling use of the camera that it tickles the intellect and electrifies the nerves."[12]

The film proved to be a popular success as well, with more than sixteen hundred prints in circulation at one juncture. All told, the film generated more than $11 million in receipts while also earning two Oscar nominations, suddenly thrusting Lester and the Beatles into cinema's highbrow crowd. "The irony was that when the film came out the Americans gave it two Academy Award nominations," George later wrote. "One was for the script, by Alun

Owen. The other was for the musical direction, by me. Dick got not a mention. Perhaps it was poetic justice." Even years later, Martin was still smarting over his treatment at Lester's hands, as well as over what he perceived to be the director's unseemly behavior throughout the production. In many ways, Martin was disgusted with Lester's antics in the same way that he had blanched at Humphrey Lyttelton's tantrum back during his days as Oscar Preuss's assistant. As it happened, George didn't even bother to attend the thirty-seventh Academy Awards, which were hosted by Bob Hope in April 1965 in Santa Monica, California. "When I found out what my opposition was I realized that there was no point in going," he wrote. "One of them was André Previn's score of the Audrey Hepburn film *My Fair Lady*, and another was *Mary Poppins*. Our little British film, Beatles or not, was lucky to get nominated really. I knew I didn't stand a chance against those two, and I was right: André Previn won." As it happened, the Academy Award nomination for Best Musical Direction would prove to be George's only Oscar nod across his long career.[13]

For George, the idea of being right had proved to be significant throughout his professional life. He placed great stock in correctness in all its forms—not merely in terms of being accurate in his assessment of a given situation but also being morally right: demonstrating tact while showing all due deference and respect. Not surprisingly, witnessing uncouth behavior by the likes of Lyttelton and Lester tended to stick in Martin's craw. To his mind, such people revealed a serious character flaw the moment that they began "throwing one's own weight about" to the chagrin of others. But being right was about much more than mere comportment. For George, being right also concerned being able to ascertain the ways in which the cultural or political winds were blowing, being able to recognize the sound of the next big hit as quickly as possible—and, even more pointedly, before anyone else did.[14]

On Friday, July 10, as the Beatles attended the premiere of *A Hard Day's Night* in the Liverpool Town Hall and Odeon Cinema, the long-player saw its first full day of release in British record stores. Up in Liverpool, the Beatles' motorcade was met by some two hundred thousand people out to support their hometown heroes. For the Beatles, the idea of returning to their roots was disconcerting, particularly for Lennon, who later remarked, "We couldn't say it, but we didn't really like going back to Liverpool. Being local heroes made us nervous. When we did shows there, they were always full of people we knew. We felt embarrassed in our suits and being very clean. We were worried that friends might think we'd sold out—which we had, in a way." After the premiere in Liverpool, the band hit the road yet again to embark upon a smattering of dates across the United Kingdom and in Sweden before meeting up with George in the United States, where Brian had booked their first full-fledged American tour.[15]

As for *A Hard Day's Night*, the LP easily picked up the baton from the Beatles' previous two chart-toppers, *Please Please Me* and *With the Beatles*. They even called Robert Freeman back to prepare the distinctive cover art for the album, which featured the faces of John, Paul, George, and Ringo in the form of twenty separate portraits by the famed photographer. At the same time, the new LP found Martin and the Beatles in fine form, sounding even more confident and electric than their previous efforts. For one thing, *A Hard Day's Night* was the first Beatles album not to feature any cover versions, including only Lennon-McCartney originals from top to bottom. The album also saw Martin break with his own design principles while sequencing the LP. For George, the placement of the band's songs on their long-players had been motivated almost entirely by strict commercial designs. His philosophy for structuring a recording for the pop-music marketplace dictated that an album hook its listeners with a dynamic opening track and conclude with a knockout punch. "My old precept in the recording business was always 'Make side one strong,' for obvious commercial reasons," he later remarked. "Another principle of mine when assembling an album was always to go out on a side strongly, placing the weaker material towards the end but then going out with a bang." While George cited commercial principles for his thinking in this regard, his ideas about song placement—like those of most A&R men during this era—likely evolved from a long-standing rule of thumb for song order vis-à-vis the nature and manufacturing of vinyl records. This rule of thumb held that a long-player's louder tracks should be strategically located at the beginning of each side of a given album, where the concentric grooves of the record enjoy considerably more real estate, thus leaving the interior of a record, where the grooves are more tightly constrained, for less dynamic tracks with fewer high-frequency sounds. In any event, for the Beatles' first two albums, George had hewn very closely to this dictum, beginning and ending *Please Please Me* with "I Saw Her Standing There" and "Twist and Shout," respectively, while bookending *With the Beatles* with "It Won't Be Long" and "Money (That's What I Want)." And while *A Hard Day's Night* explodes into being with the title track, the album concludes, rather poignantly—even artfully—with "I'll Be Back." It was a break from form, to be sure, as George opted to conclude the album with the wistful sounds of one of the band's most heartfelt, melancholic numbers to date.[16]

Like their previous albums, *A Hard Day's Night* took the charts by storm. In the United States, the LP topped the charts for an astonishing fourteen straight weeks, while the album enjoyed similar dominion over the British charts, where it held the number-one position from July 25 to December 1964. For Brian, George, and the Beatles, the upcoming American tour in August 1964 was designed to consolidate their fame on an entirely different and unprecedented scale. George took enormous pride in their incredible accomplishments at this juncture. And as always, "the music sold, and sold, and sold. Once the dam had been breached, the sales that first year in America were enormous, though only a drop in the ocean compared with what was to follow. To me, that brought great excitement and great pride. It wasn't a question of the glamour, after all. I had been used to dealing with the Peter Sellers and Sophia Lorens of this world. It was more bound up with the idea that something one had made was being heard in millions and millions of homes throughout the world; that it was, literally, becoming a part of the language. That thrilled me enormously." The month-long tour came up well short of being glamorous, with the Beatles barnstorming their way through twenty-three cities, playing thirty concerts from San Francisco to New York City. As a key indicator of both their ethics and their clout, the bandmates refused to play for segregated audiences or in venues that denied entrance to African Americans. While the group consented to press conferences in each new city, they pointedly declined, albeit politely, the opportunity to join President Lyndon B. Johnson for a wreath-laying event at the grave of John F. Kennedy, the nation's fallen leader. Brian now uniformly refused official invitations after the incident at the British embassy the previous February. Even the likes of LBJ, it turned out, was no exception.[17]

George joined the band for several dates on their triumphant first American tour, which often seemed like flying in the eye of a hurricane given the tumult that invariably surrounded the band. "An American rock tour is a whistle-stop business, and you literally don't know which town you are in," George later wrote. "You're whipped into a plane, you land somewhere, give a concert, go back to some hotel, fall into bed again, have a party—and then you're fed into another plane. The boys would ask, 'Are we in Oklahoma or Kansas? Are we in New York City or Cincinnati?' The only way to find out was by asking someone who knew, and such people were hard to find." For George, one of the highlights of the tour was the band's Sunday, August 23, performance at the renowned Hollywood Bowl. George had accompanied the band for the express purpose of making a live recording of the Beatles in concert in the hallowed clamshell venue's environs. For the purposes of the recording, he worked closely with Voyle Gilmore, the senior producer at Capitol Records whom George had met during his 1958 observation of a Frank Sinatra recording session at the Capitol Tower. While Martin and Gilmore managed to capture the recording that day, the event was filled with mayhem—particularly in terms of the unrelenting sound of thousands of screaming fans, with the official gate receipts having marked the attendance at 17,256 patrons. No stranger to live recording—*Beyond the Fringe* had more than prepared him for mobile production—George felt that a concert album by the Beatles should attempt to capture the excitement of their live act in spite of the overwhelming ambient crowd noise. "They were great as a live band," he later remarked. But that August evening at the Hollywood Bowl proved to be their undoing as far as memorializing the group's live show on record went. Despite Martin and Gilmore's best efforts, the cacophony of thousands of screaming fans proved to be too much for their equipment. Working desperately to filter out the noise, George recognized that it was all but hopeless to expect to come away with a clean recording. As he toiled with Gilmore's Capitol Records crew, Martin watched the recording desk's volume-unit meters redlining throughout the band's relatively brief twelve-song set. "It was like putting a microphone at the tail of a 747 jet," George later observed. "It was one continual screaming sound, and it was very difficult to get a good recording." As for Capitol Records' plans for releasing a live album, George "rejected the original recordings as too poor to release." Listening to the tapes, he discovered that "there were voices and instruments on every track, plus an enormous amount of screaming. It was very difficult to separate one from the other."[18]

With his hopes for capturing the Beatles live on record all but dashed for the time being, George trundled on with the band to Colorado's famed Red Rocks Amphitheatre, a breathtaking outdoor venue some ten miles outside of Denver, for the Beatles' August 26 performance. For George, the experience in Colorado proved to be unforgettable. As he later remarked, "The only time I was really frightened was in Denver," which "lies about 7,000 feet up, and to get into the airport the airplane has to do a fairly steep bank before it lands. George Harrison was not prepared for this, and he was scared out of his wits, alternately praying for deliverance and yelling 'We're going to crash!'" But as it turned out, the experience on the plane was only just the beginning. After they landed, "five Cadillacs were drawn up on the runway to meet the plane, and we piled in. But instead of going straight to the hotel, the mayor asked us if we would do a tour of the airfield perimeter. The reason was soon obvious. All the way 'round, it was packed with fans, about 10 deep, jammed up against the barbed-wire fence, like Stalag Luft III turned inside-out. We drove 'round for what seemed miles, about five feet from the fence, five feet from a sea of happy, screaming people all waving frantically." For Martin, such moments revealed the dark underbelly of living at the heart of Beatlemania, where the screams outmatched their groundbreaking music and even a motorcade seemed fraught with peril.[19]

In order to make their way into the city and hunker down for the night at Brown's Hotel, the promoters were forced to resort to a diversion in order to misdirect the horde of people awaiting their arrival. As George later recalled, the diversionary tactic "consisted of a number of people pretending to be Beatles and drawing up in limousines at the front of the hotel, while we went in at the back, through the kitchen entrance. The trouble was that all the photographers and newsmen had tumbled to what we were doing, and they piled in after us. A terrible mêlée in the kitchen resulted, with pots and pans flying in all directions. Brian, the four boys and I finally made it to a service lift, but before we could shut the doors the reporters, the most ruthless people on earth when it comes to getting a story, simply jammed themselves in with us."[20]

But for George and Brian—the men who had shepherded and packaged the Beatles for stardom—the concert itself proved to be an alarming experience, "a different kind of fear" in comparison to the scene back on the hotel elevator, which "was like the Black Hole of Calcutta" after it stalled between floors given the attendant weight of so many passengers. Later at Red Rocks, George and Brian discovered firsthand how fragile the group's lives had become in the swirling vortex of Beatlemania. A natural amphitheatre carved out of rock, Red Rocks features a stage below a rocky outcropping. On either side of the stage, two large towers contained the spotlights and amplification systems. "During the concert," George later wrote, "Brian and I decided that we would like a bird's-eye view of the proceedings. So we climbed one of the towers, whose summit was about level with the top of the crowd. Even beyond the amphitheatre we could see people perched on trees and so on, trying to see over. That was the moment when we realized just how vulnerable the boys were. We could see them below as little dots, but one sniper among all those people could have picked them off very simply. Nor is that some wild piece of over-dramatization. The whole thing was frenetic, fanatic, and slightly unreal, and Brian was already worried for their safety."[21]

While he was rightly proud of their extraordinary accomplishments by this juncture in their career together, George felt the first chill associated with the dangers lurking just beyond Beatlemania's edifice of ecstasy and fandom. As it turned out, he had been dealing with his own demons for quite some time—namely, his enduring issues with the EMI Group's inability to recognize his extraordinary work as head of Parlophone, particularly in terms of the Beatles' massive success. Indeed, unbeknownst to the bandmates, another drama had been playing itself out that would shortly impact their careers—although it had been happening in EMI House in Manchester Square while the band was thrilling audiences on their world tour back in June. At this point, George had completed the first two years of his latest three-year contract, and he was required to give a year's notice if he did not intend to re-sign with EMI. Years later, his closest friends would credit Judy with affording the A&R head with the courage to take on EMI House and demand, after all this time, that they recognize his value. He was still understandably miffed about the lack of a December 1963 bonus. "That made up my mind, in no uncertain way. 'Blow this for a lark,' I thought. I'm leaving." So in June 1964, he voiced his long-standing, pent-up anger in writing. His letter was simple and to the point: "Please take notice that in a year's time I shall no longer be working here."[22]

Oh, it was Martin's revenge all right. He had meant what he said, and while the EMI brass may have been hopeful that he would come around, they clearly had no idea about the strength of his resolve after the last contract negotiation and, worse yet, after the year-end bonus that never managed to materialize. By August 1, 1964, his productions of the UK and US soundtrack albums, along with their high-octane title track and his incidental music, were riding atop the charts in both countries and racking up millions of sales units as *A Hard Day's Night* reigned at the box office. Even during those heady days of mid-1964, many still wondered—in spite of veritable mountains of evidence—if the Beatles were a flash in the pan, as the old saying goes. But even still, it is difficult indeed to comprehend the ways in which EMI so fervently held the company line where George was concerned. It simply boggles the mind.

# 14

# OFF THE BEATLE TRACK

WHILE THE SATIRE BOOM may have reached its zenith before the cancellation of *That Was the Week That Was* in December 1963, George continued to mine for comedy gold at Abbey Road, where he took full advantage of his time away from the Beatles to work with the likes of Bernard Cribbins, Spike Milligan, Michael Flanders, and Donald Swann. For his part, George saw the satire boom as a kind of "social revolution" driven by comedy—especially of the more "biting and irreverent" vintage that he had been spearheading since the previous decade. He had been instrumental in the evolution of *That Was the Week That Was*, which featured David Frost, Millicent Martin, Lance Percival, Roy Kinnear, and Willie Rushton, among others. During its run, *That Was the Week That Was* had "put the fear of God into politicians and establishment figures," in George's words—and perhaps even in Norrie Paramor during the winter of 1962, thanks to George's March 1962 revelations to David Frost about the Columbia A&R man's questionable business practices. After the show was canceled in spite of two successful seasons, the BBC chalked up its reasoning to the fact that 1964 was an election year, and it would be difficult for the network to maintain its impartiality given its broadcast of a high-profile satirical program like *TW3*, as it was affectionately known. George had commemorated the show's influential run with a Parlophone LP in early 1963. As part of the label's Gold Stereo Collection, the *TW3* long-player was marketed for a more sophisticated demographic, particularly audiophiles who coveted the newfangled stereophonic sound. Produced by George in front of a live studio audience on January 7, 1963, the LP included Millicent Martin's famous theme song, "That Was the Week That Was, It's Over, Let It Go," with comic interludes from David Frost.[1]

By the time George began working with the Beatles and Brian's stable of artists, his available time for having a hand in comedy productions had begun to slow precipitously. In 1963—not long after the Beatles recorded their landmark "She Loves You" single—George took a respite from the Fab Four, who were touring the British countryside at the time, to take in the comedy revue *Cambridge Circus*, which opened in London's West End on July 10, 1963, later playing in New Zealand before making its way to Broadway in 1964. The show starred Graham Chapman and John Cleese—later of Monty Python fame—along with Tim Brooke-Taylor, David Hatch, Bill Oddie, Chris Stuart-Clark, and Jo Kendall. Later in the year, George produced a live album of songs and sketches by the cast, including the hilarious "Judge Not," a send-up of what the comedy troupe perceived to be the British legal system's convoluted, often venal ways. During his early years with the Beatles, George made several more forays into comedy, including his recording of Flanders and Swann's "The Gas Man Cometh." Inspired, no doubt, by Eugene O'Neill's *The Iceman Cometh*, Flanders and Swann's ditty plays a spry game of class-conscious chicken between an irate householder and the conspiracy of tradesmen who endlessly begat more work for one another:

*'Twas on a Friday morning*
*The Painter made a start;*
*With undercoats and overcoats he painted every part,*
*Every nook and every cranny,*
*But I found when he was gone*
*He'd painted over the gas tap and I couldn't turn it on!*
*Oh, it all makes work for the working man to do!*

In many ways, "The Gasman Cometh," with its witty word games and layered rhymes, typifies the gentle brand of satire inherent in so many of George's comedy productions over the years. As Flanders himself commented during a live recording of *At the Drop of Another Hat*, produced by Martin during Flanders and Swann's performance at the Haymarket Theatre: "The purpose of satire, it has been rightly said, is to strip off the veneer of comforting illusion and cozy half-truth. And our job, as I see it, is to put it back again." In a darker satiric vein, George produced Peter Lewis and Peter Dobereiner's long-player titled *Funny Games, Politics*, a comedy tour de force starring Roy

Kinnear, Millicent Martin, Lance Percival, William Rushton, and Kenneth Cope. Now a regular member of George's rotation, Millicent Martin once remarked that the Parlophone head managed to get "the best out of people because he didn't frighten them."[2]

In between Beatles projects, George continued to work with the artists in his Parlophone stable, including Matt Monro, with whom he recorded "From Russia with Love" for the 1963 James Bond flick. For the recording, Martin deployed his varispeed windup piano effect to mimic the sound of balalaikas echoing in the background of Monro's vocals. Meanwhile, George's longtime chum John Dankworth enjoyed renown for his score for the *633 Squadron* soundtrack. Directed by Walter Grauman, *633 Squadron* starred Cliff Robertson in the story of a fictional British fighter-bomber squadron, which transported George back to his love of aviation during his Fleet Air Arm days. George produced the soundtrack, which featured the work of the John Dankworth Orchestra, in Abbey Road's spacious Studio 1. Later in 1964, George saw his own singles release with "Ringo's Theme (This Boy)" backed with "And I Love Her" from the soundtrack of *A Hard Day's Night* and credited to George Martin and His Orchestra. By this time, George was receiving glowing reviews for his Beatles orchestrations, with *Billboard*'s Pop Spotlight highlighting George's work on *A Hard Day's Night* and lauding him as "an outstanding arranger and conductor." In spite of such attestations, when the single saw its release on August 7, 1964, the record failed to crack the British charts, although it managed to climb as high as the number-fifty-three spot on the American Hot 100. If nothing else, the "Ringo's Theme" single proved that the band's vast audience may have been invariably hungry for more Beatles product—but only (and increasingly) if it emanated from the real McCoy themselves.[3]

But the year's biggest hits—outside of the Fab Four, of course—belonged to Brian's stable, which continued to produce results in George's hands. He recorded three successive hit singles by Billy J. Kramer and the Dakotas, including "I'll Keep You Satisfied," which reached as high as number four. Another Lennon-McCartney throwaway, "I'll Keep You Satisfied" was produced at Abbey Road with Lennon, the primary songwriter, in attendance at the session. At one point, John kidded Billy about his singing prowess—"Adam Faith, ya fool!" Lennon shouted at the Dakotas' front man. As Billy made his apologies, George piped up over the studio talkback, saying, "I give you full permission to come to the Beatles session on Thursday and shout at John whenever you like." Billy J. Kramer and the Dakotas captured the top spot with "Little Children," which marked a departure of sorts. Breaking with his run of Beatles-authored hits, Kramer turned down the opportunity to record Lennon and McCartney's "One and One Is Two" in favor of "Little Children," which was written by a pair of American songwriters, J. Leslie McFarland and Mort Shuman. McCartney had written "One and One Is Two" back in January in the Beatles' Paris suite at the George V Hotel. Later that year, Billy J. Kramer and the Dakotas cracked the top 10 with "From a Window," another Lennon-McCartney ballad, which Martin produced in July with McCartney present. At one point, the Beatle even chimed in with a harmony vocal when Billy had trouble reaching the high notes that punctuate the song.[4]

Martin also found time to work with another one of Epstein's acts, the Fourmost, who tried their hand at Lennon and McCartney's "One and One Is Two," the Billy J. Kramer reject. Even with McCartney playing bass on the number, the Fourmost couldn't bring the composition off. As the Fourmost's guitarist Brian O'Hara later recalled, "There just wasn't any meat in the song and we couldn't get anywhere with it." George wasn't surprised at the Fourmost's inability to bring the song to fruition, later remarking that they were "a nice group, very happy fellows" who ended up proving that Brian, who "always thought that his picking was impeccable," would occasionally miss the mark. Eventually, the ornery tune found its way into the hands of a South African band, the Strangers with Mike Shannon, who recorded "One and One Is Two" for the Philips label. The group changed the key signature and made subtle alterations to McCartney's original lyrics and arrangement, but it didn't matter. When it finally saw release in May 1964, "One and One Is Two" hit the British charts with a veritable thud. There was simply no saving the Merseybeat ballad, which was saying a lot, given that Lennon and McCartney were the undisputed rulers of pop music's roost at the time.[5]

For all of their incredible run of successes in 1963 and 1964, Brian and George—still British pop music's reigning "dream team" in the Beatle manager's eyes—would occasionally meet their match. With *Ferry Cross the Mersey*, their attempt to build a rock musical around the Mersey sound, the duo was left with egg on their faces—Brian's mostly. In many ways, *Ferry Cross the Mersey* made for a blatant effort to cash in on the success of the Beatles and *A Hard Day's Night* by shifting the setting to Liverpool, Merseybeat's primal scene. With Gerry Marsden having composed a spate of songs for the soundtrack, *Ferry Cross the Mersey* acted as a vehicle for Gerry and the Pacemakers. If Brian and George held any illusions about the project's capacity for duplicating the cultural impact of *A Hard Day's Night*, they were decidedly short lived. Even in its earliest stages, *Ferry Cross the Mersey* met with trouble. Screenwriter Tony Warren eventually gave up on the script—in spite of "downing bottles of whiskey" in a desperate attempt to make the flimsy narrative work. After David Franden picked up the pieces of Warren's draft and completed the screenplay, Jerome Summers shot the film, for which the Beatles' manager received a production credit and served as musical director, on location in Liverpool. Consisting of a series of disconnected chase scenes and antiestablishment gags, the film never stood a chance, being called out for what it was by British and American critics alike. Eugene Archer, reviewing the movie for the *New York Times* after the film's limited US release in February 1965, lambasted *Ferry Cross the Mersey*, chiding it as an "unabashed imitation" of *A Hard Day's Night*. Archer described the movie as "mildly funny—but we have seen it all before. There, of course, is the problem. The Beatle movie was fresh and unconventional, and it had a point—a highly sophisticated one, too. The only point in the new effort is slavish dedication to the principle of past success."[6]

While the film proved to be a critical and commercial disappointment, the project's only genuine highlight turned out to be George's bestselling soundtrack album. Although the movie came up well short as a vehicle for celebrating the Liverpudlian origins of the Mersey sound, the soundtrack acted as a fairly impressive showcase, in retrospect, for Brian and George's stable of North Country acts. In addition to a flurry of Gerry and the Pacemakers tunes, the album featured the Fourmost's recording of "I Love You Too" and Cilla Black's "Is It Love?" The soundtrack also included George's original material, credited to the George Martin Orchestra, including the instrumental "All Quiet on the Mersey Front," a play on words regarding the 1929 novel *All Quiet on the Western Front*, by Erich Maria Remarque, as well as the Academy Award–winning film of the same title. A shimmering fanfare of mid-1960s bombast and steely, 007-tinged guitar work, "All Quiet on the Mersey Front" underscored the Beatles producer's easy knack for knocking off instrumental effusions. The album was rounded out by the composition that would emerge as one of Gerry and the Pacemakers' signature tunes, "Ferry Cross the Mersey," which Marsden had written expressly for the film. Arguably the songwriter's finest moment, "Ferry Cross the Mersey" benefited from George's typically understated production values. A top 10 hit in the US, UK, and Australian marketplaces, George recorded the song on May 27, 1964, at Abbey Road. For the recording, Martin placed Marsden's soaring, plaintive vocal front and center, with a jaunty beat counterbalanced by Martin's glistening orchestral arrangement. While the movie that bears its name was an unmitigated flop, "Ferry Cross the Mersey" demonstrated

George's unfailing pop sensibilities after so many years of toil across the previous decade.

As with Brian's obvious aspirations to position *Ferry Cross the Mersey* on the coattails of *A Hard Day's Night*, George rarely found himself drifting out from under the Beatles' all-consuming spotlight for very long during this period. They understandably loomed very large in his world, having helped to transform him from Parlophone's workaday standard-bearer and lead producer into a kind of recording juggernaut in his own right. He was regularly quoted and referenced in *Melody Maker* and *NME*, and, stateside, in such industry stalwarts as *Billboard* and *Cash Box*. But in his own mind, he was still very much at war with EMI for their long-standing penny-pinching ways in spite of his role at the veritable center of the seismic shifts being wrought by Beatlemania on both sides of the Atlantic—indeed across the globe. In many ways, the opportunity to work with Ella Fitzgerald made for a welcome respite from such tensions. After all, the chance to serve as producer for the jazz great—and at her bidding, no less—was proof positive of George's high standing in a field that he had rather nonchalantly entered fourteen years earlier. It was early April 1964, and "the First Lady of Song" was in London to record tracks for inclusion on her upcoming *Hello, Dolly!* long-player. With Ella's heart set on recording a cover version of "Can't Buy Me Love" for the album, her personal manager, Norman Granz, made arrangements for a session with George at Abbey Road on April 7, the same day on which the Beatles were gallivanting around the Twickenham set with Richard Lester. George pulled out all the stops for Ella's visit, hiring Johnny Spence, whom the A&R head held in great esteem, to conduct a studio band consisting of five saxes, eight brass, a rhythm section, a piano, and Spence working from Martin's scores. With much-in-demand freelancer Henri René handling the jazz arrangement for "Can't Buy Me Love," helpfully propelled by Spence's big-band sound, George set to work. While he was jazzed by the opportunity to record an artist of Fitzgerald's caliber, he was not so jazzed that he lost perspective about the difference between working with the American music legend and the Beatles, who were already proving themselves to be an entirely different phenomenon. Still, he would remember Ella with a special fondness as she performed live in the studio, with "the eternal handkerchief in her hand mopping her eyes, and she sang like a dream."[7]

Years later, Martin reflected on the Fitzgerald session at Abbey Road, writing, "Hundreds of artists have made cover versions of the Beatles' songs. Now, many people have felt that that was the criterion of their credibility as composers; that when someone like Ella Fitzgerald sang 'Can't Buy Me Love' it gave them an almost royal seal of approval. But I don't agree with that, because the fact is that an awful lot of people jumped on the bandwagon. Even the Ella Fitzgeralds of this world are not above that when it means increased sales." For the recording of "Can't Buy Me Love," Martin coaxed a strong performance from the vocalist, who was in fine fettle at Abbey Road with Spence's orchestra providing brisk accompaniment. Yet for all of the pomp and circumstance of having American jazz royalty under his supervision at Abbey Road, George held no illusions about the session's larger meaning in his world. He wasn't even entirely sure that she liked "Can't Buy Me Love" all that much. "She didn't necessarily think it was the greatest song ever," he wrote. "She might well have preferred to record 'Moonlight in Vermont,' but a Beatles song was a commercial certainty." But for George, the real takeaway involved the Beatles' and Fitzgerald's relative standing in an industry in which the Liverpool band was quickly altering the calculus in the pop world. It was a moment of great epiphany for him as he contemplated what the Beatles had achieved—and what potentially existed just beyond the horizon. "There is a lot of snobbery in music," he concluded about the matter. "Some people might have felt that Ella Fitzgerald was better than the Beatles, and that therefore she was doing them a favor. I don't think that was necessarily so. She is a great singer, but in terms of sheer artistry I wouldn't be too certain about the comparison." In May 1964, *Billboard* described the new Fitzgerald single as a "hot property," although it ultimately fell well short of becoming the "commercial certainty" that Martin imagined, leveling out at a paltry number thirty-four on the UK charts. A year later, Fitzgerald attempted to ride the Beatles wave yet again with "Ringo Beat," a novelty number complete with allusions to the much-ballyhooed generation gap and a coy reference to "She Loves You":

*When he smiles and shakes his head and starts that beat*
*The kids start a-screaming and stomping their feet.*
*It's the younger generation's kind of rhythm*
*So don't be a creep, come on and get with 'em.*
*It's the Ringo beat, yeah, yeah, yeah!*

Released as one of the very few remaining singles in the twilight of Fitzgerald's illustrious career, "Ringo Beat" hit the American charts with a thud in 1965, failing to capitalize on Beatlemania's zeitgeist in any meaningful way and charting at a dismal number 127.[8]

Meanwhile, Cilla Black's career continued to skyrocket, giving George a much-needed outlet for flexing his creative energies outside the Beatles' orbit. Always on the lookout for a song with hit potential, George had happened upon Umberto Bindi's "Il Mio Mondo," which sounded, to George's ears, like the perfect vehicle for Cilla's next record. Given the song's haunting romantic strains, Martin began to imagine a new life for Bindi's composition, which had been released as a single in Italy in 1963 without making any waves. In order to transform the tune for the British marketplace, he commissioned American songwriter Carl Sigman to translate and reframe the lyrics for deployment with Cilla at Abbey Road. While Sigman retained the title—rendering "Il Mio Mondo" as "You're My World"—he treated the lyrics to an expansive rewrite. In May 1964, George recorded Cilla in Studio 1 backed by Johnny Pearson and His Orchestra and guitarist Judd Proctor, along with the Breakaways, an English girl group who provided backup vocals. Cilla later wrote that her road manager, future husband Bobby Willis, also lent backing vocals on the recording. Released on May 30, 1964, "You're My World (Il Mio Mondo)" easily topped the British charts, holding the number-one slot for four weeks—one more week than Cilla's previous single, "Anyone Who Had a Heart." For Cilla, this latter fact was of special import given the earlier flap with Dionne Warwick. "A big plus, when I heard it had reached number one," Cilla later wrote, "was knowing that the hurtful remarks dished out by Dionne Warwick's fans at the time of 'Anyone Who Had a Heart' couldn't stick now that I'd made such a swift return to the top of the charts."[9]

After the chart-topping success of "You're My World," George had decided that the best course for the young chanteuse was to try her hand at yet another Beatles throwaway—his typical modus operandi for the lion's share of Brian's stable. He had sent Cilla a copy of the demo of "It's for You" that the bandmates, sans Ringo, had prepared on June 3, the fateful day that the drummer had collapsed during the *Saturday Evening Post* photo session. George had big plans for dressing the song up for Cilla's performance, including orchestration by Johnny Spence, his go-to arranger at the time. "Although Paul had sung it as a waltz," Cilla later wrote, "George Martin took a big hand in my recording of it and asked Johnny Spence to arrange it. Johnny was a famous big-band arranger, and he later went on to be Tom Jones' personal musical director. It was a fabulous arrangement, a sort of jazz waltz. I definitely wanted to do it à la Della Reece, with a Big Band sound." On July 2, 1964, George was recording a remake of "It's for You" with Cilla when John and Paul arrived at Abbey Road, jet-lagged from having just returned from their world tour down under. They good-naturedly sat in on the session, observing as yet another Lennon-McCartney original was transformed in the studio. Paul even stayed late to assist with a piano overdub. "It was great to see them," Cilla recalled, adding that "they were in awe of Johnny Spence, as well as of George Martin." As a testament to her soaring popularity, by the time that "It's for You" was released on July 31, the single had already accrued advance orders of two hundred thousand copies, landing Cilla in the British top 10 yet again.[10]

In late 1964, George would circle back around to Cilla, only this time he fell back on an age-old practice that had served him poorly on just about every occasion. As that banner year was coming to a close, he hustled Cilla into the studio to record a cover version of "You've Lost That Lovin' Feeling" to capitalize on the Righteous Brothers' American hit, which had been released in November to great fanfare and acclaim. On the one hand, George's instincts told him that Cilla was perfect for the emotional, uplifting song. But on the other, he was consumed by the fervor of competition, the impetus that had fueled his ambitions across his career with standout compositions like "Earth Angel," "Itsy Bitsy Teeny Weeny Yellow Polka Dot Bikini," and "Anyone Who Had a Heart." And besides, he reasoned with himself, "You've Lost That Lovin' Feeling" was generating a smash in the American marketplace; why not repackage it for British consumption?

In many ways, "You've Lost That Lovin' Feeling" was a quintessentially American hit. Written by producer Phil Spector, along with Barry Mann and Cynthia Weil, the record featured Spector's dramatic Wall of Sound recording ambience. Decca Records' Tony Hall was tasked with promoting the Righteous Brothers' latest single on British shores, and he quickly discovered that BBC DJs preferred Cilla's version of "You've Lost That Lovin' Feeling" to Spector's recording, which sounded like a "dirge" to the BBC record spinners. And for a while, that perspective seemed to hold sway. As it happened, Cilla's and the Righteous Brothers' versions of the song debuted on the UK charts during the very same week in January 1965, underscoring the tremendous reach of the American recording. At first, things seemed promising for Cilla and George, as Cilla's version debuted at number twenty-eight, a higher slot than that of the Righteous Brothers. Fearing that Cilla's recording would eclipse the original, Tony Hall quickly dispatched the Righteous Brothers on a UK publicity jaunt, where they performed the song on television programs in Manchester and Birmingham. Things got really interesting when Andrew Loog Oldham, the Rolling Stones' manager and producer, became smitten with the American version, taking out a full-page ad in *Melody Maker* in order to promote the Righteous Brothers' upcoming appearance on ITV's

*Ready Steady Go!* At this juncture, Cilla's single had nestled its way into the number-two slot, with the Righteous Brothers suddenly breathing down her neck at number three. The stakes went even higher after Hall encountered Brian Epstein at a party. Filled with the same bluster that prompted him to claim that the Beatles would be bigger than Elvis, the Liverpool impresario boasted that Cilla's "You've Lost That Lovin' Feeling" would clinch the top spot, telling Tony, "We'll be number one next week. You haven't a hope in hell." But his words would be all for naught, as the Righteous Brothers' version topped the UK charts the very next week, while Cilla's cover version fell to number five. Honorable in defeat, Cilla congratulated the Righteous Brothers on their accomplishment. As it was, "You've Lost That Lovin' Feeling" would notch the high-water mark for the remainder of Cilla's singing career, not to mention her partnership with George.[11]

In August 1964, George had the opportunity to work with yet another industry legend—Judy Garland. For Geoff Emerick, the chance to work with a Hollywood icon began with, of all things, what seemed like the makings of a practical joke. Tape operator Richard Langham was well known around the studio for his pranks. He was especially adept at imitating voices—often impersonating Norman Smith and sometimes even George Martin. As Emerick later wrote, "One time, his practical joking nearly backfired badly on me. George Martin was on the phone asking me if I could assist on an upcoming Judy Garland session, and since the request seemed so outrageous, I assumed it was actually Richard calling. 'Bugger off, Langham!' I shouted into the phone, chortling with glee at the thought that I'd caught him out. But it really was George, and he explained that he really wanted me to do the session because he knew that Judy and her entourage would want playback lacquers immediately afterward." The youthful Emerick was crestfallen at the thought of offending the Parlophone head. "I could feel my face turning crimson red as I apologized profusely," Geoff recalled. "'That's okay, Geoff,' he [George] said soothingly. 'I already know the kinds of things Richard gets up to. But,' he added with more than a trace of sarcasm, 'I don't think he does my voice particularly well, so you might want to get the earwax out before you come down here.'"[12]

Garland was in town with Lionel Bart, the lyricist behind *Maggie May*, the musical that was set to open later that year in London's West End at the Adelphi Theatre. For *Maggie May*, Bart had collaborated with Alun Owen, the screenwriter behind *A Hard Day's Night*. Based on a traditional ballad about a wily Liverpool prostitute, *Maggie May* narrated the trouble-ridden lives of the titular streetwalker, along with a group of Merseyside dockworkers making do in their hardscrabble environs. Although she wasn't starring in the upcoming West End production, Garland came to *Maggie May* by way of Bart, the renowned composer of *Oliver!* who was guiding the star's singing career at the time. With Bart's encouragement, Garland planned to record four numbers from the musical, including "The Land of Promises," "It's Yourself," "There's Only One Union," and "Maggie, Maggie May." After an early August session with Columbia's Norman Newell ended in a row between Garland and Newell, Martin stepped in to take over the production duties and bring the suddenly beleaguered project to fruition. On August 12, Garland recorded the latter two songs under George's supervision. The veteran singer made quick work of the numbers in Studio 2, completing "There's Only One Union" and "Maggie, Maggie May"—the very same tune that George had produced with the Vipers back in 1957—in four takes each. Once the star and the producer isolated the right key for Garland to carry off the song, the entire session passed rather smoothly, all things considered. As George later recalled, "Judy had gained a reputation for being a difficult artist, but she was sweet as pie to me. I was a great admirer. I thought she was charming, and we got on like a house on fire. The only problem was that, as she knew damn well, she could no longer sing very well, and she was apologetic, repeatedly asking for another take. She had always had a wide vibrato, but as she grew older she had trouble controlling it. She was at the end of her tether, and it was a great shame."[13]

While Geoff may have been incensed at Richard's antics that night—"I'll get that bloody Langham if it's the last thing I do!" he vowed—the opportunity to work with Judy left a lasting impression on the young engineer. After George completed the session, Geoff remembered, "I was thrilled to get a chance to meet Miss Garland, who was one of my idols. Ever since her first appearance at the London Palladium back in 1951, she'd been a star in England, and *The Wizard of Oz* was one of my favorite films. She'd lived in London on and off for many years, often booking sessions at Abbey Road when she was in town, though I'd never been lucky enough to cross paths with her before." Unfortunately, for much of the session Geoff was relegated to "that accursed machine room," where he was operating the four-track tape machine.[14]

For Geoff, the real excitement began after the session had finished, when "Miss Garland's entourage were going to the local pub to celebrate, but she had decided not to join them. Instead, to my utter astonishment, Miss Garland accompanied me down the corridor and sat there while I was cutting playback lacquers of the work we'd just completed, just the two of us in this tiny room." Years later, Emerick would recall, "I had tons of questions I wanted to ask her, but I was too shy to get the words out. Instead, I simply blushed furiously and struggled to make small talk with the fabulous Miss Garland while I tried to concentrate on getting the work done. All too soon her entourage reappeared and she was whisked away. I never saw her again." As it happened, Garland would leave Abbey Road that evening and never grace a recording studio again. In fact, "There's Only One Union" and "Maggie, Maggie May" would be the last two tracks that she would ever record for EMI, which released the four-song EP in September 1964. That same month, Garland collapsed with a stomach ailment following the after-party for the London premiere of *Maggie May* on September 23. In November, she recorded several of the *Maggie May* numbers onstage while performing with her daughter, eighteen-year-old Liza Minnelli, at the London Palladium. Just five years later, Garland succumbed to a barbiturate overdose at the age of forty-seven, having made her final two studio recordings with Martin.

Although the Parlophone head enjoyed the opportunity to work with the likes of Fitzgerald and Garland while also continuing to produce Epstein's stable of artists, he also experienced the occasional professional casualty during that incredible year at Abbey Road. Since the fall months of 1963, he had been working with veteran Welsh singer Shirley Bassey. As George later recalled, "Shirley had had a pretty checkered career. She was a very volatile person, and had already been with various recording companies including EMI, for whom Norman Newell had recorded her. Finally she came to me, because, I suppose, I was the 'hot' one at that time, with the Beatles and so on. She was very emotional, but I liked her very much, and of course she was a tremendous artist."[15]

Martin produced Bassey's cover version of "I (Who Have Nothing)," which had been recently popularized by Ben E. King. Based on the Italian composition "Uno Dei Tanti" by Carlo Donida and Giulio Rapetti, "I (Who Have Nothing)" would later emerge as a showstopping number in Bassey's stage act. The moment he first heard the song, George knew that it had hit potential for Shirley. "The Italian song stuck out a mile," he reported to the *Daily Mirror* at the time. With an arrangement by Tony Osborne, George produced the session on September 6, as a heavily pregnant Bassey completed "I (Who Have Nothing)" in only a handful of takes. Released scant weeks later at the tail end of September 1963, George's production of the song propelled Bassey into the United Kingdom's top 10, landing her at number six on the hit parade. Unfortunately, Bassey's next single, "Who Can I Turn To?"—also produced by Martin—failed to chart.[16]

Yet Martin's collaboration with Bassey would reach its greatest heights in 1964, when she was tapped to sing the title track for *Goldfinger*, the latest entry in the James Bond movie franchise. George produced the August 20, 1964, session at London's CTS Studios in Wembley with John Barry, the renowned film composer, in attendance. With Vic Flick, Jimmy Page, and Big Jim Sullivan on guitars, Bassey was backed by Barry's orchestra for the track, which took several hours to complete. The session was prolonged by Barry's exacting ways, as the composer often brought the proceedings to a halt over the faintest of technical glitches. For Bassey, the real challenge involved singing the number's final, climactic note, which Barry hadn't even devised until a break in the session that evening. By the time the musicians had finished their tea, Barry had added the song's climax into his orchestration. But for Bassey, the struggle to capture the song had only just begun. At one point, she slipped behind a studio partition between takes in order to remove her brassiere to be able to sing more comfortably. Years later, Bassey remembered the great difficulties inherent in delivering that signature, final note on record: "I was holding it and holding it—I was looking at John Barry and I was going blue in the face and he's going, 'hold it just one more second.' When it finished, I nearly passed out."[17]

For Martin and Bassey, "Goldfinger" would mark their final musical triumph together. Charting at number twenty-one in the United Kingdom, "Goldfinger" became Bassey's only top 40 US hit. Unfortunately, the producer was unable to continue their partnership. "I still had all my other artists to attend to," he later wrote. "It was inevitable that with the success of the Beatles, and to a lesser extent the other artists of Brian's stable, there should be a certain amount of frustration and jealousy, a feeling that some were getting more attention than others. Luckily, the only time that really came to a crunch was with Shirley Bassey." For his part, George had intended to continue working with the Welsh chanteuse. At one point, their creative partnership fell into a state of collapse when they were "routining" new material. "Routining meant that I would collect a number of songs I thought would be suitable for the artist, in this case Shirley," George wrote, "and then she would come to the office and we would run through them on the piano. Having agreed on the numbers she would sing, we would work out which keys they would be sung in, what the shape of the recording would be, how many choruses they would have, what kind of orchestral backing, what kind of beginning and ending, and so on. She spent the whole afternoon routining these songs with me." At the end of their work session, George pulled out his ever-handy diary to plan their next recording date. Things fell apart in a hurry as George attempted to situate Shirley's plans with his upcoming recording schedule—complicated, no doubt, by impending work on the Beatles' next long-player. For her part, Shirley insisted on recording on a particular Monday evening, remarking to her producer, "If I mean anything to you at all, you will do it when I want to. I want to do it on the Monday night." Suddenly, a line had been drawn in the sand. "I'm sorry," George answered, "but I'm not going to work that night because I've got another engagement." Turning to George, she brusquely announced, "I've lived in the shadow of the Beatles and Cilla Black far too long!" before slamming the door in her wake.[18]

For George's part, he knew exactly why Shirley had reacted so harshly over what appeared to be a simple scheduling quandary. As it happened, the engagement to which George was referring during his quarrel with Shirley was the very same evening in which Cilla Black would be singing at the London Palladium for the queen as part of the gala Royal Command Performance. "I think Shirley was testing me!" he later reflected. "We never recorded again."

While Bassey clearly wanted nothing further to do with the Parlophone head, plenty of other clients came his way that fabled year, including British pop singer Alma Cogan, who at age thirty-two had already enjoyed a long and successful career. Known as the "Girl with the Giggle in Her Voice," Cogan came George's way by virtue of her association with Brian, as well as her growing friendship with John and Paul. Under George's supervision and with Stan Foster and His Orchestra as her accompaniment, Alma recorded the single "It's You" backed with "I Knew Right Away" in the space of a single session at Abbey Road. An uncredited McCartney played tambourine on the A-side. "What I remember most of all were her bubbly personality and her infectious singing style," George later wrote, "with a little break in the voice that was very attractive." To the great shock and sadness of the Beatles and their circle, Alma was dead scarcely two years later, having succumbed to ovarian cancer at thirty-four years old.[19]

As it turned out, the likes of Cilla Black, Shirley Bassey, and Alma Cogan—not to mention Brian's stable of Liverpool acts—were hardly George's only clients. By mid-1964, and especially after his Oscar-nominated work on the soundtrack for *A Hard Day's Night*, George understandably began to imagine a musical career in his own right. As the Beatles made their way around the world, George made good use of his time apart from the bandmates, recording a dozen Fab Four instrumentals with a studio orchestra. Released in August 1964, *Off the Beatle Track*—the discarded title from the *Please Please Me* days—included high-octane orchestrations of such numbers as "She Loves You," "Can't Buy Me Love," "I Saw Her Standing There," "All

My Loving," "I Want to Hold Your Hand," and "From Me to You," among others. While the album sold rather modestly in spite of the awesome power of Beatlemania, *Off the Beatle Track* heralded a new phase in George's career as bandleader and arranger. Under the banner headline MARTIN GETTING UNITED ARTISTS' FOUR-STAR BUILDUP AS PERFORMER, *Billboard* magazine announced George's personal contract in a September 1964 issue. "Through the efforts of United Artists Records," *Billboard* reported, "George Martin is going to be his own man. After A&Ring dates in England that produced more than 100 million record sales, Martin is now being groomed by UA here as an artist in his own right. UA's start with Martin isn't bad at all. His single of 'Ringo's Theme,' out of the Beatles' soundtrack album *A Hard Day's Night* has passed the 200,000 sales mark and his LP, *Off the Beatle Track* has racked up over 20,000 copy sales to date." The only question, it seemed, involved how to market the Beatles' producer. Would it be the big-band bombast instrumentals of *A Hard Day's Night* or the sounds of easy listening? "According to a UA executive, the thoughts, right now, are to build up Martin as another Mantovani and/or Percy Faith," *Billboard* continued. "The company already has earmarked an album release date for early next year in which Martin will debut with an instrumental, 'non-Beatles-type,' along the colorful instrumental lines of Mantovani or a Faith." For his part, George was ready to jump into the pop scene and take advantage of the unexpected, albeit modest, success of "Ringo's Theme" on the American charts. As George remarked in the *Billboard* article, "Today's market requires something different, and I'm going to come up with instrumental sounds that accent a beat and that highlight the sounds that are now attracting listening interest."[20]

By this point, it had been a few months since George had laid down the law with EMI. A cold war of sorts had begun in which Len Wood would occasionally take the temperature of the situation in order to see where George stood on the matter. A firestorm had erupted in Manchester Square as George's EMI colleagues heard the news about his planned departure. "That really set the cat among the executive pigeons," George later recalled. "'What do you mean by it?' I was asked. 'After all, you've been with us for 14 years, and suddenly you do this.'" While he had given his notice back in June, in truth, George didn't treat the notion of severing his ties with EMI lightly. But the writing was on the wall—and his salary paled in comparison to the untold riches that his recordings had afforded EMI. Indeed, George's contributions in 1963 and 1964 alone had transformed Parlophone from an eclectic "third label" into ground zero for British beat music. The success of the Beatles "gave me great satisfaction," George later reflected, "even if it didn't bring me any wealth: I was still earning less than £3,000 a year with EMI." It is noteworthy that George took great pains to avoid involving Brian and the Beatles in his long-standing salary dispute. "In retrospect," he later wrote, "I think it more than likely that the Beatles thought that, because of our success, I was doing frightfully well, and that they were responsible for it. But I never discussed it with them, or indeed with Brian. Besides, in those first two years even they weren't rolling in money. Royalties take a long time to flow in, and Brian certainly wasn't rushing around ordering Rolls-Royces. Nor was there really time to think about money. We were all simply working frantically hard to build the whole thing up."[21]

Besides, George didn't want such concerns to pollute their working relationship. Caring about his financial welfare at this point in their lives simply wasn't part of the Beatles' worldview. He adored their jocularity in the summer of 1964, just as he had admired it during their first session together back in June 1962, when they had left him in tears with their collective, irreverent sense of humor. "The Beatles were never ones for showing concern about, or gratitude towards, anyone else," he later recalled. "Although they obviously did appreciate what I was doing, they were never the kind of people who would go out of their way to say: 'What a great job you've done there, George! Take three weeks off.' But then, I never expected that of them. They had an independent, cussed streak about them, not giving a damn for anybody, which was one of the things I liked about them in the first place."[22]

In any event, after serving for so many years at EMI's beck and call, George valued his creative partnership with the Beatles far too much to upset their work together over such a personal concern as his salary. "All I wanted from them was good songs. And those they gave me. At the start I thought: 'God, this can't last forever. They've given me so much good stuff that I can't expect them to keep on doing it.' But they did. They amazed me with their fertility. To begin with, the material was fairly crude, but they developed their writing ability very quickly; the harmonies, and the songs themselves, became cleverer throughout 1963." But even in such moments, George—having modeled himself on the gentlemen officers back in the Fleet Air Arm—fell on the sword of self-deprecation: "Although one obviously had to be a good producer to make the records commercially viable, there was certainly no genius attached to my role at that early stage. There were probably a number of producers who could have done it just as well." In such instances, George comes off like an unreliable narrator in his autobiographical writings. His contemporaries frequently chalked up such posturing to his innate belief that to boast was unmannerly and verboten, that the work, more than anything, should speak for itself. But even still, how could George have truly believed such a brash statement about the revolutionary work that he had already carried out with the Beatles at Abbey Road by the summer of 1964? Was he in fact acting as his own worst enemy in the very same moments when his self-interest should have rightly reached its fever pitch?[23]

# 15

# "CAN WE HAVE THAT ON THE RECORD?"

JUST A SCANT few days before the Beatles began their August 1964 American tour, George and the band regrouped at Abbey Road to begin work on a new long-player as a follow-up to *A Hard Day's Night*, which had been released only a month earlier. Recording sessions for the album that would be titled *Beatles for Sale* commenced on the evening of Tuesday, August 11, 1964, when they tried their hand at "Baby's in Black," a new Lennon-McCartney composition. In keeping with Brian and George's formula for delivering two albums per year, *Beatles for Sale* would simultaneously allow them to accomplish this goal and also release new product in time for the holiday shopping season. Years later, George commented on the band's sporadic sessions during the summer and fall months of 1964, when they were forced to piece together odd dates here and there in order to allow for the requisite time in the studio to produce new work. "They were rather war-weary during *Beatles for Sale*," George later wrote. "One must remember that they'd been battered like mad throughout 1964, and much of 1963. Success is a wonderful thing, but it is very, very tiring." As for the Beatles, they often found it difficult to maintain their creative energies during this period. As McCartney later recalled, he and Lennon developed a pattern in which they would begin to prepare new material after learning that Epstein and Martin had fixed several recording dates in advance. During the Beatles' early years, John proved to be especially adept at working within the confines of the group's incredibly busy schedule.

As Paul later remarked, "When we knew we were writing for something like an album, [John] would write a few [songs] in his spare moments. He'd bring them in, we'd check 'em. You just had a certain amount of time. You knew when the recording date was and so a week or two before then we'd get into it."[1]

It was under precisely these conditions that George and the Beatles set to work on "Baby's in Black," a number that John and Paul had written in just such a fashion. "We rather liked this one," McCartney later recalled. "We wanted to write something a little bit darker, bluesy. It was very much co-written and we both sang it. Sometimes the harmony that I was writing in sympathy to John's melody would take over and become a stronger melody." The song's despondent lyrics possibly refer to the story of Astrid Kirchherr, the bandmates' friend from Hamburg who was engaged to be married to Stuart Sutcliffe, the original Beatles bassist, at the time of his premature April 1962 death, only two months before the band first made George's acquaintance at Abbey Road. The composition's most salient feature is its waltz-like structure with a 6/8 time signature.[2]

As with "If I Fell," Martin positioned Lennon and McCartney around a single, shared microphone so that they could sing "Baby's in Black" as a duet. Martin recorded the Beatles performing the song's basic rhythm track across fourteen takes, only five of which were complete, with Lennon on acoustic guitar, McCartney on bass, Harrison on lead guitar, and Starr on drums. At this point, the group carried out several overdubs, including John and Paul's vocal duet, as well as double-tracking their voices in strategic instances throughout the song. Ringo also added a tambourine part. For the remainder of the "Baby's in Black" session, Harrison played a series of notes on his Gretsch Tennessean by bending the tremolo arm in order to establish a distinctive intro for the number. As Harrison plied away at his tremolo bar, Martin can be heard over the studio talkback saying, "You want the beginning like that, do you?"—suggesting that the Beatles were slowly but surely beginning to make their own choices about arrangement. For his part, Lennon enhanced the tremolo effect by manually turning the volume knob on Harrison's guitar as the Beatles' lead guitarist made several attempts at getting the best take.[3]

Three days later, Martin and the bandmates reconvened at Abbey Road to try their hand at "I'm a Loser," a new Lennon composition. They also worked on two cover versions, "Mr. Moonlight" and "Leave My Kitten Alone," as they completed their final session before embarking upon their American tour. For "I'm a Loser," Martin recorded the Beatles in eight takes, four of them complete, with three tracks arranged among bass, drums, and acoustic guitar; Lennon and McCartney's vocals; and Harrison's lead guitar work. At Martin's suggestion, the song begins with a brief preview of the chorus in order to establish the composition's principal hook. In describing such moments, George would typically attribute his creative contribution to "streamlining" the Beatles' arrangements, hastening to add that "it was their genius that made the songs work." In so doing, he revealed a self-deprecating posture that he deployed over and over again when discussing his efforts with the group. He would repeat this claim so often and so consistently throughout his life, that it would seem almost insincere.[4]

During the first take of "I'm a Loser," McCartney can be heard reminding Lennon where to play his various harmonica interludes, yet another indication that the Beatles were taking a stronger hand in defining their musical arrangements. Years later, John would remark, "That's me in my Dylan period. Part of me suspects I'm a loser, and part of me thinks I'm God almighty." The Beatles would, in fact, meet Bob Dylan for the first time just two weeks later at New York's Delmonico Hotel, where they would fall under marijuana's skunky spell—not to mention that of the American folk singer, whom they had been fervently listening to since January. For John, "I'm a Loser" marked a self-conscious turn toward introspection, a shift that would have lasting implications for the band. But first, he had to capture his lead vocal. At one juncture, George pointedly calls the proceedings to a halt after hearing a loud popping noise produced by John's vocals via the sensitive studio microphone—specifically, the *p* sound in the lyrics "I'm a loser, / And I'm not what I *appear* to be." Eventually, John finds himself in all manner of trouble, crying out "I'm all wrapped up!" as he shifts among singing lead vocals, playing guitar, and working his harmonica. In so doing, he harks back to the band's very first session with George, when the A&R man instructed Paul to sing lead vocals to facilitate the easy transition to John's harmonica part on "Love Me Do." But the comparisons with their early work end right there. "I'm a Loser" marks a shift of sorts toward songwriting as a subjective activity. "We got more and more free to get into ourselves," Paul later remarked. "And I think also John and I wanted to do something bluesy, a bit darker, more grown-up. Rather than just straight pop."[5]

After abandoning "I'm a Loser" for the evening, the group turned to "Mr. Moonlight," a cover song from their standing repertoire during their Hamburg residencies. Written by Roy Lee Johnson, "Mr. Moonlight" was originally released by Piano Red (William "Willie" Lee Perryman), who recorded the song under the name of Dr. Feelgood and the Interns. Martin took full advantage of four-track recording for "Mr. Moonlight," with McCartney's bass and Starr's drums on track one; Lennon's rhythm guitar on track two; Lennon's lead vocal, along with McCartney and Harrison's backing vocals on track three; and Harrison's lead guitar recorded on track four. After trying the song out across four takes, the Beatles abandoned the song for a later session.

At 10 PM that same evening, George and the group shifted their attention to "Leave My Kitten Alone," a 1959 Little Willie John tune that was later recorded by Johnny Preston in the early 1960s. As it happened, "Leave My Kitten Alone" would emerge as one of the *Beatles for Sale* sessions' most mysterious numbers. After the band played the song across five takes—including a scorching lead vocal from Lennon on the final, "best" version—Martin led them through a series of overdubs, including Lennon's double-tracked lead vocals, Starr's tambourine, and McCartney's piano part. The song ends rather abruptly, as George likely planned to fade the song out during the mixing stage. Yet after the evening of August 14, George and the Beatles would inexplicably abandon the song, which wouldn't even be mixed for potential release for some eighteen years.

As it happened, George and the bandmates didn't return to the studio until Tuesday, September 29, after the Beatles had completed their American tour the previous week. That evening, the group tackled three new compositions: "Every Little Thing," "What You're Doing," and "I Don't Want to Spoil the Party." The production of their new album was quickly moving apace, thus enabling Brian and George to feel relatively comfortable about meeting their self-imposed holiday deadline. Lennon and McCartney had written "Every Little Thing" and "What You're Doing" during a break from the tour in Atlantic City. During the band's brief respite on the Jersey Shore, Ringo had also continued working on his first composition, the rough draft of a song that dated back to 1962 titled "Don't Pass Me By." George and the group began the evening with their first attempts at recording "Every Little Thing," an elegant, folk-tinged number that had the potential to be released as the band's next single. After four takes, they abandoned the track for the night, turning their attentions toward Lennon's "I Don't Want to Spoil the Party," with its innate country-and-western flavor simmering just below the surface. George recorded "I Don't Want to Spoil the Party" across nineteen takes, only five of which were completed. The Beatles' producer arranged the bass, drums, and Lennon's acoustic guitar on one track; Harrison's lead guitar on the second; Lennon and McCartney's vocals on the third; and backing vocals and a tambourine part on the remaining track. After completing "I Don't Want to Spoil the Party" in workmanlike fashion, they turned to "What

You're Doing," which they recorded in seven takes before leaving the song unfinished for a future session.

By the next afternoon, George and the Beatles were at it again. Earlier that day, Ringo had arrived at the studio early to sit in on a session with his former bandmates, Rory Storm and the Hurricanes, who were recording a cover version of "America," the standout tune from the hit musical *West Side Story*. In a momentous turn of events, Brian Epstein briefly sat in the producer's chair as Ringo chipped in with a percussion part and shared in the backing vocals, which eventually morphed into such inside jokes as "The Beatles went out to America / Played 'Twist and Shout' in America," among other lyrical gems. That afternoon, George and the Beatles picked up where they had left off the previous evening, recording five more takes of "Every Little Thing," the last of which was marked as the best. While the bandmates had a deadline to meet, there were plenty of hijinks in evidence, including take six, in which Paul burped a portion of his vocal, and take seven, which dissolved into cascades of laughter. With Martin's guidance, the Beatles took great care in perfecting the arrangement, which Lennon enhanced with an overdubbed lead guitar while McCartney punctuated the chorus with a descant piano and Starr made his debut on the timpani, the first orchestral instrument to appear on a Beatles recording. As time would demonstrate, it wouldn't be the last. During the evening session, the bandmates returned to "What You're Doing," with take eleven being selected as the best, if only for the time being, as the song would later be remade.

The September 30 session concluded in fine style, with George and the Beatles taking a stab at John's "No Reply," a composition that had been recorded as a demo back on June 3 after Ringo had fallen ill. By the end of the evening of September 30, the group had completed "No Reply," which had originally been intended for Tommy Quickly, one of Brian's stable of Liverpool singers who had opted to record "Tip of My Tongue," an early Beatles discard, instead. Quickly's version of "Tip of My Tongue" subsequently failed to chart. But after Quickly passed on "No Reply," the song was fair game for the Beatles, who swiftly transformed the song into not only a standout track but also a clear harbinger of the more sophisticated efforts to come. With Paul singing harmony in support of John's lead vocal, "No Reply" emerged as a deeply affecting narrative about the harrowing straits of romantic dependence. Primarily authored by Lennon, "No Reply" featured a piano part from Martin that afforded the song with a much-needed sense of interpersonal tension. For Lennon, "No Reply" marked a turning point of sorts, as the Beatle began fashioning well-honed, self-conscious ballads. The

Beatles' latest track even caught the attention of their publisher. As John later recalled, "I remember Dick James coming up to me after we did this one and saying, 'You're getting better now. That was a complete story.' Apparently, before that, he thought my songs wandered off."[6]

By this time in the band's career, John was clearly picking up steam as a songwriter and churning out new, more thought-provoking material at an impressive clip. As for Dick James, he had proven himself to be a vital cog in Brian's consolidation of the Beatles' organization. But as 1964 was coming to a close, James had already begun making plans to leverage Northern Songs and make a killing. Around this time, George was approached by EMI chairman Sir Joseph Lockwood, who was asking for his counsel about how much Northern Songs was worth—and even more importantly, thinking aloud about whether or not EMI should attempt to acquire it. George didn't mince words, telling Sir Joseph, "It is worth a great deal of money." As George learned, Sir Joseph had been negotiating with Dick and had agreed to a bargain-basement price of £800,000 to purchase Northern Songs. By the end of the protracted negotiations, EMI had lowered their offer to £500,000, along with another £100,000 to be paid out over the following three years, assuming that current sales forecasts continued unabated. Having seen EMI undervalue the Beatles' publishing so dramatically, James abruptly ended the negotiations. George couldn't believe that his employers had so monumentally fumbled the opportunity to acquire Northern Songs. "It was stupid of EMI," he later wrote. But in many ways, he should hardly have been surprised. In terms of the Beatles' publishing interests, this latest instance made for yet another round in a saga that would have long-standing implications for the band—Lennon and McCartney, especially—as well as for Martin and Dick James's professional relationship.[7]

On Tuesday, October 6, George conducted a fifth session in support of the Beatles' new album. Beginning the workday at 3 PM, the band spent seven hours perfecting a new song, "Eight Days a Week," which quickly replaced "Every Little Thing" as the leading candidate for their next singles release. The song came into being during one of Paul's visits to John's estate in suburban Weybridge. As McCartney later recalled, "I remember asking the chauffeur once if he was having a good week," and the chauffer said, "'I'm very busy at the moment. I've been working eight days a week.' And I thought, 'Eight days a week! Now there's a title.'" Several years later, John would point out that they had written "Eight Days a Week" as an attempt to create a title track for their next movie, which Brian had negotiated following the commercial success of *A Hard Day's Night*. The band allotted much of the October 6 session to experimenting with the arrangement as the day progressed rather than adhering to any central vision for bringing the catchy tune to fruition. For the first six takes, the Beatles busied themselves with the song's introduction, which still seemed rather ragged after several attempts. For the next seven takes, Lennon double-tracked his vocal while the others provided a series of handclaps. John and Paul also practiced different variations of the song's distinctive harmonies as "Eight Days a Week" evolved across the evening session. Between takes, John could be heard rehearsing a nifty new guitar riff that would later emerge as "I Feel Fine."[8]

On Thursday, October 8, Martin and the Beatles made short work of McCartney's "She's a Woman," at that point the only Lennon-McCartney composition to be entirely written and recorded in the very same day. As Paul later reported, "I have a recollection of walking 'round St. John's Wood with that in my mind so I might have written it at home and finished it up on the way to the studio, finally polished it in the studio, maybe just taken John aside for a second and checked it with him, 'What d'you think?' 'Like it.' 'Good.' 'Let's do it!'" As the Beatles perfected the song in Number 2, the arrangement was enhanced at every turn. As Paul recalled, "John did a very good thing: instead of playing through it and putting like a watercolor wash over it all with his guitar he just stabbed on the off-beats. Ringo would play the snare and John did it with the guitar, which was good, it left a lot of space for the rest of the stuff. That was a distinctive sound on that." The song was rendered even more distinctive still by Ringo's deployment of yet another new percussion instrument called a chocalho, a cylindrical metal shaker of Portuguese origin. With "She's a Woman" completed in an economical seven takes, the Beatles had their next B-side in the can. At this point, all George and the bandmates needed to do was identify once and for all their next single's A-side.[9]

Across the Beatles' incredible recording career, George and the group would enjoy more than their share of landmark sessions at Abbey Road, but few stand out like the nine-hour affair that they conducted on Sunday, October 18, 1964. The marathon session was necessitated by the band's sporadic availability given the constraints of their current British tour, which had begun back on October 9 in Bradford and would run through a November 10 date in Bristol. On this day alone, they would bring eight tracks to completion, isolate their next stand-alone single, and make history in the recording studio. They may indeed have been war weary, as George had maintained about the Beatles during this period, but their industriousness more than made up for their understandable exhaustion toward the tail end of that life-changing year.

The day's work began with "Eight Days a Week," the song that they had left in an unfinished state during their previous meeting. Flush with creative energy, George and the Beatles decided to tackle the catchy composition head on. As Emerick later recalled, the session began when Martin "asked everyone to convene in the control room. The first order of business was to do some repair work" on "Eight Days a Week." "As the last note died out, we all excitedly agreed that the high-energy performance captured on tape was a definite 'keeper,'" Geoff wrote. "The only problems were with the ragged beginning and overly abrupt ending, and an intense discussion ensued about how to best fix them." As it happened, John and Paul had cooked up an idea about beginning the song with their harmonies, sung a cappella, to afford "Eight Days a Week" with an arresting intro. Recognizing that the two Beatles were making precious little progress on this latest brainchild—and with one eye focused, no doubt, on the studio clock—George redirected the band's energies back to the song's unsettled conclusion. With Smith and Emerick up in the control room with Martin, Lennon and Harrison chimed out the melody on their guitars—a Gibson "Jumbo" acoustic and twelve-string Rickenbacker, respectively—as McCartney brought the song in for a landing with a series of staccato bursts on his Höfner bass. With the issue of the outro finally resolved, the Beatles' circle set their sights on the "the problem of what to do about the ragged intro," Geoff later recalled, "and as they were pondering what to do about it, Norman came up with the brilliant suggestion of simply fading in the song, instead of having everything come crashing in at full volume." Quite suddenly, "Eight Days a Week" had come into focus, with Smith fashioning the new edit pieces onto the best take from the previous session.[10]

With "Eight Days a Week" in the can, George and the bandmates began knocking off "Kansas City"/"Hey-Hey-Hey-Hey!"—a long-standing Beatles concert staple and the first of several cover versions that they would tackle that day. Written by Jerry Leiber and Mike Stoller, "Kansas City" had been released as a single in 1952 by Little Willie Littlefield, while "Hey-Hey-Hey-Hey" had been composed and popularized by Paul's singing idol, Little Richard. The group knew the song inside and out, and with Martin lending a subtle piano, they knocked off the tune in two high-octane takes. With yet another song in the can, they returned to "Mr. Moonlight," which had remained unfinished since the August 14 session when they had also tried their hand at "Leave My Kitten Alone." With Martin in the control booth, the band remade "Mr. Moonlight," isolating the rhythm section—bass, guitars, and conga—on track one; a Hammond organ riff from McCartney on track two; Lennon's lead vocals on track three; and backing vocals on the remaining track. "Mr. Moonlight" received a final, key bit of ornamentation when Smith edited Lennon's opening scream from August 14 into the mix, affording the song with a striking intro.

Which brought George and the Beatles to "I Feel Fine," the riff that John had been rehearsing between takes during the previous session. Based on Bobby Parker's "Watch Your Step," one of Lennon's favorite songs, the ecstatic guitar sequence clearly had the makings of a hit record, but the Beatles—and especially John—had something even more groundbreaking in mind for "I Feel Fine." As McCartney later recalled, the song's innovative intro happened initially by accident during a break in the previous session. "John had a semi-acoustic Gibson guitar. It had a pick-up on it so it could be amplified," McCartney remarked. "We were just about to walk away to listen to a take when John leaned his guitar against the amp. I can still see him doing it. He really should have turned the electric off. It was only on a tiny bit, and John just leaned it against the amp when it went, 'Nnnnnnwahhhhh!' And we went, 'What's that? Voodoo!' 'No, it's feedback.' 'Wow, it's a great sound!' George Martin was there so we said, 'Can we have that on the record?' 'Well, I suppose we could, we could edit it on the front.' It was a found object, an accident caused by leaning the guitar against the amp." With this newfangled sound at their fingertips, the Beatles began to experiment with various means of controlling its duration. On October 18, Emerick observed the band from the control room as they toyed with using feedback as the introductory gambit for "I Feel Fine." "As the band began rehearsing their next song in the studio with George Martin," Emerick recalled, "I used the opportunity to sit in the control room and relax for a few minutes. I was making small talk with Norman about something or other when all of a sudden I heard this loud, buzzing sound issue forth from the speakers. 'What the bloody hell was that?' I asked him, alarmed. My first thought was that a cable had gone bad, or that a piece of equipment had failed. Norman chuckled. 'Have a look,' he said to me. I pressed my nose up against the control room glass and was astonished to see John Lennon kneeling before his amplifier, guitar in hand. We knew that if you brought a guitar too close to an amplifier, it would squeal, but John was using it in a controlled way for the first time."[11]

As the Beatles attempted to get a handle on "I Feel Fine," Martin suggested that they record the rhythm track first, which they accomplished across eight takes. For the ninth take, John added his lead vocals. The distinctive intro was achieved with Paul plucking a low note on his bass, while John controlled the feedback howling from his guitar. He was understandably proud of having captured the effect on record. Years later, he described it as "the first feedback anywhere. I defy anybody to find a record—unless it's some old blues record in 1922—that used feedback in that way. I mean, everybody played feedback on stage, and the Jimi Hendrix stuff was going on long before. In fact, the punk stuff now is only what people were doing in the clubs. So I claim for the Beatles—before Hendrix, before the Who, before anybody—the first feedback on any record."[12]

With their next standalone singles release fully in hand, Martin and the band took a dinner break before shifting to one of McCartney's oldest compositions, which he had written at age sixteen in his family's front parlor back in Liverpool. As Paul later recalled, "There were certain songs I had from way back that I didn't really finish up, but they were in the back of my mind." Titled "I'll Follow the Sun," the song was completed by the group in eight takes, with the final run-through being selected as their best effort. Lennon and McCartney sang the middle eight in an exquisite vocal duet, while Harrison overdubbed a solo in the guitar break. In yet another innovation on the day, Ringo kept time during "I'll Follow the Sun" by simply slapping his knees with the palms of his hands. Years later, Martin would single out "I'll Follow the Sun" as his favorite track from the *Beatles for Sale* album. He later admitted that he was generally tolerant of recording technical imperfections during this era, preferring to capture the best possible vocal performances, as he had done with John and Paul's memorable work on "I'll Follow the Sun." "Looking back," he later recalled, "some of the plops that we got on the mics were pretty awful, but I was out to get the performance—the excitement of the actual live action—and technical things like that didn't worry me too much."[13]

The October 18 session hurtled toward its conclusion with the recording of three more songs that evening—"Everybody's Trying to Be My Baby," "Rock and Roll Music," and "Words of Love"—all of which were accomplished in just five takes. For the first two tracks, George sweetened the songs' lead vocals by heavily treating them with STEED (single tape echo and echo delay) in order to achieve a live-sounding echo effect. The enhancement was accomplished when Smith delayed the recorded signal by directing it into Studio 2's echo chamber using a tape machine and then picking up the resultant sound using a pair of condenser microphones, which transmitted the signal back to the recording console. For "Everybody's Trying to Be My Baby," a cover version in the style of Carl Perkins, one of Harrison's guitar idols, George and the group captured the song in a single take with the STEED effect applied live during the actual recording. As a result, Harrison's vocal oozes with reverb as if he's singing in a spacious concert hall. "Not only did he sing it with enthusiasm," Emerick wrote, "but he played guitar confidently and well. Even his solo, performed live, was flawless." After adding a tambourine overdub by Ringo, they turned to another cover version, the Chuck Berry classic "Rock and Roll Music." With Lennon's vocals sweetened with a heavy dose of STEED and Martin playing a mean piano, the Beatles recorded "Rock and Roll Music" in a single, scintillating take.[14]

For John, George's deployment of STEED to treat his lead vocals was seemingly the answer to his long-standing issues with the quality of his voice. "I could never understand his attitude, as it was one of the best voices I've heard. He was a great admirer of Elvis Presley's early records, particularly the 'Heartbreak Hotel' kind of sound," George later remarked. In many ways, John was his own worst critic, fretting over the quality of his lead vocals, which he frequently attempted to camouflage and enhance via double-tracking. STEED afforded him with a means for altering his voice even more perceptibly. As George remembered, "He was always saying to me, 'Do something with my voice. Put something on it. Smother it with tomato ketchup. Make it different.' He was obsessed with tape delay—a sort of very near-echo. I used to do other things to him, and as long as it wasn't his natural voice coming through, he was reasonably happy—but he'd always want his vocals to get special treatment. However, I wanted to hear it in its own natural quality." As it turned out, John's long-standing difference with George over the natural beauty of his voice was only just getting started.[15]

With the evening growing nigh, the Beatles had time for just one more track, as they had to be in Scotland the very next day to resume their current tour. At this juncture, they turned to Buddy Holly's "Words of Love," the only time that the bandmates, who idolized the fallen Texan, would record one of his numbers. Captured in three takes—only two of which were complete—"Words of Love" featured John and Paul in a warm vocal duet. Martin sweetened the track with a series of overdubs, including Lennon and McCartney double-tracking their vocals, as well as double-tracking the distinctive chiming sound emitted by Harrison's Gretsch Tennessean. To keep time for the song, Ringo can be heard rapping the side of a packing case—not unlike the sound that the Crickets' Jerry Allison achieved on Holly's "Everyday" by slapping his hands on his lap. With the second take of "Words of Love" having been selected as the best run-through, the Beatles' incredibly productive session had come to an end after just over nine hours of work in Studio 2.

Eight days later, George and the Beatles would finish their principal recordings for *Beatles for Sale*. Taking advantage of another day off from their tour, the bandmates added yet another cover version to the album's contents—in this instance, Carl Perkins's "Honey Don't," with Ringo on lead vocals. Over the years, John had handled the song in the Beatles' set but relinquished it for *Beatles for Sale* to allow for the drummer's vocal contribution to the long-player. More often than not, Martin and the band would ensure that Starr was showcased on their album-length projects. As the drummer later recalled, "It was a case of finding a vehicle for me with the Beatles. That's why we did it ['Honey Don't'] on *Beatles For Sale*. It was comfortable. And I was finally getting one track on a record: my little featured spot." Recorded in five brisk takes during the afternoon session, "Honey Don't" offered Martin's fairly standard four-track arrangement during this era, with bass and drums on one track; Lennon and Harrison's acoustic and electric guitars, respectively, on a second track; and Starr's lead vocal on a third track. Tambourine was added to fifth take of "Honey Don't," which was marked as the best of the lot. During the evening session, the Beatles returned to "What You're Doing," which they remade across seven takes, three of which were complete run-throughs. With a similar track arrangement to "Honey Don't," "What You're Doing" proved to be a tighter, more confident rendition than the group had fashioned during the September 29 session in which it was debuted. The final take was considered the best, although for his part, McCartney felt particularly uncertain about his miniature bass solo at the end of the song, complaining to Martin, "George, what did it sound like with the bass doing a funny thing? Did it sound any good or did it sound just all ugly crap?" Without missing a beat, George replied with unflinching sincerity, "It sounded rather magnificent." With the contents of their new album all but complete, the band turned their efforts toward their annual Christmas Flexi-Disc fan club giveaway. As George rolled the tape, the four Beatles engaged in all manner of jokes and skits, along with a smattering of seasonal carols. At one point, Harrison referenced the band's filmic follow-up to *A Hard Day's Night*, which Epstein had dutifully scheduled for production in the new year. Perhaps most significantly, the October 26 session at Abbey Road marked the first time that the Beatles attended a mixing session, which George had supervised before work had begun on "Honey Don't." A shift in their studio practices—very subtle, of course, at this juncture—was underway, as the group was beginning to take a greater interest in the various processes that went into making their music.[16]

With Norman Smith and Ken Scott in tow, George held a control room mixing session for *Beatles for Sale* on October 27 in which the trio prepared the mono and stereo mixes of the album. A follow-up session on November 4 allowed George to complete the remaining stereo mixes, bringing to fruition his work on the band's fourth studio album in the space of two years. The Beatles' next singles release, "I Feel Fine" backed with "She's a Woman," hit the stores on Friday, November 27. With new Beatles product in the offing, the single sold more than eight hundred thousand copies during its first five days of release in the United Kingdom, while turning over a million more during its gala first week in the United States. *NME* heralded "I Feel Fine" as "a real gas . . . a happy-go-lucky mid-tempo swinger [with] a tremendous rhythm and a really catchy melody." At this point, George and the bandmates had succeeded in landing yet another chart-topping UK hit. "I Feel Fine" marked their seventh consecutive number-one song, following "Please Please Me," "From Me to You," "She Loves You," "I Want to Hold Your Hand," "Can't Buy Me Love," and "A Hard Day's Night." George duly recognized their incredible succession of hits as a "unique achievement," adding that "it became almost an accepted fact of nature. The question was not whether a record would get to number one, but how quickly." By this point, the numbers were simply staggering. In October, EMI had estimated that some ten million Beatles records had been shipped, while the *Daily Mail* calculated the band's international earnings somewhere north of $56 million.[17]

Released on December 4, *Beatles for Sale* marked the fourth Beatles album in the space of twenty-one months. In the United Kingdom, the long-player quickly ascended to the top of the charts, where it unseated *A Hard Day's Night*. Over the years, *Beatles for Sale* has developed a reputation for being one of the band's weakest LP releases. George attributed this impression to the fact that the Beatles "were always on the go. *Beatles for Sale* doesn't appeal to me very much now, it's not one of their most memorable ones. They perked up again after that." While George may have had his misgivings, *Beatles for Sale* was recorded and released like veritable clockwork in keeping with Brian and George's larger plan to produce two new albums and three singles in every calendar year. Neil Aspinall, the Beatles' road manager, chalked up any lingering perceptions about the album's quality to the group's indefatigable North Country work ethic, not to mention Brian and George's paradigm for Beatles success. "No band today would come off a long US tour at the end of September, go into the studio and start a new album, still writing songs, and then go on a UK tour, finish the album in five weeks, still touring, and have the album out in time for Christmas," Aspinall later observed. "But that's what the Beatles did at the end of 1964. A lot of it was down to naïveté, thinking that this was the way things were done. If the record company needs another album, you go and make one."[18]

Their producer's commentary notwithstanding, *Beatles for Sale* finds George and the band experiencing fits of innovation as they attempt to break free from Brian and George's self-imposed marketing plan. In so doing, they concocted a turning point of sorts with their most recent long-player. For one thing, the album's spate of cover versions from their stage repertoire would mark the last time that they would base their output so extensively on nonoriginal material. But perhaps most significantly, *Beatles for Sale* reveals Lennon in the throes of an intense period of change. His latest songs—"No Reply," "I'm a Loser," and "I Don't Want to Spoil the Party," to name but a few—found him entering a highly introspective phase, likely set into motion by the Beatles' meeting with Bob Dylan back in August. There would be no turning back. Lennon and his mates were already taking a greater interest in expanding the capacity of the recording studio to bring their musical ideas to life. As Martin later observed, by this time "they started getting really interested in studio techniques. They always wanted to get the thing right so it wasn't a one-take operation, they would listen to it and they'd do two or three takes until they got it pretty well right." Artistically, they were poised to enter a new and potentially exciting chapter in their career together.[19]

In its own way, the album cover photograph for *Beatles for Sale* points toward something new on the Beatles' creative horizon. Shot by Robert Freeman at dusk near London's Hyde Park, the photo depicts the bandmates in an expressionless, almost brooding pose against the autumnal colors of late fall. One can almost glimpse the shift within Freeman's grainy photograph. There was something different in the offing alright, and it was coming sooner than the group's legions of fans, still ecstatic amid Beatlemania's seemingly unremitting haze, could even possibly have guessed.

# 16

# YESTERDAY AND TODAY

FOR GEORGE, 1965 began with, of all things, a broken foot.

On January 25, George and Judy joined John and Cynthia Lennon for a gala ski trip at St. Moritz in the Swiss Alps. The couples had been friendly for quite some time by this point. In addition to sharing the experience of the Beatles' triumphant first American visit, the couples would often socialize, with John being particularly taken with Judy's upper-class demeanor. When he was composing his first book, *In His Own Write*—a collection of essays, experimental fiction, and other miscellaneous writings and cartoons—John would ask Judy to recite from his motley assortment of puns and word games. As George later remembered, "I thought they were terribly funny. I showed them to Judy, and she read one line out loud. 'Read some more, Judy,' said John, and he made her read a whole excerpt. She had the boys rolling around laughing at her cut-glass accent, pronouncing all those invented words John used." During this period, George was much closer to John than to Paul, who "was very much the *avant-garde* man, spending his time in art galleries with John Dunbar and people like that, listening to Stockhausen and so on. John seemed much more the pipe-and-slippers man, at home with Cyn in stockbroker belt Weybridge."[1]

As it happened, George's ski trip with Judy and the Lennons was off to a promising start—but only after the Beatles' producer quelled the media posse that had trailed them to St. Moritz by giving them a few hours of unfettered access to John in which they peppered him with questions and took a number of photographs. After a hearty day of skiing, the two couples retired to their luxurious suite at the Palace Hotel. Ever the prankster, John emerged from the shower wearing his black skiing tights. With his mussed hair, he fell into a comical "Max Wall walk" and left everyone in stitches. "Not to be outdone," George later wrote, "I donned my black tights and on top of them a pair of boxer shorts fluffed out a bit to look like a skirt, and put a bandeau 'round my head." With his costume in place, George executed a "Nureyev-type leap with an entrechat in the middle." But as his audience broke into laughter, George flubbed the landing. Suddenly, "there was a sharp noise like a twig breaking, and I collapsed in agony." With a fortnight of skiing left to go, George had to deal with the ignominious reality of having broken his foot—not on the pristine slopes of the Swiss Alps but in the relative safety of a hotel sitting room.

Years later, George would remember the trip for another reason altogether. In one unforgettable moment, he enjoyed the rare opportunity to witness John in the act of composing a new song "while we were all gathered around, nursing my broken foot": "I distinctly remember him strumming away on the guitar, singing, 'I once had a girl, / Or should I say, / She once had me.'" To George's mind, it sounded like "a very bitter little story." After playing "This Bird Has Flown," as he called it at the time, John turned to another new composition called "Ticket to Ride," which he debuted for the Beatles' producer. "I liked it straightaway," George remembered. "John said he would get together with Paul as soon as he got back to London and finish it off."[2]

On February 7, the couples made their return from the Swiss Alps, with George hobbling his way through customs with his leg encased in a plaster cast up to his knee. Scarcely a week later, George and the Beatles were back in the studio. As with their work on *A Hard Day's Night* a year earlier, they were under the gun to produce a spate of new songs for their upcoming feature film. On Monday, February 15, they convened at Abbey Road to begin six full days of recording sessions before flying out to the Bahamas, where they were set to begin principal photography with Richard Lester. As the bandmates prepared for their first session of the new year, John posed for photos in George's automobile in the EMI parking lot in front of the studio. The Beatle had just received his license after passing his driving test. By the time that George and the bandmates had assembled in Studio 2 that afternoon, it had been more than three full months since they had worked together. For his part, George was teeming with butterflies, later remarking, "When the sessions begin, my heart is usually in my mouth. I wonder, sometimes, whether they can keep it up time after time, but they do! They're terribly workmanlike in the studio." By this point, Abbey Road had become a safe haven for the group. As Ken Scott observed, "They were all so close, I think anywhere that all of them were away from the crowds was a refuge for them." But just as important, the Beatles were "fearless," in Scott's words. "They didn't mind change—every record changed slightly. Obviously, as it went along it changed more and more, and faster and faster. More often than not when someone is worried about getting the next hit they keep on exactly the same formula. They didn't."[3]

For the occasion of the February 15 session, George pointedly instructed Ken to leave the tape machine running as the Beatles rehearsed their latest material for the upcoming feature film. In so doing, George established a shift in the band's recording practices that would leave an indelible mark on their sound. As the tape ran unabated, the Beatles would focus their attention on perfecting the bedrock of a particular song—often concentrating purely on the backing or rhythm track. After laying down the basic track, George and the group would then overdub additional elements to the song, ranging from lead and backing vocals to guitar solos and other instrumental ornamentation. In this way, the band often resorted to many fewer takes to complete a song—although that very same recording might have been subjected to numerous additions and subtractions along the way as they tried out different sounds through processes of trial and error. With "Ticket to Ride," their first recording of the new year, the shift in George and the band's studio practices netted a quick and very palpable result. Produced during an afternoon session, "Ticket to Ride" was an electric, driving rock song. Martin arranged the first two tracks of the recording with Starr's drums and McCartney's bass on one track and Lennon and Harrison's rhythm and lead guitars, respectively, on a second. With Harrison executing the distinctive twelve-string Rickenbacker riff, Lennon taped his lead vocal on a third track, along with McCartney's backing vocal. In this way, Martin and the Beatles were literally building "Ticket to Ride" from the ground up. The remaining fourth track allowed McCartney to overdub guitar fills and a solo on his hollow-bodied Epiphone Casino, as well as tambourine and handclaps to afford the song extra punch.

With "Ticket to Ride," the Beatles' sound had changed in a hurry. Leaving the tape running and nailing down the song's relentless forward momentum allowed George and the bandmates to capture the recording in an economical two takes, with take one being a false start. As a result, the production teems with a clear sense of energy and immediacy, imbuing "Ticket to Ride" with a live, crisp sound that finds the band barreling ahead of their most recent work on *Beatles for Sale*. Rehearsing the song with the tape running in the studio also provided the creative space for several innovations—namely, the spirited coda that brings the song home in fine style. As McCartney later remarked, "I think the interesting thing was a crazy ending; instead of ending like the previous verse, we changed the tempo. We picked up one of the lines, 'My baby don't care,' but completely altered the melody. We almost invented the idea of a new bit of a song on the fade-out." As McCartney pointed out, "it was quite radical at the time."[4]

With "Ticket to Ride," the Beatles proved how truly fearless they could be in the studio, to borrow Scott's characterization, and Martin made a conscious effort during this period to provide the bandmates with a wide berth in which to exercise their evolving imaginations. As the producer later observed, "A two-way swing developed in our relationship. On the one hand, as the style emerged and the recording techniques developed, so my control—over what the finished product sounded like—increased. Yet at the same time, my need for changing the pure music became less and less. As I could see their talent growing, I could recognize that an idea coming from them was better than an idea coming from me, though it would still be up to me to decide which was the better approach. In a sense, I made a sort of tactical withdrawal, recognizing that theirs was the greater talent." "Ticket to Ride" explicitly demonstrated this point, with the Beatles taking advantage of their free rein in the studio to develop new sounds and musical textures. But the group's latest track also found George devoting more of his energies to post-production efforts—particularly in terms of enhancing the finished product. With "Ticket to Ride," these efforts involved taking great pains in honing the song's ultimate presentation to a waiting world. Two days later, Martin, Smith, and Scott conducted a control room session to engineer the song's inventive fade-out while also adding a healthy amount of reverb. In so doing, they took "Ticket to Ride" to even greater heights.[5]

The February 16 session continued after the dinner hour with two new compositions for the feature film, including McCartney's "Another Girl" and Harrison's "I Need You." With the tape running, the Beatles established a rhythm track for "Another Girl," which McCartney had written during a recent Tunisian vacation while Martin and Lennon were in St. Moritz. After nailing down a basic track, the group added numerous edit pieces—by now a near-specialty of Martin's in the Beatles' mid-1960s heyday. Later, on February 17, McCartney would overdub a new lead guitar solo for "Another Girl." Up next was "I Need You," a new Harrison composition, an acoustic version of which was recorded over five takes that evening. The next afternoon, Martin and the band remade the song, supplying it with a more electric sound. Martin later saw "I Need You" as a significant milestone for Harrison, who had long toiled in the shadows of Lennon and McCartney. As the producer later remarked, "'I Need You' worked out very well. George got a bit discouraged some time ago when none of us liked something he had written. He has got something to say as a songwriter, and I hope he keeps it up."[6]

As the sessions progressed that week, Martin and the studio personnel prepared production acetates to share with Lester and his producer, Walter Shenson, who were gearing up for principal photography on the feature film. That evening, Martin and the band devoted fourteen takes—the most that they would carry out for any song during the whole of that year—to "Yes It Is," a tender ballad written by Lennon. As with "This Boy," the song featured close harmonies, which Martin helped to perfect in the studio. Harrison's distinctive guitar sound on "Yes It Is," as with "I Need You" earlier that afternoon, was deployed using a foot-controlled tone pedal. Connected to the guitar's volume controls, the tone pedal generated volume swells with each passing chord. Harrison's plaintive guitar work imbued Lennon's wistful ballad with even greater depths of meaning.

Earlier that day, the Beatles had been honored by EMI chairman Sir Joseph Lockwood in a ceremony at the company's Manchester Square offices. With Brian and George looking on, Sir Joe, as the Beatles affectionately referred to him, presented the band with dozens of awards, including numerous commemorative gold records that they had earned the previous year. The event concluded with a series of photographs depicting the Beatles, George, and Brian posing with Sir Joseph, their gold discs arrayed in the foreground. With the clock clicking ever down on George's EMI contract, the images reveal the group's brain trust in a coming state of flux. As the EMI chairman well knew, George's stubborn inclination to leave his employment with the company promised to deliver a number of unknown outcomes should he indeed hold fast to his position and resign from the EMI Group. With the Beatles' initial contract with the British juggernaut coming due in sixteen months, George's change in status seemed to augur a period of great uncertainty not only for Martin and the bandmates but also for EMI. Brian was only just beginning to negotiate the Beatles' EMI contract, which after the fourth option year, was set to expire in June 1966. Not surprisingly, the rumors began to spiral in the trade papers. In an April 1965 *Billboard* article titled "Beatles Seen Recording for Own Company," Sir Joseph was quoted as saying that he "strongly regrets that the group was originally signed to such a comparatively short contract." Spoken with the genuine benefit of hindsight, Sir Joseph's words belied the reality of the situation back in May 1962, when

George himself had little inclination to sign the band, which in all fairness, was nothing more at the time than an unknown regional act out of Liverpool with no industry track record.[7]

On Wednesday, February 17, George and the Beatles tackled two more songs under consideration for the feature film, including McCartney's "The Night Before" and Harrison's "You Like Me Too Much." The band completed both songs in a pair of afternoon and evening sessions. While "The Night Before" emerged in two takes, much like "Ticket to Ride" on Monday, George and the group spent some five hours adding a series of overdubs to the basic rhythm track, including Paul's double-tracked lead guitar and Ringo's maracas. The song is notable for John's performance on a Hohner Pianet C electric piano, which he would reprise for "You Like Me Too Much" that same evening. Harrison and McCartney turned in layered lead guitar solos, courtesy of an overdub, with each playing in a different octave. "You Like Me Too Much" proved to be the greater challenge that day, requiring eight takes and a number of overdubs. After recording the basic rhythm track, Martin supervised a series of overdubs, including the double-tracking of Harrison's lead vocals, Harrison's lead guitar solo, and McCartney and Martin playing the studio's Steinway piano at the same time.

With six new songs under their belts, George and the Beatles returned to Abbey Road on Thursday, February 18, which would prove to be a banner day in their collaboration, even going so far as to set the stage for a slew of future innovations to come. Lennon arrived at the session armed with a new, folk-oriented composition titled "You've Got to Hide Your Love Away." He was joined by a guest that day—his childhood friend Pete Shotton. "That's me in my Dylan period," Lennon later remarked about his new composition. "I am like a chameleon, influenced by whatever is going on. If Elvis can do it, I can do it. If the Everly Brothers can do it, Paul and me can. Same with Bob Dylan." As George and the band essayed the song that afternoon, the tape was left running as the Beatles recorded a basic rhythm track with Ringo gently brushing his snare while John sang and played his twelve-string Framus Hootenanny. For the first few takes, the band suffered a series of false starts when Lennon paused to adjust a microphone and, later, after McCartney accidently broke a drinking glass. After several attempts, Martin marked take nine as "best."[8]

During the first few complete run-throughs, John continued to refine his gruff vocal stylings. At one point, George recalled, "I asked him not to sound too much like Dylan. He wasn't doing it deliberately. It was subconscious more than anything." As Shotton later recalled, by this time, Lennon had inadvertently incorporated a new lyric into the tune, having discovered that he had accidentally sung "feeling two-foot small" instead of the original phrase, "feeling two-foot tall." As Shotton looked on, Lennon said, "Let's leave that in, actually. All those pseuds will really love it," referring to the pretentious "pseudo-intellectuals" of the day. George sweetened the take with a number of overdubs, including Ringo on tambourine, Paul on maracas, and John rerecording his lead vocal. By this juncture, "You've Got to Hide Your Love Away" was already another Beatles classic in the making. And that's when John shared his vision for the coda: a flute solo to bring his splendid Dylanesque composition to a close. For George, it was a sudden opportunity to draw upon his experience as composer and arranger for a Beatles recording. According to George's production notes, they were joined in the studio two days later by flautist John Scott, a regular hired musician around the Abbey Road corridors. With Martin's arrangement in hand, Scott recorded a double-tracked flute solo. As Scott later remembered, "They told me roughly what they wanted, ¾ time, and the best way of fulfilling their needs was to play both tenor flute and alto flute, the second as an overdub." Not only was Scott the first outside musician to appear on a Beatles track since Andy White back in September 1962, but also the recording of "You've Got to Hide Your Love Away" found Martin and the band expanding their musical horizons considerably by augmenting their standard four-part sound. For Norman Smith, a clear shift in the Beatles' work was palpable. As he observed at the time, "They're absolutely determined not to duplicate tempos or intensity of sound. They want to come up with something different each time in the studio."[9]

Unfailingly industrious, they attempted two more songs after the dinner break on February 18. Always on the lookout for a vehicle for Starr to sing, Lennon and McCartney unveiled an up-tempo rock number titled "If You've Got Trouble." George and the band captured the song in a single take and added a few overdubs before abandoning the lackluster tune. In addition to double-tracking Starr's vocal, the overdubs included McCartney on his Epiphone Casino and Harrison playing the solo on his Fender Stratocaster. At one point, Ringo shouted "Rock on, anybody!" in a halfhearted attempt to breathe life into the song. The day concluded with yet another new composition, "Tell Me What You See," which found the group members playing a range of instruments, including Paul on the electric piano and Ringo working the guiro, a Latin American percussion instrument shaped like an open-ended, hollow gourd. Journalist Ray Coleman was in the studio during the song's production, and he later afforded readers of *Melody Maker* a rare glimpse into Martin and the band's working relationship: "Martin is perched on a high chair, and the four Beatles are around him, singing lightly and playing acoustic guitars. Martin sings a song with them." After further rehearsing "Tell Me What You See" with the group, George reveals the exacting attention to detail that typified his approach to making Beatles records:

> Martin: "Let's have one more go at the backing, then we'll record your voices separately. This time, we'll get it exactly right."
> McCartney: "Why—what was exactly wrong?"
> Martin: "The tuning sounded wrong. And you, George, should be coming in on the second beat every time instead of every fourth beat."
> Harrison: "Oh, I see."[10]

In its essence, this brief exchange demonstrated what people in the Beatles' inner circle understood implicitly: namely, that George was possibly the single most influential person in their world, really the only one who could impinge upon the nature of their music. Even Brian, whom they held in extraordinarily high esteem, held little, if any, sway in terms of influencing the direction of their creative lives. At one point, when Brian dared to offer an opinion about their efforts in the studio, John coolly replied, "You look after your percentages, Brian. We'll take care of the music."[11]

With only a few days remaining before the group had to leave for the Bahamas, George and the Beatles attempted two more potential songs for the soundtrack. First up was "You're Going to Lose That Girl," which they recorded on the afternoon of February 19. With the tape running, they produced the song in two takes, with the second (erroneously marked as take three) being complete. The basic track consisted of John's rhythm guitar, Paul's bass, and Ringo's drums. With Harrison turning in a guitar solo, McCartney overdubbed an electric piano part on a second track, while Lennon, McCartney, and Harrison shared lead vocals on a third. The fourth track found John overdubbing his vocals. A new guitar solo, with bongo and acoustic piano accompaniment, would be added at a later date. With "You're Going to Lose That Girl" relatively complete, Martin and the Beatles took their leave from Abbey Road, as EMI chairman Sir Joseph Lockwood was holding a gala dinner party that night in the Beatles' honor at the Connaught Hotel. The group was rightly being feted, but it is impossible not to believe, given the confluence of events regarding George's and the Beatles' contracts, that they were also being not-so-subtly wooed by the EMI brass.

On February 20, George and the band spent their last afternoon in the studio before the Beatles' departure. On the docket was a new McCartney tune titled "That Means a Lot," which the group slaved over throughout the session. As was their usual practice at this time, they recorded four rehearsal takes with the tape running before capturing a basic track consisting of McCartney's bass, Lennon's rhythm guitar, Harrison's acoustic guitar, and Starr's drums. A second track was composed of additional bass from Paul, Ringo's echoed tom-tom, and additional guitar courtesy of John's Fender Strat. At this juncture, Martin combined tracks one and two onto track three, thus freeing up space on the second track for backing vocals from Lennon and Harrison in support of McCartney's lead vocals on track four. With track one now available, Martin overdubbed a piano part, along with enhanced vocals from McCartney, Lennon, and Harrison, as well as Ringo's maracas, which were featured during the song's coda. In so doing, Martin and the bandmates had created one of their busiest recordings to date. Yet in spite of their incredible efforts that afternoon, they opted to abandon the track, which they considered to be unsatisfactory, for a later date.

Before the Beatles made their departure for a faraway film set in the Bahamas, John was interviewed by journalist Ray Coleman about their latest bout in the studio. Describing the material that they had just completed with George, John remarked, "They're just songs. If they fit the story and the sequences, some of them will be in. It's up to the film bosses. Not us. We've just concentrated this week on making records. There are a couple of obvious songs for the film, at least we think so, but nothing's been decided." In keeping with Brian and George's rudimentary plan, established during the previous calendar year, of releasing new Beatles product in the form of a new single every three months, two albums per year, and a feature film to boot, the bandmates winged their way to the Bahamas via New York City to rendezvous with the "film bosses" themselves, Richard Lester and Walter Shenson.[12]

Principal photography on the Beatles' new feature film commenced on February 23 on New Providence Island. The Beatles stayed at the Balmoral Club as the guests of their financial advisor, Dr. Walter Strach, who had taken up residence in the Bahamas as a tax shelter. Currently being filmed under the working title of *Eight Arms to Hold You*, Lester's follow-up to *A Hard Day's Night* had originally been written as a vehicle for Peter Sellers, who turned the screenplay down in favor of the frivolous *What's New Pussycat?* After being rewritten to accommodate the Beatles' silver-screen personae, the script for *Eight Arms to Hold You* attempted to capture the zany humor of *A*

*Hard Day's Night* in the guise of a Marx Brothers film. And this time around, Lester would be armed with a considerably more expansive budget of $1.5 million, enabling him to shoot in brilliant Technicolor as opposed to the previous film's low-budget black and white. But in spite of such robust resources, Lester's sophomore effort was relatively pedestrian from the start. Where *A Hard Day's Night* offered a fresh take on the jukebox movie genre, the latest screenplay was fuelled by high camp, deploying a James Bond–inspired spy narrative as its central conceit. While the Beatles publicly lauded their new movie as a "mad story," they would be forgiven for having any misgivings about a screenplay in which Ringo, it seems, has managed to come into the possession of an exotic diamond ring that is sought after by desperate people of all stripes, including a cult of Eastern mystics, hit men, and mad scientists. As the madcap movie unfolded, the drummer's mates attempted to rescue him from his life-or-death predicament while negotiating a veritable maze of car chases and skiing shenanigans.[13]

Years later, the Beatles would freely admit that their time in the Bahamas was nothing short of a "haze of marijuana." Since making Dylan's acquaintance back in August 1964, the group had emerged as potheads of the first order. In Ringo's memories, the Beatles' cannabis habit was purely recreational. "A hell of a lot of pot was being smoked while we were making the film. It was great. That helped make it a lot of fun," he later recalled. "Dick Lester knew that very little would get done after lunch. In the afternoon, we very seldom got past the first line of the script. We had such hysterics that no one could do anything." But for John, the Beatles' psychotropic turn had deeper implications involving the virtual prison of their fame. "The Beatles thing had just gone beyond comprehension," he later recalled. "We were smoking marijuana for breakfast. We were well into marijuana and nobody could communicate with us, because we were just all glazed eyes, giggling all the time. In our own world." As for George, who was back in England waiting on the precipice of momentous, highly personal events in the offing, the Beatles' pot smoking had been evident for quite some time. He hadn't failed to notice their increasingly frequent trips to Abbey Road's washroom, from whence they would return, like the foursome that they were, "grinning all over their faces." Admittedly, George hadn't noticed the change coming over his charges at first. But then he began slowly but surely to perceive the ways in which marijuana was "affecting the boys in front of my very eyes, yet my own brand of naïvety had prevented me from seeing the whole thing for what it really was. I hardly knew what pot smelled like, although it was right under my nose!"[14]

On February 25, the third day of filming on the set of Lester's feature film, the Beatles hammed it up for the camera in and around Interfield Road in Nassau. Later, John and Ringo played various scenes at the Bahamas Softball Association's stadium, while Paul was being filmed within the dank recesses of local limestone quarry caves. On that same day back in England, George learned that his divorce from Sheena had been finalized after many years of personal struggle. For George, it had to have been a bittersweet victory at best, as the competing worlds of his past and present continued to collide even after his divorce had become official. Finally, the charade that he and Sheena had concocted was coming to an end—but only at a hefty price. It was especially burdensome for George's young son, Gregory, now nine years old, who had suddenly become privy to his parents' breakup, which his older sister, Alexis, had known about for years. Even decades later, it was painful for Gregory to recall the first time he cast his eyes on Judy, who was sitting in the back of a Rolls-Royce. "Naturally, it was a difficult situation," he remembered, "for a boy who's very passionate, and very intelligent, and who was in love with his mother and his father." For Gregory, his family's predicament had become transfixing. "All I saw was my mother's enormous pain, and I saw my father living in this world that was fantastic," he recalled. "And you know it was very difficult because I was constantly being shuttled back and forth between a very, very modest lower-middle-class semi-detached house in Hatfield and a luxury townhouse and a Rolls Royce every other weekend."[15]

As principal photography on the film moved forward, the Beatles shifted from the sun-kissed beaches of the Bahamas and the snow-covered slopes of Obertauern in Austria to the remote Salisbury Plain, Greater London, and, finally, back to Twickenham, that cavernous movie studio that they knew so well from their days shooting *A Hard Day's Night*. For George Harrison, life on Lester's moveable feast of a movie set would have larger implications for his musical and spiritual lives alike. During a break in filming, Harrison first cast his eyes on a sitar, the fretted instrument of Hindustani music. As Harrison later recalled, "We were waiting to shoot the scene in the restaurant when the guy gets thrown in the soup, and there were a few Indian musicians playing in the background. I remember picking up the sitar and trying to hold it and thinking, 'This is a funny sound.'" In short order, Harrison's budding interest in the exotic instrument led him into the orbit of Ravi Shankar, the influential Hindustani classical composer. "I went and bought a Ravi record," Harrison later remarked. "I put it on and it hit a certain spot in me that I can't explain, but it seemed very familiar to me. The only way

I could describe it was: my intellect didn't know what was going on and yet this other part of me identified with it. It just called on me."[16]

Eventually, Harrison began taking lessons from Shankar after making his acquaintance through London's Asian Music Circle. By this time, the quiet Beatle had bought a sitar of his own from Indiacraft, a shop on Oxford Street: "It was a real crummy-quality one, actually, but I bought it and mucked about with it a bit." While Harrison enjoyed his first brush with the challenges and rewards of Hindustani music, Martin was an old hand at working with sitar- and tabla-playing musicians. Back in 1959, he produced a sidesplitting track by Peter Sellers and the Goons in which they lampooned *My Fair Lady*'s "Wouldn't It Be Loverly" to a disquieting Indian soundtrack. Meanwhile, as Lester and the Beatles continued their globe-trotting ways, Martin was left to his own devices back in London, as the director had pointedly hired British film and television composer Ken Thorne to write the incidental music while thumbing his nose at the Academy Award–nominated musical director of *A Hard Day's Night*. As George later wrote, "Since the director was Dick Lester again, it was hardly surprising that, to quote Sam Goldwyn, I was included out. The music was done by Ken Thorne, a buddy of Lester's." While George may have been miffed by the turn of events, he could tell that their relationship had soured: "Dick Lester and I didn't hit it off too well on *A Hard Day's Night*, and the fact that I got an Academy Award nomination for musical direction probably didn't help either."[17]

On April 9, only a scant few days after Harrison discovered the sitar on Lester's film set, the band's latest single, "Ticket to Ride" backed with "Yes It Is," was released to great fanfare. In short order, the record skyrocketed to the top of the UK charts, notching the group's eighth consecutive number-one single. In his review of "Ticket to Ride" in *NME*, Derek Johnson took special note of the song's "depth of sound" and "tremendous drive." As for George and the Beatles, "Ticket to Ride" marked a clear departure from the group's early sound. Years later, Lennon would go so far as to claim that "Ticket to Ride," with its relentless, high-octane guitar, "was one of the earliest heavy-metal records made." Fewer than two weeks later, "Ticket to Ride" would be released in the United States, where the single's A-side label announced that the song hailed "from the United Artists Release *Eight Arms to Hold You*."[18]

But by that time, the feature film's working title had been scrapped in favor of a new moniker. In addition to *Eight Arms to Hold You*, a number of titles had been bandied about on the set, including Lester's suggestion of calling the feature film *Beatles 2*, Harrison's tongue-in-cheek suggestion of *Who's Been Sleeping in My Porridge*, and Shenson's oddly forlorn recommendation of *The Day the Clowns Collapsed*. But as McCartney later recalled, everyone recognized the moment in which the eventual title finally emerged. "I seem to remember Dick Lester, Brian Epstein, Walter Shenson, and ourselves sitting around, maybe Victor Spinetti was there, and thinking, 'What are we going to call this one?' Somehow *Help!* came out. I didn't suggest it; John might have suggested it or Dick Lester. It was one of them." Regardless of the title's source, Lennon and McCartney suddenly found themselves in the very same quandary that produced "A Hard Day's Night" under duress the year before.[19]

For John, composing the title track was a burden, on the one hand, but on the other, an opportunity to continue in the introspective vein that he had begun on *Beatles for Sale* and continued with "You've Got to Hide Your Love Away." As John sat down to bring the title track to fruition, he was in the act, he would later recall, of making a literal call for help through the auspices of his music. Indeed, in its original incarnation "Help!" was a downbeat, piano-oriented tune. As John later recalled, "When 'Help!' came out in '65, I was actually crying out for help. Most people think it's just a fast rock and roll song. I didn't realize it at the time; I just wrote the song because I was commissioned to write it for the movie. But later, I knew I really was crying out for help. It was my fat Elvis period. You see the movie: He—I—is very fat, very insecure, and he's completely lost himself. And I am singing about when I was so much younger and all the rest, looking back at how easy it was. Now I may be very positive—yes, yes—but I also go through deep depressions where I would like to jump out the window, you know. It becomes easier to deal with as I get older; I don't know whether you learn control or, when you grow up, you calm down a little. Anyway, I was fat and depressed and I was crying out for help." On April 11, with the title of the feature film now in place, Lennon and McCartney put the finishing touches on "Help!" at Lennon's Weybridge estate. As with "A Hard Day's Night" a year earlier, John and Paul composed the song to order. With John's original lyrics in place, along with the up-tempo melody concocted during their latest writing session, "Help!" was born.[20]

On Tuesday, April 13, with only a scant few weeks left before the completion of principal photography, George and the bandmates reconvened at Abbey Road to record new material for the first time since March 30, when they had taken another crack at "That Means a Lot." As the March 30 session proceeded, they attempted to remake the song across several successive takes. In spite of their efforts, "That Means a Lot" failed to materialize to anyone's satisfaction. At one point, it seemed to fall apart, with Lennon abandoning his guitar in favor of banging on a studio piano. For George and the Beatles, songs like "That Means a Lot," where the magic simply wasn't happening, were remarkably few and far between. At this point in their career together, almost every new song resulted in a finished track that would be released for public consumption. Only a handful of songs—"That Means a Lot," "If You've Got Trouble," and "Leave My Kitten Alone"—would be consigned to the studio vault during this period. Generally, they were able to harvest almost every idea at this point, with songs like "That Means a Lot" being rare examples of the frustration that they might experience when nearly everything else worked so effortlessly for them in the studio.

But as events would have it, "That Means a Lot" was not destined for the rock 'n' roll graveyard just yet. Only eight days after the band had given up on the track, George invited P. J. Proby, a singer-songwriter from Houston, Texas, to Abbey Road to take his own shot at recording the orphaned tune. Proby had found his way into Epstein's stable via Jack Good, the British television producer behind such fare as ITV's *Ready Steady Go!*, as well as the TV special *Around the Beatles*. Proby had become fast friends with the bandmates on the set of *Around the Beatles*, which featured Lennon, McCartney, Harrison, and Starr vamping it up in a scene from Shakespeare's *A Midsummer Night's Dream*. After Martin and the band had come up empty with "That Means a Lot," Epstein wasted precious little time getting the song into Proby's hands. Ron Richards produced Proby's session, while Martin arranged and conducted the orchestration for the would-be teen idol's version. In addition to the orchestration, Richards and Martin also slowed the song down perceptibly. When it was released in the United Kingdom in September 1965, it charted at number thirty, Proby's weakest showing since breaking into the British music scene the previous year.

In contrast with the Beatles' work on "That Means a Lot," the April 13 session would be a dream, with George and the band bringing "Help!" to fruition in workmanlike fashion, albeit with several bumps along the way. That evening, they recorded the basic track first, with McCartney's bass and Starr's drums on one track, while Lennon played his twelve-string Framus Hootenanny and Harrison worked his Gretsch Tennessean on the other. The Beatles required several attempts to get the backing track in place, as Harrison ran into repeated difficulty attempting to capture the distinctive descending guitar figure. At one point, Martin suggested that Harrison overdub his guitar part later that evening to make things easier. Meanwhile, Lennon had begun to find his mettle with the song only to experience his guitar going out of tune. At this point, Martin halted the proceedings so that Lennon could tune his Framus Hootenanny. By take eight, Paul tried to buoy his bandmates' spirits, saying, "This is it. It's the swinging take!"—only to see their latest attempt aborted after a few seconds. To everyone's great relief, take nine offered a stellar run-through, and after the tape was rewound, the vocal tracks were recorded, along with Ringo playing tambourine. After several false starts, Harrison succeeded in overdubbing the descending guitar figure, which he finally conquered on take twelve. Clocking in at just over two minutes in length, "Help!" not only provided the title track for the feature film but also found Martin and the Beatles at the top of their game.[21]

While the Beatles were globe-trotting with Lester from one location to another, Martin enjoyed very few opportunities to work with the band in the studio. By this point, they were under the gun to complete the soundtrack album given that *Help!* was set to premiere on July 29. As far as George was concerned, they were suffering from the very same lack of continuity that had plagued the *Beatles for Sale* sessions. As George later recalled, "If it was time for a new single or album, I'd have to get in touch with Brian. He'd look through his diary and say, 'I can give you May 19th and perhaps the evening of the 20th.' I had to grab them whenever I could." As it happened, Lester's protracted shooting schedule finally came to an end during the week of May 11. But as it turned out, the *Help!* album would have to wait. Capitol Records was desperate for new material to round out the American *Beatles VI* LP. To assuage the insatiable US marketplace, Capitol execs—including Dave E. Dexter Jr., in spite of his well-known misgivings back in 1963—were demanding new Beatles product at every turn. To fill out *Beatles VI*, the band turned their attention to a pair of Larry Williams compositions, "Dizzy Miss Lizzy" and "Bad Boy," longtime staples of their Hamburg and Cavern Club stage acts. With their deep knowledge of both songs, the Beatles captured the recordings in a handful of takes. But the May 10 session was not without an unusually tense moment, heightened, no doubt, by the long day of filming that the band had endured before making their way to Abbey Road that evening. As McCartney later recalled, Martin himself was at the epicenter of the Beatles' angst. "We did occasionally get pissed off with him," Paul admitted. "As time went by, things crept in. In an out-take I heard recently—recording 'Dizzy Miss Lizzy'—John is saying, 'What's wrong with that?' and George Martin says, 'Erm . . . it wasn't exciting enough, John,' and John mumbles, 'Bloody hell'—that kind of thing was creeping in a bit. 'It wasn't exciting enough, eh? Well, you come here and sing it, then!' I think that's just pressure of work. When you've been working hard for a long time, you really start to need a break." Although John may have been perturbed by George's remonstration, the subsequent take found the Beatle raising his game and whooping it up considerably. Long after the group retired for the night, Martin, Norman Smith, and Ken Scott languished behind at Abbey Road in order to mix the tunes and airmail them stateside. Things were moving at such a breakneck pace that within forty-eight hours, the Beatles were reviewing proofs of the *Beatles VI* album cover.[22]

By the time that George and the Beatles reconvened in the studio on Monday, June 14, their worlds had been turned upside down yet again. After taking some much-needed time off, the band returned from their vacations only to learn that they had been selected by the queen to receive MBE awards designating them as members of the Most Excellent Order of the British Empire. Prime Minister Harold Wilson made the announcement, later remarking, "I saw the Beatles as having a transforming effect on the minds of youth, mostly for the good. It kept a lot of kids off the streets. They introduced many many young people to music, which in itself was a good thing. A lot of old stagers might have regarded it as idiosyncratic music, but the Mersey sound was a new important thing. That's why they deserved such recognition." When Martin and the Beatles resumed work on the *Help!* long-player on the afternoon of June 14, they took the Mersey sound to places that none of them could have imagined back in June 1962, just three years earlier when Harrison had the nerve to pipe up about Martin's tie.[23]

For Martin and the Beatles—McCartney especially—the June 14 session would be one for the ages, as the group laid down three top-drawer tracks, including a pop classic that in many ways would shift the band's musical direction for the duration of their career. For Martin, June 14 would mark the beginnings of a clear shift in his role in the group's creative calculus. Up until that point, George had acted as the bandmates' highly skilled editor, shifting verses and choruses, changing tempos, offering structural suggestions. On June 14, his role would begin to alter, slowly but surely, into something more.

But first the Beatles grappled with a pair of new, widely divergent McCartney compositions, "I've Just Seen a Face" and "I'm Down," a folk-tinged ditty and a Little Richard–inspired scorcher, respectively. The acoustic "I've Just Seen a Face" was captured in six takes, along with a percussion overdub in which Ringo played maracas. As Paul later recalled, "It was slightly country and western from my point of view. It was faster, though, it was a strange up-tempo thing. I was quite pleased with it." In many ways, the fiery "I'm Down" served as the diametric opposite of "I've Just Seen a Face." At the end of take one, an ebullient McCartney uttered, "Plastic soul, man, plastic soul." After perfecting a raucous rhythm track in seven takes with Paul turning in a searing lead vocal, John overdubbed a tantalizing organ solo, complete with Jerry Lee Lewis–like keyboard runs.[24]

But "I've Just Seen a Face" and "I'm Down" were mere appetizers on that fateful day. With "I'm Down" having come to fruition in fine style, George and the Beatles took a well-deserved dinner break. Some ninety minutes later, with Paul's voice having recovered from the larynx-tearing experience of singing "I'm Down," the group turned to a composition that had been ruminating in Paul's synapses for months, possibly even longer. As George later recalled, "I first heard 'Yesterday' when it was known as 'Scrambled Eggs'—Paul's working title—at the George V Hotel in Paris in January 1964." For his part, Paul was smitten with the melody, but the Beatle was quite certain that he had heard it somewhere before. "It came too easy," he later recalled. "I didn't believe that I had written it. I thought that maybe I had heard it somewhere before, it was some other tune. I went around for weeks playing the chords of the song for people, asking them, 'Is this like something? I think I've written it,' and people would say, 'No. It's not like anything else, but it's good.'" At one point, he even tested the song out on Alma Cogan at her Kensington flat. By this point, he had appended the words "Scrambled eggs, / Oh, my baby, how I love your legs" to the mysterious melody. Whenever he'd play it, "Scrambled Eggs" would invariably elicit a laugh over the song's puerile lyrics. A fortnight before the June 14 session, McCartney—like the other Beatles, who had just concluded principal photography for *Help!*—went on vacation. As he and Jane Asher drove from Lisbon down the coast to the small fishing village of Albufiera, the lyrics finally came to him: "Yesterday / All my troubles seemed so far away." When he arrived at his lodgings, Paul got his hands on a Martin acoustic guitar—which the left-handed Beatle strummed upside down—and he merged the newfound words with the tune that had dominated his thinking for so long. With a full-fledged composition now in hand, McCartney shared the song with Martin upon his return to London. At first, the Beatles' producer questioned the idea of titling the song "Yesterday" as it was mindful of "Yesterdays," the Jerome Kern–Otto Harbach standard popularized by Peggy Lee. But beyond the similarities of their titles, the songs had little else in common. At last, "Yesterday" was ready for its Abbey Road debut.[25]

After the dinner break on June 14, George and the Beatles prepared to record "Yesterday" for the first time, although the evening session progressed fairly awkwardly given the uncertainty about what the other bandmates would contribute to the composition. "I brought the song into the studio for the first time and played it on the guitar," Paul later recalled, "but soon Ringo said, 'I can't really put any drums on—it wouldn't make sense.' And John and George said, 'There's no point in having another guitar.' So George Martin suggested, 'Why don't you just try it by yourself and see how it works?'" And with that, Paul "sat on a high stool" in Studio 2 with his Epiphone Texan and sang "Yesterday," the producer remembered, recording the song in two swift takes, with the second being marked as "best." For the remainder of the session, Martin and the group pondered what to do with the track, which seemed rather slight in comparison with their body of work at this point. Finally, George recalled, "We agreed that it needed something more than an acoustic guitar, but that drums would make it too heavy. The only thing I could think of was strings, but Paul was unsure. He hated syrup or anything that was even a suggestion of MOR ['Middle of the Road,' in radio format lingo]. So I suggested a classical string quartet. That appealed to him but he insisted, 'No vibrato, I don't want any vibrato!'" George finally quelled Paul's concerns about using a string quartet, saying, "If we hate it, we can take it off. We'll just go back. It's very nice just with the solo guitar and your voice."[26]

The next day, Paul joined George at his London residence, where they sat down at the piano to compose the orchestration for "Yesterday." As Paul later recalled, "People tend to think that we did the music and George did all the arrangements. The thing people don't generally know was that me or John or whoever it was involved in the orchestral angle would go 'round to George's house or he would come 'round to ours, and we would sit with him, and I did on this. I went 'round to George's house and we had a pleasant couple of hours, had a cup of tea, sat there with the manuscript paper on the piano." On this day, George was clearly moving into uncharted territory with the Beatles, uniting his long-honed knowledge of orchestration with the pop band that had turned his world upside down. Sitting together at the piano, George and Paul shaped the score as the Beatles' producer handled the notation. "Paul worked with me on the score," George later recalled, "putting the cello here and the violin there. There is one particular bit which is very much his—and I wish I'd thought of it!—where the cello groans onto the seventh the second time around. He also liked the idea of holding the very high note on the first [upper] violin in the last section. To be honest, I thought that was a bit boring, but I acceded to his request. The rest of the arrangement was pretty much mine." When they completed their work, the Beatle hastily scrawled "by Paul McCartney, John Lennon, George Martin, Esq., and Mozart" across the original orchestration.[27]

As promised, George arranged for a string quartet to join the Beatles in Studio 2 on the afternoon of June 17. George had booked four session players from the Top of the Pops orchestra, with Tony Gilbert and Sidney Sax on violin, Kenneth Essex on viola, and Francisco Gabarro on cello. After walking the musicians through their parts, George headed for the control room, only to be intercepted by Paul, who was still concerned about the vibrato sounds with which the session men were liberally ornamenting their parts. For Paul, "it sounded a little too gypsy-like." After George instructed the musicians thusly, Paul was satisfied, feeling that the accompaniment now "sounded stronger" than before. With the string quartet's work having been completed, "we overdubbed the strings," George remembered, "while Paul had another go at the vocal. But because we didn't use headphones there was leakage from the studio speaker into his microphone, giving the impression of two voices or double-tracking." Afterward, George supervised a pair of mono mixes of the song with Norman Smith and Phil McDonald. The next day, McCartney's twenty-third birthday, Martin, Smith, and McDonald carried out the stereo mix, and "Yesterday," for all intents and purposes, was complete. For his part, George was brimming with pride at the finished product. He had not only assisted Paul in bringing his creation to life but also succeeded in concocting a score that accented the Beatle's composition without being overly obtrusive. To George's mind, the string accompaniment was "utter simplicity" itself.[28]

While George had finally captured Paul's wayward song in the studio—and ultimately, for inclusion on the *Help!* long-player—"Yesterday" would have long-standing implications for the group and their producer. As the Beatles' brain trust rounded out the album, George took Brian aside, telling him, "You know, this isn't the Beatles. This is Paul McCartney." George even went so far as to suggest that they release the song under the bass player's name. "Shall we call it Paul McCartney?" George asked, to which Brian replied, "'No, whatever we do we are not splitting up the Beatles. This is the Beatles—we don't differentiate.' So even though none of the others appeared on the record," George added, "it was still the Beatles—that was the creed of the day." But as for releasing "Yesterday" as their next British single, the Beatles simply weren't having it, feeling that the song's classical pretensions didn't fit their image. As it happened, they played the song on an August 14 appearance on *The Ed Sullivan Show* before a live audience of some seventy-three million viewers, with McCartney accompanied by a string quartet culled from the Ed Sullivan Orchestra. When it was released the next month as a Capitol single, "Yesterday" soared to the top of the *Billboard* charts. As the song reigned over the American airwaves that fall, the Beatles managed to do the unthinkable, expanding their demographic considerably beyond teens and young adults. Paul's fears about the Beatles falling prey to radio's MOR format had become a reality—but in ways that even he could scarcely have imagined. Now, *everyone* was listening to the Beatles—from children and preteens all the way through the middle-aged and beyond.[29]

For Brian, "Yesterday" was proof positive that the Beatles were the most daring and original act of their era, that there were quite literally no boundaries that they couldn't traverse. The Beatles' manager chalked up their unbroken string of successes to George and the group's tireless, unrelenting work in the studio. "This hasn't happened by accident," Brian wrote, "and it can only be sustained by taking the greatest care, for though success breeds success we could easily topple if we tried to flood the market with shoddy goods. The public is no fool." Perhaps George himself had finally learned this most valuable of lessons after so many years of trying to ride the latest fad to the top of the charts. It had only been a matter of months since he had played his most recent gambit with Cilla Black's cover version of "You've Lost That Lovin' Feeling" only to come up just short in an international showdown with Phil Spector and the Righteous Brothers. And besides, George was barely removed from so many years of knee-jerk moves like the "Earth Angel" and "Itsy Bitsy Teeny Weeny Yellow Polka Dot Bikini" fiascos.[30]

But things were different now. For George especially, "Yesterday" was a watershed moment in his creative life with the Beatles. "That was when, as I can see it in retrospect, I started to leave my hallmark on the music, when a style started to emerge which was partly of my making," he later wrote. "It was on 'Yesterday' that I started to score their music. It was on 'Yesterday' that we first used instruments other than the Beatles and myself. On 'Yesterday,' the added ingredient was no more nor less than a string quartet; and that, in the pop world of those days, was quite a step to take. It was with 'Yesterday' that we started breaking out of the phase of using just four instruments and went into something more experimental, though our initial experiments were severely limited by the fairly crude tools at our disposal, and had simply to be molded out of my recording experience." With "Yesterday," the Beatles' producer was finally making the "sound pictures" that he had longed to create in the studio since his earliest days with the EMI Group. And the lesson of the "Yesterday" episode, if one were to be gleaned, was that—in the world of musical artistry, at least—quality and originality trump everything. It was a lesson that George would not soon forget.[31]

# 17

# SOMETHING IN THE AIR

WITH "YESTERDAY" SAFELY tucked away in the Abbey Road vault, George and the Beatles turned their attention toward rounding out the contents of the *Help!* album, which was slated for release on August 6 in order to synchronize its appearance in the marketplace with the feature film's premiere on July 29. But the Beatles had an even more pressing scheduling issue on their hands: on Sunday, June 20, they were set to play the first date on their latest European tour at Paris's Palais des Sports. The *Help!* soundtrack LP had to be completed at once if they were going to meet Brian and George's self-imposed deadlines.

Working at their usual harried pace, George and the group convened at Abbey Road on Tuesday, June 15, for an afternoon session. They recorded John's latest composition, "It's Only Love," in six takes, only four of which were complete. Written under the working title of "That's a Nice Hat (Cap)," the song collapsed during take five after the normally sure-handed Ringo made a drumming error, apologizing to John and exclaiming, "We all make mistakes." As with the earlier "I Need You" and "Yes It Is," Harrison accented his guitar part on "It's Only Love" using a tone pedal. With their European tour looming in just a few days, the Beatles took Wednesday off to afford John with some much-needed PR time to publicize his second book, *A Spaniard in the Works*, which was scheduled for release on June 24, when the group would be appearing at Milan's Velodromo Vigorelli. John may have been caught up in the malaise of his "fat Elvis" period, but he certainly wasn't sitting idle. On Thursday, June 17, Martin and the Beatles turned to Starr's contribution to the long-player, a cover version of Buck Owens's "Act Naturally," which they recorded in thirteen takes. Lennon was notably absent from the afternoon's proceedings. Much of the session was spent nailing down the rhythm track, which featured Harrison on his Gibson "Jumbo" acoustic, McCartney on his Höfner bass, and Starr on drums. A series of overdubs included Starr's vocal, McCartney's harmony vocals, and Harrison's solo on his Gretsch electric.[1]

As the Beatles worked to round out the contents of the *Help!* album in short order, the only disappointment on the day belonged to Norman Smith, who had been led to believe that Martin and the bandmates were on the verge of recording one of Smith's original compositions. Suffice it to say that in a band where the spoils of authorship had been writ large, even their engineer was prompted into action. As Smith later recalled:

> I'd been writing songs since I was a small boy, and in 1965 I wrote one with John Lennon in mind. They were coming to the end of the *Help!* LP and needed one more song. George Martin and I were in the control room waiting for them to make up their minds and I said, "I know they've heard all this before, but I happen to have a song in my pocket." George said, "Get on the talkback and tell them." But I was too nervous so George called down, "Paul, can you come up? Norman's got a song for you." Paul looked shocked. "Really, Normal?"—that was one of their nicknames for me—"Yes, really." So we went across to Studio 3 and I sat at the piano and bashed the song out. He said, "That's really good, I can hear John singing that!" So we got John up, he heard it, and said, "That's great. We'll do it."

Not missing a beat, McCartney asked Smith to record a demo version of the song so that they could make it their own. As it happened, Dick James was on the premises, and before Smith went home to record the demo, the music publisher offered to purchase the song outright for £15,000. Shocked by James's sudden largesse, Smith was rendered speechless. "I couldn't talk but I looked across to George and his eyes were flicking up towards the ceiling, meaning 'ask for more.'" The next day, Smith was ready to present the Beatles with the demo only to be met by Lennon and McCartney, who said, "Look, we definitely like your song but we've realized that Ringo hasn't got a vocal on the LP, and he's got to have one. We'll do yours another time, eh?" And with that, Smith's £15,000 was "gone in a flash. By the next LP, they'd progressed so much that my song was never even considered again."[2]

As it turned out, the Beatles wouldn't be recording a cover version by *anybody* in the foreseeable future, much less Smith. With the likes of "Yesterday" and "You've Got to Hide Your Love Away" seemingly raising George and the bandmates' expectations for their original compositions at nearly every turn, the high stakes of authorship would increasingly define the direction of their creative lives. After the dinner break on June 17, they attempted one more song before putting the *Help!* LP to bed. Titled "Wait," the song had been composed primarily by Paul during the Beatles' stay at New Providence Island's Balmoral Club. In four quick takes, the group captured the rhythm track, which consisted of McCartney on bass, Lennon playing rhythm guitar, Starr on drums, and Harrison playing his Sonic Blue Fender Stratocaster with his tone pedal deployed. After Lennon and McCartney overdubbed their vocals, Martin and the band called it quits for the night.

As it turned out, the saga involving the fate of "Wait" was only just beginning—and wouldn't be resolved until much later in the year. The next day, Martin conducted a control room mixing session in Studio 2 with assistance from Smith and Phil McDonald. Mono mixes were carried out for all of the *Help!*-era Beatles recordings, including "Wait." But by the time George turned to the album's stereo mixes, he had opted to discard "Wait" from consideration for inclusion on the long-player. Perhaps George felt that the track wasn't ready for release—or even more likely, George might have felt that "Wait" didn't fit his more immediate needs for sequencing the album. Still unsatisfied with "If You've Got Trouble" and "That Means a Lot"—and with "Wait" suspended in mothballs for the moment—George turned to the fiery "Dizzy Miss Lizzy," one of the cover versions that they had recorded back in May expressly for American release, to close out the album. As with "Twist and Shout," "Money (That's What I Want)," and "Everybody's Trying to Be My Baby," "Dizzy Miss Lizzy" fit George's bill for closing out the group's LPs with an up-tempo rocker.

For whatever reason, the most recent Lennon-McCartney composition would have to wait for another day. As the episode with "Wait" demonstrates, even by the time of the band's fifth studio album, George was still calling many of the shots regarding the sequencing of their music, even going so far as to make editorial decisions about choosing the songs themselves for inclusion—or in the case of "Wait," for deferral. As the Beatles winged their way to Paris and the onset of their European tour, Martin was understandably concerned about their capacity for maintaining the torrid pace of their professional lives during this period. In many ways, he was surprised that they kept coming back, yet again, with one classic song after another given the extraordinarily demanding circumstances of being at the eye of the Beatles' storm. But even still, George could already recognize a clear shift in his relationship with the band, as well as the nature of his contributions to their efforts in the studio. In the early days, he had functioned in a more authoritarian capacity, but now things were clearly different. "After that time, rather than just writing a song and asking me what they should do with it, John and Paul started thinking more in terms of structure and composition," he later wrote.[3]

Sensing the increasing role of authorship and craft in their working life together, the Beatles' producer devoted greater attention to assisting them in bringing their visions to life in the studio. He was especially cognizant of the different approaches that Lennon and McCartney took in creating their music: "Paul would think of a tune and then think 'What words can I put to it?' John tended to develop his melodies as the thing went along. Generally, he built up a song on a structure of chords which he would ramble and find on his guitar until he had an interesting sequence. After that, the words were more important than anything else," George added. "He never set out to write a melody and put lyrics to it. He always thought of the structure, the harmonic content, and the lyrics first, and the melody would then come out of that." With five albums under their belts, George knew—with greater authority and evidence than virtually anyone else—that the Beatles were engaged in pursuing a remarkable path, one that was already leaving an indelible mark on the history of popular music. And as far as George and the group were concerned, it was still early days indeed.[4]

On the evening of July 29, *Help!* premiered at the London Pavilion, where ten thousand fans congregated outside on the streets to catch a glimpse of the Four Mop-Tops. As with *A Hard Day's Night*, the *Help!* premiere had morphed into a society affair, with the band arriving in a Rolls-Royce and later hobnobbing with the likes of Princess Margaret and Lord Snowdon. But that is where the comparisons with their first feature film end. As it turned out, the Beatles' camp wasn't fooling anybody with *Help!* Writing in the *London Sun*, Ann Pacey astutely observed that the Beatles seem "as trapped as four flies" in *Help!* In an August 24 review in the *New York Times*, Bosley Crowther also saw right through their facade. "Funny? Exciting? Different? Well, there's nothing in *Help!* to compare with that wild ballet of the Beatles racing across a playground in *A Hard Day's Night*, nothing as wistful as the ramble of Ringo around London all alone. Those were episodes that gave a welcome respite to the frantic pace and mood of that film. This one, without sense or pattern is wham, wham, wham all the way," Crowther wrote. "The boys themselves are exuberant and uninhibited in their own genial way. They just become awfully redundant and—dare I say it?—dull."[5]

If the Beatles were going through the motions in *Help!*—fueled, by their own admission, on a steady diet of marijuana—it should hardly be surprising that their attempts at self-caricature were coming off as "dull." Pacey's words were equally perceptive. By the summer of 1965, the Beatles had become imprisoned by the celebrity that they had coveted for so very long through their early days in Liverpool, Hamburg, and beyond. And by this point, given the unique circumstances of their fame, the Beatles' only genuine solace seemed to emanate from their pioneering work in the studio with George. For Lennon and McCartney especially, their most authentic selves were playing out within the safe, creative spaces of Abbey Road as opposed to their seemingly endless progress from one hotel room to another across the globe. George intuitively recognized the vast psychological disjunction that they must have been experiencing between their faux celluloid images and their groundbreaking efforts with him back in the friendlier confines of the recording studio. At times, George would ponder the bandmates' lives in a whimsical light, chalking their trials and tribulations up to "the craziness of the relentless Beatles roller coaster." But by the time that *Help!* premiered, George recognized the absurdity inherent in the group's unusual brand of fandom. Their concerts, awash in the unchecked abandon of the screaming multitudes, were parodies of performance. For his part, George was particularly troubled by the unbridled adulation focused on the Beatles, who at times were treated like messianic figures. "It was almost like going to Lourdes," he later wrote. "There were people who actually wanted to touch the hems of the clothes they were wearing. Royalty are trained from birth to cope with that sort of thing; the Beatles were not. They can hardly be blamed for wanting to put up a barrier against the world." Since the previous year's events at Colorado's famed Red Rocks Amphitheatre, George had been genuinely worried for the band's safety. And as events would show, George was right to be concerned. Life on the road could actually get worse for the Beatles. The boredom of another nondescript hotel in Anywhere, USA, could turn out to be the least of their problems.[6]

As the Beatles made short work of their summer European tour—and with yet another visit to American shores in the offing—the *Help!* long-player finally saw its release into the arms of their fans, who were insatiable, as always, for new Beatles product. Writing in *Record Mirror*, Richard Green lauded the LP's wide-ranging contents and the band's growing eclecticism: "This album could easily be titled *The Many Moods of the Beatles*. Showcased in 14 tracks are ballads, rock and roll, folk, country and western and a helping of straight pop." The soundtrack quickly shot to the top of the UK charts upon its release on August 6, following suit in the United States just a week later. Once again, the cover featured a photograph of the band by Robert Freeman, who posed the Beatles in the act of spelling out a word via semaphore. As Freeman later remarked, "I had the idea of semaphore spelling out the letters 'HELP.' But when we came to do the shot, the arrangement of the arms with those letters didn't look good. So we decided to improvise and ended up with the best graphic positioning of the arms." As it turned out, the UK cover depicted the Beatles spelling out the incomprehensible word *NUJV*, as opposed to *HELP*—Lennon's seminal outcry during those "fat Elvis" days. In the United Kingdom, the album resulted in not only a hit film but also a pair of chart-topping singles in "Ticket to Ride" and "Help!" In the United States, that number was complemented with the release of "Yesterday" backed with "Act Naturally." Within five weeks, the single would turn over a million copies stateside. In the longer term, "Yesterday" would emerge as a game changer for the band—not only becoming one of the most covered songs in the history of popular music but also widening the Beatles' demographic considerably in the bargain.[7]

As for Martin himself, while Lester had "included him out" as the *Help!* feature film's musical director, Lester's slight didn't stop the Beatles' producer from recording instrumental versions of the album's contents on his own accord. Indeed, in keeping with *Billboard*'s reportage back in September 1964, George had devoted many of his non-Beatles working hours to creating instrumental versions of their music with studio orchestras. While the "Ringo's Theme (This Boy)" single had bubbled under the top 40 in the US charts, George's instrumental follow-up from the United Artists soundtrack for *A Hard Day's Night*—"I Should Have Known Better" backed with "A Hard Day's Night"—faired even more poorly, failing to crack *Billboard*'s Hot 100 at all. Apparently, the public's unquenchable appetite for Beatles music by this point no longer extended beyond the genuine article. Released on February 19, 1965, under George's new contract with United Artists, *A Hard Day's Night: Instrumental Versions of the Motion Picture Score* sold only moderately well, containing the four instrumentals from George's Oscar-nominated score, along with orchestral versions of nine other tracks from the original soundtrack. With liner notes describing George as "the Beatles' brilliant musical director," the sleeve copy for *A Hard Day's Night: Instrumental Versions of the Motion Picture Score* notes that "the songs are superb and already well-loved, and the George Martin touch is happily present for all to delight in time and time again."[8]

George released his collection of *Help!*-themed instrumentals on EMI's Columbia TWO label in mid-1965. Marketed as "easy listening," George's *Help!* long-player hardly succeeded in burning up the charts, but as with his instrumentals from *A Hard Day's Night*, the latest collection blazed new trails by igniting interest in the Beatles beyond their original teenaged and young adult demographic. As yet another 1965 release for United Artists, *George Martin Scores Instrumental Versions of the Hits* featured George's orchestrations of a wide range of contemporary works, including the Beatles' "I Feel Fine," "P.S. I Love You," and "No Reply," as well as his own original contribution to the *Ferry Cross the Mersey* soundtrack, "All Quiet on the Mersey Front." For the first time, George's compilation found him spreading his musical wings, if only slightly, to cover such numbers as Petula Clark's "Downtown" and the Rolling Stones' "Time Is on My Side." At the same time, his latest orchestrations saw him staying rather close to home with instrumental cover versions of the Righteous Brothers' "You've Lost That Lovin' Feeling"—arranged in the style of his Cilla Black recording—and "Walk Away," a recent top 5 British hit for Matt Monro.

Meanwhile, George operated at his usual frenzied pace with Brian's stable of acts, not to mention his regular slate of Parlophone artists. As it turned out, several of Brian's Liverpool bands were on their last legs after being celebrated as genuine hitmakers at the height of Beatlemania and the British Invasion. In the summer of 1965, George began working on *First and Fourmost*, the long-player that would be the only full-length album in the Fourmost's discography. Consisting of fourteen cover versions selected by George as vehicles for the struggling band, *First and Fourmost* included the band's spirited attempts at Jackie DeShannon's "Till You Say You'll Be Mine," Gerry Goffin and Carole King's "Some Kind of Wonderful" (as popularized by the Drifters), Jerry Lieber and Mike Stoller's "Yakety Yak" (as popularized by the Coasters), and Bobby Troup's "The Girl Can't Help It" (as popularized by Little Richard).

Perhaps most significantly, "Yakety Yak," with its aural effects and comic overtones, found the Fourmost attempting to make a name for themselves as a quasi-novelty act. In spite of George's reputation as the United Kingdom's comedy producer du jour, he did very little to support their movement in this direction. At the time, he was still trying to help them find their footing as a bona fide pop act as opposed to a chart-topping wannabe that had made their name on the Beatles' coattails. As Brian O'Hara later recalled, "George

Martin didn't encourage us to do comedy records, but nobody would have known what to do with a comedy group at the time." George selected "Girls! Girls! Girls!"—which had been previously popularized as the title track of Elvis Presley's 1962 musical comedy of the same name—as the LP's lead single. But the Fourmost's recording, with its novelty aspirations, failed to resonate with the record-buying public. Topping out at number thirty-three on the UK charts, "Girls! Girls! Girls!" made for the band's last appearance in the top 40. As with Shirley Bassey's rebuke of George back in 1964, the Fourmost attributed their slide to Brian and George's inattention to the band—especially blaming Brian for putting his energies into the Beatles rather than into his Liverpool stable of one-time hitmakers. At one juncture, even Gerry Marsden, with whom Brian and George got along famously, had made a gentle point of his concerns about the NEMS pecking order. As press officer Tony Barrow later observed, "They all felt that, but, whereas Gerry Marsden would be facetious, the Fourmost would whinge and moan. And it did them no good. Brian certainly didn't like them moaning to me, a humble press officer, and it just made both sides more resentful." While the Fourmost had hardly given up the ghost of fame during this period, they would be dealt a near-fatal blow as a working band the following year when Mike Millward succumbed to leukemia at just twenty-three years old.[9]

As it happened, the Fourmost weren't the only Mersey act at the end of their rope as far as George was concerned. In contrast with the Fourmost, Billy J. Kramer and the Dakotas were coming off a string of Martin-produced hits, including "I'll Keep You Satisfied," "Little Children," and "From a Window." As 1965 wore on—and with a break, as usual, in the Beatles' tightly knit schedule—George brought Billy J. Kramer and the Dakotas back into the studio to record what would be their final long-player under his supervision. The impetus for the sessions was the latest Burt Bacharach–Hal David confection, a wistful tune titled "Trains and Boats and Planes." The song made its way into George and Billy's orbit by way of Brian Epstein. As luck would have it, Bacharach was recording a television special for Granada TV when producer Johnnie Hamp heard the song and tried to facilitate a British cover version with a Mersey beat band known as Four Just Men. After they turned down the opportunity, "Trains and Boats and Planes" caught Brian's attention, and he promptly recommended it as the next vehicle for Billy J. Kramer and the Dakotas. Not missing a beat as usual, George invited the band to Abbey Road, where they recorded the *Trains and Boats and Planes* long-player in fairly short order. In addition to the title track, which George marked as the album's lead single, *Trains and Boats and Planes* was filled out by a variety of other cover versions, including the old Platters tune "Twilight Time," the Drifters' "Under the Boardwalk," and Jackie DeShannon's "When You Walk in the Room," among others. For "Trains and Boats and Planes," George pulled out all the stops. As with "Ferry Cross the Mersey," he adorned the track with soaring violins, which afforded "Trains and Boats and Planes" with a nostalgic mien. Always endeavoring to camouflage any "offending phrase from the Kramer tonsils"[10]—as he had observed during the making of "Do You Want to Know a Secret"—George doubled the lead singer's vocals, in key instances, with violin flourishes in order to bolster the track. With the gloss of Martin's production in place, "Trains and Boats and Planes" made a serious run at the UK charts, topping out at number twelve in spite of solid competition from Bacharach's recording, which charted at number four. When the single was released stateside, however, Billy J. Kramer and the Dakotas' "Trains and Boats and Planes" barely made a dent in the US marketplace, charting at a dismal number forty-seven. As it turned out, the *Trains and Boats and Planes* LP marked the end of George and the group's collaboration. Within a year, they would disband, joining so many other North Country acts who had tried their hand at the music business during the high tide of Beatlemania only to see their moment in the sun dwindle almost as quickly.

In truth, the beat-music boom and the British Invasion were not enough to keep acts such as the Fourmost and Billy J. Kramer and the Dakotas afloat. In stark contrast with the Beatles, much of Brian's stable simply lacked the talent or the versatility to innovate and remain relevant—no matter how assiduously George attempted to dress them up for an ever-shifting pop-music marketplace. If there were exceptions to the challenging circumstances of living in the Beatles' shadow among Brian's acts, they came in the form of Cilla Black and Matt Monro. But even the likes of Cilla and Matt presented special difficulties all their own. As George observed, "One of the main problems for the record producer is finding suitable material. This is especially true when you are recording someone like Matt Monro or Shirley Bassey, who don't write their own songs. It is the job of the producer to find them the right ones. If you are a professional producer and people in the business know that you record Matt, or Shirley, or Cilla Black, they will send you songs with those people in mind. Even the public sends offerings. But that is not enough. You still have to search. You still have to ring up the publishers' offices." As 1964 transitioned into 1965, George went a step further, taking matters into his own hands. After producing a raft of hit singles with the Liverpool singer, George invited Cilla to Abbey Road to record her debut long-player.

Titled *Cilla*, it topped out at number five in the UK charts, proving that the Liverpool lass was no flash in the pan. In addition to a cover version of the Shirelles' "Baby It's You," the album included a new composition titled "Come to Me," cowritten by none other than George along with Cilla's fiancé, fellow Liverpudlian Bobby Willis. With Cilla's voice on full-throated display, "Come to Me" pulsated with the dramatic, swinging verve of mid-1960s pop.[11]

But George wasn't done by a long shot. Later that same year, he also produced Monro's debut album, titled *I Have Dreamed*. While the long-player charted at number twenty, coming up well short of Cilla's success with her own debut, *I Have Dreamed* featured such cover versions as Monro's rendering of the Academy Award–winning tune "Love Is a Many Splendored Thing," along with the contemporary Lennon-McCartney classic "All My Loving." And then there was "Once in Every Long and Lonely While," coauthored by George and Tin Pan Alley standout Hal Shaper. With George's soaring strings arrayed against Matt's velvet tones, "Once in Every Long and Lonely While" benefits from George's shrewd pairing of the singer with Johnny Spence, who conducted the orchestration. As a close cousin of "Once in Every Long and Lonely While," "If This Should Be a Dream" finds Martin writing especially for Monro yet again. Coauthored with Dick James—no stranger to composing music himself—George's "If This Should Be a Dream" proved to be another winning vehicle for the artist who came to be known as "the Man with the Golden Voice." For George, seeing his compositions in the public main proved to be gratifying on a variety of fronts. Perhaps most important, in contrast with Norrie Paramor, who peppered his artists' records with pseudonymous compositions, George's contributions on Matt's behalf were right out in the open.

Although *I Have Dreamed* was only a modest chart success by mid-1965, Monro enjoyed even greater heights with his Martin-produced rendition of the Beatles' "Yesterday." As the very first in a long line of cover versions of the Lennon-McCartney classic, "Yesterday" became a top 10 UK hit for Monro. For his part, Monro shrewdly capitalized on the Beatles' decision not to release "Yesterday" as a single in the British marketplace. He had seen McCartney perform "Yesterday" on television's *Blackpool Night Out*, and he jumped at the chance to record his own version. When the baritone vocalist asked George to prepare an arrangement, the producer was briefly taken aback. "That was most difficult," George later admitted, "because I had already scored it for Paul and I didn't want to do it any other way. I did re-score it for Matt and produced his record with a string orchestra. We had French horn and I changed the harmonies. All the things Paul would hate were there, but it worked for Matt Monro." By autumn, Monro's bravura turn with "Yesterday" was experiencing its own heyday on the United Kingdom's airwaves. But by that time, with 1965 coming to a close, the Beatles had already moved well beyond their work on *Help!*[12]

As the summer of 1965 roiled on, George turned his attention from his studio efforts to the thorny issue of his professional affiliation. George's standing contract with EMI was in limbo, having expired at the end of April, although Len Wood still held out hope that the juggernaut would manage to retain George's services and perhaps most significantly for the EMI Group, not jeopardize their relationship with Brian and the Beatles in the bargain. But in spite of the very high stakes on the line with George's contract status, EMI remained oblivious to his demands, which he had plainly stated for so long. Victor Carne's words, which he had generously shared with George all those years ago when he first joined EMI's ranks, were surely ringing in the producer's ears. "Always remember, George, that if you are needed by the company you can do pretty much as you like," Carne had advised him. "But if you need the company more than they need you, then you really have to toe the line!" As the musical architect of Beatlemania, George suddenly didn't need EMI so much anymore, not as he had back in 1962, when he was juggling his secret life with Judy and his family was out in the suburbs. At that point, he clearly had to toe the line, and he had re-signed with the multinational company as expected. But now the EMI Group needed him desperately, yet the tone-deaf record giant simply couldn't find its way clear to securing his services without insulting him at nearly every turn.[13]

During this same period, George's faithful A&R assistant Ron Richards traveled to California to record a live album with Gerry and the Pacemakers. As it turned out, Richards's West Coast visit brought him into the orbit of a host of American producers who confirmed what he and George had suspected for so long: not only that their American counterparts earned royalties from the records that they supervised but also that residuals and other production fees were built directly into their own contracts. When he returned to England, Richards shared the news with Martin, who was still caught up in the tumult of his ongoing negotiations with EMI, as well as with Peter Sullivan, who had only recently left the EMI Group for the comparatively greener pastures of Decca. In his new post, Sullivan had hit the ground running, discovering a nightclub singer called Tommy Scott and overseeing his transition into the legendary Tom Jones, who topped the UK charts in early 1965 with "It's Not Unusual." Richards also shared his American reconnaissance with EMI assistant John Burgess. In fairly short order, an idea began to percolate among the four producers: What would happen if a quartet like themselves dared to go independent? How would they be able to earn residuals yet still interface with a generally conservative British recording industry that was all too comfortable with its existing hierarchies of management, production staff, and artists—and in that rank, no less?

As George tried to make sense of his professional life during that fateful summer, he found himself dealing with Len Wood at nearly every juncture, with EMI's managing director slowly coming to realize that the producer was committed to making a break with the multinational company. In spite of their vexed association during this period, Martin never lost respect for Wood, although he would always feel befuddled by the other man's unyielding fiscal perspective. As George later recalled, "There's a curious ambivalence about my relationship with Len. I have bitter experiences from my negotiations with him. At the same time, the fact is that I grew up in the business with him. When I started with Parlophone, he was the sales manager for Columbia, and I've always been very fond of him. I think that the way in which he always conducted business is just his misfortune, part of the way he is made. He has a puritanical streak which has always disapproved of the raciness of the business, and he tries to exert his own restraint upon it."[14]

While Martin had given notice a year earlier, Wood continued to press him about renegotiating his contract with EMI and remaining in the company's fold. And in spite of his "puritanical" business approach, Wood begrudgingly admitted that the Beatles' producer clearly merited a raise of some kind. Holding fast to his position, George told the managing director, "It's very simple. I've had EMI right up to here." At that point, Wood demanded to know if a third party was attempting to procure Martin's services:

> They wanted to know who was after me. I told them that no one was, and they clearly didn't believe it. When I told them I was going out on my own, I got remarks like "Oh-oh, you won't last long." Then the tack changed. Throughout the following 12 months, at regular three-or four-week intervals, I was treated to lunches and drinks, and blandishments like "Come on now, old chap, I think you're being a little silly about this. I mean, you should have more money, you're quite right."

It was at this juncture that Wood made his fatal mistake as far as Martin was concerned. "I don't want more money, Len," George told him for the umpteenth time. "I just want commission. I want tangible results from my efforts, that's all. I want to see something off each record that is mine. I don't care how small it is, but that's what I want."[15]

And that's when Wood made his final gambit to retain the most successful producer—even at that comparatively early date—in the EMI Group's history. "Look. I know you're being very stubborn about this," he told George. "But I'm determined to keep you on. You're a good producer, and a good chap, and too good to lose. You're definitely going to stay with us. I'll tell you that right now." For the first time in his dealings with the Parlophone head, Wood seemed to be on the verge of acceding to Martin's long-held desire for a commission on his artists' record sales—and for the briefest of moments, it all seemed so promising, as if it might be possible for him to stay with EMI after all. Wood proposed that Martin receive 3 percent of the profits generated by his recordings, albeit with one proviso: the producer's percentage would be computed after deducting the overhead expenses associated with his work. Not surprisingly, George asked for further clarification:

> "Well, that's a bit vague," I said. "Can you tell me what it amounts to?"
>
> "Yes, yes, hold on," he said, like some angler convinced that the fish is about to take the bait. "Let's take last year, for example. If this had been operating last year, 1963, you'd have ended up with a bonus of £11,000. How does that sound to you?" he asked, triumphantly.
>
> "It sounds very good," I said. "But how do you arrive at that?"
>
> "Well, take your salary, and your secretary's salary, and your assistant, and his typist, and for the sake of argument we'll double that, to allow for overheads. To that we add the musicians' fees that you paid during the year for session work. I've worked out that on that basis, your department cost us roughly £55,000 last year."
>
> "I know what I did last year, and how hard I worked, but I think I've been jolly economical!"
>
> "Yes, you were very good," he said. "You always are. No problem about that. Now, on the other side of the sum, you'd have had three percent commission on our profits. Okay? Last year, that would have amounted to £66,000. From that we take away the £55,000, which leaves you with £11,000."

Now, Martin was positively thunderstruck by Wood's admission. As he sat there in front of Wood's massive polished desk, Martin began to do the math. With his mind spinning with numbers and percentages, "the truth was that the sheer horror of what he had just said was slowly beginning to seep into my brain." And then suddenly, he got it. The figures were ineluctably clear: £66,000 was 3 percent of £2.2 million. As if to make matters worse, Wood underscored his own words, admitting, "That's the profit we made from the sales of your records last year."[16]

In that very instant, the back and forth of Martin's long negotiations with Wood went up in smoke. George knew exactly where he stood with EMI—and he was disgusted both with the implications as well as with the small-mindedness of Wood's thinking regarding the matter. He simply couldn't get over the managing director's last remark. "With that simple sentence, he cut straight through whatever vestige of an umbilical cord still bound me to EMI," George observed. And that's when his last-ditch discussion with Wood reached its sad nadir. "There's one other thing, Len. You seem to be putting net against gross—the net of your profits against the gross of my costs. If, for example, the profits had been only one and a half million, then three percent of that would be 50,000. So with costs of 55,000, the theory would be that I'd pay you back 5,000!" As Wood allowed that Martin's conclusion was accurate, the producer's resolve had been once and truly hardened vis-à-vis EMI: "I was flabbergasted. First, the meanness of the whole thing was so transparent. Second, I could hardly believe the stupidity of the man in letting me know what I was worth. 'Thank you, very much,' I said. 'I haven't changed my mind at all. I'm leaving.'" Even at that late juncture—and after the utter pettiness of Wood's unflagging position—Martin made his exit with a great deal of sadness. As he later wrote, "It is difficult, looking back, to describe the depths of my bitterness. I really had been devoted to the company, and always valued loyalty in other people. But there comes a moment when you realize that your idea of being a good, loyal worker without complications is being misconstrued, and you are being taken for a ride. I was bitter; I was sad—sad for the company that I knew I had to leave."[17]

But finally emboldened by his decision to effect his departure from EMI, George made quick work of charting his untethered future beyond the company that had given him his start some fifteen years earlier. There was no question that he would become a freelancer. Wood's penny-pinching attitude notwithstanding, the industry simply wasn't ready for what Martin had in mind. Like the Beatles, their producer was simply ahead of his time in terms of his business outlook. By August 1965, when George's severance from EMI's employ became official, he had a fairly radical plan in mind. Looking around the EMI ranks, he realized that a small handful of people carried out the company's pop-music efforts. On the production side, there was George himself, along with Columbia's Norman Newell, HMV's Wally Ridley, and, of course, the disgraced Norrie Paramor. And then there were the production assistants, including Ron Richards, John Burgess, and Decca's Peter Sullivan. George also took special note of the administrative assistants who made EMI's pop-music machine hum, including Burgess's secretary Carol Weston, longtime Parlophone staffer Shirley Burns (née Spence), and the indispensible Judy, who by his own admission had afforded George with the confidence and the tenacity to see his departure from EMI through.

As George took stock of the EMI personnel, he made a conscious decision to invite the company's young guns to make a break along with him. He had little in common with Ridley, who was more than a dozen years his senior, not to mention, an old-school, big band–oriented producer. And there was nary a thought about inviting Paramor. No, that wasn't going to happen, as far as George was concerned. In addition to the Beatles' producer and Judy Lockhart Smith, the ranks of the EMI refugees included Newell, Richards, Burgess, Sullivan, Weston, and Burns. "With our going, EMI was stripped of all its young blood," George later wrote. "Only the old remained. In a sense, it was Martin's Revenge." By George's reasoning, his little coterie enjoyed direct access to many of the leading recording artists of the day. Burgess's stable included Adam Faith, Manfred Mann, and Peter and Gordon, while Richards served as the producer for the likes of P. J. Proby and the Hollies. Sullivan counted newcomers Lulu, Tom Jones, and Engelbert Humperdinck among his acts. And, of course, George himself served as the group's anchorman, with the Beatles, Cilla Black, Gerry and the Pacemakers, Billy J. Kramer and the Dakotas, and the Fourmost to his name.[18]

With three other leading producers in tow, George was left to devise an administrative scheme for their uncharted venture. In George's mind, they would be establishing a kind of "producer's organization" that would be "four for all, and all for one." George self-consciously modeled his business plan on the Associated London Scripts cooperative that Spike Milligan and Eric Sykes had founded in the 1950s. In its heyday, Associated London Scripts served as the premier agency for the most celebrated comedy and television writers of its time. While George recognized his key role as the new organization's main draw, he opted to take a chance on brute egalitarianism. "We will pool our income, and we will distribute it according to the way we are earning," he told his new production partners. "I'm still very keen on incentives, but to start off with we'll have equal shares in the company, 25 percent each," adding, "I reckon I'm equal to you, but on the other hand, as George Orwell would have put it, I reckon I'm a bit more equal. All the same, we'll have 25 percent each." After his experience with EMI, George simply couldn't cotton to any business concept that didn't favor fairness and equity as its backbone. In terms of income, George pointed out that as they would generally be producing recordings on their own, they would each need to contribute 25 percent of their income to maintaining the business's overhead. For example, if George earned £10,000 from his recordings, he would syphon £2,500 back into the company. As a further incentive for paying themselves as evenhandedly as possible, he suggested an upper limit of £10,000 for any of the producers, along with a lower limit of £3,000, below which none of them could sink. As a final rule, any remaining earnings would be invested back into the business.[19]

With the parameters of the new company in place, the group settled on a name for their venture, which they christened Associated Independent Recording or AIR for short. "Our motto was 'Built by producers, for producers,'" according to George. Perhaps most explicitly, AIR wouldn't be "a place where engineers told you what to do, like EMI used to be." But as it turned out, AIR—for all of its maverick origins—couldn't exist without EMI as its de facto partner. On the one hand, EMI held the recording contracts of the lion's share of AIR's artists. On the other hand, AIR had everything going for it but capital, that most essential of ingredients for affording their start-up a fighting chance. George fully realized that to establish "a company you need money for wages, rent, stationery, furniture, typewriters. And money was what we didn't have. There had certainly been no golden, silver, or even lead handshake from EMI." All George had to show for his fifteen years at EMI were the contributions to his pension fund, which amounted to £1,800. It was a beginning, of course, but it wouldn't be nearly enough for what George had in mind. With the daunting challenge of locating the requisite start-up funds, he turned back to EMI—and in the bargain found himself in another lengthy round of negotiations with the juggernaut. As he later recalled, the new arrangement was defined "by the sheer logic of the situation" in spite of their recent adversarial relationship. As George well knew, "I was probably the most successful producer EMI had. I guess they were frightened of changing horses in midstream, of splitting a winning partnership." When the EMI brass broached the question of who would end up handling the Beatles' production duties, George played it cool. "That's up to them, isn't it?" he informed Wood.[20]

With EMI's full attention in his grasp, George proposed that they hash out a royalty deal in which he and his partners would be paid exclusively via residuals. The heart of the new agreement dictated that EMI had the right of first refusal on any of AIR's productions. He advised Wood that he and his colleagues would make a concerted effort to discover and produce new acts in addition to their existing stable and that EMI would be given first dibs on issuing the rookie artists' recordings in the marketplace. While Wood quickly ascertained the logic of Martin's proposition, Martin couldn't help feeling that the managing director made the entire process seem "needlessly complex," as the eventual agreement contained an extremely complicated schedule that attempted to account for different territories and nearly every conceivable type of recording. In broad strokes, the resulting contract enabled AIR to produce records that George and his partners financed themselves. If EMI opted to release the recordings, AIR would receive a royalty of 7 percent of the product's retail price. Things became even more dicey, though, when it came to AIR's production of existing EMI artists. In that case, they would receive a producer's royalty amounting to 2 percent of the retail price. In George's reasoning, "The highest royalty payable to an artist at that time was five percent, so we were asking for two-fifths of that. Considering that artists in those days were not making much of a living out of their records, and that record sales were not all that high, it wasn't an extortionate demand, and EMI agreed." In a final, calculated move, George requested an advance of £5,000 against AIR's contract.[21]

As they wrapped up their negotiations regarding Martin's new venture, Wood only offered one caveat: How, indeed, would the Beatles, given their enormous value, be allocated under the agreement? Wood made it clear that Martin's proposed 2 percent royalty simply wasn't on the table. As Martin later recalled, Wood "took the view, which some might find curious in the circumstances, that I was not entitled to cash in on something that was already established; they overlooked the thorny question of who had established it in the first place!" As the most difficult aspect of his negotiations with EMI, George finally succeeded in proposing a producer's royalty on Beatles product that held different percentages for Great Britain, the United States, and the rest of the world. In the United Kingdom, Wood agreed to a royalty on Beatles records of 1 percent of the wholesale price, which amounted to 0.5 percent retail. In the United States, with its comparatively larger pop-music marketplace, EMI proved to be even less generous, agreeing to compensate AIR to the tune of 5 percent of the pressing fees that EMI gleaned from its American licensees.[22]

With a deal finally in place, George apprised Brian of his new status vis-à-vis the EMI Group. For his part, Brian had long been aware of George's dissatisfaction with EMI and his plans to leave the company at the conclusion of three-year contract he had signed back in 1962. Not surprisingly, George took comfort in Brian's brave initial foray into the music business in the days when the Beatles were still John, Paul, George, and Pete. Indeed, as Martin followed through with his plans to make a go of AIR, he couldn't help reflecting on the incredible level of risk that had driven Epstein into making his successful run with the Beatles. As George observed, Brian "was pitchforked into the rough end of the business without a great deal of training or experience, and he did remarkably well. Suddenly, from being a kind of failed dramatic student, he found something that he felt he could cope with. Being unsure for most of his life up to that time, suddenly he realized that there was something that he could do really rather well." With these last words, George might as well have been talking about himself and his own circuitous journey toward finding his mettle as a record producer. In any event, with his long-standing respect for the Beatles' manager, George comported himself by refusing to put any undue pressure on Brian, who had remained loyal and sympathetic throughout George's ordeal with his former employer. "This doesn't mean that you have to stay with me," he informed Brian. "EMI may well choose another producer for the Beatles, someone on the staff. It'll be up to you to decide. I don't want my leaving to be an embarrassment. But I intend to leave whatever happens, whether I record the Beatles or not." George's careful approach to Brian and the Beatles' interest notwithstanding, there was little doubt about the outcome. Brian had struggled for far too long and against fearsome odds to break up their winning partnership just yet.[23]

Not surprisingly, the news of George's departure from EMI and the formation of AIR sent a veritable chill across the business. In its pages, *NME* described the momentous events as "a shock to the recording industry." Wood admitted that the whole affair had been "a tricky situation. We had not agreed to a new contract with the Beatles and here was their producer about to leave the company. I agreed to a deal which retained his services on projects for EMI including the Beatles and we agreed to pay him a royalty." In the United States, the news generated a shockwave from coast to coast. By the time the news broke in a September 1965 article in *Billboard*, Martin and Wood had tempered their remarks to connote a spirit of generosity and collaboration. Headlined FOUR TOP BRITISH A&R MEN FORM PRODUCTION CONCERN, the *Billboard* article found George offering a fairly benign purpose for founding AIR in the first place, chalking it up to a kind of revolution against slipshod recording practices. "During the past 18 months or so there has been a spate of disk issues, many of which just clutter up the market," George remarked. "Anyone can go into a recording studio and make a tape.

We consider ourselves professional people who will concentrate on producing quality material." And then there was Wood, who gladly pointed out that AIR's productions would undoubtedly be a great boon for the EMI Group. "As the new company would record mainly for EMI," he observed, AIR's future activities couldn't help but "have considerable benefit to EMI."[24]

But no matter how the incredible events of the late summer and early fall of 1965 were parsed, George implicitly understood that his liberation and the subsequent establishment of AIR had come at a "great loss for EMI." After all, nearly every one of the AIR producers' artists had chosen to stay with the selfsame A&R men who had shared in their development and success over the years. In spite of everything, George must have known that it simply didn't have to be this way, that another, more equitable outcome had been possible all along. As Martin and the Beatles prepared to go back into the studio that autumn, the producer had little time to lament the ways in which Wood's long-standing shortsightedness had left EMI in a highly vulnerable position. When he reconvened with the Beatles back at Abbey Road in mid-October, he was flush with excitement—not only at making a go of it with AIR, which was reason enough to be hopeful after so many years of toil at EMI, but also at the remarkable new sound vistas that the bandmates were only just beginning to fashion with Big George, as they lovingly called him, in the studio.[25]

# 18

# PLASTIC SOUL

When GEORGE AND THE BAND reconvened at Abbey Road on Tuesday, October 12, 1965, they were collectively exhausted. But as usual, there was no time to lose. In keeping with their practice during the previous two years, Brian and George had promised a new long-player for EMI in time for the holiday shopping season. As they made their way to St. John's Wood that afternoon, they were coming off an intense period that included the tremendous shadow cast by George's highly complex disentanglement from the EMI Group. For the bandmates, much of the year had been characterized by the breakneck pace of shooting *Help!*, not to mention the long hours in the studio to bring off the soundtrack. And then there was the band's latest American tour, a two-week affair that brought the dark side of Beatlemania to the fore. Consisting of stadium and arena bookings, the tour was highlighted by the group's August 15 performance at New York City's Shea Stadium. As promoter Sid Bernstein proudly pointed out, "Over 55,000 people saw the Beatles at Shea Stadium. We took $304,000, the greatest gross ever in the history of show business" (at the time). In spite of the event's record-breaking stature, the Shea Stadium gig found the Beatles at the eye of an increasingly constricting hurricane. To get to the venue, they were transported to the Port Authority Heliport at the World's Fair, where they were packed into a Wells Fargo armored truck, which transported them to the stadium. At Shea, they were protected by some two thousand security personnel, who were responsible for crowd control even though the bandmates were situated comparatively far away from their audience, playing from a tiny stage in the middle of the ball field.[1]

And that's when they took their show out west. The Beatles played a second residency at the Hollywood Bowl, where the sound was overwhelmed yet again by the screaming tumult. In a lackluster meeting with Elvis Presley, the band members were unimpressed by the rock god—especially John, who concluded, "It was a load of rubbish. It was just like meeting Engelbert Humperdinck." On a more convivial note, the bandmates met the Beach Boys' Mike Love and Carl Wilson before their second show at the Portland Coliseum on August 22. For their part, the Beach Boys were in the early stages of making a new long-player of their own—an album that, even in its incipient moments, promised to reshape their surf-rock sound in new and unexpected ways. Also on hand that day was celebrated American poet Allen Ginsberg, who later composed a poem about the experience titled "Portland Coliseum." Not long afterward, the tour mercifully ended following a particularly raucous show at San Francisco's Cow Palace on August 31. And then the Beatles winged their way back to the United Kingdom, where they promptly collapsed, save for Ringo and his wife, Maureen, whose son Zak was born on September 13. As their date with George back at Abbey Road loomed large on the horizon, John and Paul finally got back to business, cranking out a bushel of songs in the space of a fortnight. It was under these harried conditions that George and the band began recording their sixth studio album together. And while the Beatles' long-player started out rather inauspiciously, George and his charges soon realized that something special was afoot.[2]

On that first evening, they tried their hand at a new Lennon number that he and McCartney had only recently polished off at the former's Weybridge estate. Picking up where they had left off with the *Help!* soundtrack, George continued allowing the tape machine to run while the Beatles worked out the kinks with their latest compositions before recording a basic rhythm track and then enhancing it via multitrack technology. As Ringo later observed, "It was getting to be really exciting in the studio. We did it all in there: rehearsing, recording and finishing songs. We never hired a rehearsal room to run down the songs, because a lot of them weren't finished. The ideas were there for the first verse, or a chorus, but it could be changed by the writers as we were doing it, or if anyone had a good idea."

By this time, George had become keenly aware that other clientele had taken notice of the Beatles' increasingly long hours in Studio 2, although he tried to act as peacekeeper, a role that was no doubt impacted by his new status as AIR's de facto leader. "We were given very much *carte blanche* with Studio 2," he later recalled, "but didn't really chuck people out, although there were times when pressure was brought to bear and somebody who had the studio booked was told that the Beatles wanted it. I didn't approve of this at all but sometimes the boys would steam-roller people. EMI contributed to this by demanding product and we were often unfairly accused of being arrogant. Personally, I always tried to play the game."[3]

On that first afternoon, they took a stab at recording "Run for Your Life," which John had based, ironically enough, on an Elvis Presley cover version that "the King" had released back in 1955. As John later recalled, "It was inspired from 'Baby, Let's Play House.' There was a line in it, I used to like specific lines from songs, 'I'd rather see you dead, little girl, than to be with another man.' I wrote it around that—a line from an old blues song that Presley did." Even in its finished state, "Run for Your Life" hardly presaged the incredible originality to come—even as soon as a few hours later with "This Bird Has Flown"—during that very first evening back in the studio. As for "Run for Your Life," George and the Beatles quickly dispatched the song in five takes, with the final attempt being the only complete version. After overdubbing acoustic guitar, backing vocals, and tambourine, they turned their attention to "This Bird Has Flown," which John had debuted for the Beatles' producer during their January ski trip to St. Moritz.[4]

While "Run for Your Life" had seemed rather forced as Beatles compositions go, "This Bird Has Flown" was anything but. For more than four hours, George and the bandmates toiled over John's creation. Although they only managed to complete a single take, the session made for a revolutionary moment in Beatles recording history, as Harrison lugged his sitar into Studio 2 at Lennon's express invitation. As Starr later recalled, "We were all open to anything when George introduced the sitar: you could walk in with an elephant, as long as it was going to make a musical note. Anything was viable. Our whole attitude was changing. We'd grown up a little, I think." The backing track consisted of Lennon playing acoustic guitar on the first track, along with McCartney's bass and Starr's percussion on a second. The third track featured Lennon's lead vocal, McCartney's harmony vocal, and Harrison's sitar. A fourth track was later overdubbed and included an additional lead vocal from Lennon, McCartney on maracas, Starr on finger cymbals, and Harrison's sitar performed in a call-and-response fashion with Lennon's lyrics, which narrated the story of a cosmopolitan love affair: "I once had a girl / Or should I say, she once had me?" The take concludes with Harrison, still a novice at working the exotic instrument, complaining about how difficult it is to play the sitar. As Norman Smith later recalled, it was even more difficult to tape the instrument, commenting, "It is very hard to record because it has a lot of nasty peaks and a very complex wave form. My meter would be going right over into the red, into distortion, without us getting audible value for money. I could have used a limiter but that would have meant losing the sonorous quality." For his part, Martin was well aware of the challenges of recording the sitar, having first captured the instrument on tape back in 1959 for Sellers's "Wouldn't It Be Loverly."[5]

When the evening session finally concluded, Martin and the band agreed to shelve "This Bird Has Flown" for the time being. The very next evening, everyone was back in Studio 2 to take a stab at yet another new Lennon-McCartney number titled "Drive My Car." Written in the bluesy style of Otis Redding—complete with Harrison's aping of "Respect" in his lockstep guitar part with McCartney's bass—"Drive My Car" picks up where "This Bird Has Flown" left off, telling the story of yet another woman, this time with movie-star pretensions, who knows exactly what she wants in the world of men. Lennon and McCartney had completed the song only days earlier at Lennon's estate, and the composition finally came together when they happened upon "drive my car," an "old blues euphemism for sex," in McCartney's words. With Martin and Smith up in the control room, they captured the number in four takes—with take four being the only complete run-through. The basic track featured McCartney's bass, Harrison's lead guitar, Lennon's tambourine, and Starr's drums. "Drive My Car" is particularly noteworthy because of an early appearance of Paul's Rickenbacker 4001S bass. The Beatle had been given the guitar back in August 1964 when the band first played the Hollywood Bowl. As Paul later recalled, Mr. Rickenbacker himself had presented him with "a special left-handed bass. It was the first left-handed bass I'd ever had, 'cause the Höfner was a converted right-hand." But that wasn't the only difference between the two different makes of guitars. While it was heavier than his "Beatle bass," the Rickenbacker also had more versatility and definition in its sound. Along with the changing studio technology that Martin navigated across the band's career, their various shifts in instrumentation contributed to their evolving sound, as well as to their growing desire to challenge the boundaries of the studio.[6]

Across the long evening in which they recorded "Drive My Car," Martin and the Beatles tried their hands at numerous overdubs, including Lennon and McCartney's lead vocals, Harrison's harmonies, and McCartney's piano. In addition to a well-timed cowbell part, "Drive My Car" zipped into life with Paul's funky guitar intro and sizzling slide guitar solo, which he later echoed during the outro. In only their second day of recording their new long-player, it was already clear that George and the Beatles were navigating their way into very different territory from the musical world of *Help!* The October 13 session also marked the first time that George and the Beatles worked beyond the tolling of the midnight hour at Abbey Road.

By this point, the studio had become the bandmates' one great sanctuary from a world of turmoil and sameness. As George later recalled, "Coming to the studio was a refuge for them. It was the time and place when nobody could get at them. The strange hours for their sessions were really necessary because of the frenetic life they were forced into. Just look at what they used to pack into a year; tours here and overseas, TV, radio, press, and general promotion. Recording was important but it had to be squeezed in between everything else, and they enjoyed recording much more than touring. They got fed up with the vulnerability of it all—the continual pawing—and needed to escape from time to time." Not surprisingly, this need for escape had reached its fever pitch by the latter months of 1965. And besides, with each passing album, the group was altering their sound perceptibly, growing their musical output by leaps and bounds. Under those conditions, who wouldn't want to spend every possible hour chasing after their art at Abbey Road? In their own way, the Beatles "changed the discipline of the place," Smith recalled. Previously, "the local council had imposed a midnight ban on recording, this was after EMI had eased their own 10 o'clock curfew, not because of the noise, although the echo chamber still leaked a bit, but mainly because it was a residential area and car doors slamming and people shouting used to annoy the neighbors." But George and the band had flexed their muscles and managed to shatter the midnight curfew as well. Before long, sessions inching into the wee hours of the morning would become the norm.[7]

On Saturday, October 16, they hit pay dirt yet again with "Day Tripper," which had been written explicitly as their next single. As with "Drive My Car," "Day Tripper" worked from an ear-catching guitar hook. And also like "Drive My Car," the Beatles' latest number signaled how far the band had progressed as a musical fusion since the *Help!* sessions. Lennon recognized the place of "Day Tripper" in the group's evolving sound, proudly recalling, "That's mine. Including the lick, the guitar break, and the whole bit. It's just a rock and roll song. Day trippers are people who go on a day trip, right? Usually on a ferryboat or something. But it was kind of—you know, you're just a weekend hippie. Get it?" With George up in the control booth, Ringo kicked the song into action, exclaiming, "Let's really rock it this time!" As it happened, the Beatles captured the song in three takes before aiming their sights on Harrison's latest composition, "If I Needed Someone." In a single take, they managed to create a rhythm track consisting of McCartney's bass,

Starr's drums, Lennon's rhythm guitar, and Harrison's chiming twelve-string guitar. As he later reported in *NME*, the songwriter self-consciously based the number on the Byrds' "The Bells of Rhymney," which he mimicked with his standout Rickenbacker part.[8]

By this comparatively early stage of recording the Beatles' new long-player, it was abundantly clear that their sessions were already starkly different from their previous efforts, which had been broken up by a grueling array of concert appearances and movie shoots. George and the bandmates were quickly establishing a sense of momentum in which each passing day at Abbey Road seemed to promise something new and even more innovative than the last. The afternoon session on Monday, October 18, proved to be a revelation, as the group swiftly dispatched "If I Needed Someone" with Harrison's overdubbed lead vocals, along with Lennon and McCartney's backing vocals and Starr's tambourine. For Harrison, "If I Needed Someone" proved to be a significant confidence builder. For far too long, he had been pigeonholed as a subordinate player in the Beatles' creative nexus. "Songwriting for me," he later admitted, "was a bit frightening because John and Paul had been writing since they were three years old. It was hard to come in suddenly and write songs. They'd had a lot of practice. They'd written most of their bad songs before we'd even got into the recording studio. I had to come from nowhere and start writing, and have something with at least enough quality to put on the record alongside all the wondrous hits. It was very hard." For the Beatles' lead guitarist, "If I Needed Someone" was a harbinger of things to come.[9]

The rest of that productive Monday afternoon was allotted to recording John's exquisite new composition "In My Life." Lennon later recalled writing a first draft of the song in which he "struggled for days and hours trying to write clever lyrics." As Lennon remembered, "'In My Life' started out as a bus journey from my house on 250 [*sic*] Menlove Avenue to town, mentioning every place that I could remember. And it was ridiculous. This is before even 'Penny Lane' was written and I had Penny Lane, Strawberry Field, Tram Sheds—Tram Sheds are the depots just outside of Penny Lane—and it was the most boring sort of 'What I Did on My Holiday's Bus Trip' song and it wasn't working at all." In Lennon's estimation, the song's lyrics improved after he began waxing nostalgically about the friends, lovers, and places of his Liverpudlian past. And for Lennon, "In My Life" was nothing short of a watershed moment. As he later recalled, "It was, I think, my first real major piece of work. Up till then it had all been sort of glib and throwaway. And that was the first time I consciously put my literary part of myself into the lyric." And that's when Paul picked up the baton at John's Weybridge estate:

"I went down to the half-landing, where John had a Mellotron, and I sat there and put together a tune based on Smokey Robinson and the Miracles. Songs like 'You Really Got a Hold on Me' and 'Tears of a Clown' had really been an influence. You refer back to something you've loved and try and take the spirit of that and write something new. So I recall writing the whole melody. And it actually does sound very like me, if you analyze it. I was obviously working to lyrics. The melody's structure is very me."[10]

When he rejoined the Beatles at Abbey Road on October 18, Martin led the band through a series of brief rehearsals before laying down "In My Life" in a quick succession of takes on Studio 2's four-track mixing desk. For the first take, the group tackled the song's rhythm section, with Lennon strumming his Gibson "Jumbo" acoustic guitar and McCartney playing his Rickenbacker bass. Meanwhile, Harrison picked the song's melodic introductory notes on his Sonic Blue Fender Stratocaster and Starr kept time with his Ludwig Oyster Black Pearl Drums. For the second track, Lennon recorded a superb rendering of his lead vocal—in a single, magnificent take, no less—with McCartney and Harrison providing gentle harmonies and Starr contributing a tambourine part.

As Martin observed from the control room, Lennon delivered a breathtaking performance, to say the least, with the singer's lyrics deftly examining the power and inevitable failure of memory. While some places and people remain vivid, the lyrics tell us, others recede and disappear altogether. "And these memories lose their meaning," Lennon sings during the plaintive refrain, "when I think of love as something new." For the third take, Lennon and Martin set about the business of recording a keyboard solo for "In My Life." And that's when things got even more interesting. To Lennon's mind, the solo was an essential feature—a highly melodic means for underscoring the song's nostalgic power. With the studio's Hammond organ on hand, Lennon opted for a classical sound in the spirit of J. S. Bach. As the Beatles collectively lacked the ability to score music—much less read it—Martin sat beside Lennon at the grand piano in Studio 2. As Lennon sang the notes of a potential keyboard solo, Martin doubled the sounds on the grand piano with one hand while charting them in his notebook with the other. With the keyboard solo having been fully realized, George sat before the Hammond organ as Norman Smith cued up the existing first and second takes of "In My Life" in the second-floor control room. But as he listened to the playback with Smith and the Beatles, Martin was decidedly underwhelmed. "In My Life" was a magisterial recording, to be sure, but the organ solo sounded thin and lifeless in contrast with the song's moving lyrics. As the October 18 session came to a close, the Beatles nonchalantly shrugged their shoulders. Perhaps the organ solo was merely a space saver until something better came along.

With "In My Life" in stasis for the moment, the Beatles took a day off to join Tony Barrow at London's Marquee Studio to record their annual Christmas record. The very next day, Wednesday, October 20, George and the Beatles turned in yet another one of their patented landmark sessions, in which they devoted nearly nine hours to a single track, Lennon and McCartney's thoughtful, ear-catching composition "We Can Work It Out." Recorded across some 525 minutes during the afternoon and evening sessions, "We Can Work It Out" demonstrated not only that the bandmates' songwriting was improving exponentially but also that their musicianship was becoming even more precise and melodic with each passing day. When they finished up that evening, George and the group had only recorded two takes, with the first one breaking down after Ringo momentarily fumbled the song's intricate shift from 4/4 to waltz time. But all in all, they were remarkable takes indeed, with the second being marked as "best." Much of the evening session involved overdubbing John and Paul's lead vocals, in which the two songwriters' senses of stark reality and optimism, respectively, came into full bloom. As with such earlier songs as "You've Got to Hide Your Love Away," "We Can Work It Out" saw the band expanding their instrumental repertoire, with Martin turning in a standout harmonium part. As Harrison later recalled, "The studio itself was full of instruments: pedal harmoniums, tack pianos, a celesta, and a Hammond organ. That's why we used all those different sounds on our records—because they were *there*."[11]

With the sterling "We Can Work It Out" under their belts, George and the Beatles were faced with a conundrum, having seemingly already decided upon "Day Tripper" as the A-side of their final 1965 singles release. While they were still enthralled with the earlier number, "We Can Work It Out" clearly had plenty of commercial potential on its own, and George and the bandmates began to settle on the new song as their next A-side. But just as quickly, the Beatles brain trust's thinking shifted yet again. As Harrison later recalled, "After a lot of talk, we decided 'Day Tripper' is really the top track. This is what I had wanted all along," the lead guitarist admitted. For his part, John believed that "Day Tripper"—with its progressive rock 'n' roll sound—was more emblematic of the Beatles at that time and merited being showcased as the single. And that's when they hit upon the idea of releasing both songs as a double A-side, forcing the British record industry to bend to their will by giving both songs a shot at topping the UK charts. As George later remarked, "After we gave both titles to EMI, the boys decided that they preferred 'Day Tripper,' but both sides are extremely good and worth a lot of plays. As far as EMI's official policy is concerned, there is no A-side, and both will be promoted equally." And the Beatles had their way, of course. Released on December 3, the double A-sided "Day Tripper" backed with "We Can Work It Out" saw both songs topping the British charts, and George and the band had made history yet again.[12]

On Thursday, October 21, the incredible string continued as they remade "This Bird Has Flown"—shortly to be retitled—which they had first attempted nine days earlier. As the session got underway, Norman Smith announced the track as "'This Bird Has,' er . . . er . . . 'Norwegian Wood,' take three." Ultimately, Lennon chose to combine the song's titles as "Norwegian Wood (This Bird Has Flown)." Remade across three takes, with the last one being marked as "best," "Norwegian Wood" had evolved considerably since the earlier session. In the first take that afternoon, the Beatles recorded the song with a pronounced sitar introduction sans bass and drums. The next iteration featured a pair of acoustic guitars, Paul's bass, and John and Paul's vocals. For the final, "best" attempt of the day, "Norwegian Wood" came to life with Lennon's exquisite acoustic guitar introduction, which he perfected after several tries. The final take featured McCartney's bass and Harrison's twelve-string acoustic on the first track; Harrison's sitar prominently arrayed on the second track; John and Paul's vocals, along with the acoustic guitar intro, on the third track; and bass drum and tambourine flourishes on the fourth track. As for the song's acoustic introduction, John had affixed a capo on the neck of his Gibson "Jumbo" to raise the pitch. With its lilting guitar and mysterious narrative, "Norwegian Wood" found the Beatles' folk-oriented soundscapes on the *Help!* long-player progressing dramatically in only a matter of months.[13]

During the five-hour evening session that same day, Martin and the band took a stab at yet another gem, Lennon's "Nowhere Man." Even in its earliest manifestations, "Nowhere Man" offered yet another reminder of the embarrassment of riches that the Beatles had at their disposal—and which they regularly debuted for George in Studio 2. As he later remarked, "The material the Beatles gave to me was gold; there was practically no dross at all. I've worked with other people who've brought me something and I've said 'I think you ought to go back and re-write that.' Or that we ought to scrap it completely." But not with the boys from Liverpool. "They came forward with the most wonderful material," George exclaimed. "It was brilliant; it was different. Every one took a new twist." With "Nowhere Man," Lennon and McCartney's songwriting prowess abandoned the common theme of romantic love, instead concentrating on the human condition and how it is so often beset by loneliness and isolation. As John recalled, writing the song was initially frustrating: "I'd actually stopped trying to think of something. Nothing would come. I was cheesed off and went for a lie down, having given up. Then I thought of myself as Nowhere Man—sitting in this Nowhere Land." After rehearsing the song with the tape running, the band's first complete attempt at "Nowhere Man" featured an electric guitar–inflected rhythm track. Before the session ended, Lennon, McCartney, and Harrison tried their hands at devising a three-part harmony, which they sang in a difficult upper register. As the hour grew later, Martin and the bandmates took their leave for the evening, vowing to remake the song the next day.[14]

But in the hours before the Beatles arrived at Abbey Road on Friday, October 22, to continue work on "Nowhere Man," George had other plans in mind. Getting down to business at 10:30 AM, the band's producer turned his attentions back to "In My Life." George was determined to unseat the Hammond organ solo that he had recorded as the song's musical interlude back on October 18. George had convinced himself that he could do better, that a stunning and glorious song such as "In My Life" deserved a much grander fate. As he awaited the Beatles' appearance that day, George knew exactly what he had to do. It was time to break out his old and trusted friend: the windup piano. That George felt free and confident enough to contribute to the song's musicality outside of the Beatles' presence underscores his substantial and continuing role in orchestrating their musical direction. As with "A Hard Day's Night," deploying the technique in the service of "In My Life" was a painstaking and at times frustrating process, as it required George to contend with the limits of an existing recording as he played the grand piano in Studio 2. Even more troubling, performing at half speed forced the producer to play the keyboard at a lugubriously slow pace, requiring him to restart several times before perfecting the solo for full-speed playback during the mixing process. But the result was nothing short of a bravura performance. In many ways, "In My Life" found George's technique in its finest manifestation. Years later, he explained his use of the windup piano in order to "get a harpsichord sound by shortening the attack of everything, but also because I couldn't play it at real speed anyway. So I played it on piano at exactly half normal speed, and down an octave. When you bring the tape back to normal speed again, it sounds pretty brilliant. It's a means of tricking everybody into thinking you can do something really well."[15]

With his magnificent solo flown in to the "In My Life" mix, George waited expectantly for the Beatles' arrival that afternoon. "I played it back to them when they returned, and they said, 'That's great!' So, we left it like that."[16]

With "In My Life" having come to fruition, George and the band returned to "Nowhere Man," which they worked on throughout the evening. In remaking the song, the Beatles recorded three more takes, with take four being selected as the "best." For the basic rhythm track, "Nowhere Man" featured John's acoustic guitar, Paul's bass, and Ringo's drums. As Martin and the group carefully built each layer of the "Nowhere Man" remake, Lennon, McCartney, and Harrison returned to the three-part harmony a cappella introduction—only this time they sang it in their natural registers to perfection, affording the number with an arresting preview of the tune. "Nowhere Man" took on its unique musical sheen when Lennon and Harrison happened upon the idea of playing their Fender Stratocasters in unison, thus imbuing their guitars with the effect of being double-tracked. At this point, things got even more interesting when the bandmates decided to enhance their guitar sound via several sets of faders devised by the Abbey Road engineering team to give them a highly trebled, silvery sheen. Quite suddenly, the Beatles' producer and their engineers were engaging in the kind of studio trickery that would evolve significantly in 1966 and beyond. As McCartney later recalled:

> I remember we wanted very treble-y guitars—which they are—they're among the most treble-y guitars I've ever heard on record. The engineer said, "Alright, I'll put full treble on it," and we said, "That's not enough," and he said, "That's all I've got, I've only got one pot and that's it!" And we replied, "Well, put that through another lot of faders and put full treble up on that. And if that's not enough we'll go through another lot of faders." . . . So we were always doing that, forcing them. They said, "We don't do that," and we would say, "*Try it.* Just try it for us. If it sounds crappy, OK, we'll lose it, but it just might sound good." I always wanted things to be different because we knew that people, generally, always want to move on, and if we hadn't pushed them the guys would have stuck by the rule books and still been wearing ties. Anyway you'd then find, "Oh, it worked!" and they were secretly glad because they had been the engineer who put three times the allowed value of treble on a song. I think they were quietly proud of those things.[17]

With the guitars having been treated with maximum treble, "Nowhere Man" saw George and the Beatles pushing the technological limits of Abbey Road even further. And as events would show, they were only just beginning to see how far they could go with their sound.

On Sunday, October 24, they reconvened for a nine-hour session on behalf of Paul's "I'm Looking Through You," another song that had been slated for their still-untitled long-player. A folk-oriented number in keeping with many of their songs during that period, "I'm Looking Through You" found its origins in Paul's flagging relationship with Jane Asher, who was frequently away from London pursuing her acting career. As McCartney later recalled, "She went down to the Bristol Old Vic quite a lot around this time. Suffice it to say that this was probably related to that romantic episode and I was seeing through her façade. And realizing that it wasn't quite all that it seemed. I would write it out in a song and then I've got rid of the emotion. I don't hold grudges so that gets rid of that little bit of emotional baggage." Over the duration of the long session, the band made a strong first attempt at the song, recording a first take in the afternoon and adorning it with a feast of sounds later that evening, including acoustic and electric guitars, not to mention maracas, organ, handclaps, and a poignant vocal contribution from Paul. Yet by the end of the night, the composer still wasn't entirely satisfied, and the Beatles left "I'm Looking Through You" for another day.[18]

The Beatles were away from the studio on Monday, October 25, when George, Norman Smith, and Ken Scott produced mono mixes of "Drive My Car," "In My Life," "If I Needed Someone," "Day Tripper," "Norwegian Wood (This Bird Has Flown)," and "Nowhere Man" in preparation for the imminent release of the band's next single and LP in time for the holiday rush. The next day, as "Yesterday" reigned atop the American charts, they created stereo mixes in the Studio 2 control room. As for the Beatles themselves, they were absent yet again, having been delivered to Buckingham Palace in order to receive their MBEs from Queen Elizabeth II. After the ceremony, Brian convened a press conference at London's Saville Theatre, where the Beatles, channeling their buoyant press reception in the Pan Am lounge back in February 1964, held sway and narrated their audience with Her Majesty:

> The Queen: "It is my pleasure to give you this award."
> Harrison: "Thank you, ma'am."
> The Queen: "Have you been working hard?"
> Lennon: "No, we've been having a holiday."
> The Queen: "How long have you been together?"
> McCartney: "Many years."
> Starr: (breaking into song with the old vaudeville tune "My Old Dutch")
> "We've been together now for forty years!"

The Queen: (pausing in her confusion) "Did you start it all?"

Starr: "No, they did. I was the last to join. I'm the little fella."[19]

As the Beatles' drummer later recalled, the group didn't quite know what to make of the queen's reaction as they took their leave: "She had this strange, quizzical look on her face, like either she wanted to laugh or she was thinking 'Off with their heads!'"[20]

On Thursday, October 28, George supervised another mixing session—this time, devoted to making a remix of "We Can Work It Out" especially created for John and Paul to sing along with during an upcoming Granada television special to be titled *The Music of Lennon and McCartney*. When the Beatles heard the playback, they were aghast at their vocals, deciding to rerecord them at the next possible instant. The following day, they convened with George for an afternoon session in order to overdub new vocals onto "We Can Work It Out." Later that afternoon, the Beatles' producer supervised remixes of both "We Can Work It Out" and "Day Tripper" for the television special, which was recorded in front of a live studio audience on November 1 and 2 at the Granada TV Centre in Manchester. As filming commenced, the Beatles' work on their new LP was postponed until later in the week, as everyone was in on the act, including Martin, who conducted the George Martin Orchestra's version of "I Feel Fine" to kick off the show. Directed by Philip Casson, the program was scheduled for a December 19 broadcast and celebrated the budding Lennon-McCartney songbook. Featured guests included Cilla Black, Peter and Gordon, Lulu, Henry Mancini, Billy J. Kramer and the Dakotas, Marianne Faithfull, Peter Sellers, and, of course, the Beatles themselves.

As November came into focus, the band's latest album remained untitled—even though it was due with EMI in only a matter of days by this juncture. During a November 1 press conference, Paul didn't have the first clue about what to name the album, "the title of which could be *It's the Bloody Beatles Again!* or *Eight Feet Away*," he exclaimed. By Wednesday, November 3, they were back in the studio to try their hands at a brand-new number that ironically had been in the Lennon-McCartney ether for quite some time. Titled "Michelle," the tune had been in Paul's mind for years, dating back to at least 1959. As Paul later recalled, "There used to be a guy called Austin Mitchell who was one of John's tutors at art school and he used to throw some pretty good all-night parties. You could maybe pull girls there, which was the main aim of every second; you could get drinks, which was another aim; and you could generally put yourself about a bit. I remember sitting around there, and my recollection is of a black turtleneck sweater and sitting very enigmatically in the corner playing this rather French tune." By 1965, John and Paul were invariably searching for new material in order to keep up with the hefty pace that Brian and George had established. At one point, John said to Paul, "D'you remember that French thing you used to do at Mitchell's parties?" Needing lyrics to bring the memorable tune into being, Paul turned to Jan Vaughan, the wife of his childhood mate Ivan, who worked as a French teacher. She not only provided the songwriter with the idea of "Michelle, ma belle" but also gave him the translation of the phrase, "these are words that go together well," which she derived as "*Sont des mots qui vont très bien ensemble.*" Later, John concocted the song's moving middle eight after hearing Nina Simone's recording of "I Put a Spell on You." And voilà, "Michelle" was once and truly born.[21]

During the afternoon session on November 3, Martin and the band concentrated their efforts on the basic rhythm track, which came to consist of acoustic guitar, bass, and drums, along with McCartney's lead vocal. In a moment of creative caprice, Paul attempted to play his Rickenbacker with a capo applied to the neck. "I'd try anything once," he later remarked. "I would just mess around with any experimental effect." Having exhausted all four tracks on the tape, Martin and Smith copied the tape onto a second one while mixing the recording down to three tracks. Across the long evening session, George and the Beatles turned their attention to several overdubs. At one point, tape operator Jerry Boys recalled listening in the control room as Paul crafted his lead vocals: "I stood there quite spellbound. It sounded lovely. George asked me what I thought of the Beatles singing a song with French lyrics, and I got the impression that with me being a young chap he was sounding me out, perhaps because they weren't too sure themselves. I said it sounded very pleasant, which it certainly did!" As they continued to shape the recording, McCartney suggested that Martin enhance the song by slowing down the tempo of the basic rhythm track toward the end of "Michelle." In this way, George afforded more "emphasis" to the number's emotional climax. Satisfied with George's enhancement, Paul later recalled that "we thought it sounded better that way." But George wasn't finished just yet. Still lacking a solo at the heart of the song, the Beatles happened upon an idea. As Martin later pointed out, "The guitar solo in 'Michelle' is my composition, actually. I wrote down the notes and said [to Harrison], 'I'll play this. You can do these notes with me on guitar. We'll play in unison.'" With Martin working the studio piano without benefit of a microphone, Harrison brought the beautiful solo to life, and "Michelle" was complete.[22]

By Thursday, November 4, George and the Beatles had the makings of a truly exquisite, even groundbreaking long-player on their hands. But they were also quickly running out of time. The album was due to be released at the beginning of December, and at this point they had no more than a week to round out the LP. They began work that night at 11 PM and continued into the wee hours, finally closing up shop around 3:30 AM. At this point, they were fairly desperate, having nothing in the way of new material to make their deadline. With nothing to lose, they reached all the way back to March 5, 1963, when they had abandoned "What Goes On" in favor of recording "The One After 909." Still in search of a vehicle for Ringo to sing, "What Goes On" seemed to fit the bill while they played for time to write new songs. The song was credited to "Lennon-McCartney-Starkey" after the drummer provided some lyrics—"about five words," in Starr's memory. A rockabilly tune in the vein of Carl Perkins, "What Goes On" featured a moment of self-conscious levity when Ringo sings, "It's so easy for a girl like you to lie, / Tell me why." In the background, John can be heard responding "We already told you why" in a knowing reference to "Tell Me Why" from *A Hard Day's Night*. The rest of the evening was devoted to the band's first attempt at an instrumental since their prefame days. Announced by Smith over the talk-back as "12-Bar Original," the recording was exactly that: a twelve-bar blues effusion. Recorded live in Studio 2 without benefit of overdubs, the number featured Harrison playing a tone pedal–driven lead guitar, with Lennon on rhythm guitar, McCartney on bass, Starr on drums, and Martin working the harmonium. After the first attempt broke down, take two clocked in at 6:36 PM. By the time that they called it quits for the night, "12-Bar Original" had been abandoned by Martin and the bandmates for consideration for the upcoming long-player. After Smith prepared acetate versions for the group's private consumption later in the month, the instrumental wouldn't be mixed for potential release for some thirty years.

On Saturday, November 8, with less than a month before the LP's release date, George and the Beatles reconvened for an evening session at Abbey Road, where they attempted a remake of "I'm Looking Through You." During a six-hour session that lasted until after midnight, the band performed a more acoustic-oriented version of the song, complete with a newly crafted middle eight. In the end, the group remained unsatisfied with the latest version of "I'm Looking Through You." But the writing was on the wall: the bandmates needed to concoct new material—and quickly if they were going to hit the mark. After the bandmates took the weekend to try and generate new material, George and the group met up at Abbey Road on the evening of Monday,

November 10. As it happened, the LP was not the only tardy product at the time, as the Beatles were also due to record their latest Christmas Flexi-Disc installment for their fan club. In addition to engaging in jokes and tomfoolery until three in the morning in order to record their latest Christmas record, the Beatles spent the lion's share of the evening taking a stab at Harrison's latest composition, tentatively titled "Won't Be There with You."

With George leaving the tape running, as was their usual practice, the group rehearsed the song, all the while cracking one joke after another, speaking in exaggerated Scouse accents, and kidding their producer that they intended to replace him with Ron Richards. Eventually, the hilarity abated, and they managed to capture the rhythm track in a single take. But when Harrison made his first pass at recording his lead vocal track, things began to fall apart, with Martin and the bandmates succumbing to their understandably frayed nerves given their impending deadline. The first crack in their edifice occurred when John ran into trouble singing his backing vocal. After another failed attempt, they managed to complete the first verse, followed closely on its heels by the second verse. But the final verse proved to be their undoing, with John requesting an a cappella rehearsal in order to nail down the part. And then—eureka!—they seemed to have finally done it, only to be thwarted by Martin himself, who accidentally deleted the third verse when he was cuing up the playback. During the next attempt, Paul fell prey to the studio gremlins, botching his vocals after having been pitch perfect for much of the night.

After finally capturing the vocal tracks for "Won't Be There with You"—later retitled as "Think for Yourself"—George and the group turned to the song's overdubs, which made for a landmark moment in their own right, with Paul deploying a fuzz box on his Rickenbacker bass. The distorted sound of his bass part dominates the song, proving to be its most salient feature after Harrison's searing vocals. The fuzz box itself had been custom built by Abbey Road technicians. As Ken Townsend later observed, "It was an electronic device in which you could have controlled distortion. You actually made the sound overload." As the Beatles trundled home early the next morning, they left George alone in the studio to mix their Christmas record the next day while they went about the desperate business of concocting new material. Although their backs were clearly against the wall, the songs slated for release at this point were a marvel all their own. First, there was their next singles release, "Day Tripper" backed with "We Can Work It Out." And then there were the makings of a stellar long-player consisting of "Drive My Car," "Norwegian Wood (This Bird Has Flown)," "Nowhere Man," "Think for

Yourself," "Michelle," "What Goes On," "In My Life," "If I Needed Someone," and "Run for Your Life." But for all that, they were still five songs short.[23]

On Wednesday, November 10, George and the band managed to whittle that number down by two, working until four the next morning. Up first was a new Lennon-McCartney composition titled "The Word." Primarily written by John, the song made for an early attempt at the peace anthems that would typify his later work. As John observed, "You read the words. It's all about getting smart. It's the marijuana period. It's love. It's a love and peace thing. The word is 'love,' right?" They captured the song in three takes, including McCartney on piano and Martin playing a treble-riven harmonium part to accent the song's wicked musical bridge. In its finest moments, the tune's perceptive middle eight, sung by John in all his power and fury, muses on love's shifting contexts and connotations: "Everywhere I go, I hear it said / In the good and bad books that I have read." With "The Word" in the can, they turned to their old friend "I'm Looking Through You." With the adrenaline of an encroaching deadline, they recorded the rhythm track in a single take, save for a couple of false starts courtesy of John. The basic track consisted of Lennon on acoustic guitar, McCartney on bass, and Starr on drums. The only thing left was the vocals, which could wait for one more day.[24]

On Thursday, November 11, George and the Beatles spent some thirteen hours in the studio in a breakneck effort to bring the long-player, finally, to fruition. In many ways, the session—which began at six in the evening and ended the next morning at seven, just in time for a much-deserved English breakfast—harked back to that fabled *Please Please Me* session on February 11, 1963, when the bandmates were only just beginning to find their way as a working unit with George at Abbey Road. In spite of the pressure, they managed to capture three more songs on that day while putting the finishing touches on a fourth. In many ways, it was a prototypical session for the Beatles, who would find their mettle time and time again and come up aces when everything seemed to be on the line. The first number of the day involved a new McCartney composition, "You Won't See Me." By the second take, a basic rhythm track had been recorded, consisting of Lennon's piano, McCartney's bass, Harrison's electric guitar, Starr's drums, and a brief Hammond organ part courtesy of longtime roadie Mal Evans. The remaining tracks were devoted to McCartney's lead vocals; McCartney's double-tracked lead along with Lennon and Harrison on falsetto harmonies; and additional backing vocals from McCartney and Harrison.

With "You Won't See Me" under their belts, Martin and the band turned to "Girl," another standout composition from Lennon, who had written it in just the nick of time. As John later observed, "I definitely find I work better when I've got a deadline to meet. It really frightens you, and you've got to churn them out. All the time, I'm sort of arranging things in my mind." Within two takes, they had captured the basic track, which was comprised of McCartney's bass, Starr's drums, Lennon's acoustic guitar, and Harrison's finely arrayed, bouzouki-like guitar sound on his Hootenanny. In this manner, the quiet Beatle afforded the song with an intricate Greek melody in keeping with the group's evolving soundscapes of late. After Lennon recorded his lead vocal, along with a double-tracked middle eight, McCartney and Harrison provided an irreverent backing vocal that, momentarily at least, caught Martin's attention. As Paul later remarked, "It was to get some light relief in the middle of this real big career that we were forging. If we could put in something that was a little bit subversive then we would. George Martin might say, 'Was that "dit dit" or "tit tit" you were singing?' 'Oh, "dit dit," George, but it does sound a bit like that, doesn't it?' Then we'd get in the car and break down laughing." As it turned out, "Girl" wasn't the first time that they had considered infusing their records with a well-concealed bit of smut. Years later, McCartney would take special note of a sexually suggestive lyric that his songwriting partner had considered singing in "Day Tripper" by subtly crooning "she's a prick teaser" in place of "she's a big teaser." "We thought, 'That'd be fun to put in,'" Paul later recalled. "That was one of the great things about collaborating; you could nudge-nudge, wink-wink a bit, whereas if you're sitting on your own, you might not put it in."[25]

And just like that, they were out of new material. With "You Won't See Me" and "Girl" in states of completion, George and the Beatles were back up against the wall. With nothing else in the coffers, they turned to "Wait," the track that they had abandoned during the final stages of recording the *Help!* soundtrack back in June. In short order, they adorned the song with additional guitar work and another vocal from Paul, along with maracas and tambourine. And suddenly, the only thing left to do was apply a little varnish to "I'm Looking Through You," which they completed in the wee hours of November 12. In many ways, it was fitting that the recording sessions for the band's sixth studio album concluded with "I'm Looking Through You"—in itself the subject of so much toil in recent days. Having superimposed one last set of vocals on the song, the long-player finally had its full complement of fourteen tracks, ready and waiting to be mixed for the Beatles' seemingly unquenchable marketplace. On Monday, November 15, George did just that, mixing the long-player, which now went under the name *Rubber Soul*, with the indefatigable Norman Smith and Richard Lush assisting him in the Studio

1 control room. The session resulted in one particular oddity during the mixing of "I'm Looking Through You." George left John's two false acoustic guitar starts from November 10 at the beginning of the mix, reasoning that the Beatles' distributors would edit them out when preparing the masters. As it happened, the folks at Capitol Records left the recording intact—false starts and all—and the band's vast American audience was treated to a rare, unintended version of the song right out of the gate.

On November 16, *Rubber Soul* finally left George's custody after he established the album's running order, the last time he would exert such authority over the sequencing of a Beatles album. As was his practice, he kicked the LP off with the catchy, up-tempo "Drive My Car" and brought it to the finish line with the rock 'n' roll sounds of "Run for Your Life." In a final bit of irony—as EMI had done everything in its power to make the December 3 release date—the company's pressing plant encountered manufacturing problems while cutting the mono record. On November 19, disc cutter Harry Moss finally succeeded in cutting the mono LP. By the twenty-third, the stereo version of *Rubber Soul* had been cut. And with that, lacquer discs were hastily delivered to the manufacturing plant. At the same time, the album's sleeve, with its innovative cover photograph, was printed en masse. And by December 3—like clockwork, as if Brian and George had planned it so smoothly all along—both *Rubber Soul* and the Beatles' latest single were ready to hit the stores. From start to finish, the long-player had gone from its first recording session to the record shops in slightly more than fifty days. And in that decidedly analog era, it was an incredible turnaround by any measure.

For George and the group, *Rubber Soul* was a turning point in nearly every possible way. First, there was the significant matter of the title, which in and of itself was different from the band's previous forays, albums that most often parroted their title tracks—*Please Please Me*, *A Hard Day's Night*, and *Help!*, for example—or simply broadcast the group's name writ large (as in *With the Beatles* and *Beatles for Sale*). But *Rubber Soul* was, rather pointedly, neither of those things. The long-player's title connoted the very aspect that Paul had exclaimed after recording the raucous "I'm Down" back on June 14: "Plastic soul, man, plastic soul." Years later, Paul elaborated on the point, remarking, "I think the title *Rubber Soul* came from a comment an old blues guy had said of Jagger. I've heard some out-takes of us doing 'I'm Down' and at the front of it I'm chatting on about Mick. I'm saying how I'd just read about an old bloke in the States who said, 'Mick Jagger, man. Well you know they're good—but it's plastic soul.' So 'plastic soul' was the germ of the *Rubber Soul* idea." For his part, John described the title as being a pun on the concept of "English soul"—as a kind of intercultural approximation of stateside rhythm and blues in British hands, as an attempt to borrow from and appropriate a well-honed, thoroughly American genre but in a recognizably different (even less authentic) transatlantic fashion.[26]

Indeed, when listened to as a whole, *Rubber Soul* finds George and the Beatles mining all sorts of new sounds and flavors on the LP—not merely their plasticine brand of English soul but folk, exquisitely rendered ballads, Indian classical music, and country as well. As George later observed, "I think *Rubber Soul* was the first of the albums that presented a new Beatles to the world. Up to this point, we had been making albums that were rather like a collection of their singles and now we really were beginning to think about albums as a bit of art in their own right. We were thinking about the album as an entity of its own, and *Rubber Soul* was the first one to emerge in this way."[27]

The manner in which George and the Beatles concentrated their energies during the recording sessions for *Rubber Soul* no doubt contributed to the album's resounding quality—and in spite of a host of issues, namely the lack of new material at various junctures during the long-player's creation. *Rubber Soul* also marked their first LP since *Please Please Me* to be recorded in a fairly steady and uninterrupted fashion during a continuous period from October 12 through November 15. But while this ceaseless, highly compacted pace clearly had an impact on the album's achievement as the finest Beatles LP to date, it was not without toil. As George later observed, "My workload was enormous so that I was spending more time in the studio than I was anywhere else. And I found myself completely and utterly wrapped up in my work." And the existing technology at the time didn't always help, as George and the group's ideas for innovation so often outperformed the equipment at their disposal at Abbey Road. Ever practical, George didn't allow technological challenges to prevent him from bringing the Beatles' sonic visions to life. With nothing to lose, he simply drew upon so many years of experience and well-earned studio know-how, resorting to "manipulations of the resources we had at the time." After bringing in such a magisterial album in the eleventh hour and under a host of competing constraints, George and the Beatles couldn't be blamed if they got to thinking—after everything that they had gone through to launch *Rubber Soul* into being—what making an album would be like if they could work in the studio without limitations. Indeed, what could they accomplish within a context in which their only boundaries were the depths of their imaginations and the existing recording technologies of the day?[28]

The Beatles themselves quickly realized the remarkable nature of their creation, recognizing that they had clearly turned a corner from their days as mere mop-top idols. "This was the departure record," Ringo remarked, "what was happening elsewhere was nothing like it." For Harrison, the band's latest achievement was no surprise. "We certainly knew we were making a good album. We did spend a bit more time on it and tried new things. But the most important thing about it was that we were suddenly hearing sounds that we weren't able to hear before. Also, we were being more influenced by other people's music and everything was blossoming at that time; including us, because we were still growing." For his part, McCartney could feel a sea change in the group's working relationship with Martin, who was formerly an authority figure, only to morph, as *Rubber Soul* came into focus, into a collaborator—a partner of sorts in evolving their musical fusion together. Previously, George "had a lot of control—we used to record the stuff, and leave him to mix it, pick a single, everything," Paul later remarked. "After a while though, we got so into recording we'd stay behind while he mixed it, watching what he was doing." For Lennon, especially, *Rubber Soul* had proven to be a watershed moment, as his "fat Elvis" days began to slowly recede behind him. While McCartney had been the artistic force behind such gems as "Drive My Car" and "Michelle," Lennon spearheaded many of the LP's most sophisticated tracks, including "Norwegian Wood (This Bird Has Flown)," "Nowhere Man," and "In My Life," which Martin had transformed from an instant classic into the sublime via his windup piano technique. "We were getting better technically and musically, that's all," Lennon observed. "We finally took over the studio. In the early days, we had to take what we were given. We had to make it in two hours or whatever it was. And three takes was enough, and we didn't know about 'you can get more bass,' and we were learning the technique. With *Rubber Soul*, we were more precise about making the album—that's all. We took over the cover and everything."[29]

Shot in the garden of John's Weybridge estate, *Rubber Soul*'s poignant photograph was taken by Robert Freeman as his final cover art for the band. He attributed "the distorted effect in the photo" to being "a reflection of the changing shape of their lives." Paul later recalled how the distorted effect came to pass, remarking, "When we came to choose which of Bob's photos we should use for the cover of *Rubber Soul*, he visited us at a friend's flat one evening. Whilst projecting the slides on to an album-sized piece of white cardboard, Bob inadvertently tilted the card backwards. The effect was to stretch the perspective and elongate the faces. We excitedly asked him if it was possible to print the photo in this way. Being Bob, he said, 'Yes,' and the cover to our album *Rubber Soul* was decided."[30]

And with that, the Beatles' transformation was complete. The concept of the record album, previously viewed by rock 'n' roll musicians and their handlers as a mere collection of songs to hawk for the music-buying public, had been elevated—first, via the band's groundbreaking work in the studio and second, by the imaginative creation of their cover art. Quite suddenly, the long-player was an artifact as opposed to simply existing as a commercial vehicle. As a cohesive album, *Rubber Soul* redefined the imprimatur of the Beatles as "recording artists." And while a few contemporary reviewers found the group's bold new soundscapes to be perplexing, for the most part the extent of George and the bandmates' latest accomplishment was resoundingly clear to the record journalists of the day. In *NME*, Allen Evans raved that the Beatles were "still finding different ways to make us enjoy listening to them," calling the album "a fine piece of recording artistry and adventure in group sound." At the same time, *Record Mirror* gushed that "one marvels and wonders at the constant stream of melodic ingenuity stemming from the boys, both as performers and composers. Keeping up their pace of creativeness is quite fantastic."[31]

As it happened, British music critics weren't the only ones who noticed a change afoot in the Beatles' sound, not to mention the trailblazing aspects of *Rubber Soul*. Perhaps most significantly given everything that would happen in just a few short months, the Beach Boys' Brian Wilson, the architect of the American band's evolving sound, absolutely marveled at the Beatles' new LP. It was "the first album I listened to where every song was a gas," he later remarked, adding, "I liked the way it all went together, the way it was all one thing. It was a challenge to me." Wilson continued, "It didn't make me want to copy them but to be as good as them." By this point, the Beach Boys were already in the midst of recording their follow-up LP to *Summer Days (And Summer Nights!!)*. For a short while, their next album would go under the working title of *Our Freaky Friends* until a fateful visit to the San Diego Zoo caused them to take another tack and call it *Pet Sounds*. But after Wilson heard *Rubber Soul*, his ambitions for the Beach Boys' recording grew exponentially. In a moment of inspiration, he sought out his wife, Marilyn, exclaiming, "I'm gonna make the greatest album! The greatest rock album ever made!" In fairly short order, the Beach Boys would capture George and the band's attention, and the Beatles' sound would shift yet again in vastly unexpected ways.[32]

But by then, they would be well into a new and very different year. For now, *Rubber Soul* was making its way into the waiting arms of the British faithful, followed shortly thereafter by their American counterparts. In England, *Rubber Soul* was released on December 3, the very same day in which the Beatles embarked upon a nine-day tour of the British Isles. On December 12, the curtain closed in front of the group at the Capitol Cinema in Cardiff, Wales. The show ended in fine fettle, with Paul delivering a blistering performance of "I'm Down," but as usual scarcely anyone could hear the Fab Four among the din of screams. But what nobody knew—save for the Beatles and their innermost circle—was that "I'm Down" would be the last song of the last concert on the very last tour that the Beatles would ever play in their homeland.

# EPILOGUE

# LIFE BEGINS AT FORTY

THE DAY AFTER THE BEATLES' CARDIFF SHOW, Brian and the bandmates met with Walter Shenson, the producer who brought them to the big screen in *A Hard Day's Night* and *Help!* While the meeting was certainly less climactic than the previous evening's concert, the day's events held great portents nonetheless. Brian had arranged the meeting so that Walter could pitch a third feature film to the group. This time, the deal involved another property for United Artists titled *A Talent for Loving*. Based on Richard Condon's novel of the same name, *A Talent for Loving* would depict the four lads from Liverpool transplanted into an 1870s-era western as pioneering frontiersmen. But for the first time, the Beatles weren't having it, voting unanimously—all for one and one for all, as was their practice—to reject Shenson's gambit outright. And in so doing, for the first time since achieving global fame, they upset Brian and George's formula divining their annual output to be a pair of studio albums, a fresh parcel of singles, and a major movie release. Simply put, there would be no Beatles feature film in 1966. The winds of change were clearly blowing in the bandmates' camp.

*Rubber Soul* had ushered in a new era for the Beatles all right, and in more ways than one. But as forward-thinking as the band may have been, December 1965 also proved to be a time for wistfully considering their recent past, which by any measure was a unique achievement all its own. On December 17, the Granada television special aired, broadcasting *The Music of Lennon and McCartney* into homes all across Great Britain. As one act after another, including the George Martin Orchestra, saluted the songwriters' embarrassment of musical riches that evening, John and Paul had much to celebrate at this comparatively early date in their recording career. They had already been feted in numerous ways and in nearly every medium. They had even famously won over William Mann, the classical music critic for the *Times*, back in December 1963. In his article, Mann interpreted Lennon's work on "Not a Second Time" as being akin to the Aeolian cadence that concludes Gustav Mahler's *The Song of the Earth*. John would later joke that an "Aeolian cadence" meant nothing to him, sounding for all the world like "exotic birds." But he would be lying if he said that he wasn't secretly chuffed by receiving such select attention. And then there was Paul's "Yesterday," for which BBC critic Deryck Cooke extolled John and Paul as "serious" composers of a "new music."[1]

Perhaps the greatest compliment that the songwriters enjoyed that night came from the lips of no less than Peter Sellers, the innovative comedian who had helped to propel George Martin and Parlophone back into EMI's good graces all those years ago. Arguably the highlight of *The Music of Lennon and McCartney* TV special, Sellers turned in a sidesplitting performance of "A Hard Day's Night." The comedian's performance acted as a satire of the Beatles' chart-topper to be sure, but in such moments of parody invariably lay a nodding affirmation of the original text. As it happened, Sellers's "A Hard Day's Night" marked the comic's final recording with George. The idea for lampooning "A Hard Day's Night" came from one John Junkin, a scriptwriter friend of Martin's and the actor who played Shake in the Beatles' first feature film. As Martin later recalled, one day Junkin said to him, "You know, a lot of these Beatles lyrics are quite funny if you read them" aloud. For his part, George had never considered the group's songs in that fashion, later remarking, "I'd never looked at them like that before, but there was something in what he said, so I spoke to Peter about it. He tried a few lyrics in different voices, and we both saw the possibilities. He was really funny, and we ended up giggling like schoolboys. His impersonation of Laurence Olivier was uncanny, and when he read 'A Hard Day's Night' in that voice—as Olivier would have interpreted *Richard III*—I knew it was the one to go for." For the recording of Sellers's Olivier rendition of the song, Martin pulled out all of the stops in order to heighten the comedic effect. "I wrote a special score using the music of the song," he said, but he arranged it purposefully to "sound like a medieval accompaniment, using muted violins to give the sound of viols and recorders instead of flutes." For the television special, Sellers sat aloft on a throne as the camera slowly closed in and he began reciting Lennon and McCartney's lyrics. With the locks of his Elizabethan wig in full bloom, he accented the words in a theatrical English accent, suggestively drawing them out as he imbued their language with even more alluring connotations than even the Beatles' original version could ever have sustained. "When I'm home . . . feeling you . . . holding me . . . tight . . . tight," Sellers recited, as the studio audience went wild and Martin's intentionally whimsical score echoed about the soundstage.[2]

If Sellers's parody proved nothing else, it demonstrated that the Beatles had once and truly arrived, that they were worthy of such a lofty send-up courtesy of one of their homeland's most esteemed comedians and satirists. In the same vein, *The Music of Lennon and McCartney* celebrated John and Paul as the most renowned popular songwriters of their day. As Martin unabashedly remarked, "Great talent it was. They were the Cole Porters and George Gershwins of their generation, of that there is no doubt. Somebody compared them to Schubert, which sounds a bit pretentious, but I would go along with that to the extent that their music was perfectly representative of the period in which they were living." By then, even John and Paul knew it, too. After the accolades had been heaped upon "Yesterday" and *Rubber Soul*, there was really no looking back. For so long, they had been writing in close quarters—"nose to nose" and "eyeball to eyeball"—but even those days were rapidly coming to a close. For Lennon and McCartney, the stakes of authorship—and the myriad rewards that it brought—were growing ever more competitive with each new recording.[3]

As it happened, the increasing shifts in the band's calculus—and the role of authorial stakes in these changes—were hardly lost on Norman Smith either. For his part, Smith had had just about enough of the Beatles by this time. For a while he had chalked it up to being at a creative impasse with the group: "*Rubber Soul* wasn't really my bag at all." But in truth, it was much more than that. In a less guarded moment, he would admit that "when *Rubber Soul* came around it was taking a lot longer to record each title. I could see the friction building up and I didn't like it at all. I thought, 'To hell with this,' and I told George Martin, 'I don't like what I see and I want to get off this train.' He said, 'They're going to be very upset about this,' but I said, 'Well, that's the way it is.'" In the engineer's reckoning, "something had happened between *Help!* and *Rubber Soul*. There had been one hell of a change in the relationship between the boys—mainly between John and Paul. It was very noticeable, and it made me quite sad in actual fact." In earlier days, "the four boys, George, and myself had formed a sort of family, and, as you can probably imagine, it was wonderful to be part of all that." But as far as he was concerned, the writing was already the wall—and had been for a while. Smith had recognized a change in the band's chemistry as McCartney, in particular, seemed to be emerging as the "main musical force." Even Harrison—the junior member in the Beatles' songwriting contest for so long by this point—was getting into the act. None of this was lost on Martin, of course. He may have been hoodwinked by the smutty backing vocals in "Girl," but by this juncture he had observed the group up close, day after day, for literally hundreds of hours inside and outside the studio. No, he knew exactly what was going on. But at the same time, he recognized their increasing tension as a central element in the Lennon-McCartney partnership—and in a larger sense, in the music of the Beatles. "Imagine two people pulling on a rope, smiling at each other and pulling all the time with all their might," he once observed. "The tension between the two of them made for the bond."[4]

Ever true to his word, Smith made his exit from the Beatles' brain trust in the new year. "I told George and George told Eppy, and the next thing I received a lovely gold carriage clock inscribed 'To Norman. Thanks. John, Paul, George and Ringo.'" As fate would have it, Smith wouldn't roam very far from Martin and the bandmates' orbit. In a few short months, he would be promoted to Parlophone A&R head—George's old job. In short order, he would take up offices with the other record execs at EMI's Manchester Square location. With George having left the EMI Group to form AIR, someone had to take the reins of Parlophone, the "third label" that wasn't nearly as browbeaten as it had been so many years earlier, before George found his mettle with comedy records and later when the Beatles took the world by storm. As for Smith, administrative life wasn't without its pitfalls. After being elevated as head of Parlophone, "The first thing I had to do was get an artists' roster together, and I had this idea of sending out a letter to all the agents and managers telling them I was now the producer and that I was looking for new acts. Unfortunately," Smith related, "one of the letters went to an executive of a rival record company who was listed as an agent. He wrote to the chairman of EMI alleging that I was attempting to illegally poach artists from other record companies. I got my knuckles severely rapped for that, and I'd only been in the job two weeks." It may have been an inauspicious beginning, but even George—already being hailed as the world's preeminent record producer—made a mistake or two along the way, as evinced most recently by the mishap with the tape machine during the "Think for Yourself" session back in early November. While George and the Beatles may have been understandably sad to see "Normal" Smith leave their inner circle, his departure created a natural and much-deserved opportunity for young Geoff Emerick, who would turn twenty years old in 1966, to take his own crack at being the Beatles' engineer.[5]

But on January 3, 1966, as George celebrated his fortieth birthday, the effects of such changes had yet to be realized—and wouldn't be for days, if not weeks or months or even years. With the triumph of *Rubber Soul* still fresh as the album reigned atop the charts, the man who had brought Parlophone back from the brink of obsolescence had succeeded beyond his wildest dreams, having crawled out from behind EMI's shadow and made a name for himself in the wide world of pop music and Western culture. And he had done so with a beat-music band of his own—with a group of Liverpool musicians upon whom the rest of the industry had turned its back. He had piloted them beyond their modest Mersey-sound origins into something that none of them could have even reasonably imagined. Yes, they had come a long way from the simple, bluesy sound of "Love Me Do" and eclipsed George's expectations many times over. With each passing session—from *Please Please Me* through *Rubber Soul*—they had marched into the studio, brimming with new and often breathtaking compositions, and unveiled a seemingly endless array of musical riches in the friendly confines of Studio 2. And to think that by January 1966 they were only just getting started.

As George marked his fortieth birthday, there was much to be thankful for and even more untold possibilities lurking just beyond the horizon. Fewer than four years earlier, he had begrudgingly taken a risk on the band, and the bet had paid off handsomely and then some. While George and Judy celebrated the producer's birthday, the Beatles were, for the most part, taking a much-deserved break from the studio and that wearisome road that they knew so well. But come April, they were poised to fire the whole enterprise up again and see where it might lead to next. As for George, having finally been untethered from the EMI group and with his divorce from Sheena finalized the previous February, the Beatles' producer was at a crossroads. With marriage to his beloved Judy no doubt in the offing, George could afford to look at the world with a gleam in his eye and plenty of untapped ambition left in that secret, working-class heart of his. With Len Wood and EMI in his rearview mirror and his partners at AIR eager to support his vision for unbridled pop-music production, one thing was certain: after years of toiling at the behest of others, he was finally going into business for himself.

# ACKNOWLEDGMENTS

A PROJECT OF THIS MAGNITUDE could never come to fruition without the encouragement and support of a host of friends and colleagues. I owe special debts of thanks to Patrick Alexander, William Baker, Brian Black, Amanda Brockriede, Eileen Chapman, John Christopher, Lynne Clay, James Collins, Todd Davis, Chris DeRosa, Phil Dunn, Jackie Edmondson, Furg, Daphne Keller, Michele Kennedy, Laura Moriarty, Nancy Mezey, Jacob Michael, Nicolle Parsons-Pollard, Vaune Peck, Judy Ramos, Joe Rapolla, George and Kathy Severini, Michael Thomas, Rich Veit, and Kurt Wagner.

A number of Beatles specialists and music scholars have shared their time and expertise on behalf of this project, including Jim Berkenstadt, Adrian Brown, Walter Everett, Larry Feibel, Michael Frontani, Laurence Juber, Katie Kapurch, Jude Southerland Kessler, Allan Kozinn, Howard Kramer, Jason Kruppa, Richard Langham, Mark Lapidos, Spencer Leigh, Staffan Olander, Kit O'Toole, Tim Riley, Robert Rodriguez, and Bob Santelli. I am especially grateful to Mark Lewisohn, whose groundbreaking work and painstaking scholarship continue to benefit music historians around the world. This book simply would not have been possible without his lifelong devotion to getting the Beatles' story right.

I am thankful for the steadfast encouragement of my extraordinary agent, Isabel Atherton; my indefatigable publicist, Nicole Michael; and Yuval Taylor, senior editor at Chicago Review Press. My deepest thanks are due to Gregory Paul Martin, a true artist in his own right, for generously sharing his memories and family photographs. With his wife, Cherie Rose, Gregory has been invaluable to this project.

Finally, I am thankful, as always, for the love and support of my family—Fred, Jennifer, Andy, Becca, Peter, Tori, Josh, Ryan, Chelsea, Emma, Landon, Justin, and Mellissa—and especially to my wife, Jeanine, who makes all things possible.

# NOTES

## Prologue: "Good God, What've We Got 'Ere?"

1. Mark Lewisohn, *Tune In: The Beatles—All These Years* (Boston: Little, Brown, 2013), 1:666.
2. Mark Lewisohn, *The Complete Beatles Recording Sessions: The Official Abbey Road Studio Session Notes, 1962–1970* (New York: Harmony, 1988), 18.
3. Ibid.
4. Ibid.
5. Bob Spitz, *The Beatles: The Biography* (Boston: Little, Brown, 2005), 318; Kevin Ryan and Brian Kehew, *Recording the Beatles: The Studio Equipment and Techniques Used to Create Their Classic Albums* (Houston, TX: Curvebender, 2006), 349.
6. George Martin, *All You Need Is Ears*, with Jeremy Hornsby (New York: St. Martin's, 1999), 124.

## 1: Made in Great Britain

1. Francis Hanly, dir., *Produced by George Martin* (BBC, 2012).
2. George Martin, *Playback: An Illustrated Memoir* (Guildford, England: Genesis, 2003), 9.
3. Ibid., 9–10.
4. Ibid., 10; Hanly, *Produced by George Martin*; Gregory Paul Martin, interview with author (hereafter cited as Martin interview), March 10, 2016.
5. Martin, *Playback*, 10–11.
6. Ibid., 11.
7. Martin, *All You Need Is Ears*, 13; Martin, *Playback*, 13.
8. Martin, *Playback*, 13; Hanly, *Produced by George Martin*.
9. Martin, *Playback*, 13.
10. Ibid., 15.
11. Martin, *All You Need Is Ears*, 15.

12. George Martin, "The Tingle Factor," interview with Jeremy Nicholas, BBC Radio Four Extra, 1992, www.bbc.co.uk/programmes/b07cmbyg; Martin, *All You Need Is Ears*, 30.
13. Martin, *All You Need Is Ears*, 15.
14. Martin, *Playback*, 15–16; Hanly, *Produced by George Martin*; Lewisohn, *Tune In*, 1:254.
15. Martin, *Playback*, 16.
16. Ibid., 18; Martin, *All You Need Is Ears*, 17.
17. Martin, *Playback*, 16–17; Hanly, *Produced by George Martin.*
18. Martin, *All You Need Is Ears*, 17.
19. Martin, *Playback*, 18; Martin, *All You Need Is Ears*, 18; Hanly, *Produced by George Martin.*
20. Martin, *All You Need Is Ears*, 18; Martin, *Playback*, 18–19.
21. Martin, *Playback*, 19.
22. Hanly, *Produced by George Martin*; Martin, *All You Need Is Ears*, 19.
23. Martin, *All You Need Is Ears*, 21; Lewisohn, *Tune In*, 1:253.
24. Martin, *All You Need Is Ears*, 22.
25. Ibid.
26. Martin, *Playback*, 20.
27. Martin, *All You Need Is Ears*, 23; Martin interviews, April 22, 2016, and March 10, 2016.
28. Martin interview, March 22, 2016.
29. Ibid.
30. Martin, *All You Need Is Ears*, 23.
31. Ibid., 25.
32. Martin, *Playback*, 23.

## 2: The Big Smoke

1. Martin, *Playback*, 22.
2. Ibid.
3. Ibid., 23.
4. Martin interview, March 22, 2016.
5. Martin, *All You Need Is Ears*, 26–27.
6. Ibid., 27; Martin interview, March 22, 2016.
7. Martin, *All You Need Is Ears*, 28.
8. Ibid.
9. Sheet music provided by Gregory Paul and Cherie Rose Martin, March 22, 2016.
10. Ibid.
11. Martin, *All You Need Is Ears*, 34.
12. Ibid., 28.

13. Martin, *Playback*, 24–25; Martin, *All You Need Is Ears*, 36–37; for the corporate history of EMI and Parlophone, see Alistair Lawrence, *Abbey Road: The Best Studio in the World* (London: Bloomsbury, 2012), and Brian Southall, *Abbey Road: The Story of the World's Most Famous Studios* (Wellingborough, England: Patrick Stephens, 1982).
14. Martin, *All You Need Is Ears*, 36.
15. Ibid., 37; Lewisohn, *Tune In*, 1:638.
16. Martin, *Playback*, 29.
17. Martin, *All You Need Is Ears*, 38.
18. Ibid., 38.
19. Martin, *Playback*, 31–32.
20. Ron Goodwin, "Ron Goodwin," interview by Christopher Ritchie, *Soundtrack!* 8, no. 30 (1989), www.runmovies.eu/?p=1812.
21. Martin, *All You Need Is Ears*, 48.
22. Ibid., 40.
23. Ibid., 40.
24. Ibid., 40–41.
25. Ibid., 43.
26. Ibid., 44–45.

## 3: A House in St. John's Wood

1. Spitz, *The Beatles*, 372.
2. Martin, *Playback*, 36.
3. Martin, *All You Need Is Ears*, 44; Hanly, *Produced by George Martin*.
4. Martin, *All You Need Is Ears*, 47.
5. Lewisohn, *Tune In*, 1:261.
6. Hanly, *Produced by George Martin*.
7. Martin interview, March 22, 2016, and February 2, 2017.
8. Martin interview, March 22, 2016.
9. Ibid.
10. Martin, *All You Need Is Ears*, 60.
11. Martin, *Playback*, 35.
12. Ibid., 36; Lewisohn, *Tune In*, 1:265.
13. Hanly, *Produced by George Martin*.
14. Martin, *All You Need Is Ears*, 56.
15. Lewisohn, *Tune In*, 1:262.
16. Martin, *All You Need Is Ears*, 82; Southall, *Abbey Road*, 69.
17. Martin, *All You Need Is Ears*, 63.
18. Hanly, *Produced by George Martin*; Lewisohn, *Tune In*, 1:266.
19. Martin, *Playback*, 47.

20. Ibid.; Hanly, *Produced by George Martin.*
21. Martin, *Playback*, 48.
22. Martin, *All You Need Is Ears*, 89–90.
23. Martin, *Playback*, 48; Martin, *All You Need Is Ears*, 87.
24. Martin, *All You Need Is Ears*, 88; Lewisohn, *Tune In*, 1:279.
25. Hanly, *Produced by George Martin*; Martin, *All You Need Is Ears*, 88.
26. Martin, *Playback*, 48; Martin, *All You Need Is Ears*, 88–89.
27. Martin, *Playback*, 55.
28. Ibid., 124.
29. See Humphrey Carpenter, *That Was Satire That Was: The Satire Boom of the 1960s* (London: Faber and Faber, 2001).
30. Spitz, *The Beatles*, 297; Southall, *Abbey Road*, 52.

## 4: "Frustration Has Many Fathers"

1. Martin, *All You Need Is Ears*, 179; Lewisohn, *Tune In*, 1:278.
2. Martin, *All You Need Is Ears*, 120–21.
3. Mark Lewisohn, *Tune In: The Beatles—All These Years*, extended ed. (Boston: Little, Brown, 2013), 1:294.
4. Lewisohn, *Tune In*, 1:266.
5. Martin, *Playback*, 58.
6. Martin, *All You Need Is Ears*, 100.
7. Martin, *Playback*, 60.
8. Ibid., 60–61.
9. Ibid., 61; Howard Massey, *The Great British Recording Studios* (Milwaukee, WI: Hal Leonard, 2015), 322.
10. Martin, *Playback*, 63.
11. Lewisohn, *Tune In*, extended ed., 1:641.
12. Ibid.
13. Martin, *All You Need Is Ears*, 27; Martin interview, March 22, 2016.
14. Southall, *Abbey Road*, 77–78.
15. Spencer Leigh, *The Cavern Club: The Rise of the Beatles and Merseybeat* (Carmarthen, Wales: McNidder and Grace, 2016), 62.
16. Martin, *All You Need Is Ears*, 100.
17. Martin, *Playback*, 63.

## 5: An Instant Friendship

1. Martin, *Playback*, 63.
2. Justin Wm. Moyer, "What the Late George Martin Really Did for the Beatles," *Washington Post*, March 9, 2016, www.washingtonpost.com/news/morning-mix/wp/2016/03/09/what-george-martin-who-died-tuesday-really-did-for-the-beatles/.
3. Martin, *Playback*, 71.

4. Lewisohn, *Tune In*, 1:637.
5. Martin, *Playback*, 68; Martin, *All You Need Is Ears*, 100; Lewisohn, *Tune In*, 1:696.
6. Hanly, *Produced by George Martin*; Lewisohn, *Tune In*, 1:637.
7. Brian Epstein, *A Cellarful of Noise: The Autobiography of the Man Who Made the Beatles* (New York: Pocket, 1998), 42.
8. Lewisohn, *Tune In*, 1:326, 512, 517.
9. Lewisohn, *Tune In*, 1:590–91.
10. Martin, *All You Need Is Ears*, 122; Hanly, *Produced by George Martin*.
11. Epstein, *A Cellarful of Noise*, 62; Martin, *All You Need Is Ears*, 122.
12. Epstein, *A Cellarful of Noise*, 62; Lewisohn, *Tune In*, 1:592–93.
13. Martin, *Playback*, 74; Andy Babiuk, *Beatles Gear: All the Fab Four's Instruments, from Stage to Studio* (San Francisco: Backbeat, 2001), 61; Lewisohn, *Tune In*, 1:612.
14. Spitz, *The Beatles*, 297.
15. Michelle Monro, *Matt Monro: The Singer's Singer* (New York: Titan Books, 2012), 85.
16. Ibid., 141–42.
17. Lewisohn, *Tune In*, 1:531.
18. Martin, *All You Need Is Ears*, 99, 120.
19. Lewisohn, *Tune In*, 1:638.
20. Ibid., 1:270.
21. Martin interview, March 22, 2016.
22. Martin interview, January 28, 2017; Jane Warren, "Family Feud of 'Fifth Beatle': Sir George Martin's Children in Furious Inheritance Row," *Express*, September 22, 2016, www.express.co.uk/comment/expresscomment/713193/family-feud-fifth-beatle-sir-george-martin-children-furious-inheritance-row.
23. Martin, *Playback*, 176.
24. Lewisohn, *Tune In*, 1:637.
25. Martin, *All You Need Is Ears*, 220–21.
26. Ibid., 221.
27. Martin interview, March 22, 2016.
28. Ibid.
29. Ibid.
30. Lewisohn, *Tune In*, 1:637.
31. Ibid., 1:638–39.

## 6: "I Don't Like Your Tie"

1. Lewisohn, *Tune In*, 1:594.
2. Ibid.
3. Ibid., 1:640.
4. Martin interview, March 22, 2016; Alistair Taylor, *With the Beatles* (London: John Blake, 2003), 55; Lewisohn, *Tune In*, 1:613; John Lennon and Yoko Ono, *All We*

*Are Saying: The Last Major Interview with John Lennon and Yoko Ono*, interview by David Sheff, ed. G. Barry Golson (New York: Griffin, 2000), 159.

5. Taylor, *With the Beatles*, 156; Lewisohn, *Tune In*, 1:647; Martin, *Playback*, 76.
6. Lewisohn, *Tune In*, 1:648; Elvis Costello, foreword to *Here, There, and Everywhere: My Life Recording the Music of the Beatles*, by Geoff Emerick and Howard Massey (New York: Gotham, 2006), x.
7. Lewisohn, *Tune In*, 1:656.
8. Epstein, *A Cellarful of Noise*, 62.
9. Brian Southall, *Northern Songs: The True Story of the Beatles Song Publishing Empire*, with Rupert Perry (London: Omnibus, 2009), 275.
10. Ibid., 282.
11. Lewisohn, *Tune In*, 1:665–66.
12. Ibid.; Lewisohn, *Complete Beatles*, 6, 17–18.
13. Babiuk, *Beatles Gear*, 65; Lewisohn, *Complete Beatles*, 17; Ryan and Kehew, *Recording the Beatles*, 348.
14. Hanly, *Produced by George Martin*.
15. Lewisohn, *Tune In*, 1:663.
16. Ibid., 1:668.
17. Ibid., 1:669; Lewisohn, *Complete Beatles*, 6.
18. Lewisohn, *Tune In*, 1:670.
19. Ibid.; Lewisohn, *Complete Beatles*, 18. The Beatles likely sped up the tempo of "Love Me Do" at George's recommendation on June 6. As John later remarked, "Love Me Do" was originally "a slower number like Billy Fury's 'Halfway To Paradise,' but George Martin suggested we do it faster. I'm glad we did. We all owe a great deal of our success to George, especially for his patient guidance of our enthusiasm in the right direction." See Alan Clayson, *John Lennon* (London: Sanctuary, 2003), 103–4.
20. Lewisohn, *Tune In*, 1:670.
21. Hanly, *Produced by George Martin*; Lewisohn, *Tune In*, 1:670–71.
22. Lewisohn, *Tune In*, 1:671.
23. Martin, *All You Need Is Ears*, 124.

## 7: "Liverpool? You're Joking!"

1. Lewisohn, *Tune In*, 1:673; Martin, *All You Need Is Ears*, 123.
2. Martin, *Playback*, 49.
3. Lewisohn, *Tune In*, 1:676; Hanly, *Produced by George Martin*.
4. Lewisohn, *Tune In*, 1:698.
5. Ibid.; Tony Bramwell, *Magical Mystery Tours: My Life with the Beatles*, with Rosemary Kingsland (New York: St. Martin's, 2005), 78.
6. Lewisohn, *Tune In*, 1:726.
7. Philip Norman, *John Lennon: The Life* (London: Ecco, 2008), 270; according to the *Oxford English Dictionary*, a "Liverpool kiss" connotes a "blow delivered to the head or face"—a head-butt.

8. Lewisohn, *Tune In*, 1:725; The Beatles, *The Beatles Anthology* (San Francisco: Chronicle, 2000), 90; Lewisohn, *Complete Beatles*, 18.
9. Walter Everett, *The Beatles as Musicians: The Quarry Men Through Rubber Soul* (Oxford: Oxford University Press, 2001), 123; Lewisohn, *Tune In*, 1:725.
10. John Lennon, *Lennon Remembers*, interview by Jann Wenner (1970; repr., New York: Verso, 2000), 27; Lewisohn, *Tune In*, 1:727–28; Lewisohn, *Complete Beatles*, 7.
11. Martin, *Playback*, 88.
12. Lewisohn, *Tune In*, 1:728; Lewisohn, *Complete Beatles*, 18.
13. Spitz, *The Beatles*, 352.
14. Lewisohn, *Tune In*, 1:730.
15. Ibid., 1:730–31; Beatles, *Beatles Anthology*, 90.
16. Chris Salewicz, *McCartney: The Biography* (London: Queen Anne, 1986), 135; Lewisohn, *Tune In*, 1:779, 782.
17. Hunter Davies, *The Beatles* (New York: Norton, 2004), 171; Hanly, *Produced by George Martin*.
18. Lewisohn, *Tune In*, 1:800.
19. Martin, *All You Need Is Ears*, 127; Southall, *Northern Songs*, 376, 390.
20. Lewisohn, *Tune In*, 1:803.
21. Gordon Thompson, *Please Please Me: Sixties Pop, Inside Out* (Oxford: Oxford University Press, 2008), 120–21; Martin, *All You Need Is Ears*, 130.
22. Martin, *All You Need Is Ears*, 130; Lewisohn, *Tune In*, 1:809.

## 8: 585 Minutes

1. Epstein, *A Cellarful of Noise*, 65.
2. Lewisohn, *Tune In*, 1:822.
3. Ibid., 1:806.
4. Martin, *All You Need Is Ears*, 125.
5. Epstein, *A Cellarful of Noise*, 77; Martin, *Playback*, 105.
6. Lewisohn, *Tune In*, 1:835.
7. Don Wedge, "Telstar Reaches Two Millionth Orbit," *Billboard*, January 26, 1963, 28; Martin, *All You Need Is Ears*, 130.
8. Martin, *All You Need Is Ears*, 130.
9. Martin, *Playback*, 88.
10. George Martin, *With a Little Help from My Friends: The Making of Sgt. Pepper*, with William Pearson (Boston: Little, Brown, 1994), 77; Lewisohn, *Complete Beatles*, 24.
11. Lewisohn, *Complete Beatles*, 24.
12. Ibid., 26; Martin, *All You Need Is Ears*, 131.
13. Beatles, *Beatles Anthology*, 96; Lewisohn, *Complete Beatles*, 26.
14. Martin, *All You Need Is Ears*, 142.
15. Geoff Emerick and Howard Massey, *Here, There, and Everywhere: My Life Recording the Music of the Beatles* (New York: Gotham, 2006), 60.

16. Ibid.
17. Ibid.; Lewisohn, *Complete Beatles*, 28.
18. Lewisohn, *Complete Beatles*, 32.
19. Martin, *With a Little Help*, 121; "Get Back to the Staircase," *The Genealogy of Style* (blog), December 8, 2014, https://thegenealogyofstyle.wordpress.com/2014/12/08/get-back-to-the-staircase/?iframe=true&preview=true.
20. Beatles, *Beatles Anthology*, 93.

## 9: Yeah, Yeah, Yeah!

1. Spitz, *The Beatles*, 386; Lewisohn, *Complete Beatles*, 28.
2. Martin, *Playback*, 123; Martin, *All You Need Is Ears*, 132.
3. Martin, *All You Need Is Ears*, 132; Spitz, *The Beatles*, 396.
4. Martin, *Playback*, 82.
5. Southall, *Northern Songs*, 476, 487.
6. Epstein, *A Cellarful of Noise*, 71; Martin, *All You Need Is Ears*, 134.
7. Martin, *All You Need Is Ears*, 133, 135; Epstein, *A Cellarful of Noise*, 107.
8. Martin, *All You Need Is Ears*, 134.
9. Debbie Geller, *In My Life: The Brian Epstein Story*, ed. Anthony Wall (New York: Thomas Dunne Books, 2000), 55; Hanly, *Produced by George Martin*.
10. Emerick and Massey, *Here, There, and Everywhere*, 64.
11. Chris Hutchins, "From Liverpool?—You're a Hit," *Billboard*, June 29, 1963, 52.
12. Lewisohn, *Complete Beatles*, 32, 69; Everett, *Beatles as Musicians*, 175.
13. Emerick and Massey, *Here, There, and Everywhere*, 67.
14. Martin, *With a Little Help*, 46.
15. Lewisohn, *Complete Beatles*, 28.
16. Emerick and Massey, *Here, There, and Everywhere*, 69.
17. Barry Miles, *Paul McCartney: Many Years from Now* (New York: Holt, 1997), 152; Kenneth Womack, *The Beatles Encyclopedia: Everything Fab Four* (Santa Barbara, CA: Greenwood, 2014), 2:425.
18. Miles, *Paul McCartney*, 148.
19. "Obituaries: Brian O'Hara," *Independent*, July 1, 1999, www.independent.co.uk/arts-entertainment/obituaries-brian-ohara-1103691.html.
20. Cilla Black, *What's It All About?* (London: Ebury 2003), 76.
21. Martin, *All You Need Is Ears*, 135; Black, *What's It All About?*, 79.
22. Womack, *Beatles Encyclopedia*, 1:224.
23. Spitz, *The Beatles*, 421; Martin, *All You Need Is Ears*, 159.
24. Martin, *All You Need Is Ears*, 135; Black, *What's It All About?*, 89.
25. Martin, *All You Need Is Ears*, 136; Black, *What's It All About?*, 88–89.
26. Martin, *All You Need Is Ears*, 136.
27. Southall, *Northern Songs*, 670.
28. Everett, *Beatles as Musicians*, 194.

29. Emerick and Massey, *Here, There, and Everywhere*, 69.
30. Spitz, *The Beatles*, 427.

## 10: El Dorado

1. Everett, *Beatles as Musicians*, 197; Emerick and Massey, *Here, There, and Everywhere*, 70; Lewisohn, *Complete Beatles*, 36.
2. Emerick and Massey, *Here, There, and Everywhere*, 76; Miles, *Paul McCartney*, 108; Spitz, *The Beatles*, 424.
3. Emerick and Massey, *Here, There, and Everywhere*, 72.
4. Lewisohn, *Complete Beatles*, 36; Martin, *Playback*, 90.
5. Emerick and Massey, *Here, There, and Everywhere*, 75.
6. Beatles, *Beatles Anthology*, 107.
7. Womack, *Beatles Encyclopedia*, 2:1009.
8. Martin, *All You Need Is Ears*, 136.
9. Keith Badman, *The Beatles Off the Record: Outrageous Opinions and Unrehearsed Interviews* (London: Omnibus, 2001), 74.
10. Martin, *All You Need Is Ears*, 180.
11. Hanly, *Produced by George Martin*; Martin, *All You Need Is Ears*, 180.
12. Spitz, *The Beatles*, 413–14; Southall, *Northern Songs*, 706.
13. Lewisohn, *Complete Beatles*, 38.
14. Ibid.
15. Tony Barrow, "The Story Behind *A Hard Day's Night*," *Beatles Monthly Book* 204 (September 1993): 5.
16. Martin, *All You Need Is Ears*, 133.
17. Emerick and Massey, *Here, There, and Everywhere*, 81.
18. Martin, *All You Need Is Ears*, 243.
19. Ibid., 36, 254.
20. Ibid., 158.
21. Ibid.

## 11: A Really Big Shew

1. Beatles, *Beatles Anthology*, 105; Epstein, *A Cellarful of Noise*, 23.
2. Martin, *All You Need Is Ears*, 159.
3. Spitz, *The Beatles*, 459.
4. Martin, *All You Need Is Ears*, 160.
5. Ibid.; Martin, *Playback*, 112–13.
6. Martin, *All You Need Is Ears*, 161.
7. Ibid.
8. Ibid.
9. Ibid.
10. Spitz, *The Beatles*, 478; Martin, *All You Need Is Ears*, 162.

11. John C. Winn, *Way Beyond Compare: The Beatles' Recorded Legacy*, vol. 1, *1957–1965* (Sharon, VT: Multiplus, 2003), 142; The Beatles, *The Beatles Anthology*, television documentary (ABC, 1995); Spitz, *The Beatles*, 478; Epstein, *A Cellarful of Noise*, 129.
12. Martin, *All You Need Is Ears*, 164.
13. Ibid., 164–65.
14. Womack, *Beatles Encyclopedia*, 1:170.
15. Philip Norman, *Shout! The Beatles in Their Generation* (New York: Simon and Schuster, 1981), 258.
16. Martin, *Playback*, 112–13.
17. Ray Coleman, *Lennon: The Definitive Biography* (New York: Harper, 1993), 369.
18. Badman, *Beatles Off the Record*, 90.
19. Lewisohn, *Complete Beatles*, 40; Spitz, *The Beatles*, 40.
20. Everett, *Beatles as Musicians*, 233.
21. Lewisohn, *Complete Beatles*, 40; Spitz, *The Beatles*, 40.

## 12: The Four Mop-Tops

1. Winn, *Way Beyond Compare*, 160.
2. Spitz, *The Beatles*, 489, 491.
3. Peter Tonguette, "Richard Lester," *Senses of Cinema* 26 (May 2003), http://sensesofcinema.com/2003/great-directors/lester/.
4. Michael R. Frontani, *The Beatles: Image and the Media* (Jackson: University Press of Mississippi, 2007), 25; "Beatle Hair-Do Draws Cutting Remarks," *Washington Post*, January 26, 1964, B1; James Feron, "Singing Beatles Prepare for US," *New York Times*, February 6, 1964, www.nytimes.com/1964/02/06/singing-beatles-prepare-for-us.html?_r=0; Peter Lyne, "Beatles . . . Ahem . . . a Secret Weapon," *Christian Science Monitor*, February 21, 1964, 1–2.
5. Martin, *All You Need Is Ears*, 222.
6. Ibid.
7. Beatles, *Beatles Anthology*, 124.
8. Mark Espiner, "Sounds and Vision," *Guardian*, June 30, 2001, www.theguardian.com/books/2001/jun/30/books.guardianreview1.
9. Badman, *Beatles Off the Record*, 93; Damian Fanelli, "Song Facts: The Beatles' 'A Hard Day's Night,'" *Guitar World*, April 16, 2013, www.guitarworld.com/song-facts-beatles-hard-days-night.
10. Maureen Cleave, "Did I Break Up the Beatles?," *Daily Mail*, December 18, 2009, www.dailymail.co.uk/tvshowbiz/article-1237097/Maureen-Cleave-Did-I-break-The-Beatles.html; Emerick and Massey, *Here, There, and Everywhere*, 83; Lewisohn, *Complete Beatles*, 43.
11. Lewisohn, *Complete Beatles*, 43; Emerick and Massey, *Here, There, and Everywhere*, 83; "100 Greatest Beatles Songs," *Rolling Stone*, September 29, 2011, www.rollingstone.com/music/lists/100-greatest-beatles-songs-20110919.
12. Beatles, *Beatles Anthology*, 124; Winn, *Way Beyond Compare*, 170
13. Ryan and Kehew, *Recording the Beatles*, 381; Emerick and Massey, *Here, There, and Everywhere*, 84.

14. Emerick and Massey, *Here, There, and Everywhere*, 84.
15. Ibid.
16. Ibid., 82; Cleave, "Did I Break Up the Beatles?"
17. Cleave, "Did I Break Up the Beatles?"

## 13: Martin's Revenge

1. Hanly, *Produced by George Martin.*
2. Winn, *Way Beyond Compare*, 1:185.
3. Badman, *Beatles Off the Record*, 91
4. Lewisohn, *Complete Beatles*, 44.
5. Spitz, *The Beatles*, 505, 909–10; Jim Berkenstadt, *The Beatle Who Vanished* (Madison, WI: Rock and Roll Detective, 2013), 3. In a May 6, 2016, e-mail to the author, Berkenstadt wrote, "In my opinion, this crisis was Epstein's greatest moment. His solution to get a stand-in drummer was the *only* option. George Harrison resisted the idea until Epstein explained the do-or-die business aspects of the need for a stand-in."
6. Berkenstadt, *Beatle Who Vanished*, 3, 61; Womack, *Beatles Encyclopedia*, 2:661.
7. Berkenstadt, *Beatle Who Vanished*, 60, 78; Taylor, *With the Beatles*, 111.
8. Womack, *Beatles Encyclopedia*, 2:661; Berkenstadt, *Beatle Who Vanished*, 63.
9. Spitz, *The Beatles*, 507; Beatles, *Beatles Anthology*, 140.
10. Martin, *Playback*, 120; "Why Don't We Do It on the Road? On Tour with Paul McCartney," *Musician*, May 1990, 46.
11. Martin, *All You Need Is Ears*, 222–23.
12. Spitz, *The Beatles*, 511; Bosley Crowther, "The Four Beatles in *A Hard Day's Night*: British Singers Make Debut as Film Stars," *New York Times*, August 12, 1964, www.nytimes.com/movie/review?res=990DE7DE1E30E033A25751C1A96E9C946591D6CF.
13. Martin, *All You Need Is Ears*, 223.
14. Ibid., 45.
15. Beatles, *Beatles Anthology*, 144.
16. Martin, *With a Little Help*, 148–49.
17. Martin, *All You Need Is Ears*, 165.
18. Martin, *Playback*, 130.
19. Martin, *All You Need Is Ears*, 162.
20. Ibid., 163.
21. Ibid.
22. Ibid., 180; Martin interview, March 10, 2016.

## 14: Off the Beatle Track

1. Martin, *Playback*, 124.
2. Hanly, *Produced by George Martin.*
3. "Pop Spotlight: *A Hard Day's Night*," *Billboard*, September 7, 1964, 52.
4. Winn, *Way Beyond Compare*, 1:83.

5. Womack, *Beatles Encyclopedia*, 2:697; Martin, *Playback*, 105.
6. Martin, *Playback*, 105; Anthony Hayward, "Obituary: Tony Warren," *Guardian*, March 2, 2016, www.theguardian.com/tv-and-radio/2016/mar/02/tony-warren-obituary-coronation-street-creator; Eugene Archer, "*Ferry Cross the Mersey*: New Film Stars Gerry and the Pacemakers," *New York Times*, February 20, 1965, www.nytimes.com/movie/review?res=9C01EEDA1E38E13ABC4851DFB466838E679EDE.
7. Martin, *Playback*, 126.
8. Martin, *All You Need Is Ears*, 167–68.
9. Black, *What's It All About?*, 96.
10. Ibid., 113.
11. Mick Brown, *Tearing Down the Wall of Sound: The Rise and Fall of Phil Spector* (London: Bloomsbury, 2008), 170.
12. Emerick and Massey, *Here, There, and Everywhere*, 88.
13. Martin, *Playback*, 127.
14. Emerick and Massey, *Here, There, and Everywhere*, 89.
15. Martin, *All You Need Is Ears*, 169.
16. John L. Williams, *Miss Shirley Bassey* (London: Quercus, 2013), 251.
17. Ibid., 270.
18. Martin, *Playback*, 128.
19. Ibid., 129.
20. "Martin Getting United Artists' Four-Star Buildup as Performer," *Billboard*, September 19, 1964, 15.
21. Martin, *All You Need Is Ears*, 166, 181.
22. Ibid., 166.
23. Ibid.

## 15: "Can We Have That on the Record?"

1. Womack, *Beatles Encyclopedia*, 1:109; Miles, *Paul McCartney*, 163.
2. Miles, *Paul McCartney*, 175.
3. Lewisohn, *Complete Beatles*, 47.
4. Hanly, *Produced by George Martin*.
5. Womack, *Beatles Encyclopedia*, 1:446; Miles, *Paul McCartney*, 175.
6. William J. Dowlding, *Beatlesongs* (New York: Simon and Schuster, 1989), 83.
7. Martin, *Playback*, 83; Beatles, *Beatles Anthology*, 98.
8. Everett, *Beatles as Musicians*, 262; John Lennon and Yoko Ono, "Lennon/McCartney Songalong: Who Wrote What," interview by Alan Smith, *Hit Parader*, April 1972; Beatles, *Beatles Anthology*, 98.
9. Miles, *Paul McCartney*, 173.
10. Emerick and Massey, *Here, There, and Everywhere*, 91–92.
11. Miles, *Paul McCartney*, 172; Emerick and Massey, *Here, There, and Everywhere*, 94–95.
12. Lennon and Ono, *All We Are Saying*, 173.

13. Miles, *Paul McCartney*, 39; Ryan and Kehew, *Recording the Beatles*, 378.
14. Emerick and Massey, *Here, There, and Everywhere*, 96.
15. Clayson, *John Lennon*, 103–4.
16. Beatles, *Beatles Anthology*, 160; Winn, *Way Beyond Compare*, 1:281.
17. Spitz, *The Beatles*, 541; Martin, *All You Need Is Ears*, 168.
18. Lewisohn, *Complete Beatles*, 53; Beatles, *Beatles Anthology*, 161.
19. Beatles, *Beatles Anthology*, 92.

## 16: Yesterday and Today

1. Martin, *Playback*, 132, 138.
2. Ibid., 138; Spitz, *The Beatles*, 585; Badman, *Beatles Off the Record*, 148.
3. Badman, *Beatles Off the Record*, 140; Ken Scott, "Beatles' Recording Engineer Ken Scott Reveals Behind the Scenes Details on Working with the Fab Four," interview by Marshall Terrill, *Day Trippin'*, July 25, 2012, https://daytrippin.com/2012/07/25/beatles-recording-engineer-ken-scott-reveals-behind-the-scenes-details-on-working-with-the-fab-four/.
4. Miles, *Paul McCartney*, 193.
5. Martin, *All You Need Is Ears*, 167.
6. Badman, *Beatles Off the Record*, 165.
7. "Beatles Seen Recording for Own Company," *Billboard*, April 3, 1965, 1.
8. Badman, *Beatles Off the Record*, 164.
9. Womack, *Beatles Encyclopedia*, 2:1107; Badman, *Beatles Off the Record*, 165; Lewisohn, *Complete Beatles*, 55; Ryan and Kehew, *Recording the Beatles*, 386.
10. Everett, *Beatles as Musicians*, 289–90.
11. Norman, *John Lennon*, 412. In his autobiography, Brian took special note of John's remark, writing: "And he meant it. I was terribly annoyed and hurt because it was in front of all the recording staff and the rest of the Beatles. We all looked at one another and felt uncomfortable and John turned away, indicating that there was no apology coming. I left the studios in a sort of sullen rage. Later we had it out, but he told me quite emphatically that it was not cruelly intended and only meant in fun." See Epstein, *A Cellarful of Noise*, 100.
12. Ray Coleman, "Here We Go Again," *Melody Maker*, February 27, 1965, 13, 20.
13. Spitz, *The Beatles*, 550.
14. Ibid.; Moyer, "What the Late George Martin"; Martin, *All You Need Is Ears*, 199.
15. Martin interview, March 10, 2016.
16. Babiuk, *Beatles Gear*, 169; Badman, *Beatles Off the Record*, 190.
17. Beatles, *Beatles Anthology*, 196; Martin, *All You Need Is Ears*, 226.
18. Womack, *Beatles Encyclopedia*, 2:909.
19. Miles, *Paul McCartney*, 199.
20. Everett, *Beatles as Musicians*, 296.
21. Winn, *Way Beyond Compare*, 1:315.
22. Norman, *John Lennon*, 408; Beatles, *Beatles Anthology*, 194.

23. Coleman, *Lennon*, 402.
24. Miles, *Paul McCartney*, 200; Lewisohn, *Complete Beatles*, 69.
25. Lewisohn, *Complete Beatles*, 59; Ryan and Kehew, *Recording the Beatles*, 395.
26. Beatles, *Beatles Anthology*, 175; Everett, *Beatles as Musicians*, 301.
27. Miles, *Paul McCartney*, 205; Everett, *Beatles as Musicians*, 301.
28. Spitz, *The Beatles*, 562; Lewisohn, *Complete Beatles*, 59; Hanly, *Produced by George Martin*.
29. Beatles, *Beatles Anthology*, 175; Martin, *Playback*, 147.
30. Epstein, *A Cellarful of Noise*, 108.
31. Martin, *All You Need Is Ears*, 166–67.

## 17: Something in the AIR

1. Lewisohn, *Complete Beatles*, 60.
2. Ibid.
3. Badman, *Beatles Off the Record*, 140.
4. Norman, *John Lennon*, 409.
5. Bob Neaverson, *The Beatles Movies* (London: Cassell, 1997), 42; Bosley Crowther, "Singers Romp Through Comic Adventures," *New York Times*, August 24, 1965, www.nytimes.com/movie/review?res=9B0CEEDC103CE733A25757C2A96E9C946491D6CF.
6. Martin, *All You Need Is Ears*, 165.
7. Richard Green, "The Beatles: *Help!*," *Record Mirror*, July 24, 1965, www.rocksbackpages.com/Library/Article/the-beatles-ihelpi-parlophone; Robert Freeman, *The Beatles: A Private View* (New York: Barnes and Noble, 2003), 62.
8. Years later, George's *Help!* LP would enjoy a strange afterlife when his orchestral version of "Ticket to Ride" made an unexpected appearance on Pink Floyd's legendary album *The Dark Side of the Moon* (1973). As the heartbeat fades away at the conclusion of "Eclipse," George's "Ticket to Ride" instrumental can be heard very faintly. Audiophiles theorize that this residue occurred because the original tape had been recycled for use during the recording of *The Dark Side of the Moon* at Abbey Road.
9. "Obituaries: Brian O'Hara," *Independent*.
10. Martin, *All You Need Is Ears*, 134.
11. Ibid., 248.
12. Ray Coleman, *McCartney: Yesterday . . . and Today* (London: Boxtree, 1996), 56.
13. Martin, *Playback*, 29.
14. Martin, *All You Need Is Ears*, 185.
15. Ibid., 181.
16. Ibid., 181–82.
17. Ibid., 182–83.
18. Ibid., 183.
19. Ibid., 184.
20. Ibid., 184–85.
21. Ibid., 185–86.

22. Ibid., 186.
23. Geller, *In My Life*, 63.
24. Spitz, *The Beatles*, 589; "Four Top British A&R Men Form Production Concern," *Billboard*, September 4, 1965, 18.
25. Martin, *All You Need Is Ears*, 183.

## 18: Plastic Soul

1. Roy Carr and Tony Tyler, *The Beatles: An Illustrated Record* (New York: Harmony, 1976), 46.
2. Coleman, *Lennon*, 212.
3. Beatles, *Beatles Anthology*, 159; Southall, *Abbey Road*, 92.
4. Lennon, *Lennon Remembers*, 85.
5. Beatles, *Beatles Anthology*, 197; Lewisohn, *Complete Beatles*, 65.
6. Miles, *Paul McCartney*, 270; Tony Scherman, *The Rock Musician: 15 Years of the Interviews—the Best of* Musician *Magazine* (New York: St. Martin's/Griffin, 1994), 37.
7. Southall, *Abbey Road*, 91.
8. Everett, *Beatles as Musicians*, 316; Winn, *Way Beyond Compare*, 1:364.
9. Beatles, *Beatles Anthology*, 194.
10. Lennon and Ono, *All We Are Saying*, 152, 178–79; Miles, *Paul McCartney*, 277.
11. Spitz, *The Beatles*, 590.
12. Badman, *Beatles Off the Record*, 194–95.
13. Lewisohn, *Complete Beatles*, 65.
14. George Martin, "Insights: Sir George Martin Celebrating 45 Years in the Music Business," interview by Mel Lambert, *Media and Marketing* 13 (1994), www.mediaandmarketing.com/13Writer/Interviews/MIX.George_Martin.htm; Badman, *Beatles Off the Record*, 191.
15. Babiuk, *Beatles Gear*, 169.
16. Badman, *Beatles Off the Record*, 193.
17. Lewisohn, *Complete Beatles*, 13.
18. Miles, *Paul McCartney*, 276.
19. Winn, *Way Beyond Compare*, 1:369.
20. Beatles, *Beatles Anthology*, 183.
21. Badman, *Beatles Off the Record*, 186; Miles, *Paul McCartney*, 273.
22. Babiuk, *Beatles Gear*, 173; Lewisohn, *Complete Beatles*, 67; Martin, *George Martin: Den Femte Beatlen* [George Martin: The fifth Beatle] (Sweden, 1993), television documentary.
23. Lewisohn, *Complete Beatles*, 67.
24. Badman, *Beatles Off the Record*, 190.
25. John Lennon, "Beatles Music Straightforward on Next Album," interview by Alan Smith, *Hit Parader*, December 1969, www.beatlesinterviews.org/db1969.0503.beatles.html; Miles, *Paul McCartney*, 209–10, 276.

26. Beatles, *Beatles Anthology*, 193.
27. Badman, *Beatles Off the Record*, 188.
28. Hanly, *Produced by George Martin*; Spitz, *The Beatles*, 591.
29. Beatles, *Beatles Anthology*, 194; Ryan and Kehew, *Recording the Beatles*, 402.
30. Badman, *Beatles Off the Record*, 189.
31. Allen Evans, "Beatles Tops," *NME*, December 3, 1965, 8; "The Beatles: *Rubber Soul*," *Record Mirror*, December 4, 1965, www.rocksbackpages.com/Library/Article/the-beatles-rubber-soul.
32. Robert Rodriguez, *Revolver: How the Beatles Re-imagined Rock 'n' Roll* (Milwaukee, WI: Hal Leonard, 2012), 75; Keith Badman, *The Beach Boys: The Definitive Diary of America's Greatest Band, on Stage and in the Studio* (San Francisco: Backbeat, 2004), 104.

## Epilogue: Life Begins at Forty

1. William Mann, "What Songs the Beatles Sang," *Times*, December 27, 1963, http://jolomo.net/music/william_mann.html; Dowlding, *Beatlesongs*, 57; Deryck Cooke, "The Lennon-McCartney Songs," *Vindications: Essays on Romantic Music* (Cambridge: Cambridge University Press, 1982), 196–200.
2. Martin, *Playback*, 156; Beatles, *Beatles Anthology*, 158.
3. Martin, *All You Need Is Ears*, 167; Joshua Wolf Shenk, "Two Is the Magic Number: A New Science of Creativity," *Slate*, September 14, 2010, www.slate.com/articles/life/creative_pairs/features/2010/two_of_us/inside_the_lennonmccartney_connection_part_2.html.
4. Lewisohn, *Complete Beatles*, 69; Joshua Wolf Shenk, *Powers of Two: Finding the Essence of Innovation in Creative Pairs* (Boston: Houghton Mifflin Harcourt, 2014), 167.
5. Southall, *Abbey Road*, 103; Lewisohn, *Complete Beatles*, 69.

# BIBLIOGRAPHY


"100 Greatest Beatles Songs." *Rolling Stone*, September 29, 2011. www.rollingstone.com/music/lists/100-greatest-beatles-songs-20110919.

Archer, Eugene. "*Ferry Cross the Mersey*: New Film Stars Gerry and the Pacemakers." *New York Times*, February 20, 1965. www.nytimes.com/movie/review?res=9C01EEDA1E38E13ABC4851DFB466838E679EDE.

Babiuk, Andy. *Beatles Gear: All the Fab Four's Instruments, from Stage to Studio*. San Francisco: Backbeat, 2001.

Badman, Keith. *The Beach Boys: The Definitive Diary of America's Greatest Band, on Stage and in the Studio*. San Francisco: Backbeat, 2004.

———. *The Beatles Off the Record: Outrageous Opinions and Unrehearsed Interviews*. London: Omnibus, 2001.

Barrow, Tony. "The Story Behind *A Hard Day's Night*." *Beatles Monthly Book* 204 (September 1993): 5.

"Beatle Hair-Do Draws Cutting Remarks." *Washington Post*, January 26, 1964, B1.

Beatles, The. *The Beatles Anthology*. San Francisco: Chronicle, 2000.

———. *The Beatles Anthology*. ABC, 1995. Television documentary.

"The Beatles: *Rubber Soul*." *Record Mirror*, December 4, 1965. www.rocksbackpages.com/Library/Article/the-beatles-rubber-soul.

"Beatles Seen Recording for Own Company." *Billboard*, April 3, 1965, 1.

Berkenstadt, Jim. *The Beatle Who Vanished*. Madison, WI: Rock and Roll Detective, 2013.

Black, Cilla. *What's It All About?* London: Ebury, 2003.

Bramwell, Tony. *Magical Mystery Tours: My Life with the Beatles*. With Rosemary Kingsland. New York: St. Martin's, 2005.

Brown, Mick. *Tearing Down the Wall of Sound: The Rise and Fall of Phil Spector*. London: Bloomsbury, 2008.

Carpenter, Humphrey. *That Was Satire That Was: The Satire Boom of the 1960s*. London: Faber and Faber, 2001.

Carr, Roy, and Tony Tyler. *The Beatles: An Illustrated Record*. New York: Harmony, 1976.

Clayson, Alan. *John Lennon*. London: Sanctuary, 2003.

Cleave, Maureen. "Did I Break Up the Beatles?" *Daily Mail*, December 18, 2009. www.dailymail.co.uk/tvshowbiz/article-1237097/Maureen-Cleave-Did-I-break-The-Beatles.html.

Coleman, Ray. "Here We Go Again." *Melody Maker*, February 27, 1965, 13, 20.

———. *Lennon: The Definitive Biography*. Rev. ed. New York: Harper, 1993.
———. *McCartney: Yesterday . . . and Today*. London: Boxtree, 1996.
Cooke, Deryck. "The Lennon-McCartney Songs." In *Vindications: Essays on Romantic Music*, 196–200. Cambridge: Cambridge University Press, 1982.
Costello, Elvis. Foreword to *Here, There, and Everywhere: My Life Recording the Music of the Beatles*, by Geoff Emerick and Howard Massey, ix–xi. New York: Gotham, 2006.
Crowther, Bosley. "The Four Beatles in *A Hard Day's Night*: British Singers Make Debut as Film Stars." *New York Times*, August 12, 1964. www.nytimes.com/movie/review?res=990DE7DE1E30E033A25751C1A96E9C946591D6CF.
———. "Singers Romp Through Comic Adventures." *New York Times*, August 24, 1965. www.nytimes.com/movie/review?res=9B0CEEDC103CE733A25757C2A96E9C946491D6CF.
Davies, Hunter. *The Beatles*. 1968. Reprint, New York: Norton, 2004.
Dowlding, William J. *Beatlesongs*. New York: Simon and Schuster, 1989.
Emerick, Geoff, and Howard Massey. *Here, There, and Everywhere: My Life Recording the Music of the Beatles*. New York: Gotham, 2006.
Epstein, Brian. *A Cellarful of Noise: The Autobiography of the Man Who Made the Beatles*. 1964. Reprint, New York: Pocket, 1998.
Espiner, Mark. "Sounds and Vision." *Guardian*, June 30, 2001. www.theguardian.com/books/2001/jun/30/books.guardianreview1.
Evans, Allen. "Beatles Tops." *NME*, December 3, 1965, 8.
Everett, Walter. *The Beatles as Musicians: The Quarry Men Through Rubber Soul*. Oxford: Oxford University Press, 2001.
Fanelli, Damian. "Song Facts: The Beatles' 'A Hard Day's Night.'" *Guitar World*, April 16, 2013. www.guitarworld.com/song-facts-beatles-hard-days-night.
Feron, James. "Singing Beatles Prepare for US." *New York Times*, February 6, 1964. www.nytimes.com/1964/02/06/singing-beatles-prepare-for-us.html?_r=0.
"Four Top British A&R Men Form Production Concern." *Billboard*, September 4, 1965, 18.
Freeman, Robert. *The Beatles: A Private View*. New York: Barnes and Noble, 2003.
Frontani, Michael R. *The Beatles: Image and the Media*. Jackson: University Press of Mississippi, 2007.
Geller, Debbie. *In My Life: The Brian Epstein Story*. Edited by Anthony Wall. New York: Thomas Dunne Books, 2000.
"Get Back to the Staircase." *The Genealogy of Style* (blog), December 8, 2014. https://thegenealogyofstyle.wordpress.com/2014/12/08/get-back-to-the-staircase/?iframe=true&preview=true.
Goodwin, Ron. "Ron Goodwin." Interview by Christopher Ritchie. *Soundtrack!* 8, no. 30 (1989). www.runmovies.eu/?p=1812.
Green, Richard. "The Beatles: *Help!*" *Record Mirror*, July 24, 1965. www.rocksbackpages.com/Library/Article/the-beatles-ihelpi-parlophone.
Hanly, Francis, dir. *Produced by George Martin*. BBC, 2012.
Hayward, Anthony. "Obituary: Tony Warren." *Guardian*, March 2, 2016. www.theguardian.com/tv-and-radio/2016/mar/02/tony-warren-obituary-coronation-street-creator.
Hutchins, Chris. "From Liverpool?—You're a Hit." *Billboard*, June 29, 1963, 52.
Lawrence, Alistair. *Abbey Road: The Best Studio in the World*. London: Bloomsbury, 2012.
Leigh, Spencer. *The Cavern Club: The Rise of the Beatles and Merseybeat*. Carmarthen, Wales: McNidder and Grace, 2016.
Lennon, John. *Lennon Remembers*. Interview by Jann Wenner. 1970. Reprint, New York: Verso, 2000.

Lennon, John, and Yoko Ono. *All We Are Saying: The Last Major Interview with John Lennon and Yoko Ono*. Interview by David Sheff. Edited by G. Barry Golson. New York: Griffin, 2000.

———. "Beatles Music Straightforward on Next Album." Interview by Alan Smith. *Hit Parader*, December 1969. www.beatlesinterviews.org/db1969.0503.beatles.html.

———. "Lennon/McCartney Songalong: Who Wrote What." Interview by Alan Smith. *Hit Parader*, April 1972.

Lewisohn, Mark. *The Complete Beatles Recording Sessions: The Official Abbey Road Studio Session Notes, 1962–1970*. New York: Harmony, 1988.

———. *Tune In: The Beatles—All These Years*. Vol. 1. Boston: Little, Brown, 2013.

———. *Tune In: The Beatles—All These Years*. Vol. 1. Extended ed. Boston: Little, Brown, 2013.

Lyne, Peter. "Beatles . . . Ahem . . . a Secret Weapon." *Christian Science Monitor*, February 21, 1964, 1–2.

Mann, William. "What Songs the Beatles Sang." *Times*, December 27, 1963. http://jolomo.net/music/william_mann.html.

Martin, George. *All You Need Is Ears*. With Jeremy Hornsby. New York: St. Martin's, 1979.

———. *George Martin: Den Femte Beatlen* [George Martin: The Fifth Beatle]. Television documentary. Sweden, 1993.

———. "Insights: Sir George Martin Celebrating 45 Years in the Music Business." Interview by Mel Lambert. *Media and Marketing* 13 (1994). www.mediaandmarketing.com/13Writer/Interviews/MIX.George_Martin.htm.

———. *Playback: An Illustrated Memoir*. Guildford, England: Genesis, 2003.

———. "The Tingle Factor." Interview by Jeremy Nicholas. BBC Radio Four Extra, 1992. www.bbc.co.uk/programmes/b07cmbyg.

———. *With a Little Help from My Friends: The Making of Sgt. Pepper*. With William Pearson. Boston: Little, Brown, 1994.

Martin, George, and His Orchestra. *A Hard Day's Night: Instrumental Versions of the Motion Picture Score*. United Artists, 1965.

"Martin Getting United Artists' Four-Star Buildup as Performer." *Billboard*, September 19, 1964, 15.

Massey, Howard. *The Great British Recording Studios*. Milwaukee, WI: Hal Leonard, 2015.

Miles, Barry. *Paul McCartney: Many Years from Now*. New York: Holt, 1997.

Monro, Michelle. *Matt Monro: The Singer's Singer*. New York: Titan Books, 2012.

Moyer, Justin Wm. "What the Late George Martin Really Did for the Beatles." *Washington Post*, March 9, 2016. www.washingtonpost.com/news/morning-mix/wp/2016/03/09/what-george-martin-who-died-tuesday-really-did-for-the-beatles/.

Neaverson, Bob. *The Beatles Movies*. London: Cassell, 1997.

Norman, Philip. *John Lennon: The Life*. London: Ecco, 2008.

———. *Shout! The Beatles in Their Generation*. New York: Simon and Schuster, 1981.

"Obituaries: Brian O'Hara." *Independent*, July 1, 1999. www.independent.co.uk/arts-entertainment/obituaries-brian-ohara-1103691.html.

"Pop Spotlight: *A Hard Day's Night*." *Billboard*, September 7, 1964, 52.

Rodriguez, Robert. *Revolver: How the Beatles Re-Imagined Rock 'n' Roll*. Milwaukee, WI: Hal Leonard, 2012.

Ryan, Kevin, and Brian Kehew. *Recording the Beatles: The Studio Equipment and Techniques Used to Create Their Classic Albums*. Houston, TX: Curvebender, 2006.

Salewicz, Chris. *McCartney: The Biography*. London: Queen Anne, 1986.

Schechter, Scott. *Judy Garland: The Day-by-Day Chronicle of a Legend*. New York: Cooper Square, 2002.

Scherman, Tony. *The Rock Musician: 15 Years of the Interviews—the Best of* Musician *Magazine*. New York: St. Martin's/Griffin, 1994.

Scott, Ken. "Beatles' Recording Engineer Ken Scott Reveals Behind the Scenes Details on Working with the Fab Four." Interview by Marshall Terrill. *Day Trippin'*, July 25, 2012. https://daytrippin.com/2012/07/25/beatles-recording-engineer-ken-scott-reveals-behind-the-scenes-details-on-working-with-the-fab-four/.

Shenk, Joshua Wolf. *Powers of Two: Finding the Essence of Innovation in Creative Pairs*. Boston: Houghton Mifflin Harcourt, 2014.

———. "Two Is the Magic Number: A New Science of Creativity." *Slate*, September 14, 2010. www.slate.com/articles/life/creative_pairs/features/2010/two_of_us/inside_the_lennonmccartney_connection_part_2.html.

Southall, Brian. *Abbey Road: The Story of the World's Most Famous Studios*. Wellingborough, England: Patrick Stephens, 1982.

———. *Northern Songs: The True Story of the Beatles Song Publishing Empire*. With Rupert Perry. London: Omnibus, 2009.

Spitz, Bob. *The Beatles: The Biography*. Boston: Little, Brown, 2005.

Taylor, Alistair. *With the Beatles*. London: John Blake, 2003.

Thompson, Gordon. *Please Please Me: Sixties Pop, Inside Out*. Oxford: Oxford University Press, 2008.

Tonguette, Peter. "Richard Lester." *Senses of Cinema* 26 (May 2003). http://sensesofcinema.com/2003/great-directors/lester/.

Warren, Jane. "Family Feud of 'Fifth Beatle': Sir George Martin's Children in Furious Inheritance Row." *Express*, September 22, 2016. www.express.co.uk/comment/expresscomment/713193/family-feud-fifth-beatle-sir-george-martin-children-furious-inheritance-row.

Wedge, Don. "Telstar Reaches Two Millionth Orbit." *Billboard*, January 26, 1963, 28.

"Why Don't We Do It on the Road? On Tour with Paul McCartney." *Musician*, May 1990, 46.

Williams, John L. *Miss Shirley Bassey*. London: Quercus, 2013.

Winn, John C. *Way Beyond Compare: The Beatles' Recorded Legacy*. Vol. 1, *1957–1965*. Sharon, VT: Multiplus, 2003.

Womack, Kenneth. *The Beatles Encyclopedia: Everything Fab Four*. 2 vols. Santa Barbara, CA: Greenwood, 2014.

# INDEX